Transcultural Research – Heidelberg Studies on Asia and Europe in a Global Context

Series Editors:

Madeleine Herren
Axel Michaels
Rudolf G. Wagner

For further volumes:
http://www.springer.com/series/8753

Antje Flüchter · Susan Richter
Editors

Structures on the Move

Technologies of Governance
in Transcultural Encounter

Editors

Antje Flüchter
Karl Jaspers Centre
Voßstr. 2
69115 Heidelberg
Germany

Susan Richter
Karl Jaspers Centre
Voßstr. 2
69115 Heidelberg
Germany

ISSN 2191-656X ISSN 2191-6578 (electronic)
ISBN 978-3-642-19287-6 ISBN 978-3-642-19288-3 (eBook)
DOI 10.1007/978-3-642-19288-3
Springer Heidelberg New York Dordrecht London

Library of Congress Control Number: 2012940194

© Springer-Verlag Berlin Heidelberg 2012
This work is subject to copyright. All rights are reserved by the Publisher, whether the whole or part of the material is concerned, specifically the rights of translation, reprinting, reuse of illustrations, recitation, broadcasting, reproduction on microfilms or in any other physical way, and transmission or information storage and retrieval, electronic adaptation, computer software, or by similar or dissimilar methodology now known or hereafter developed. Exempted from this legal reservation are brief excerpts in connection with reviews or scholarly analysis or material supplied specifically for the purpose of being entered and executed on a computer system, for exclusive use by the purchaser of the work. Duplication of this publication or parts thereof is permitted only under the provisions of the Copyright Law of the Publisher's location, in its current version, and permission for use must always be obtained from Springer. Permissions for use may be obtained through RightsLink at the Copyright Clearance Center. Violations are liable to prosecution under the respective Copyright Law.
The use of general descriptive names, registered names, trademarks, service marks, etc. in this publication does not imply, even in the absence of a specific statement, that such names are exempt from the relevant protective laws and regulations and therefore free for general use.
While the advice and information in this book are believed to be true and accurate at the date of publication, neither the authors nor the editors nor the publisher can accept any legal responsibility for any errors or omissions that may be made. The publisher makes no warranty, express or implied, with respect to the material contained herein.

Printed on acid-free paper

Springer is part of Springer Science+Business Media (www.springer.com)

Editors Note

The present volume is the proceedings of a conference (26–28 October) organised by two research groups of the Heidelberg Cluster of Excellence "Asia and Europe in a Global Context", that is A4: "The Fascination of Efficiency: Migrating Ideas and Emerging Bureaucracies in Europe and Asia since the Early Modern Era" and A 9: "Cultural Transfer as a Factor of State Building". Discussions took place concerning concepts of statehood, methods to analyse transcultural statehood, and case studies applying these concepts and methods. It has been possible to include many of the papers in this book, and we would like to thank all the authors for their articles. The sequence of the articles is modelled on the conference's program. Our thanks extend to all participants for the inspiring and sometimes intense discussions, most of all to Reinhard Blänkner (Frankfurt/Oder), Susanna Burghartz (Basel), Angelika Epple (Bielefeld), Jan-Peter Hartung (London), Farhat Hasan (New Delhi), Ulrike Lindner (Bielefeld), Thomas Simon (Vienna), Sven Trakulhun (Zürich), Peer Vries (Vienna) and especially to Thomas Maissen (Heidelberg), who summarised and commented on the entire conference in the final discussion. For the inclusion of this volume in the Cluster's series *Transcultural Research. Heidelberg Studies on Asia and Europe in a Global Context* we would like to thank the Cluster's directorial board, Madeleine Herren, Axel Michaels and Rudolf Wagner. We received lots of help and support from Andrea Hacker, Douglas Fear and Chris Allen in the publication process and would also like to thank our student researchers: Carolin Matjeka for the organisational support and Elena Allendörfer, Michael Roth, Christian Stoll, Shuo Wang, Rouven Wirbser for their friendly and supportive attendance. Finally, we are grateful to Steve Bahn and Carolin Matjeka for their help in proofreading and editing the manuscripts.

Heidelberg, August 2011   Antje Flüchter & Susan Richter

Contents

Structures on the Move 1
Appropriating Technologies of Governance in a Transcultural Encounter
Antje Flüchter

Part I Statehood: Conceptual Approaches

**New Perspectives on State-Building and the Implementation
of Rulership in Early Modern European Monarchies** 31
Stefan Brakensiek

State and Political History in a Culturalist Perspective 43
Barbara Stollberg-Rilinger

Part II Case Studies: Knowledge

Pater patriae sinensis. **The Discovery of Patriarchal Rule in China
and Its Significance for German Theories of State in
the Eighteenth Century** 61
Susan Richter

Survey the People 87
The Emergence of Population Statistics as Technology
of Government in Early Twentieth-Century China
Nicolas Schillinger

**China and Constitutional Monarchy: Four Short Encounters
Around 1900** 105
Guido Mühlemann

Europe–Mughal India–Muslim Asia: Circulation of Political Ideas and Instruments in Early Modern Times 127
Corinne Lefèvre

Weighing the Mughal 147
German Perception of Governmental Structures and the Staging
of Power in Early Modern Indian Mughal Empire
Antje Flüchter

Part III Case Studies: Interaction

Technology, Tactics and Military Transfer in the Nineteenth Century ... 169
Qing Armies in Tonkin, 1884–1885
Barend Noordam

Exporting Military Revolutions and the Changing Clausewitzian Triad between People, Armed Forces and Ruler at the Turn of the Nineteenth Century 189
Peter I. Trummer

Approaches to State-Building in Eighteenth Century British Bengal 219
Sebastian Meurer

State-Building in a Transcultural Context: The Case of the French in India during the Early Eighteenth Century 243
Gauri Parasher

Visualising "State-Building" in European-Ottoman Diplomatic Relations 251
Visual Ceremonial Descriptions and Conflicting Concepts of Early Modern
Governance in the Late Seventeenth and Early Eighteenth Centuries
Dorothee Linnemann

The Consequences of Early Modern Diplomacy: Entanglement, Discrimination, Mutual Ignorance—and State Building 271
Christian Wieland

Structures on the Move

Appropriating Technologies of Governance in a Transcultural Encounter[1]

Antje Flüchter

1 Introduction

The starting point of this book is an understanding of state, statehood, and technologies of governance as resulting from transcultural processes. Accordingly, we challenge the conception of *state building* as a European singularity, that is brought into existence by exclusively European driving forces, by European factors, and structured only by European actors. The academic aim of the present volume, as well as the conference *Early Modern State (Building) in Asia and Europe—Comparison, Transfer and Entanglement* from which it emerged, is to outline the new research field of transcultural state structures and state building, as well as to probe several promising fields for further research.[2] We apply a two-pronged approach: first we discuss the modern, academic conceptualisation of *state* and *state building*; secondly, we describe ways and methods to analyse state and technologies of governance. The latter include the contemporary perception, the appropriation of knowledge of foreign statehood, state structures, and technologies of governance as transcultural results of communication and interaction. *Technology*, in this context, serves as an umbrella term for anything that structures the distribution of power and resources in states, as well as the life and security of

---

[1] Many thanks for critical reading and discussions to Susan Richter and Christoph Dartmann, Andrea Hacker, Isabella Löhr, Carla Meyer, Jenny Oesterle, Gauri Parasher, Barbara Stollberg-Rilinger.

[2] The relevance of including state formation in a project about both entangled history and the broader view of making of Europe as a result of non-European influences was stressed by Sven Beckert at the recent conference at the Frias in Freiburg: "Making Europe: The Global Origins of the Old World", Freiburg 27/5/–29/5/2010. In the fourth volume of the new WBG *Weltgeschichte*, Walter Demel writes about global empires and state building in a comparative perspective (Demel 2010).

A. Flüchter (✉)
Karl Jaspers Centre, University of Heidelberg, Voßstr. 2, 69115 Heidelberg, Germany
e-mail: fluechter@asia-europe.uni-heidelberg.de

A. Flüchter and S. Richter (eds.), *Structures on the Move*,
Transcultural Research – Heidelberg Studies on Asia and Europe in a Global Context,
DOI 10.1007/978-3-642-19288-3_1, © Springer-Verlag Berlin Heidelberg 2012

members of a particular state. As a concept, technology is wide enough to encompass institutions, knowledge and practices.[3]

In view of the fact that transculturality of state structures as a field of research has yet to be surveyed, the first part of this introduction tackles the conceptual problems concerning the English term *state* and the German *Staat*. This conceptual discussion proceeds in two steps: first, fundamental definitions of German *Staat* as well as alternative terms are discussed and we explain why even with misgivings we shall still use the terms *state* and *Staat*; in a second step, we present and contrast research about state and state formation deriving from European and Asian contexts, to find comparable concepts and structures as criteria for analysing state in a transcultural context. Only once this terminology has been clarified can we properly introduce the articles collected in this volume. We differentiate between *state* as a research concept (1), as a topic of contemporary discourse (2), and *states* as phenomena produced by social actions, as spaces of interaction, and as networks of institutions that structure action (3). Even though they are closely connected, these aspects must be heuristically distinguished. While concepts structure and re-structure research and lead it in a specific direction, they also tend to obscure other perspectives. To analyse state and state building in a transcultural context, it is necessary to strip away the concepts of their limited reference to Europe, modernity and national state and instead broaden them in a transcultural and transepochal manner. The aim of this conceptualisation of *state* is not to form a specific model and to test it in the past, but rather to outline the institutional and discursive context of particular case studies. This is why *state* is not taken as a socio-scientific model, but as a result of communication and interaction.

Since the advent of modern times, it can be assumed that states, rulers and office-holders have aimed to improve technologies of governance and have been open to new ideas, especially in times of crisis. As a consequence, state structures are always changing, turning state building into a perpetual process that is never finished at any given point in time, and is thus always incomplete and unfulfilled in the modern national state. Comparably state and state building constitute an important topic in historic research, most of all in German historiography. Classic concepts for European history understand the Early Modern period as a formative period of state building from above (Reinhard 2002; Tilly 1990). Nevertheless, such state building is not only a process planned from above, but also demanded from

---

[3] Foucault's concept of technology in the context of his studies of governmentality (Foucault 2000) provided an impetus, but this is not the main basis for the way technologies of governance are understood in this volume. Within the concept of governmentality it may well be important for a project about the transcultural state to understand the state as a technology of government (Lemke et al. 2000). Another important and helpful aspect of this concept is its overruling of the contrast between theory and reality. Instead, the concept starts with the assumption of different rationalities and heterogeneous strategies. The combination of these two leads to unexpected results. In this way, the binary structure of implementation versus failure is placed in a new perspective. Thus a space evolves, open to breaks and discontinuities. However, the concept of governmentality must also be modified in a transcultural way, because one of its bases is Christian pastoral power.

below. In other words, subjects ask for solutions to special problems by writing a supplication, or they modify governmental institutions by using them on their terms. Social actors produce, reproduce, and modify structures through their use and actions. Therefore, institutions change not only because of some governmental plan, but also because of many kinds of social practices (Giddens 2009), which in turn are intertwined with perception and concepts. For example, while making use of any governmental institution, actors refer to their ideal concepts of *state* and *good governance*.[4] This process is, so we claim, not solely intra-European, and any wider research about state and governance needs to integrate experiences from non-European world regions.

The transfer of modern state structures, concepts and models from Europe into many world regions has been frequently analysed and demonstrated. The modern national state is even considered a sort of European export hit (Reinhard 2002: 15–20, 480–509). However, we understand the process of state formation as part of a shared and entangled history. "Entangled history" is a term and a concept that reaches back to Sidney W. Mintz's important study *Sweetness and Power* (Mintz 1986) in which he proved that the history of the Caribbean has always been entangled with the wider world. However, the term "entangled history" was introduced into the German-speaking academic community by Shalini Randeria and Sebastian Conrad (Conrad and Randeria 2002; Randeria 2002). Conrad outlined that the term *entangled* aims at more than the collection of global contacts and exchange, "rather, intercourse and exchange contributed to the production of the units we still operate with today" (Conrad 2003: 275). The present volume claims a similar connection regarding state and state formation.[5] This has several consequences for our subject: firstly, flows must be looked for and analysed in all directions, not only those from Europe to the rest of the world. Secondly, it is

---

[4] The perspective "from above" and "from below" touches, but is not congruent with the difference between intentional and non-intentional, as discussed in the context of early modern state-building, however, this difference only slightly restricts the transculturality of the process. The circulation of knowledge is certainly greater or at least more obvious, if early modern counsellors or writers about state theory refer to Asian concepts than if a rural community writes a supplication to its duke. However, conversely, the (intended) demand for better governmental structures from below between Indian communities and European rulers must be understood as a transcultural empowering interaction.

[5] It is by now well established in German academia, in English-language publications, however, the term is used rather rarely (for example in a discussion in the *American Historical Review* from 2007: Cañizares-Esguerra 2007; Gould 2007; or Carlier 2010). If you look up "entangled" in Google books, tellingly the first pages present mostly fantasy adventures or romances; the first academic books that show up are about physics. More common in the US discourse is *connected* (Subrahmanyam 1997) or *braided history* (Davis 1998). Monica Juneja has tried to introduce the term *braided* into the German discourse, but *entangled* seems there to be too well established (Juneja 2004). The newly-coined concept for *entangled history* is an example for a kind of academic pidgin, following the increasing use of English in German academia. In the context of new fields of research new terms are created that sound English, but are more common in Germany than in English usage.

necessary to understand these processes not as bilateral, but as embedded in a multipolar network. Furthermore, these processes cannot be limited to modern history, which is why the focus of this volume lies with the Early Modern period. This central epoch in the history of European state-building witnessed important changes in modes of rulership and governance, which were, however, not limited to Europe, but also occurred in Asia (Osterhammel 2009: 565–646). It was a time when European-Asian encounters and mutual knowledge increased significantly and contemporary European travellers regularly discussed structures and institutions of the territories they experienced: the ubiquitous problems with customs officers, unfamiliar weapons and military systems, or the representation of power and wealth at Asian courts. They reported not simply an encounter with foreign state structures, but with superior state structures. These pre-modern Asian-European encounters were shaped by power asymmetries that differed from those in colonial times: the Europeans were far from being dominant in Asia in the sixteenth and seventeenth centuries (Subrahmanyam 2005) and had to make considerable efforts to gain access to Asian trade and power centres. At Asian courts, Europeans were forced to adapt to indigenous rules, to particular systems of political and courtly communication. Thus, at a time when European rulers and their counsellors were looking for ways to improve the state institutions and technologies of governance, these European travellers witnessed efficient and superior state structures in Asia. It is therefore quite possible that there was a European interest in these technologies of governance. In other words: the experience in Asia could lead to processes of learning or appropriation; Asian structures could, therefore, be integrated into processes of change and development in European systems of governance until the shift in power asymmetries between Asia and Europe during the second half of the eighteenth century. It is this reversal in the asymmetry of flows that would lead to the broadly accepted transfer of European ideas and concepts all over the world in the nineteenth and twentieth centuries. In summary: to better understand the shifting power asymmetries and their effect on the transfer processes between Asia and Europe, we need to look at a longer period than is usually applied in studies of state structures. Therefore, the articles assembled in this book cover the period from the sixteenth to the twentieth centuries with the main focus, as mentioned above, squarely centred on Early Modern times, because before 1750 European interest in Asian structures outweighed that of later periods.

2 State as a Transcultural Concept

State, particularly the German word *Staat*, is a term that has been, and is, extensively discussed as well as being fraught with numerous meanings. Research on *state* in a transcultural context, when used in German academia, struggles with a special translational problem: in English the term *state* has been used without deep critical discussion until recently. Philip Lime explicitly bemoaned the fact that in English historical studies scholars rarely define their concept of *state* at all (Line

2007: 9). Even though this has changed in recent research (Brewer and Hellmuth 1999; Bayly 2006: 306; Bayly 2009: 249–252), the depth of inquiry is still not comparable with the German discourse. This confronts us with yet another challenge: if we use the concept of state as a major focus for comparative and transculturally entangled research, we need a clear understanding of our terminology, its options and limitations. Moreover, this intensive discussion in German discourse brought about much important research that offers new insights into the functioning of state and governance. Therefore, so as to somewhat bridge this linguistic and discursive discrepancy, some of the main problems and discussions surrounding *Staat* within German History studies will be outlined below.

The problem with the term *Staat* in German discourse lies in the persistence or even essentialisation of legal philosopher Georg Jellinek's so-called *Drei-Elemente-Lehre*, or doctrine of three elements, according to which a state consists of (a) the fixed borders that surround its territory (*Staatsgebiet/state territory*), (b) a single and, presumably, homogeneous population that lives inside these borders (*Staatsvolk/state people*), and (c) the governmental power that rules over this territory (*Staatsgewalt/state authority*).[6] This concept of an ideal type of central state also includes a monopoly on legitimate use of force as a consequence of the sovereignty of state (Reinhard 1992; Reinhard 1999: VIII–X).[7] The theory was virtually sacrosanct in German historical discourse on the state until certain criticism was levelled against a universal understanding of this definition. The crucial landmark in German historiography was Otto Brunner's book *Land und Herrschaft*, where Brunner proved that the universal use of the concept of modern *state* is anachronistic when applied, for example, to the medieval dynasty of the Staufer (Brunner 1939; cf. the new editions after 1945 with rather small changes: Brunner 1959; in English: Brunner 1992).[8] In other words, the *Staat* concept, as defined by Jellinek and other experts of jurisprudence, shows several deficits when applied to non-modern periods. The same can be said about its application to non-European areas. In this volume, therefore, we argue that it is not the term *Staat* that is problematic in itself, but the fact that its understanding is mostly restricted to this nineteenth century German definition, which often serves as an argument for the

---

[6] It is significant for the translational problem mentioned that there is no comparable translation in English for these three terms that has the same parallel structure. Most often suggested are national territory, people and public authority or sovereignty.

[7] The term *sovereignty* is even more discussed as a topic, cf. besides Reinhard (1992) and Reinhard (1999); Quaritsch (1986); Maissen (2008); Maissen (2009); Petersson and Schröder (2007). However, the concept of sovereignty—and its problems—can be ignored for this research project that focuses on state formation as the result of a cultural encounter and not as a constitutional question.

[8] Mention should also be made here of the attempt to replace the concept of the absolutistic state by the concept of *Sozialdisziplinierung*, a concept that is also an important step in the development of the idea of state building (Oestreich 1969; Schulze 1987). Brunner and Oestreich have their academic roots in the so-called *Volksgeschichte*, an attempt to challenge historicism in the 1930s (Miller 2002).

modern state being a genuinely and exclusively European phenomenon. If German experts in constitutional law defined *Staat* in the nineteenth century according to the governmental structures they themselves experienced, i.e. the model of the modern European national state, it is not surprising, but rather self-explanatory, that this kind of a *state* could only evolve in Europe and is thus inadequate for analysing transcultural processes.

The second problem with using both the German term *Staat* and the English *state* is that even beyond the narrow definition of constitutional law just described it implies a homogeneous development of European states and neglects that within Europe, too, modern statehood was shaped in very different ways. But even if the above-mentioned definition of state fails as a description of a "real" institution, it is nevertheless often the starting point for an analysis of deficiency and for the argument that pre-modern or non-European ruling systems cannot be considered states.[9] Results of studying global and entangled history show that the assertive central state, which functions on a system of order and obedience, is not only an ideal type, but basically a myth (Bayly 2006: 309–312); nevertheless these conclusions are only rarely taken on board in national historic studies. The modern national state, as an existing system or as an ideal, is broadly accepted as an exception in history (Anderson 1990); at the same time it continues to serve as a code of distinction in the global context.[10]

Because *Staat* is still mostly understood in the previously outlined, very narrow definition, the term can hardly be applied to non-modern and non-European contexts. Therefore, other, alternative terms have been taken into consideration in German discourse. In the following, two of these alternatives will be examined: first, the concept of *Herrschaft*, a crucial term in research on pre-modern German territories. Comparable terms like *rule*, *rulership* or *authority* are not as established in English discourse (Bayly 2006: 306). Secondly, *empire* as a concept has gained increasing importance as a characterisation of Asian rule.

Otto Brunner's term *Herrschaft* is frequently used in German discourse as a pre-modern alternative to *Staat*. While this term suggests an awareness and possible circumvention of the problematic term *Staat*, it does not entirely resolve the issue. *Herrschaft*, *rulership*, *chiefdom* and similar terms allude, in general use, to the centre of rule, or to the person of the ruler. In doing so, they essentially imply the existence of an individual actor, or a group of actors planning and organising the rule "from above". Even more problematic is that they, most of all the term *chief*, often imply an evolution, as it is expressed in sequences like chiefdom—early

---

[9] Also the discussion about failed states is often a check for which criteria must be fulfilled by a state in order for it to constitute a "real" state system. Bernhard Zangl and Philip Genschel admit that hardly any state would be able to monopolise all these competences (Genschel and Zangl 2007).

[10] The discussion about the ideal modern national state could be compared to concepts like early modern Absolutism (Duchhardt 1994; Asch and Freist 2005) or its negative foil, oriental despotism (Schnepel 1997: 15–19; Rubiés 2005; Richter 1974).

kingdom—imperial kingdom (Kulke 1995) or band—tribe—chiefdom—state (Hastorf 1992: 6). Here the terms can be understood as characterising an as yet incomplete and deficient modern state. To sum up, not only can the term *Staat* imply a theory of modernisation that views the European national state as an implicit goal of history, but a similar danger also arises if we use the term *Herrschaft*, because of its implications for evolutionary development.

It is often claimed that the concept of *Staat* cannot be applied to non-European territories. In this article it has already been argued the reason for this lies in a very narrow, Eurocentric definition of *Staat*. Nevertheless, if we regard the research project to establish a conceptualisation of *state* as a result of transcultural processes, it is important to consider what terms are used for non-European territories. In studies of Asian history, the concept of *empire* often supplants *state* (Bayly 2009; Osterhammel 2009). The concept of empire implies that there is a fundamental structural difference between large Asian territories and smaller European territories in Early Modern times, without, however, considering this difference to be a flaw, but rather a characteristic of the power and importance of these Asian state structures.[11] The problem with highlighting the differences between Asian empires and European states is that it stabilises constructed cultural boundaries between the so-called Orient and the so-called Occident. Thus using the terms *Herrschaft* or *empire* and avoiding the *state* concept altogether, can block the perception of similarities, entanglement and the evolution of transcultural phenomena and practices between Asia and Europe.[12] The danger of choosing terms that define very precisely a particular cultural case or system is to lose the possibility of taking into account other, related phenomena. The present volume therefore attempts to do for the *state* what Margrit Pernau, an area scholar and historian, argued for the term *citizen*. In her study of the Muslim elite in Delhi, Pernau grappled with the fact that the term *citizen* is used for inter-European comparisons, but not in a more globally entangled context.[13] Area studies circumvent the problem by using the term *ashraf* to describe the part of the Indian population that Pernau researches. The term derives from the original Indian sources, and is thus considered to be correct. But, as Pernau argues, using such a correct and culturally specific term freezes the alterity of an Asian phenomenon, because *ashraf* seems conceptually so different from a European *citizen*. Pernau instead operates

---

[11] Empires are often ethnically heterogeneous and therefore follow a different, internal logic from smaller territories or homogeneous modern states (Münkler 2004: 8; Osterhammel 2006).

[12] Frank Perlin described his astonishment when he found that Eastern European state phenomena he read about were similar to structures he had analysed in India, and which he had hitherto considered typically Asian. He concluded that "a whole number of false contrasts have been generated which undermine the validity of traditional assumptions about India" (Perlin 1985: 472).

[13] Pernau refers here to the European broadening of the German *Bürgertumsforschung* in the context of the Collaborative Research Centre Bielefeld 177, "Sozialgeschichte des neuzeitlichen Bürgertums: Deutschland im internationalen Vergleich" (Social History of modern Citizenship: Germany in the international Comparison), cf. Kocka (1995).

with the term *citizen with turban* for the Indian context. She argues that by using this term, the social elites of India and Europe become comparable (Pernau-Reifeld 2008; Pernau 2007). In the present volume we suggest a similar strategy concerning the concept of *state*: to analyse states and statehood in a transcultural context, they must lose their narrow identification with the modern European national state and be transculturally broadened. In short: we need state not only to sport tricorns, but turbans too.

The second part of this introduction will examine important concepts of *statehood* and *rulership* that research on non-modern times and non-European world regions has developed for aspects outside the limits of the modern national state; these concepts will also be probed for their usefulness in formulating a transcultural concept of *state*. While there are different ways to broaden the latter, two in particular have been chosen here: first, the analogy of family, which facilitates a contemporary understanding of the *state* as a pre-modern system of good rule; second, the influence of recent culturalistic approaches to research on state and state building.

The specific conceptualisation of *rule* and *state* in a culture or an epoch and the criteria of their legitimisation are important perspectives in developing a transcultural concept of *state*. These culturally specific concepts have to be related to each other in an entangled history. Sometimes comparison or entanglement seems obvious. For example, one central concept of rulership was the analogy between family and *state*, father and *ruler*. The charm of the analogy lies in the fact that many similar concepts exist in Asian state theory. One example is the concept of patrimonial bureaucratic empires which is an application of Max Weber's ideas on patrimonialism to the Islamic rule of the Indian Mughal emperors (Hardy 1987; Schluchter 1987; Blake 1979, 1991). In this manner, experiences from different cultural and geographic origins can be related and brought together in a concept of state that is broadened through the analogy of family. The German context features the Christian ideal of the *Landesvater*, a term that makes the analogy between father and ruler explicit. This notion, already important in medieval Europe, became even more influential after the Reformation (Münch 1982; Frühsorge 1982; Duchhardt 1991). Otto Brunner utilised this analogy as a heuristic instrument for historical research when he outlined his concept of *ganzes Haus* (Brunner 1968), the "whole household". Brunner used the term to describe and analyse the noble organisation of a household including extended family and servants as the fundamental unit of pre-modern societies. His concept has often been criticised, because it relies mostly on normative texts (Groebner 1995; Opitz 1994). These criticisms are relevant, if the concept is understood as a model for social interaction. If, however, we want to integrate contemporary and culturally specific concepts of good rule in a transcultural, historiographic concept of state, Brunner's concept appears to be rather fruitful just because it relies on normative texts. Moreover, there are similar approaches in Asian historiography. Brunner based his ideas almost exclusively on the so-called *Hausväterliteratur*—housefather or *pater familiae* literature, normative texts with advice on husbandry for rural knights—as a means to conceptualise European rule. Similarly, Stephen Blake interprets Mughal rule based on his reading of Abu al-Fazl's book *A'in-i Akbari*, also normative and historiographic, and a Persian text about the Mughal Court and its government.[14] Thus, *family* is an important analogy for evaluating *rule* and *state* as they are conceptualised in various cultures. It allows for different cultural perceptions to be linked, which makes intercultural translation and transcultural understanding easier. However, it would be misleading to understand this apparent conformity without further analysing the cultural and temporal difference in the shaping of family as well as comparable social phenomena. The analogy between *state* and *family* can unsettle the goal-oriented juridical image of a central state, but family itself is a historical institution shaped by cultural context and, thus, always changing. Therefore, the analogy of *family* can carry different norms and meanings in different cultural contexts.

Besides the contemporary perception of *state*, recent culturalistic approaches are important for the project of transcultural state-building, because they understand *state* as a process and a result of interaction, rather than as a static model. They view the political world as socially constructed, as reproduced in every action, and as performatively regenerated (e.g. Stollberg-Rilinger 2005, 2008, 2009; Asch and Freist 2005; Landwehr 2003; Holenstein 2009; Steinmetz 2007; Flüchter 2005).[15] These studies bring new insights into the process of state building, but their results are mostly restricted to the European context. There are similar approaches and concepts regarding Asian history that also challenge the above-mentioned concepts of the modern European state. Unfortunately, despite these common conceptual grounds, the mutual perception between these research areas is still very rare. To illustrate the potential of such a combination, the following paragraphs will contrast and combine culturalist approaches from the European experience with similar concepts derived from research on statehood and rule in Asia.[16] The aim is to achieve some possible characteristics and categories for *state* and *state building* in a transcultural context. Two aspects of these studies seem particularly fruitful: first, the necessity of staging and representing governance and power by means of symbolic communication and cultural representations; secondly, the understanding of state and politics as a network of actors, of state building as a dialectical and contingent process, instead of a top-down, hierarchical, and intentionally planned process.

---

[14] In this book, Abu al Fazl, who was the main historiographer and political strategist at the court of the Great Mughal Akbar, portrayed Akbar's concept of state. He started with the imperial household, and continued with the description of the military, concluding the text with a description of the whole Empire.

[15] However, there are also opposing voices: Nicklas (2004); Rödder (2006). Cf. also the bibliographies in Stefan Brakensiek's and Barbara Stollberg-Rilinger's articles in this volume. Important theoretical concepts for these approaches are Giddens (2009); Berger and Luckmann (1967); Bourdieu (1990); Goffman (1959); Chartier (1988).

[16] The point of reference in this case is mostly studies about South Asian History. In future research that will need to be widened, and more Asian areas and other world regions will have to be included.

The first of these views social and political institutions as a result of communicative construction, and as constituted by a system of symbols. Barbara Stollberg-Rilinger and others (Stollberg-Rilinger 2005, 2008) argue that Early Modern statehood and governance needed to be staged and performatively produced, so that the audience could experience it as something real and tangible.[17] Court society during a diplomatic ceremonial meeting, or the population of a town during a procession come to mind as examples. This research perspective strips institutions of their "objectively" factualist character, and supposes that interaction and communication follow not only a means-end oriented rationale, but a symbolic logic as well. The success of the pre-modern state and its institutions depended, therefore, not only on the implementation of their instrumental goals, but also on their being understood and evaluated in the broader context of symbolic actions and performative rule. For example, we can evaluate laws not only regarding the implementation of their literal aim, that is their instrumental goals, but also as performing the right to enact a law. Thus, practices of rule can be and must be analysed beyond their instrumental goals. Nevertheless, instrumental and symbolic aims must not be understood as separated and mutually exclusive, but as intertwined.

The second important insight from the culturalist approach regarding *state building* in a transcultural context concerns the understanding of *state building* as empowering interaction, that is that not only the ruler and his counsellor planned or initiated a process of state building, but that institutions, institutional change and thus, last but not least statehood was also demanded from below. Hardly anybody still agrees with the concept of an omnipotent state, or describes the relation of ruler and ruled with the simple scheme of order and obedience in the European context.[18] This applies to the modern and even more so to the pre-modern state. In non-European contexts, however, state building from above is rarely questioned, neither from a Eurocentric nor a post-colonial view. Both views mostly assume a European superiority. In the process of European state building, the Early Modern state reduced the power of competing power-holders—most important were churches and estates, although there were also other power-holders. By these means the rulers and their counsellors, presumably tried to accumulate responsibility and power. Whether the Early Modern state was successful in this attempt is open to debate, because rule has to be understood as an interaction and negotiation between

---

[17] The so-called *performative turn* is an important element of the recent culturalistic approaches (cf. Martschukat/Patzold 2003), and refers to Austin's speech act theory and its further development in anthropology (for example Tambiah 1981). It has often been used on the subject of identity and is one of the core ideas of the SFB/Collaborative Research Centre 496 "Symbolic Communication and Social Value Systems. From the Middle Ages to the French Revolution" in Münster where it was applied to political rituals and procedures (Althoff 2007; Stollberg-Rilinger 2005).

[18] Many approaches, besides the culturalistic and praxeological ones that are mentioned above in more detail, share the understanding that the state is not the only actor in the space of politics, cf. recent studies in a conceptional history of politics in Bielefeld (Albert and Steinmetz 2007), the results of research on governance by political scientists (Mayntz 2006; Schuppert 2006), or the research on the so-called failed states (e.g. Risse and Lehmkuhl 2007).

the ruler and his elite or the competing power-holders. Negotiations between rulers and estates were not just considered to be very important in the European context, but also characteristic for the European system. However, comparable processes of negotiation between rulers and their political elites have been equally determined for pre-modern rule in Asia. This notion often goes hand in hand with the above-mentioned analogy between state and family, ruler and father. Patriarchal rule is constituted by political communication between the ruler and the ruled. The concept of a patrimonial bureaucratic empire, as mentioned above regarding the Mughal Empire, encompassed more dynamics and interactions than earlier concepts of a central state (Schnepel 1997: 26). Research on patronage in the European context has given important impulses to the understanding of state as a network and a system of interaction and negotiation (Reinhard 1979, 1996).

Studies on processes of negotiating rule and statehood are not exclusively European. However, studies employing such culturalistic approaches are deeply influenced by anthropological concepts and theories. Nevertheless, it is astounding that there is barely any exchange within the field of research on state and rule in different cultures, even though these studies have achieved very similar results with regard to symbolic communication, ritual, and performative action.[19] Comparable phenomena in different world regions must be correlated to a much greater degree than is presently the case. Like Stefan Brakensiek, Farhat Hasan, too, challenges every kind of state determinism and understands state and society as intimately interwoven (Hasan 2004; Brakensiek 2005a,b). He describes Mughal rule as poly-centric, with a claim to central sovereignty, but lacking absolute control. This picture is familiar to European historians of the Early Modern period who deal with the Holy Roman Empire and its feudal system (Stollberg-Rilinger 2006). André Wink's observation that, in the late eighteenth century, Mughal rule was still accepted as *de jure* universal, but political and regional sovereignty were disputed by regional power-holders (Wink 1986), is reminiscent of the functions of the German emperor in Early Modern times. Frank Perlin questions the orientalised picture of a completely dependent Mughal elite; his results remind us of the Janus-faced heads of European office-holders (Perlin 1985: 452–458; Rublack 1997). However, to get deeper into similar and different processes, the different kinds of competing power-holders and therefore also the process of elite formation in Asia and Europe must also be considered.

Many more examples of comparable phenomena in Asia and Europe concerning the political sphere and the process of state building could be outlined, to relativise the claim of European particularity. However, this list of resemblances does not imply that these structures were the same in Asia and in Europe. Similar structures should not be identified too quickly as connected history. Nevertheless, they

---

[19] The studies of Nicolas Dirks are based on a comparable theoretical approach (Dirks 1987, 2001). An important example from research on South Asia is the concept of the segmentary state. The pyramid-like structure of its rule is bound by a ritual sovereignty (Stein 1977; Cohn 1990; cf. also Schnepel 1997: 32–42; Mann 2005: 33–43). Very important on symbolic communication as part of Indian rule is still Ronald Inden (1978, 1992).

provide us with a starting point to look for entanglement and for the development of a transcultural concept of state and statehood. Several approaches to Early Modern European history have challenged the hierarchical and centre-oriented concept of rule and government in an even more fundamental way. Not only did rulers negotiate with elites, but also with various other groups in society. From the 1980s, Peter Blickle highlighted the political importance of urban and rural communities in Upper Germany (Blickle 2000; Blickle and Fuhrmann 1998). Even though recent research has built further on the central role that negotiation plays in governance,[20] the results have yet to be applied to a transcultural context. All these approaches challenge the idea of an omnipotent, ruling centre that created the modern state. In some cases, authoritarian aims and strategies are even neglected altogether. However, it is striking that these studies cover almost exclusively intra-European interactions. Studies on European rule outside of Europe portray the respective states as shaped much more intentionally from above and as much more powerful in implementing their strategies. It is, then, time to include the above-mentioned approaches in a transcultural context and in an entangled history.[21]

Governance and statehood comprise many different aspects in political discourse and historiography. The concept of *state*, deriving from the modern European national *state*, has no universal value, and it (this ideal or special case) can hardly function as a heuristic model outside modern times. However, the powerful, centrally organised national state became an ideal of modern statehood worldwide. This potency of the *state* concept is the reason that historians and other researchers have looked for this kind of *state* in different times and different places—and found it.[22] The existence of state structures was, and is, considered a proof of modernity and development. As was discussed above, to choose an alternative term, like *Herrschaft* or *empire*, is not satisfactory; the problems associated with the term *state* remain unsolved. Moreover, studies that leave out the term *state* entirely may find themselves being sidelined from historiographically and politically important discussions, e.g. the rise of the West, the great divergence, and the question of modernity in general. To challenge these master narratives, it is reasonable to maintain the use of the term *state*, although understood not as a fixed model, but

---

[20] There are many studies based on this approach, for example, Brakensiek (2005a); Landwehr (2000), Dinges (2000).

[21] This was also one of the demands that Gerd Schwerhoff phrased in a review of studies on a cultural history of politics. He asked how these patterns could be applied to other world regions and to non-European social actors: "Der interkulturelle Vergleich auf diesem Gebiet wäre ein nächster spannender Schritt innerhalb einer fruchtbaren Forschungsrichtung" (Schwerhoff 2006).

[22] This can be said for many studies on medieval or early modern states, as well as with regard to pre-modern non-European regions. For example, in Scandinavia historians wanted to prove that they had an as "rich and powerful [a] state" as those in central Europe; cf. on this, with biographical notes: Line (2007), XIX; or the Indian Aligarh school which understood the early modern Indian state as a more or less modern central state (cf. about that concerning this, plus and with bibliographical notes: Hasan 2004: 3).

as a space for interaction and as a result of interactive processes. Thus, we understand state as an organised socio-political system, above the family level, with one government that structures the life of its members and the distribution of power and resources. The system reached a differentiation of such a degree that the delegation of power is necessary—not only to individuals but also in an institutionalised form. Therefore at least the early stages of an executive, a bureaucracy, a legal system, and some kind of a military organisation is needed, though we want to ignore the question of some form of religious organisation, because the concept of religion as an institution is characteristic of the European or rather Christian context and is debatable for many parts of Asia (King 2002; Masuzawa 2005). This system has a centre, but the centre is not the only actor. Processes of state building consist of interactions between networks of actors and institutions. Therefore, we need action and communication theory for our research. Our main interest lies in the functioning and changing of such systems. While improvement is one possible direction of change, in general, change is understood as contingent.

3 State as an Object of Transcultural Research

3.1 Conceptual Approaches to State as an Object of a Culturalist History

Departing from these conceptual ideas on state formation, research can focus on the transcultural interaction. The quite multifaceted case studies collected in this book aim to outline a new research field, offering different topics and testing different approaches as a first step towards a new, transcultural conceptualisation of state and statehood. The volume starts with two contributions as examples of the culturalist approaches concerning *state* and *state formation*: Barbara Stollberg-Rilinger explains her concept of a culturalistic approach by applying it to the development of a European system of sovereign actors at the Westphalian peace negotiations. She also demonstrates how her approach can be combined with entangled history. Stefan Brakensiek surveys new approaches to German and European state building from below. The crucial point of his argument is that state building is not a planned action "from above", but the result of communicative processes. The empirical studies based on this approach prove as well that this interaction and communication took very different forms throughout Europe. Thus, Brakensiek is able to challenge the image of a unique European way of state building.

In the second part of this book, state and the technologies of governance are the objects of enquiry. The goal is to analyse the evolution and development of technologies of power, state and government. As explained earlier, a fixed and universally valid definition of state is of less importance for questions concerning transcultural phenomena, institutions and practices in the field of governance. In this respect, Roger Chartier's praxeologic concept of representation (Chartier 1992:

14   A. Flüchter

7–23, 1994) is promising. And if one applies this concept to state building, one can assume that contemporary concepts of state and rulership outline an ideal behaviour of the ruling classes and a kind of profile of the requirements of good governance. By means of different social practices, these ideals or requirements are accepted (in different degrees) and, in turn, institutionalised, and can thus be described by researchers.[23] It is also important to consider the fact that theoretical models and social reality are interwoven, as the Cambridge school of intellectual history points out (Pocock 1962, 1973; Skinner 1969, 1978). The case studies in the empirical part of this volume follow and test some of the above-mentioned approaches. The articles at the beginning of this book analyse different forms and ways of appropriating knowledge about foreign states and their technologies of governance, and the others examine whether, and how intercultural interaction and communication lead to transcultural forms and practices.

3.2   *State as a Topic of a Transcultural History of Knowledge*

In situations of competition or in times of crises, state systems look for ways to increase their resources of power and the efficiency of their technologies of governance. One of the strategies to fulfil that aim is to look at foreign systems and appropriate particular technologies or stocks of knowledge. The transfer of knowledge and technologies is not to be understood as a simple import. In the context of a cultural encounter, the transfer of knowledge consists of processes of perception, translation and appropriation; it can be accompanied by mutual understanding or misunderstandings. But regardless of whether the participants understood or misunderstood each other, the outcome becomes transcultural, something beyond or additional to the cultural framework as it was before the encounter. The cultural transfer approach advanced by Matthias Middell and Michel Espagne can be fruitfully employed to analyse such processes (Middell 2000, 2001; Espagne 2003). However, approaches like these must be complemented by theories of transcultural perception and translation (Bachmann-Medick 1997; Budich and Iser 1996; Asad 1986; Chakrabarty 2008: 83–90). Secondly, these processes are not simply bilateral and must be regarded as a network consisting of flows of knowledge and of technology. In this sense, the *Histoire Croisée* attempts to combine transfer with the concept of entangled history (Werner 2009: 19–22). Experiences of different cultures, their state structures and technologies of governance, have to be embedded within knowledge systems of the receiving culture. Whether the appropriation relies on a misunderstanding or a true understanding of the perceived culture, is secondary, because all products of perception and recording are results of transcultural processes. Underlying rationalities, norm systems,

---

[23] The usefulness of this approach is impressively shown in a study on symbolic practices in early modern universities by Marian Füssel (2006).

and practices of perception that shape the limiting boundaries of these structures have to be considered as contingent; therefore it is always necessary to historicise them. The methods of a history of knowledge and perception (Landwehr 2004) provide us with important instruments; however, they must also be transculturally broadened (Burghartz 2004).

Experience and knowledge of foreign state systems feed local state theory, as well as political practice. In her contribution to this volume, Susan Richter examines the discourse in German theories of state about the ideal of rulership and governance. She outlines the integration of knowledge of the Chinese state in theoretical modelling bearing on the concept of state, using texts by Christian Wolff and Johann Heinrich Gottlob von Justi. Her case study shows the complexity of these transfers and the entanglement of social practice within a theoretical discourse on state. To serve as a role model, the donor culture had to be accepted as equal or superior to the receiving culture. To analyse this, she connects studies of symbolic communication with intellectual history. In the media of diplomatic ceremonies, the Chinese emperor was acknowledged as an equal of European kings. The appropriation of Chinese knowledge into European model-building was facilitated because several aspects of the Chinese concept of the state were similar to those of the Europeans—for example, a shared analogy between family and state. The epistemological changes in European discourse on state in the eighteenth century and the new physiocratic thought structured the selective integration of knowledge about China. Guido Mühlemann's and Nicolas Schillinger's contributions to this volume focus in the opposite direction. Mühlemann analyses the transfer of political ideas relating to constitutional monarchy from Europe to China around 1900. He traces different forms of this kind of monarchy in Europe, and explains the relevance of Chinese structures and ideas, as well as individual actors for the (failed) attempts to introduce it to China. Schillinger examines the application of European methods of statistics in modern China. He analyses the process of Chinese reception and the selective appropriation of foreign technologies of governance. Although European and American methods of statistical investigation were mostly accepted as role models, each method was tested and the one that suited the Chinese best was chosen. The selection criteria depended on the methods offered and on Chinese strategies. It is significant that in one context the relevance of traditional Chinese methods was highlighted, and in another context the same method, in comparison with European methods, was considered inappropriate. Schillinger also demonstrates that there was hardly a bilateral relation between Europe and China. Firstly, the Chinese selected among the European possibilities, and secondly, much of the knowledge came to China via Japan.

Such flows of knowledge and the curiosity about foreign solutions to similar problems can be found in most state systems. In her paper, Corinne Lefèvre analyses the circulation of political ideas and instruments in seventeenth century Mughal India. Contrary to older studies that claim that the Mughal Empire was hardly interested in Europe and European institutions, Lefèvre examines how Mughal emperors commissioned texts on Europe. She describes an interesting collaboration between a Jesuit and an Indo-Persian scholar. This knowledge about Europe, however, circulated in the Mughal Empire only as an object of curiosity, and was not among the sources that the Mughals referred to in relation to state and state building. As Lefèvre explains in the second part of her article, impulses from the Safavid Empire were much more important in such matters. Thus, the existence of foreign knowledge does not, *per se*, provide sufficient proof of transfer. Knowledge can also be of practical use, or serve as entertainment. The process of selection, the structures of this process, and the underlying criteria will have to be analysed in future research. Perception is the first step in the process of appropriation of foreign knowledge. It is accompanied by reading about the foreign culture and by integrating this experience in one's own system of reference. My contribution to this volume investigates an example of this process. It analyses the perception of seventeenth century Indian Mughal technologies of governance and their integration into European knowledge. To this end, knowledge of institutions such as the general administrative system, the customs administration and judiciary, as well as the description of court ceremonials, particularly those courtly festivities of central importance, is examined and analysed. When searching for non-European threads in European state-building, it is important to know what was interesting for a European audience about Indian statehood. Travellers reported on things they considered interesting and things they hoped their audience also would be interested in. For the discourse on state building, it is important to ask which aspects of this information were integrated into wider or more specific theoretical knowledge, that is, what was transferred from travelogues to compilations, and, even more importantly, to encyclopedias and theoretical texts. A selective perception may be observed, as the methods of learning and forgetting were closely linked to European interests and the development of international power asymmetries.

3.3 State as a Result of Interaction

In Early Modern Europe, the transfer of knowledge must be considered the most important source of transculturality. Europeans brought home knowledge from different regions of the world. Some of it was integrated into general discourse and was socially accepted as truth, and modified in this process.[24] Apart from a few non-European diplomatic missions to Europe, much of the face-to-face communication and interaction took place in other world regions. This asymmetry hardly changed until modern times. However, the power asymmetries that structured the encounter changed a great deal between the sixteenth and the twentieth centuries. Prior to the eighteenth century, the encounter was often dominated by Asian

---

[24] Individual visitors from far-away regions, such as the Polynesian Omai, Greenlanders at the Danish Court, North American Indian chieftains (or the famous Pocahontas) at the English court, etc., made these regions perhaps "more real" for the Europeans. However, most of these impressions were exotic, rather than transcultural.

partners. This changed in modern times—from the eighteenth century onward in India, and from the nineteenth in China. The development of transcultural structures and technologies of governance can be analysed using various examples from different fields: in this book we chose the military, technologies of administration, and diplomacy. These are areas where intercultural interaction took place and they are also assumed to be central to modern state building.[25] In the light of the concepts of negotiation discussed earlier, it remains to be asked how the interaction was perceived, which structures shaped them, which groups were involved.

In the personal encounter, the Europeans learned about Asian technologies of governance. They built factories in towns under Asian rule, paid taxes or tributes, presented themselves at the court etc. In this context the Europeans were forced to subordinate themselves to the rule of Asian empires. Because of these restrictions Europeans faced in their factories situated under Indian rule, most European companies wanted to build an independent base, where they could exercise their rule. For example, in India, this happened in Goa (Portuguese), Pondicherry (French), Tranquebar (Danish) and Bombay (British). To rule these towns the Europeans had to build administrative structures and institutions. Research often misleadingly terms this kind of state building as colonial state building, because it implies as yet non-existing colonial power relations. However, there were hardly any real new foundations in Asia, the areas where the Europeans built their settlements cannot be defined as empty or devoid of forms of governance. On the contrary, the European usually had to begin their building on structures already in existence. Different concepts are used to analyse these first steps of this type of state building. In her case study, concerning the French in Pondicherry during the early eighteenth century, Gauri Parasher applies the concepts of appropriation and state building from below. The French had to negotiate with Indians on different levels: with Indian rulers as well as regional inhabitants. This process of state building must be enlarged by taking into account intercultural communication, the role of brokers, and must be understood as an interaction and an appropriation. It remains to be analysed if the new rulers linked their technologies of governance to old patterns of rule and order to be accepted as rulers. It also remains to be asked how the ruled coped with this new set of rulers and with their new ways of ruling: did they resist some aspects of the new rule? Did they instrumentalise other institutions? To what extent can the evolving structures and institutions, planned by the ruling elite, be considered as transcultural? Were they perceived or even justified as transcultural? These questions have to be answered in the context of shifting asymmetries as becomes apparent in Sebastian Meurer's case study on British rule in Bengal. At the beginning, the EIC's rule in Bengal was at least *de jure* subordinated to the structures of the Mughal Empire. Warren Hastings' plans

---

[25] This is the case for the model of the developing fiscal-military state. This model, developed by Charles Tilly and Michael Mann, has become very influential; in German discourse, the most important studies are those cited above, by Wolfgang Reinhard (Tilly 1990; Tilly and Ardant 1975; Mann 1986).

for effective governance made use of the Mughal empire's old structures—which he understood as an ancient constitution comparable to similar invented traditions in the British discourse. This understanding changed thoroughly under Charles Cornwallis who conceptualised his rule as a distinct break with the Indian past. This shift had practical consequences, for example in the way information about India was gathered. It also manifested in a striking change in the evaluation of theoretical concepts, most of all the concept of Asiatic despotism. To phrase it more provocatively: in the first phase of their rule in Bengal, the British established transcultural state structures; in the second phase, they perceived them, at the least, as an alternative British draught to Indian despotism.

The military is considered an important aspect of state building in Europe (Tilly 1990), but also in India (Stein 1998: 156–160). In general, armies were—at least, before the time of national armies—organisations where many different kinds of people and groups met and mingled. These organisations represent a space where many transcultural practices evolved. The military is also a field where rulers and army chiefs had to keep track of developments and improvements in foreign armies, because inferiority in this field could be, and often was, disastrous. Development in the military field, such as a standing army, is considered a very important aspect of modern state building. Thus, a special relevance is attributed to the so-called Military Revolution, and, together with the superiority of Western weaponry, it is understood as a major factor in the *Rise of the West* (Parker 1996: 115–145). This relation is evaluated differently in research by specialists of non-European warfare (e.g. Gommans 2002). However, military technology is often considered to be one of the few European developments that aroused the interest of Asian rulers (Trakulhun 2003). This is doubtless true for the seventeenth century; in the nineteenth century, the Chinese military was, especially after their defeat in the Sino-French war, undergoing a process of modernisation, and was interested in European technology. The conditions and routes of this transfer are analysed by Barend Noordam who uses the concepts of tasking and military culture to emphasise that transfer depended to a large extent on the culture and mentality of the receiving society. The failure of such transfers—or the lack of military success following a transfer of technology—is often explained by the corresponding lack of strategy and training; this, however, was not only a Chinese or non-European problem, but also occurred in the course of intra-European transfers. Thus, the dichotomy of European and non-European in this process has to be re-evaluated. The second article concerning the transfer of military knowledge also focuses on the relation between military ideas and society. Peter Trummer examines the transfer of military ideas using the example of the Clausewitzian Triad. Prussian reformer Carl von Clausewitz argued that military changes lead to consequences regarding the relation between ruler and people, an idea that he based on contemporary notions in France. This model interested China in the nineteenth century. The author stresses that the term "military revolution" should not be limited to military development and modernisation; the process of evolution in this field can only be called a revolution when social change is involved.

Structures on the Move

The third field of transcultural state building to be highlighted in this volume concerns diplomacy. This is a field where, for a long time, European historiography claimed to have a special and distinct system as a consequence of either the Westphalian treaty of 1648, the so-called Westphalian System or the congress of Vienna in 1815 (Vec 2001; Stollberg-Rilinger in this volume). Even so, diplomatic relations with non-European territories had always existed, and this interaction required the development of transcultural forms of communication and negotiation.[26] Again, for a long time, the exclusive power of defining this symbolic language was in Asian hands. Therefore, to examine this field and to understand the creation of a transcultural space where the diplomatic mission could take place, symbolic communication and performative actions must be incorporated in the analysis. There are important studies on individual embassies, but such single intercultural diplomatic relations are not really integrated into the development of a European state system, state building in Europe, or the possibilities of pre-modern global diplomatic networks. In this volume, the relevance of intercultural relations and the process of developing transcultural forms of diplomacy are tackled from the European side. The closing article by Christian Wieland's returns to a more general view. He highlights the characteristics of European diplomacy within which interaction with foreign cultures and customs was part of diplomatic practice. Wieland analyses this encounter with the foreign in a European context and also indicates how his results could be applied to a broader, global context. Interestingly, he challenges the hypothesis that diplomats necessarily became experts on foreign cultures. On the contrary, their qualifications and their duty towards their masters made it necessary to avoid any form of acculturation to the foreign culture. Intercultural diplomacy, in fact, stabilised the boundary between cultures, and was thus very important for the internal differentiation within the diplomatic system.

Dorothee Linnemann has a somewhat different view of intercultural diplomacy. She shows that, even if the so-called Westphalian system be understood as strictly European, non-European courts, such as the Ottoman court, provided important arenas to negotiate and represent European differences. She applies the approaches of symbolic communication to intercultural contact and analyses the ways ambassadors dealt with foreign diplomatic ceremonial, and, more importantly, integrates the visualisations of the diplomatic encounters into the context of state building. She shows convincingly that because a wide variety of groups was involved, this sort of diplomatic interaction cannot be understood as a clear-cut East–West dichotomy.

---

[26] There is an increasing number of studies on intercultural diplomacy. Christian Windler applied network concepts to intercultural diplomatic interaction and the formation of transcultural diplomatic forms (Windler 2001, 2006; Burschel 1998, 2007).

4 Conclusion

The starting point of this volume is the assumption that state, statehood and technologies of governance result from transcultural processes and are not a European particularity or an exclusively European achievement. The articles in this volume test this assumption by investigating concepts of statehood and state formation, as well as offering case studies of knowledge transfer and intercultural interaction. In European as well as in Asian historical studies, state and state building are nowadays mostly understood as processes of interaction between rulers and different groups of the societies involved; of both implementations of governmental intentions and of appropriation from below. The discussions at the conference showed, however, that historical research restricts itself too much to its own specific area. The functioning of governance, as well as the concepts of its structure, its ideals and its aims, have to be broadened transculturally. It is time to get rid of the hegemonic position held by the concept of the modern national state and to develop a transcultural concept of state, before and beyond the hegemony of nations. On the one hand, it is very important to include non-European concepts of state in European research, to challenge certain cherished beliefs about European governance using similarities or alternative models from Asian regions of the world. On the other hand, research into Asian statehood should not only challenge the modern European nation state, but also include pre-modern European structures and institutions in its conceptualisation and discussion. Only then can the pre-modern understanding of state and governance be analysed without anachronistic notions, and also help us to understand the possibilities of a post-national state.

The case studies of knowledge transfer showed how much knowledge of the state and technologies of governance in other world regions was available, and how detailed it was, not only in modern, but also in pre-modern times. Three main results appeared in the articles and should be more deeply examined in future research: firstly, they underlined the importance of thinking in terms of networks, rather than in terms of bilateral relations. China received much of its European knowledge via Japan, German texts embodied English and French information. Future research mustfocus much more on networks of knowledge transfer and avoid focusing exclusively on Europe. At the same time, Europe and Asia should not be seen as monolithic entities; rather, the exchange processes within and between these larger cultural areas must be involved, as well. Secondly, it was shown that knowledge repeatedly changes its content and immanent hierarchies, during the process of moving. Transfer has to be understood as a permanent process of selection, appropriation and alteration. It is therefore important to investigate the historical character of knowledge, of the institutions and the concepts of state and governance, in order to understand this selectivity. Here, it is important that research from different disciplines is combined to an even greater degree. Thirdly, analysing what cultures know about each other constitutes an important first step when examining the idea of a transcultural state; future research will have to go much deeper into the question of how this knowledge was transformed into political action. Some of the articles presented show how much European history can reap from research on transfer from other parts of the world. In European political history, studies of state building from above, as well as from below, have mostly ignored non-European influences. Only if we include them, or at least take their possibility into account, can we decide whether the modern state was a genuine European phenomenon or rather a result of transcultural processes as this book postulates.

Based on the assumption that everything is transcultural in one way or another and results from processes that are at least partly transcultural, it is not necessary to prove that there are transcultural elements in governmental structures, technologies and images of statehood. However, the question still remains of how they evolved, how they were shaped, which factors, structures, intentions and narratives were involved. The case studies in this volume show how new culturalist approaches of state and state building from below can be fruitfully applied to statehood and the transfer of technologies in a transcultural context. It is a starting point for a new understanding of state and governance in a globally entangled world.

Bibliography

Albert, Mathias and Willibald Steinmetz. 2007. "Be- und Entgrenzungen von Staatlichkeit im politischen Kommunikationsraum." *APuZ* 20–21: 17–23.

Althoff, Gerd. 2007. "Medieval Studies in Germany and the 'performative turn'." Vortrag gehalten anlässlich eines Symposiums der Universität Tokio vom 8. bis 10. Oktober 2004, published in Japanese, Tokyo.

Anderson, Benedict R. O'G. 1990. *Imagined Communities: Reflections on the Origin and Spread of Nationalism*. London: Verso.

Asad, Talal. 1986. "The Concept of Cultural Translation in British Social Anthropology." In *Writing Culture: The Poetics and Politics of Ethnography*, ed. James Clifford, 151–164. Berkeley: California University Press.

Asch, Ronald G. and Dagmar Freist. 2005. *Staatsbildung als kultureller Prozeß*. Cologne: Böhlau.

Bachmann-Medick, Doris. 1997. *Übersetzung als Repräsentation fremder Kulturen*. Berlin: Schmidt.

Bayly, Christopher A. 2006. *Die Geburt der modernen Welt: eine Globalgeschichte: 1780–1914*. Frankfurt am Main [u.a.]: Campus.

Bayly, Christopher A. 2009. *The Birth of the Modern World, 1780–1914: Global Connections and Comparisons*. Malden [etc.]: Blackwell.

Berger, Peter L. and Thomas Luckmann. 1967. *The Social Construction of Reality: A Treatise in the Sociology of Knowledge*. New York: Doubleday.

Blake, Stephen P. 1979. "The Patrimonial-Bureaucratic Empire of the Mughals." *Journal of Asian Studies* 39: 77–94.

Blake, Stephen P. 1991. *Shahjahanabad: the Sovereign City in Mughal India 1639–1739*. Cambridge [u.a.]: Cambridge Univ. Press.

Blickle, Peter. 2000. *Kommunalismus. Skizzen einer gesellschaftlichen Organisationsform. Vol.1: Oberdeutschland, Vol. 2: Europa*. Munich: Oldenbourg.

Blickle, Peter and Rosi Fuhrmann. 1998. *Gemeinde und Staat im Alten Europa*. München: Oldenbourg.

Bourdieu, Pierre. 1990. "Einsetzungsriten". In *Was heisst sprechen? Die Ökonomie des sprachlichen Tausches*, ed. Pierre Bourdieu, 84–93. Vienna: Braumüller.

Brakensiek, Stefan. 2005a. *Ergebene Diener ihrer Herren? Herrschaftsvermittlung im alten Europa*. Köln, Weimar, Wien: Böhlau.

Brakensiek, Stefan. 2005b. "Lokale Amtsträger in deutschen Territorien der frühen Neuzeit. Institutionelle Grundlagen, akzeptanzorientierte Herrschaftspraxis und obrigkeitliche Identität". In *Staatsbildung als kulturelle Praxis. Strukturwandel und Legitimation von Herrschaft in der Frühen Neuzeit*, ed. Ronald A. Asch and Dagmar Freist, 49–67. Köln, Weimar, Wien: Böhlau.

Brewer, John and Eckhart Hellmuth. 1999. *Rethinking Leviathan*. New York, Oxford: Oxford University Press.

Brunner, Otto. 1939. *Land und Herrschaft: Grundfragen der territorialen Verfassungsgeschichte Südostdeutschlands im Mittelalter*. Baden bei Wien, Leipzig [u.a.]: Rohrer.

Brunner, Otto. 1959. *Land und Herrschaft: Grundfragen der territorialen Verfassungsgeschichte Österreichs im Mittelalter*. Wien [u.a.]: Rohrer.

Brunner, Otto. 1968. "Das 'Ganze Haus' und die alteuropäische Ökonomik." In *Neue Wege der Verfassungs- und Sozialgeschichte*, ed. Otto Brunner, 103–127. Göttingen: Vandenhoeck & Ruprecht.

Brunner, Otto. 1992. *Land and Lordship. Structures of Governance in Medieval Austria*. Philadelphia: Univ. of Pennsylvania Press.

Budich, Sanford and Wolfgang Iser. 1996. *The Translatability of Cultures. Figurations of the Space Between*. Stanford: Standford University Press.

Burghartz, Susanna. 2004. "Aneignung des Fremden: Staunen, Stereotypen und Zirkulation um 1600." In *Integration des Widerläufigen*, ed. Elke Huwiler and Nicole Wachter. Hamburg: LIT.

Burschel, Peter 1998. "Das Eigene und das Fremde. Zur anthropologischen Entzifferung diplomatischer Texte." In *Kurie und Politik: Stand und Perspektiven der Nuntiaturberichtsforschung*, ed. Alexander Koller, 260–271. Tübingen: Niemeyer.

Burschel, Peter. 2007. "Topkapi Sarayi oder Salomon Schweiggers Reise ans Ende der Zeit." In *Räume des Selbst: Selbstzeugnisforschung transkulturell*, ed. Andreas Bähr, Peter Burschel and Gabriele Jancke, 29–40. Köln, Weimar, Wien: Böhlau.

Canizares-Esguerra, Jorge. 2007. "AHR Forum: Entangled Histories: Borderland Historiographies in New Clothes?" *The American Historical Review June 2007* http://www.historycooperative. org/journals/ahr/112.3/canizaresesguerra.html *(29 Oct. 2010)*.

Chakrabarty, Dipesh. 2008. *Provincializing Europe: Postcolonial Thought and Historical Difference*. Princeton, New York: Princeton University Press.

Carlier, Julie. 2010. "Forgotten Transnational Connections and National Contexts: an 'entangled history' of the political transfers that shaped Belgian feminism, 1890–1914." *Women's History Review* 19: 503–522.

Chartier, Roger. 1988. *Cultural History. Between Practices and Representations*. Ithaca, New York: Polity Press.

Chartier, Roger. 1992. *Die unvollendete Vergangenheit. Geschichte und die Macht der Weltauslegung*. Frankfurt am Main: Fischer-Taschenbuch-Verlag.

Chartier, Roger. 1994. "Die Welt als Repräsentation." In *Alles Gewordene hat Geschichte. Die Schule der Annales in ihren Texten 1929–1992*, ed. Matthias Middell, 320–347. Leipzig: Reclam.

Cohn, Bernhard S. 1990. "Political Systems in Eighteenth-Century India: The Benaras Region (1962)." In *An Anthropologist among the Historians and Other Essays*, ed. Bernhard S. Cohn, 483–499. New Delhi, Oxford: Oxford University Press.

Conrad, Sebastian. 2003. "Circulation, 'National Work', and Identity. Debates About the Mobility of Work in Germany and Japan, 1890–1914." In *Entangled Histories and Negotiated Universals. Centers and Peripheries in a Changing World*, ed. Wolf Lepenies, 260–280. Frankfurt am Main [u.a.]: Campus.

Conrad, Sebastian and Shalini Randeria. 2002. "Einleitung. Geteilte Geschichten - Europa in einer postkolonialen Welt." In *Jenseits des Eurozentrismus. Postkoloniale Perspektiven in der Geschichts- und Kulturwissenschaft*, ed. Sebastian Conrad and Shalini Randeria, 9–49. Frankfurt, New York: Campus.

Demel, Walter. 2010. "Reichs- und Staatsbildung." In *Entdeckungen und neue Ordnungen 1200–1800*, ed. Walter Demel. Darmstadt: WBG.

Dinges, Martin. 2000. "Justiznutzung als soziale Kontrolle in der frühen Neuzeit." In *Kriminalitätsgeschichte. Beiträge zur Sozial- und Kulturgeschichte der Vormoderne*, ed. Andreas Blauert, 503–544. Konstanz: UVK.

Dirks, Nicholas D. 1987. *The Hollow Crown. Ethnohistory of an Indian Kingdom.* Cambridge: Cambridge University Press.

Dirks, Nicholas D. 2001. *Castes of Mind. Colonialism and the Making of Modern India.* Princeton: Princeton University Press.

Duchhardt, Heinz. 1991. "Das protestantische Herrscherbild des 17. Jahrhunderts im Reich." In *Das Herrscherbild im 17. Jahrhundert*, ed. Konrad Repgen, 26–42. Münster: Aschendorff.

Duchhardt, Heinz. 1994. "Absolutismus – Abschied von einem Epochebegriff." *HZ* 258: 113–123.

Espagne, Michael. 2003. "Der theoretische Stand der Kulturtransferforschung." In *Kulturtransfer. Kulturelle Praxis im 16. Jahrhundert*, ed. Wolfgang Schmale, 63–75. Innsbruck etc.: Studien-Verlag.

Flüchter, Antje. 2005. "Konfessionalisierung in kulturalistischer Perspektive? Überlegungen am Beispiel der Herzogtümer Jülich-Berg im 16. Jahrhundert." In *Was heißt Kulturgeschichte des Politischen?*, ed. Barbara Stollberg-Rilinger, 225–252. Berlin: Duncker & Humblot.

Foucault, Michel. 2000. "Die Gouvernementalität." In *Gouvernementalität der Gegenwart. Studien zur Ökonomisierung des Sozialen*, ed. Ulrich Bröckling et al., 41–67. Frankfurt am Main: Suhrkamp.

Frühsorge, Gotthardt. 1982. "Oeconomie des Hofes. Zur politischen Funktion der Vaterrolle des Fürsten im Oeconomus prudens et legalis des Franz Philipp Florinus." *Daphnis* 11: 41–48.

Füssel, Marian. 2006. *Gelehrtenkultur als symbolische Praxis: Rang, Ritual und Konflikt an der Universität der Frühen Neuzeit.* Darmstadt: Wissenschaftliche Buchgesellschaft.

Genschel, Philip and Bernhard Zangl. 2007. "Die Zerfaserung von Staatlichkeit und die Zentralität des Staates." *APuZ* 20–21: 10–16.

Giddens, Anthony. 2009. *The Constitution of Society: Outline of the Theory of Structuration.* Cambridge [u.a.]: Polity Press.

Goffman, Erving. 1959. *The Presentation of Self in Everyday Life.* New York [u.a.]: Doubleday.

Gould, Eliga H. 2007. "Entangled Atlantic Histories: A Response from the Anglo-American Periphery." *The American Historical Review June 2007* http://www.historycooperative.org/journals/ahr/112.3/canizaresesguerra.html *(29 Oct. 2010)*.

Gommans, Jos. 2002. *Mughal Warfare: Indian Frontiers and Highroads to Empire 1500–1700.* London, New York: Routledge.

Groebner, Valentin. 1995. "Außer Haus. Otto Brunner und die 'alteuropäische Ökonomik'." *GWU* 46: 69–80.

Hardy, Peter. 1987. "Islamischer Patrimonialismus. Die Mogulherrschaft." In *Max Webers Sicht des Islams: Interpretation und Kritik*, ed. Wolfgang Schluchter, 190–216. Frankfurt am Main: Suhrkamp.

Hasan, Farhat. 2004. *State and Locality in Mughal India. Power Relations in Western India, c. 1572–1730.* Cambridge: Cambridge Univ. Press.

Hastorf, Christine A. 1992. *Agriculture and the Onset of Political Inequality before the Inka.* Cambridge: Cambridge Univ. Press.

Holenstein, André. 1998. "Die 'Ordnung' und die 'Mißbräuche'. 'Gute Policey' als Institution und Ereignis." In *Institutionen und Ereignis. Über historische Praktiken und Vorstellungen gesellschaftlichen Ordnens*, ed. Reinhard Blänkner, 253–275. Göttingen: Vandenhoeck & Ruprecht.

24 A. Flüchter

Holenstein, André. 2009. "Empowering Interactions: Looking at Statebuilding from Below." In *Empowering Interactions. Political Cultures and the Emergence of the State in Europe, 1300–1900*, ed. André Holenstein et al., 1–31. Farnham: Ashgate.

Inden, Ronald. 1978. "Ritual, Authority and Cyclic Time in Hindu Kingship." In *Kingship and Authority in South Asia*, ed. John F. Richards, 41–91. Wisconsin: University of Wisconsin-Madison.

Inden, Ronald B. 1992. "Divine Kingship, the Hindu Type of Government." In *Imagining India*, ed. Ronald B. Inden, 162–212. Oxford: Blackwell.

Juneja-Huneke, Monica. 2004. "Verwobene Geschichte oder: Was hat das Fremde mit der eigenen Geschichte zu tun?" In *Migration und Fremdverstehen*, ed. Bettina Alavi. Idstein: Schulz-Kirchner: 193–206.

King, Richard. 2002. *Orientalism and Religion. Postcolonial Theory, India and "the Mystic East"*. London [u.a.]: Routledge.

Kocka, Jürgen. 1995. *Bürgertum im 19. Jahrhundert: Deutschland im europäischen Vergleich*. München: Dt. Taschenbuch-Verl.

Kulke, Hermann. 1995. "Introduction: The Study of the State in Pre-modern India." In *The State in India, 1000–1700*, ed. Hermann Kulke, 1–47. Delhi: Oxford University Press.

Landwehr, Achim. 2000. *Policey im Alltag. Die Implementation frühneuzeitlicher Polizeyordnungen in Leonberg*. Frankfurt am Main: Vittorio Klostermann.

Landwehr, Achim. 2003. "Diskurs - Macht - Wissen. Perspektiven einer Kulturgeschichte des Politischen." *Archiv für Kulturgeschichte* 85: 71–117.

Landwehr, Achim. 2004. *Geschichte des Sagbaren. Einführung in die Historische Diskursanalyse*. Tübingen: Ed. Diskord.

Lemke, Thomas et al. 2000. "Gouvernementalität, Neoliberalismus und Selbsttechnologie. Eine Einleitung." In *Gouvernementalität der Gegenwart. Studien zur Ökonomisierung des Sozialen*, ed. Ulrich Bröckling et al., 7–40. Frankfurt am Main: Suhrkamp.

Line, Philip. 2007. *Kingship and State Formation in Sweden, 1130–1290*. Leiden [u.a.]: Brill.

Maissen, Thomas. 2008. *Die Geburt der Republic: Staatsverständnis und Repräsentation in der frühneuzeitlichen Eidgenossenschaft*. Göttingen: Vandenhoeck & Ruprecht.

Maissen, Thomas. 2009. "Souveräner Gesetzgeber und absolute Macht. Calvin, Bodin und die mittelalterliche Tradition." In *Konfessionalität und Jurisprudenz in der frühen Neuzeit*, ed. Christoph Strohm and Heinrich de Wall, 91–113. Berlin: Duncker&Humblot.

Mann, Michael. 1986. *A History of Power from the Beginning to A.D. 1760*. Cambridge: Cambridge Univ. Press.

Mann, Michael. 2005. *Geschichte Indiens. Vom 18. bis zum 21. Jahrhundert*. Paderborn, München, Wien, Zürich: Schöningh.

Masuzawa, Tomoko. 2005. *The Invention of World Religions, or, How European Universalism was Preserved in the Language of Pluralism*. Chicago [u.a.]: University of Chicago Press.

Martschukat, Jürgen and Steffen Patzold. 2003. *Geschichtswissenschaft und "performative turn": Ritual, Inszenierung und Performanz vom Mittelalter bis zur Neuzeit*. Cologne, Weimar, Vienna: Böhlau.

Mayntz, Renate. 2006. "Governance Theory als fortentwickelte Steuerungstheorie?" In *Governance-Forschung. Vergewisserung über Stand und Entwicklungslinien*, ed. Gunnar Folke Schuppert, 11–20. Baden-Baden: Nomos.

Middell, Matthias. 2000. Kulturtransfer und Historische Komparatistik. Thesen zu ihrem Verhältnis. *Comparativ* 10: 7–41.

Middell, Matthias. 2001. "Von der Wechselseitigkeit der Kulturen im Austausch. Das Konzept des Kulturtransfers in verschiedenen Forschungskontexten." In *Metropolen und Kulturtransfer im 15./16. Jahrhundert. Prag - Krakau - Danzig - Wien*, ed. Andrea Langer and Georg Michels, 15–51. Stuttgart: Steiner.

Miller, Peter N. 2002. "Nazis and Neo-Stoics: Otto Brunner and Gerhard Oestreich before and after the Second World War." *Past and Present* 176: 144–186.

Mintz, Sidney Wilfred. 1986. *Sweetness and Power. The Place of Sugar in Modern History*. Harmondsworth: Penguin.

Münch, Paul. 1982. "Die 'Obrigkeit im Vaterstand' - Zu Definition und Kritik des 'Landesvaters' während der Frühen Neuzeit." *Daphnis* 11: 15–40.

Münkler, Herfried. 2004. *Imperien. Die Logik der Weltherrschaft vom alten Rom bis zu den Vereinigten Staaten*. Berlin: Rowohlt.

Nicklas, Thomas. 2004. "Macht – Politik – Diskurs. Möglichkeiten und Grenzen einer Politischen Kulturgeschichte." *AKG* 86: 1–25.

Oestreich, Gerhard. 1969. "Strukturprobleme des europäischen Absolutismus." In *Geist und Gestalt des frühmodernen Staates. Ausgewählte Aufsätze*, ed. Gerhard Oestreich, 179–197. Berlin: Duncker & Humblot.

Opitz, Claudia. 1994. "Neue Wege der Sozialgeschichte? Ein kritischer Blick auf Otto Brunners Konzept des 'ganzen Hauses'." *Geschichte und Gesellschaft* 20: 88–98.

Osterhammel, Jürgen. 2006. "Imperien." In *Transnationale Geschichte. Themen, Tendenzen und Theorien*, ed. Gunilla Budde et al., 56–67. Göttingen: Vandenhoeck & Ruprecht.

Osterhammel, Jürgen. 2009. *Die Verwandlung der Welt: eine Geschichte des 19. Jahrhunderts*. München: Beck.

Parker, Geoffrey. 1996. *The Military Revolution. Military Innovation and the Rise of the West. 1500–1800*. Cambridge: Cambridge University Press.

Perlin, Frank. 1985. "State Formation Reconsidered." *Modern Asian Studies* 19: 415–480.

Pernau, Margrit. 2007. "Transkulturelle Geschichte und das Problem der universalen Begriffe. Muslimische Bürger im Delhi des 19. Jahrhunderts." In *Area Studies und die Welt. Weltregionen und neue Globalgeschichte*, ed. Birgit Schäbler, 117–149. Wien: Mandelbaum Verlag.

Pernau-Reifeld, Margrit. 2008. *Bürger mit Turban: Muslime in Delhi im 19. Jahrhundert*. Göttingen: Vandenhoeck & Ruprecht.

Petersson, Niels P. and Wolfgang M. Schröder. 2007. "Souveränität und politische Legitimation. Analysen zum 'geschlossenen' und zum 'offenen' Staat." In *Legitimationsgrundlagen einer europäischen Verfassung. Von der Volkssouveränität zur Völkersouveränität*, ed. Georg Jochum, 103–150. Berlin: Duncker & Humblot.

Pocock, John G. 1962. "The History of Political Thought. A Methodological Enquiry." In *Philosophy, Politics and Society*, ed. Peter Laslett and Walter G. Runcimann, 183–202. Oxford: Blackwell.

Pocock, John G. 1973. *Politics, Language and Time. Essays on Political Thought and History*. New York: Atheneum.

Quaritsch, Helmut. 1986. *Souveränität: Entstehung und Entwicklung des Begriffs in Frankreich und Deutschland vom 13. Jahrhundert bis 1806*. Berlin: Duncker und Humblot.

Randeria, Shalini. 2002. "Entangled Histories of Uneven Modernities: Civil Society, Caste Solidarities and Legal Pluralism in Postcolonial India." In *Unraveling Ties*, ed. Yehuda Elkana et al., Frankfurt: am Main: Campus.

Reinhard, Wolfgang. 1979. *Freunde und Kreaturen. "Verflechtung" als Konzept zur Erforschung historischer Führungsgruppen. Römische Oligarchie um 1600*. München: Voegel.

Reinhard, Wolfgang. 1992. "Das Wachstum der Staatsgewalt. Historische Reflexionen." *Der Staat* 31: 59–75.

Reinhard, Wolfgang. 1996. *Power Elites and State Building*. Oxford: Clarendon Press.

Reinhard, Wolfgang (ed.). 1999. *Verstaatlichung der Welt? Europäische Staatsmodelle und außereuropäische Machtprozesse*. München: Oldenbourg.

Reinhard, Wolfgang. 2002. *Geschichte der Staatsgewalt. Eine vergleichende Verfassungsgeschichte Europas von den Anfängen bis zur Gegenwart*. München: Beck.

Richter, Melvin. 1974. "Despotism." In *Dictionary of the History of Ideas: Studies of Selected Pivotal Ideas, Vol. 2*, ed. Philip P. Wiener, 1–18. New York: Charkes Scribner's Sons.

Risse, Thomas and Ursula Lehmkuhl. 2007. "Governance in Räumen begrenzter Staatlichkeit." *APuZ* 20/21: 3–9.

Rödder, Andreas. 2006. "Klios neue Kleider. Theoriedebatten um eine Kulturgeschichte der Politik in der Moderne." *HZ* 283: 657–688.

Rubiés, Joan-Pau. 2005. "Oriental Despotism and European Orientalism: Botero to Montesquieu." *Journal of Early Modern History* 9: 109–180.

Rublack, Ulinka. 1997. "Frühneuzeitliche Staatlichkeit und lokale Herrschaftspraxis in Württemberg." *Zeitschrift für Historische Forschung* 24: 347–376.

Schluchter, Wolfgang. 1987. *Max Webers Sicht des Islams: Interpretation und Kritik*. Frankfurt am Main: Suhrkamp.

Schnepel, Burkhard. 1997. *Die Dschungelkönige ethnohistorische Aspekte von Politik und Ritual in Südorissa, Indien*. Stuttgart: Steiner.

Schulze, Winfried. 1987. "Gerhard Oestreichs Begriff Sozialdisziplinierung in der Frühen Neuzeit." *Zeitschrift für Historische Forschung* 14: 265–302.

Schuppert, Gunnar Folke. 2006. *Governance-Forschung: Vergewisserung über Stand und Entwicklungslinien*. Baden-Baden: Nomos.

Schwerhoff, Gerd. 2006. "Rezension zu: Asch, Ronald G.and Freist, Dagmar: Staatsbildung als kultureller Prozess. Köln 2005; Stollberg-Rilinger, Barbara (Hrsg.): Was heißt Kulturgeschichte des Politischen? Berlin 2005; Brakensiek, Stefan and Heide Wunder (Hrsg.): Ergebene Diener ihrer Herren? Herrschaftsvermittlung im alten Europa. Köln 2005." H-Soz-u-Kult, 07.10.2006, http://hsozkult.geschichte.hu-berlin.de/rezensionen/2006-4-021.

Skinner, Quentin. 1969. "Meaning and Understanding in the History of Ideas." *History and Theory* 8: 3–53.

Skinner, Quentin. 1978. *The Foundations of Modern Political Thought*. Cambridge: Cambridge University Press.

Stein, Burton. 1977. "The Segmentary State in South Indian History." In *Realm and Region in Traditional India*, ed. Richard G. Fox, 3–51. New Delhi: Vikas.

Stein, Burton. 1998. *A History of India*. Oxford: Blackwell.

Steinmetz, Willibald. 2007. *"Politik": Situationen eines Wortgebrauchs im Europa der Neuzeit*. Frankfurt am Main, New York: Campus.

Stollberg-Rilinger, Barbara. 2005. *Was heißt Kulturgeschichte des Politischen?* Berlin: Duncker & Humblot.

Stollberg-Rilinger, Barbara. 2006. "Das Reich als Lehnssystem." In *Altes Reich und neue Staaten. Begleitband zur Ausstellung im Deutschen Historischen Museum*, ed. Heinz Schilling and Hans Ottomeyer, 55–67. Berlin: Sandstein.

Stollberg-Rilinger, Barbara. 2008. *Des Kaisers alte Kleider: Verfassungsgeschichte und Symbolsprache des Alten Reiches*. München: Beck.

Stollberg-Rilinger, Barbara. 2009. "The Impact of Communication Theory on the Analysis of the Early Modern Statebuilding Processes." In *Empowering Interactions. Political Culture and the Emergence of the State in Europe, 1300–1900*, ed. Wim Blockmans et al., 313–318. Farnham: Ashgate.

Subrahmanyam, Sanjay. 1997. "Connected Histories. Notes towards a Reconfiguration of Early Modern Eurasia." *Modern Asian Studies* 31: 735–762.

Subrahmanyam, Sanjay. 2005. *Explorations in Connected History: Mughals and Franks*. New Delhi [u.a.]: Oxford Univ. Press.

Tambiah, Stanley Jeyaraja. 1981. *A Performative Approach to Ritual*. London: British Academy.

Tilly, Charles and Gabriel Ardant. 1975. *The Formation of National States in Western Europe*. Princeton: Princeton Univ. Press.

Tilly, Charles. 1990. *Coercion, Capitaal, and European States. AD 990–1990*. Oxford: University Press.

Trakulhun, Sven. 2003. "Kanonen auf Reisen. Portugal und die Kunst des Krieges auf dem südostasiatischen Festland. 1500–1600." In *Das eine Europa und die Vielfalt der Kulturen. Beiträge zur Kulturtransferforschung in Europa 1500–1850*, ed. Thomas Fuchs and Sven Trakulhun, 307–327. Berlin: BWV.

Vec, Miloš. 2001. "'Technische' gegen 'symbolische' Verfahrensformen? Die Normierung und Ausdifferenzierung der Gesandtenränge nach der juristischen und politischen Literatur des 18. und 19. Jahrhunderts." In *Vormoderne politische Verfahren*, ed. Barbara Stollberg-Rilinger, 559–588. Berlin: Duncker & Humblot

Werner, Michael. 2009. "Zum theoretischen Rahmen und historischen Ort der Kulturtransferforschung." In *Kultureller Austausch. Bilanz und Perspektiven der Frühneuzeitforschung*, ed. Michael North, 15–23. Köln, Weimar, Wien: Böhlau.

Windler, Christian. 2001. "Diplomatic History as a Field for Cultural Analysis: Muslim-Christian Relations in Tunis, 1700–1840." *Historical Journal* 44: 79–106.

Windler, Christian. 2006. "Diplomatie als Erfahrung fremder politischer Kulturen. Gesandte von Monarchen in den eidgenössischen Orten (16. und 17. Jh.)." *Geschichte und Gesellschaft* 32: 5–44.

Wink, André. 1986. *Land and Sovereignity in India. Agrarian Society and Politics under the Eigteenth-Century Maratha Svarajya.* Cambridge: Cambridge University Press.

Part I
Statehood: Conceptual Approaches

New Perspectives on State-Building and the Implementation of Rulership in Early Modern European Monarchies

Stefan Brakensiek

This article tries to outline some recent approaches which claim to explain the modes the process of state-building took in early modern Europe. A comparison with any of the Asian experiences could not be offered, so this is no attempt to explicate entangled or connected histories between Europe and Asia, but just a comparative note about European monarchies, which is challenging enough.

Traditionally, the state-building process in Europe has been conceptualised as the emergence of the fiscal-military state, characterised by a distinct set of political ideas and religious beliefs, fostered by growing taxes and bureaucracies, and accompanied by increasing numbers of laws and ordinances (Reinhard 1999; Wilson 2000; Contamine 2000). These customary ideas are not incorrect at all, but they are not sufficient to explain all the peculiarities of state-building in Europe. For this reason, in recent decades a number of supplementary approaches have been evolved. Firstly, the impact of personal networks on the process of decision-making at the princely courts and as a means of communication between centres and peripheries has been investigated (Reinhard 1979; Mączak 1988; Giry-Deloison and Mettam 1995; Bulst 1996). Secondly, the question of how justice and "good policy" were implemented has to a large extent now been answered (Stolleis et al. 1996; Härter 2000; Iseli 2003; Simon 2004), not only in central arenas, but on all regional scales, and most importantly on the local scale (Chittolini 1979; Aylmer 1996; Landwehr 2000; Holenstein et al. 2002; Hindle 2004). Thirdly, the concept of "empowering interactions" has most recently been worked out, which links neatly to the first and to the second proposal (Holenstein 2009). And finally, the idea has been amply discussed that ritual, ceremonies, and all kinds of cultural representations shaped princely rule in a way that set early modern politics fundamentally apart from its modern counterparts (Stollberg-Rilinger 2000; Asch and Freist 2005).

S. Brakensiek
Fakultät für Geisteswissenschaften, Historisches Institut, Universität Duisburg-Essen, 45117 Essen, Germany
e-mail: stefan.brakensiek@uni-due.de

A. Flüchter and S. Richter (eds.), *Structures on the Move*,
Transcultural Research – Heidelberg Studies on Asia and Europe in a Global Context,
DOI 10.1007/978-3-642-19288-3_2, © Springer-Verlag Berlin Heidelberg 2012

There is no reason to emphasise the differences between these four conceptions. They are all actor-orientated, as they are all interested in the interaction and in the agency of individuals, groups and corporations. Any one of them tries to explain how politics worked, how deference and obedience was installed (Muchembled 1992; Braddick and Walter 2001). But they also try to answer such questions as who was involved in policy-making, what kind of participation was enabled, and what kind of communication errors caused serious trouble (Koenigsberger 1971; Blickle 1997). All added approaches have bid farewell to any kind of teleology. In this perspective, the absolute monarchy is no longer interpreted as a necessary step towards the modern nation-state. As a common goal, these recent approaches try to aggregate their findings into what one could term the specific political culture of the European princely state (Beik 1985; Brewer and Hellmuth 1999; Black 2004; Collins 2009; Blockmans et al. 2009).

Because Barbara Stollberg-Rilinger, in her article in this volume on the culturalist perspective of state and political history, gives an insight into the meanings of rituals and ceremonies, my paper centres on the problem of how more or less daily communication between authorities and subjects was established either by personal interaction or by writing, and to what ends it was used (Becker and Clark 2001; Brakensiek and Wunder 2005). All recent research on this area starts from the simple observation that every kind of authority has to rely on the cooperation of at least some of its subjects (Lüdtke 1991). This universal law applies equally to European monarchies, principalities, and noble estates of the early modern period. To rule meant to organise interchanges of rights an liberties between the holders of the ruling power and those affected by them on a more or less regular basis. Moreover, and this was a crucial part of the occidental tradition, princes and lords sought to define themselves as acting not like tyrants, but rather like Christian authorities endowed by God with the office of maintaining the public peace, administering justice, and promoting the common weal (Weber 1998; Reinhard 1999). Certainly, this cannot be understood without examininig the communication process as presented by European political theorists (Pagden 1987; Dreitzel 1992; Nitschke 2000; Schorn-Schütte 2004; Goldie and Wokler 2006; Schorn-Schütte and Tode 2006). Furthermore it has been elaborated that encounters with the great Asian powers and increasing knowledge of their political systems shaped European self-understanding in a particular way (Osterhammel 1998).

To facilitate interchanges between the rulers and the ruled, specific institutional arrangements were set up that included policies specifically designed for these purposes, administrative bodies (or other kinds of organisations) that could implement the policies, and channels of communication to articulate consensus or conflict. The actual type of rule that resulted in specific cases thus rested on prevailing ruling concepts and their symbolic representations, as well as on bureaucratic developments, and no less on customary habits of communication. Looking at this institutional arrangement, the term "state-formation" is not entirely comfortable, since recent research has failed to reveal any kind of demiurge that could have directed any such process in a coherent way. Instead, we can observe a tacit process of trial and error that involved not only the governors, but also their public servants and many of their subjects at every step (Reinhard 2001; Emich 2005). This process affected the whole arrangement of a given ruler's policies, public offices, and channels of communication.

To reformulate it with André Holenstein: "One of the most specific characteristics of the early modern state was the absence of a uniform state authority. We observe instead a complicated, fragmented and multi-layered structure of authority and political agency; [. . .] the houses, the guilds and corporations, the communities, the estates and various groups of functional elites participated in the process of rule, thereby inducing a significant layering and fragmentation of political power" (Holenstein 2009: 5). Several attempts have been made to explore these complex relations. Since the 1980s, a number of studies have shown that the state-building process can be interpreted as resulting from personal interactions at the princely courts (Asch 1991; Cosandey and Descimon 2002; Duindam 2003; Hengerer 2004), and between the centres of rule and administrative peripheries (Kettering 1986; Windler 2000; Reinhard 2004). These studies focusing on the impact of personal networks contribute in a specific way to understanding political culture. Wolfgang Reinhard describes the role of power elites in the papal state and in secular monarchies, as reliable supporters of the expansion of state authority: by serving the crown, these elites were able to climb up the social hierarchy; in consequence, increasing the power of their employer would have seemed to be in their own best interest (Reinhard 1996). Correspondingly, Heiko Droste suggests comprehending the early modern state as a joint enterprise of crown and servants, held together by common benefits and common values, structured by a culture of patronage and loyalty (Droste 2003).

These considerations can be substantiated if one looks at how relations between peripheries and centres were shaped by certain local holders of office who functioned as an interface between central authorities and the local population. Such studies have been carried out for a number of regions in the Habsburg Empire (Neugebauer 1996; Mat'a and Winkelbauer 2006; Brakensiek 2009b), in some German territories (Robisheaux 1989; Holenstein 2003), in Spain (Lambert-Gorges 1993), France (Fontaine 2003), Italy (Grendi 1993; Astarita 1999; Castiglione 2005), England (Wrightson 1996; Hindle 2004) and Scandinavia (Gustafsson 1994; Kujala 2003). All these studies have highlighted the ability of local or regional holders of office to integrate their own activities as commissioners of the crown within the complex network of relations and local power structures as crucial for the state-building process (Brakensiek and Wunder 2005). As Christian Windler states, using a large Andalusian dominion as an example, local holders of office were the critical interfaces between local systems and larger entities (Windler 1992). Lower officials, in particular, had to balance the demands and requirements of their office against their considerations of local circumstances. Michael Braddick states for the English case that the great strength of government by holders of office was their discretion, their ability of fitting central policy to local needs (Braddick 2000). From a central European perspective, this judgement can be accepted with no reservations: *Herrschaftsvermittlung*, the mediating of power, was far more important than any kind of direct rule managed by state bureaucracies or the armed forces (Brakensiek 2009a).

At the very end of the chain of command, communal officials in towns and villages were increasingly integrated into regular communication with the authorities of the princely states (Les communautés rurales—Rural communities 1987; Blickle 1997, 2000). Traditionally, this has been interpreted as a loss of autonomous power of the communes, which is certainly true. But alongside the rising power of the princely states, the functions of the communes increased, because the few local state officials could not avoid relying upon communal functionaries to implement the multiplied state agenda. In the villages, this could be the parish priest as the traditional provider of writing, but normally peasant village officials were held responsible for the collection of taxes and tithes, the construction and maintenance of paths and ditches, the recruitment of soldiers, and the organisation of schools and poor-relief. From the sixteenth century onwards, these communal officials were obliged to record their transactions, and from the seventeenth century they were increasingly able to do so. Usually, these were unsalaried offices, only occasionally remunerated by reduction of taxes and services, or by exemption from military service. The early modern rural commune was thus deeply integrated into the emerging territorial state. And this was also increasingly true in the case of the urban communes. There, communal politics lay in the hands of local dignitaries who attained their positions by cooptation, normally combined with princely confirmation.

Territorial authorities maintained regular cooperation with towns and villages to such an extent that communal authorities became increasingly integrated into their hierarchies. But the emerging states also depended to a great extent on the functioning of the communities. For this relation, German historiography has coined the term *beauftragte Selbstverwaltung* (Wiese-Schorn 1976) which may be translated as "local self-government at the prince's command, mandated self-government, self-government mandated by the ruler, vel sim." (Hindle 2001). It must be emphasised that even those mayors, town councillors and village officials who were involved in permanent cooperation with the territorial states could scarcely claim to hold fixed and documented rights of political participation. But they could rely on pragmatic habits of participation, which were a by-product of the everyday business of governing.

Interaction between centres and peripheries was not confined to princely holders of office and communal officials. Recent research emphasises that state governance rested on selective cooperation between these officials and a great number of individual people, normally the heads of households, who were made responsible for delivering taxes, labour, military services, and information. But again, this was no communicational one-way street. Subjects in subordinate positions participated in the political process, sometimes through violent conflicts, frequently through legal disputes, mostly in the form of consensual proceedings (Lüdtke 1991). A great variety of means enabled and shaped the communication between the bureaucracies, the local notables of towns and villages, and individual subjects: visitations by commissions (Zeeden and Molitor 1977; Zeeden and Lang 1984; Menne 2007), reports by office-holders (Holenstein 2003; Tantner 2007), written petitions (Kümin and Würgler 1997; Nubola and Würgler 2005), "running to court"

(Blickle 1998), accusations and censure by the subjects (Ulbrich and Hohkamp 2001; Collin and Horstmann 2004). All these means contributed to a lively process of communication between the governments and the population.

These interactions of subjects with communal and princely officials permitted considerable opportunities for participation; local dignitaries as well as "ordinary people" could address themselves to state authorities using these legal proceedings. Recent research on the practices of the *gute Policey* has detected that many statutes promulgated by the German principalities had been substantially influenced by the persons affected (Landwehr 2000; Holenstein et al. 2002). On the one hand, the expanding agenda of "good policy" and the existence of several competing authorities, which was typical for the situation in the Holy Roman Empire, created an institutional framework that widened the scope of action for the subjects, and, to some extent, opened the gates for their participation. On the other hand, these interactions contributed to the intensification of dominion: a petition from "ordinary" villagers and town-dwellers only had a chance of being received if it complied with legal proceedings, respected a humble style, and used a "permitted" political language. One has to take into account that all these forms of participation were embedded in a non-egalitarian concept of a *societas civilis cum imperio*. In this concept, the growing lower classes normally were viewed as clear objects for discipline, and not as possible partners in the bargaining process. Consequently, the offer to participate was first and foremost addressed to the better-off heads of households (Shennan 1986).

Another important area of bargaining was jurisdiction, which was used by subjects on their own initiative (Dinges 2000). By appealing to courts, subjects took up an offer and an opportunity provided by the public authorities. In doing so, they pushed the state into the position of a mediator with sufficient authority and legitimacy to decide a conflict. Communities, corporations and individuals were most likely to adopt such instruments when local mechanisms to maintain order and to settle disputes were under pressure and reaching their limits. By calling in the state's legal authority, the litigating parties from a local society sanctioned state authority as a whole.

To summarise, the early modern state was not a result of princely will, but the outcome of a multitude of practices, which succeeded in transforming individual or group interests into court judgements, laws, or administrative measures, so that these particular interests gained authoritative validity and legitimacy. In this perspective, the early modern state resulted from communicative processes which André Holenstein suggests characterising as "empowering interactions." There was a strong, empowering reciprocity between the use of state power as embodied in the holders of office and incorporated in state authorities by groups and members of the local society, on the one hand, and the increasing authority and legitimised power of the state, on the other hand. Whether these "empowering interactions" resulted in a global change of common attitudes towards the emerging states, or, to use Michel Foucault's term, whether *gouvernementalité* arose, is a matter for discussion (Foucault 1989).

One should bear in mind that early modern Europe was not as uniform as this paper, for the sake of making some general remarks, suggests. If one compares different territories, it becomes clear how the diverging institutional arrangements shaped the scope for action available to the various estates, groups and individuals. Important variations can be detected by investigating comparatively small territories like most of the German principalities, but also the Danish or the English monarchies on the one hand, compared with larger, more complex empires like the Spanish or the Austrian Habsburg monarchies on the other hand (Elliott 1992). In the latter, the population was usually left in the custody of their aristocratic lordships. It was the local lords, and not the crown, who directed the maintenance of public order (Evans 1979; Schramm 1996).

In the lands of the Habsburg monarchy, it was not before the middle of the eighteenth century that regional courts and administrative offices were built that opened the gates for empowering interactions between the court in Vienna and individual subjects or corporations, for example, in Bohemia or Lower Austria (Winkelbauer 2003). And if we look at Hungary, the situation is even more complex, because of the deeply segmented structure of this country. There, Hungarians of the Calvinist or Catholic creeds lived alongside Catholic Swabians who spoke German, Wallachians of the Romanian Orthodox Church who spoke Romanian, Ruthenians of the Uniate church, and smaller groups of Greeks, Gypsies, Jews and Armenians (Radvánszky 1990; Fata 2000). This profoundly affected the communication between the authorities and their different subjects, because each of the populations acted as a corporate and privileged group, rather than individually or as village communities, which might have formed larger unified associations. The segmented units of society raised the agreed tributes and paid them to the nobility, but apart from that, they sustained church and communal life on their own (Vári 2005).

Under these conditions it becomes clear why the self-governing bodies of the gentry, called *comitatus*, were absolutely central to the administration, jurisdiction and politics of the Hungarian kingdom (Schimert 1995; Dominkovits 2006). The assemblies of these counties elected representatives to the Diet of the kingdom, which met at Pressburg (modern Bratislava), and this Diet was the counterpart for the bargaining process with the Habsburg crown (Bérenger 1973; Tóth 1996; Pálffy 2003). Because of the long distances between each county and the government departments at Vienna or Pressburg, and because of the denominationally, ethnically, and socially segmented character of Hungarian society, the *comitatus* became the essential unit in the indirect rule of the Habsburg monarchs (Kubinyi 1996). This might sound familiar to historians dealing with the history of empires in Asia. There seems to be a common experience of "indirect rule" inside empires, which is far older than the colonial policies of the eighteenth and nineteenth centuries. It should be remembered that this may well have nothing to do with connected histories, but with the trivial point that size matters. Compared to complex empires mostly consisting of unions of monarchies, in most German principalities (Burkhardt 2006; Brakensiek 2009a), but also in the comparatively small and uniformly structured Danish monarchy (Gustafsson 1994), empowering interactions between the central and the local spheres were more easily undertaken. Here, jurisdiction and administration was in the hands of legally trained officials, who were appointed by the prince and controlled by central government bodies. The small scale of administrative districts made it possible for the subjects to contact the local officials of the prince directly. The same holds true in a reverse direction. The individual subject could be integrated much more deeply into communication, which enhanced the ability of the princes and their bureaucracy to penetrate the country to a high degree, exceeding the possibilities of the greater European empires. This style of government was of some importance for the survival of minor powers, which cannot completely be explained by their position in the system of the European military powers.

Bibliography

Asch, Ronald G. 1991. *Princes, patronage, and the nobility. The court at the beginning of the modern age c. 1450–1650*. Oxford: Oxford University Press.

Asch, Ronald G. and Freist, Dagmar 2005. *Staatsbildung als kultureller Prozess. Strukturwandel und Legitimation von Herrschaft in der Frühen Neuzeit*. Cologne: Böhlau.

Astarita, Tommaso 1999. *Village Justice. Community, Family, and Popular Culture in Early Modern Italy*. Baltimore: Johns Hopkins University Press.

Aylmer, Gerald Edward 1996. "Centre and Locality: The Nature of Power Elites". In *Power Elites and State Building*, ed. W. Reinhard, 59–77. Oxford: Clarendon.

Becker, Peter and Clark, William 2001. *Little Tools of Knowledge. Historical Essays on Academic and Bureaucratic Practises*. Ann Arbor: University of Michigan Press.

Beik, William 1985. *Absolutism and society in seventeenth-century France. State power and provincial aristocracy in Languedoc*. Cambridge: Cambridge University Press.

Bérenger, Jean 1973. *Les "Gravamina". Remontrances des diètes de Hongrie de 1655 à 1681. Recherches sur les fondements du droit d'Etat au 17e siècle*. Paris: PUF.

Black, Jeremy 2004. *Kings, Nobles and Commoners. States and societies in early modern Europe, a revisionist history*. London: Tauris.

Blickle, Peter 1997. *Resistance, Representation, and Community*. Oxford: Clarendon.

Blickle, Peter 2000. *Kommunalismus. Skizzen einer gesellschaftlichen Organisationsform*. 2 vols. Munich: Oldenbourg.

Blickle, Renate 1998. "Laufen gen Hof. Die Beschwerden der Untertanen und die Entstehung des Hofrats in Bayern. Ein Beitrag zu den Varianten rechtlicher Verfahren im späten Mittelalter und in der frühen Neuzeit". In *Gemeinde und Staat im Alten Europa*, ed. Peter Blickle, 241–266. Munich: Oldenbourg.

Blockmans, Wim, Holenstein, André and Mathieu, Jon 2009. *Empowering Interactions. Political cultures and the Emergence of the State in Europe, 1300–1900*. Famham: Ashgate.

Braddick, Michael 2000. *State formation in early modern England, c. 1550–1700*. Cambridge: Cambridge University Press.

Braddick, Michael and Walter, John 2001. *Negotiating Power in Early Modern Society. Order, Hierarchy and Subordination in Britain and Ireland*. Cambridge: Cambridge University Press.

Brakensiek, Stefan and Wunder, Heide 2005. *Ergebene Diener ihrer Herren? Herrschaftsvermittlung im alten Europa*. Cologne: Böhlau.

Brakensiek, Stefan 2009a. "Akzeptanzorientierte Herrschaft. Überlegungen zur politischen Kultur der Frühen Neuzeit". In *Die Frühe Neuzeit als Epoche*, ed. Helmut Neuhaus, 395–406. Munich: Oldenbourg.

Brakensiek, Stefan 2009b. "Communication between Authorities and Subjects in Bohemia, Hungary and the Holy German Empire, 1650–1800: A Comparison of Three Case Studies". In *Empowering Interactions. Political Cultures and the Emergence of the State in Europe 1300–1900*, eds. Wim Blockmans, André Holenstein and Jon Mathieu, 149–162. Famham: Ashgate.

Brewer, John and Hellmuth, Eckhart 1999. *Rethinking Leviathan. The Eighteenth-Century State in Britain and Germany*. Oxford: Oxford University Press.

Bulst, Neithard 1996. "Rulers, Representative Institutions, and their Members as Power Elites: Rivals or Partners?" In *Power Elites and State Building*, ed. Wolfgang Reinhard, 41–58. Oxford: Clarendon.

Burkhardt, Johannes 2006. *Vollendung und Neuorientierung des frühmodernen Reiches 1648–1763*. Stuttgart: Klett-Cotta.

Castiglione, Caroline 2005. *Patrons and adversaries. Nobles and villagers in Italian politics, 1640–1760*. Oxford: Oxford University Press.

Chittolini, Giorgi 1979. *La formazione dello stato regionale e le instituzioni del contado*. Turin: Einaudi.

Collin, Peter and Horstmann, Thomas 2004. *Das Wissen des Staates*. Baden-Baden: Nomos.

Collins, James B. 2009. *The State in Early Modern France*, 2nd edn. Cambridge: Cambridge University Press.

Contamine, Philippe 2000. *War and competition between states*. Oxford: Clarendon.

Cosandey, Fanny and Descimon, Robert 2002. *L'absolutisme en France. Histoire et historiographie*. Paris: Éditions du Seuil.

Dinges, Martin 2000. "Justiznutzungen als soziale Kontrolle in der Frühen Neuzeit" In *Kriminalitätsgeschichte. Beiträge zur Sozial- und Kulturgeschichte der Vormoderne*, eds. Andreas Blauert and Gerd Schwerhoff, 503–544. Konstanz: UVK.

Dominkovits, Péter 2006. "Das ungarische Komitat im 17. Jahrhundert. Verfechter der Ständerechte oder Ausführungsorgan zentraler Anordnungen?" In *Die Habsburgermonarchie 1620 bis 1740. Leistungen und Grenzen des Absolutismusparadigmas*, eds. Petr Mat'a and Thomas Winkelbauer, 401–442. Stuttgart: Steiner.

Dreitzel, Horst 1992. *Absolutismus und ständische Verfassung in Deutschland. Ein Beitrag zu Kontinuität und Diskontinuität der politischen Theorie in der Frühen Neuzeit*. Mainz: Zabern.

Droste, Heiko 2003. "Patronage in der Frühen Neuzeit. Institution und Kulturform". *ZHF* 30/4: 555–590.

Duindam, Jeroen 2003. *Vienna and Versailles. The Courts of Europe's Dynastic Rivals, 1550–1780*. Cambridge: Cambridge University Press.

Elliott, John H. 1992. "A Europe of Composite Monarchies". *Past & Present* 137: 48–71.

Emich, Birgit 2005."Frühneuzeitliche Staatsbildung und politische Kultur. Für die Veralltäglichung eines Konzepts". In *Was heißt Kulturgeschichte des Politischen?*, ed. Barbara Stollberg-Rilinger, 191–205. Berlin: Duncker & Humblot.

Evans, Robert J.W. 1979. *The Making of the Habsburg monarchy, 1550–1700. An Interpretation*. Oxford: Clarendon.

Fata, Márta 2000. *Ungarn, das Reich der Stephanskrone, im Zeitalter der Reformation und Konfessionalisierung. Multiethnizität, Land und Konfession 1500 bis 1700*. Münster: Aschendorff.

Fontaine, Laurence 2003. *Pouvoir, identités et migrations dans les Alpes occidentales (XVIIe-XVIIIe siècle)*. Grenoble: Presses Universitaire.

Foucault, Michel 1989. *De la gouvernementalité. Leçons d'introduction aux cours des années 1978 et 1979*. Paris: Éditions du Seuil.

Giry-Deloison, Charles and Mettam, Robert 1995. *Patronages et clientélismes 1550–1750 (France, Angleterre, Espagne, Italie)*. Lille: Centre d'Histoire de la Région du Nord.

New Perspectives on State-Building

Goldie, Mark and Wokler, Robert 2006. *The Cambridge History of Eighteenth-Century Political Thought.* Cambridge: Cambridge University Press.

Grendi, Eduardo 1993. *Il Cervo e la repubblica. Il modello ligure de antico regime.* Turin: Einaudi.

Gustafsson, Harald 1994. *Political interaction in the old regime. Central power and local society in the eighteenth-century Nordic states.* Lund: Studentlitteratur.

Härter, Karl 2000. *Policey und frühneuzeitliche Gesellschaft.* Frankfurt: Klostermann.

Hengerer, Mark 2004. *Kaiserhof und Adel in der Mitte des 17. Jahrhunderts. Eine Mikrogeschichte der Macht in der Vormoderne.* Konstanz: UVK.

Hindle, Steve 2001. "The Political Culture of the Middling Sort in English Rural Communities, 1550–1700". In *The Politics of the Excluded, 1500–1850*, ed. Tim Harris, 125–152. Basingstoke: Palgrave.

Hindle, Steve 2004. "County Government in England". In *A Companion to Tudor Britain*, eds. Norman L. Jones and Robert L. Tittler, 98–115. Oxford: Blackwell.

Holenstein, André et al. 2002. *Policey in lokalen Räumen. Ordnungskräfte und Sicherheitspersonal in Gemeinden und Territorien vom Spätmittelalter bis zum frühen 19. Jahrhundert.* Frankfurt: Klostermann.

Holenstein, André 2003. *"Gute Policey" und lokale Gesellschaft im Staat des Ancien Régime. Das Fallbeispiel der Markgrafschaft Baden(–Durlach).* Epfendorf: Bibliotheca Academica.

Holenstein, André 2009. "Introduction. Empowering Interactions: Looking at Statebuilding from Below". In *Empowering Interactions. Political cultures and the Emergence of the State in Europe, 1300–1900*, eds. Wim Blockmans, André Holenstein and Jon Mathieu, 1–31. Famham: Ashgate.

Iseli, Andrea 2003. *Bonne Police. Frühneuzeitliches Verständnis von der guten Ordnung eines Staates in Frankreich.* Epfendorf: Bibliotheca Academica.

Kettering, Sharon 1986. *Patrons, Brokers and Clients in Seventeenth-Century France.* Oxford: Oxford University Press.

Koenigsberger, Helmut G. 1971. *Estates and revolutions. Essays in early modern European history.* Ithaca NY: Cornell.

Kubinyi, András 1996. "Landesherr, Reichstag bzw. Landtag und Komitatsversammlungen in Ungarn und Siebenbürgen 1542–1681". In *Ständefreiheit und Staatsgestaltung in Ostmitteleuropa. Übernationale Gemeinsamkeiten in der politischen Kultur vom 16.-18. Jahrhundert*, eds. Joachim Bahlcke, Hans-Jürgen Bömelburg and Norbert Kersken, 81–94. Leipzig: Leipziger Universitäts-Verlag.

Kümin, Beat and Würgler, Andreas 1997. "Petitions, Gravamina and the early modern state: local influence on central legislation in England and Germany (Hesse)". *Parliaments, Estates and Representation*: 39–60.

Kujala, Antti 2003. *The Crown, the Nobility and the Peasants, 1630–1713 Tax, rent and relations of power.* Helsinki: SKS.

Lambert-Gorges, Martine 1993. *Les élites locales et l'Etat dans l'Espagne moderne du XVIe au XIXe siècle.* Paris: CNRS Édition.

Landwehr, Achim 2000. "„Normdurchsetzung" in der Frühen Neuzeit? Kritik eines Begriffs". *ZfG* 48: 146–162.

Lüdtke, Alf 1991. "Einleitung". In *Herrschaft als soziale Praxis. Historische und sozialanthropologische Studien*, ed. Alf Lüdtke, 9–63. Göttingen: Vandenhoeck & Ruprecht.

Mączak, Antoni 1988. *Klientelsysteme im Europa der Frühen Neuzeit.* Munich: Oldenbourg.

Mat'a, Petr and Winkelbauer, Thomas 2006. *Die Habsburgermonarchie 1620 bis 1740. Leistungen und Grenzen des Absolutismusparadigmas.* Stuttgart: Steiner.

Menne, Mareike 2007. *Herrschaftsstil und Glaubenspraxis. Die bischöflichen Visitationen im Hochstift Paderborn 1654–1691.* Paderborn: Bonifatius.

Muchembled, Robert 1992. *Le temps des supplices. De l'obéissance sous les rois absolus. XVe-XVIIIe siècles.* Paris: Colin.

Neugebauer, Wolfgang 1996. "Raumtypologie und Ständeverfassung. Betrachtungen zur vergleichenden Verfassungsgeschichte am ostmitteleuropäischen Beispiel". In *Ständefreiheit*

40   S. Brakensiek

und Staatsgestaltung in Ostmitteleuropa. Übernationale Gemeinsamkeiten in der politischen Kultur vom 16.-18. Jahrhundert, eds. Joachim Bahlcke, Hans-Jürgen Bömelburg and Norbert Kersken, 283–310. Leipzig: Leipziger Universitäts-Verlag.

Nitschke, Peter 2000. *Einführung in die politische Theorie der Prämoderne 1500–1800*. Darmstadt: Wissenschaftliche Buchgesellschaft.

Nubola, Cecilia and Würgler, Andreas 2005. *Bittschriften und Gravamina. Politik, Verwaltung und Justiz in Europa (14.-18. Jahrhundert)*. Berlin: Duncker & Humblot.

Osterhammel, Jürgen 1998. *Die Entzauberung Asiens. Europa und die asiatischen Reiche im 18. Jahrhundert*. Munich: Beck.

Pagden, Anthony 1987. *The Languages of political theory in early-modern Europe*. Cambridge: Cambridge University Press.

Pálffy, Geza 2003. "Der ungarische Adel und der Kaiserhof in der frühen Neuzeit (Eine Skizze)". In *Šlechta v habsburské monarchii a císarsky dvur (1526–1740)*, eds. Václav Bůzek and Pavel Král, 133–152. České Budějovice: Historický úustav Jihoceské univerzity.

Radvánszky, Anton 1990. *Grundzüge der Verfassungs- und Staatsgeschichte Ungarns*. Munich: Trofenik.

Reinhard, Wolfgang 1979. *Freunde und Kreaturen. "Verflechtung" als Konzept zur Erforschung historischer Führungsgruppen. Römische Oligarchie um 1600*. Munich: Vögel.

Reinhard, Wolfgang 1996. *Power Elites and State Building*. Oxford: Clarendon.

Reinhard, Wolfgang 1999. *Geschichte der Staatsgewalt. Eine vergleichende Verfassungsgeschichte Europas von den Anfängen bis zur Gegenwart*. Munich: Beck.

Reinhard, Wolfgang 2001. "Was ist europäische politische Kultur? Versuch zur Begründung einer politischen Historischen Anthropologie". *GG* 27/4: 593–616.

Reinhard, Wolfgang 2004. *Römische Mikropolitik unter Papst Paul V. Borghese (1605–1621) zwischen Spanien, Neapel, Mailand und Genua*. Tübingen: Niemeyer.

Robisheaux, Thomas 1989. *Rural Society and the Search for Order in Early Modern Germany*. Cambridge: Cambridge University Press.

Schimert, Peter 1995. "The Hungarian Nobility in the Seventeenth and Eighteenth Centuries". In *The European Nobilities in the Seventeenth and Eighteenth Centuries*, Vol. 2: *Northern, Central and Eastern Europe*, ed. Hamish M. Scott, 144–182. London: Longman.

Schorn-Schütte, Luise 2004. *Aspekte der politischen Kommunikation im Europa des 16. und 17. Jahrhunderts. Politische Theologie – Res Publica-Verständnis – konsensgestützte Herrschaft*. Munich: Oldenbourg.

Schorn-Schütte, Luise and Tode, Sven 2006. *Debatten über die Legitimation von Herrschaft. Politische Sprachen in der Frühen Neuzeit*. Berlin: Akademie.

Schramm, Gottfried 1996. "Polen – Böhmen – Ungarn: Übernationale Gemeinsamkeiten in der politischen Kultur des späten Mittelalters und der frühen Neuzeit". In *Ständefreiheit und Staatsgestaltung in Ostmitteleuropa. Übernationale Gemeinsamkeiten in der politischen Kultur vom 16.-18. Jahrhundert*, eds. Joachim Bahlcke, Hans-Jürgen Bömelburg and Norbert Kersken, 13–38. Leipzig: Leipziger Universitäts-Verlag.

Shennan, Joseph H. 1986. *Liberty and order in early modern Europe. The subject and the state 1650–1800*. London: Longman.

Simon, Thomas 2004. *"Gute Policey". Ordnungsleitbilder und Zielvorstellungen politischen Handelns in der Frühen Neuzeit*. Frankfurt: Klostermann.

Stollberg-Rilinger, Barbara 2000. "Zeremoniell, Ritual, Symbol. Neue Forschungen zur symbolischen Kommunikation in Spätmittelalter und Früher Neuzeit". *ZHF* 27/3: 389–405.

Stolleis, Michael, Härter, Karl and Schilling, Lothar 1996. *Policey im Europa der Frühen Neuzeit*. Frankfurt: Klostermann.

Tantner, Anton 2007. *Ordnung der Häuser, Beschreibung der Seelen. Hausnummerierung und Seelenkonskription in der Habsburgermonarchie*. Innsbruck: Studien-Verlag.

Tóth, István György 1996. "Der wechselnde Spielraum des ungarischen Adels im 17./18. Jahrhundert". In *Ständefreiheit und Staatsgestaltung in Ostmitteleuropa. Übernationale Gemeinsamkeiten in der politischen Kultur vom 16.-18. Jahrhundert*, eds. Joachim Bahlcke,

Hans-Jürgen Bömelburg and Norbert Kersken 149–159. Leipzig: Leipziger Universitäts-Verlag.

Ulbrich, Claudia and Hohkamp, Michaela 2001. *Der Staatsbürger als Spitzel. Denunziation während des 18. und 19. Jahrhunderts aus europäischer Perspektive.* Leipzig: Leipziger Universitäts Verlag.

Vári, András 2005. "Ergebene Diener ihrer Herren. Wandel der Machtausübung im Komitatsleben und in der privaten Güterverwaltung im Ungarn des 18. Jahrhunderts". In *Ergebene Diener ihrer Herren? Herrschaftsvermittlung im alten Europa*, eds. Stefan Brakensiek and Heide Wunder, 203–231. Cologne: Böhlau.

Weber, Wolfgang E.J. 1998. *Der Fürst. Ideen und Wirklichkeiten in der europäischen Geschichte.* Cologne: Böhlau.

Wiese-Schorn, Luise 1976. "Von der autonomen zur beauftragten Selbstverwaltung. Die Integration der deutschen Stadt in den Territorialstaat am Beispiel der Verwaltungsgeschichte von Osnabrück und Göttingen in der frühen Neuzeit". *Osnabrücker Mitteilungen* 82: 29–59.

Wilson, Peter H. 2000. *Absolutism in Central Europe.* London: Routledge.

Windler, Christian 1992. *Lokale Eliten, seigneurialer Adel und Reformabsolutismus in Spanien (1760–1808). Das Beispiel Niederandalusien.* Stuttgart: Steiner.

Windler, Christian 2000. "Une république de fiefs?" Lokalismus und Zentralismus in Frankreich'. *Francia* 27/3: 119–134.

Winkelbauer, Thomas 2003. *Ständefreiheit und Fürstenmacht. Länder und Untertanen des Hauses Habsburg im konfessionellen Zeitalter. Österreichische Geschichte 1522–1699.* 2 vols. Vienna: Ueberreuter.

Wrightson, Keith 1996. "The Politics of the Parish in Early Modern England". In *The Experience of Authority in Early Modern England*, eds. Paul Griffiths, Adam Fox and Steve Hindle, 10–46. Basingstoke: Macmillan.

Zeeden, Ernst Walter and Molitor, Hansgeorg 1977. *Die Visitation im Dienste der kirchlichen Reform.* Münster: Aschendorff.

Zeeden, Ernst Walter and Lang, Peter Thaddäus 1984. *Kirche und Visitation.* Stuttgart: Klett-Cotta.

Les communautés rurales - Rural communities 1987. Recueils de la Société Jean Bodin, Paris.

State and Political History in a Culturalist Perspective

Barbara Stollberg-Rilinger

What is the significance of the so-called "cultural turn" for political history in general and the history of early modern state-building in particular? The cultural turn has meanwhile become quite well established in the humanities—this is why the term "cultural studies" is now preferred. Culturalist research has moved from the periphery of the discipline to become almost mainstream. Despite this—or perhaps because of it—fierce criticism and, especially, numerous misunderstandings remain.

But it is beyond doubt, especially when seeking to overcome the Eurocentric perspective, that the cultural turn has provided the most important methodological stimuli and continues to do so. For this reason, it seems justified to recall a couple of the fundamental assumptions that characterise the cultural turn. Although there are a lot of differences and even contradictions between the theoretical approaches the label seeks to bring together under one umbrella, I believe it is nonetheless possible to present some broadly shared basic assumptions.

In what follows I would therefore like, firstly, to state what I mean by cultural turn and show which fundamental features, in my opinion, the various relevant theoretical approaches have in common. Secondly, I would like to ask how these assumptions change the historian's perspective on all subjects, and which new ways of investigation result as far as political history is concerned. Both subjects are two sides of the same coin. Then, thirdly, I would like to illustrate this by way of a concrete micro-historical example, turning to a central moment within European political history, the Peace of Westphalia, and to show how the phenomenon of sovereignty and the so-called "European state system" is seen from a culturalist perspective. The question of what can be learned from this about the entanglement between Europe and Asia has to be left for another occasion.

B. Stollberg-Rilinger (✉)
Westfälische Wilhelms-Universität Münster, Domplatz 20-22, 48143 Münster, Germany
e-mail: stollb@uni-muenster.de

A. Flüchter and S. Richter (eds.), *Structures on the Move*,
Transcultural Research – Heidelberg Studies on Asia and Europe in a Global Context,
DOI 10.1007/978-3-642-19288-3_3, © Springer-Verlag Berlin Heidelberg 2012

1 The Cultural Turn and Political History

Culture is one of the worst concepts ever created, Niklas Luhmann supposedly once said. Many would be inclined to agree, having gradually had their fill of the cultural turn, and finding that it can mean everything and nothing. Indeed there have been several attempts to define the subject area of culture, none of which has proved altogether satisfying. For—and here I can draw upon Luhmann as well as others—if culture is defined as a special, classifiable group of social objects, then as such it loses any possible scholarly conciseness (Luhmann 1995; Walz 2005). For what, according to this definition, in the realm of human life, is *not* culture? It makes much more sense to use the term "culture" to denote a specific perspective, a form of observation.

It is well known that, historically, the term "culture" emerged in the late eighteenth century, when all social phenomena began to be observed comparatively, thus opening up the possibility (at least) of treating them on an equal footing—Lessing's Nathan comes to mind here. That is to say that—at the time of an Enlightenment understanding of the world—culture for the first time appeared as something fundamentally open and contingent. The concept of culture had its second boom around 1900, when comparative religion, ethnology, and language theory focused once again on the openness, contingency, and relativity of all social phenomena—this was a well-known concomitant to European colonialism. What we have been experiencing since the end of the twentieth century is thus actually already the third "cultural turn". It has been accompanied, not incidentally, by a new wave of social pluralisation and the dissolution of time-honoured certainties, and by a new quality of confrontation with the foreign and unfamiliar, which has for a long time been found not beyond the European borders, but in the midst of Europe itself (Tschopp and Weber 2007; Bachmann-Medick 2009).

This seems to me essential for the concept of culture that makes up the cultural turn. Culture is not one subject field among others; it is a question of the perspective from which one observes. This—"culturalist"—perspective is characterised by its tendency to make any kind of stable essence appear questionable. Instead, the focus lies on the ways in which social phenomena are produced and performed (Hunt 1989; Daniel 2001).

Central to this is the fundamental human ability to generate symbols—whether by means of language, or other codes or systems of symbols (symbol understood in the broadest sense of the term, including everyday practices, as well as scientific languages, etc.). The concept of culture thus attempts to grasp human beings' unlimited and dynamic ability to continuously construct their world themselves as an ordered and meaningful one through symbolisation. It must be emphasised that the symbolic construction of the world always has both a subjective and an objective side at the same time; these are related to one another in a state of permanent interaction, and are utterly inseparable. This means, on the one hand,

State and Political History in a Culturalist Perspective 45

that every individual is born into a world of pre-existing collective symbol systems, and grows into this world through her or his socialisation, facing it as something objectively predetermined and commonly shared. On the other hand, this shared world is reproduced only through perception, interpretation, and communication on the part of the individual subjects. It has no independent existence beyond the individuals who continuously fill it with life and, in so doing, constantly change it. If social reality in this sense is understood as a dialectical interrelationship, then it becomes clear that the customary oppositions between individual and structure dissolve: individuals are always subjectively generating anew the structures that then, conversely, confront them as something objective.[1]

The ability to produce symbols is fundamental, in that it has always shaped every human connection to the world, indeed, making it possible to participate in a shared reality at all. This, of course, is not to somehow question the existence of a reality outside of human beings, rather, it is to say that without symbol systems there is no access to it—at least no access that can be communicated.

Understood in this way, the cultural turn also encompasses what are referred to as the linguistic turn and the performative turn. The linguistic turn emphasises that there is no perception of reality outside of language (thus privileging one, particularly powerful symbol system over others). The performative turn stresses that every meaning is always generated within a concrete individual act of communication, thus that there is no fixed social structure beyond its concrete reproduction by individuals.

---

[1] This approach is based on several cultural theories. I only name but a few of the most important authors, who—despite the differences in detail—converge on this very crucial point: Weber, Max (1988) *Gesammelte Aufsätze zur Wissenschaftslehre*, ed. Johannes Winckelmann, 7th Edition, Tübingen: Mohr Siebeck (cf. ibid. 332: "Der Umstand, daß ,äußere' Zeichen als ,Symbole' dienen, ist eine der konstitutiven Voraussetzungen aller sozialen Beziehungen.") – Cassirer, Ernst (1953) *Philosophie der symbolischen Formen*. Darmstadt: Wissenschaftliche Buchgesellschaft. – Schütz, Alfred (1975) *Strukturen der Lebenswelt*. 2 vols. Neuwied: Luchterhand. – Schütz, Alfred (1993) *Der sinnhafte Aufbau der sozialen Welt. Eine Einleitung in die verstehende Soziologie*. 6th edition Frankfurt/Main: Suhrkamp. – Berger, Peter and Luckmann, Thomas (1979) *The Social Construction of Reality. A Treatise in the Sociology of Knowledge*. Harmondsworth: Penguin. – Giddens, Anthony (1986) *The Constitution of Society. Outline of the Theory of Structuration*. Cambridge: Polity Press. – Bourdieu, Pierre (1980) *Le sens pratique*. Paris: Minuit. – Geertz, Clifford (1973) "Thick Description: Toward an Interpretive Theory of Culture." In *The Interpretation of Cultures: Selected Essays*: 3–30. New York: Basic Books. – Rehberg, Karl-Siegbert (2001) "Weltrepräsentanz und Verkörperung. Institutionelle Analyse und Symboltheorien – eine Einführung in systematischer Absicht." In *Institutionalität und Symbolisierung. Verstetigungen kultureller Ordnungsmuster in Vergangenheit und Gegenwart*, ed. Gert Melville: 3–49. Cologne/Weimar/Vienna: Böhlau.—For further references see: Stollberg-Rilinger, Barbara (2004) "Symbolische Kommunikation in der Vormoderne. Begriffe – Thesen – Forschungsperspektiven." *Zeitschrift für historische Forschung* 31: 489–527.

2 Cultural History of Politics-Some Common Misunderstandings

What are the consequences of all this for the study of history, especially for those fields concerned with the state and politics?

First: if one takes the idea of culture outlined above as a basis, then cultural history too is not to be defined in terms of its specific subjects, but rather according to its specific perspective on *all* possible subjects.

This perspective consists essentially of regarding historical phenomena at a fundamental level not as static, objective facts, but instead treating them as processes of ascribing meaning, both collectively and individually. In this sense, even political history can be written as "cultural history". However, this must also take into account that "politics" itself is not some—as it were—naturally predetermined, unquestioningly applicable category, but already presupposes ascriptions of meaning, carried out either by historical contemporaries or by ourselves as historians.

From this perspective, for politics or "the political" as well, there can thus no longer be any question of an essentialist, not to mention normative, definition. This, of course, is not to say that it is possible to get by without definitions, quite the contrary. In order to be understood, after all, clearly defined terms are necessary. We should just realise that it is necessary to choose our definitions according to their usefulness. A definition of "politics" that is heuristically useful and has a reasonable hope of consensus might be that politics always has to do with both a collective whole (a polity) as well as with decision-making. According to this, the political is the sphere of activity in which collectively binding decisions are produced and implemented. As the work of the Bielefeld Research Center has shown, this definition takes into account the fact that the political sphere has historically been separated from other spheres to very different degrees and has been formulated in very different ways (SFB 1831 "Das Politische als Kommunikationsraum in der Geschichte" in Bielefeld; Lehmkuhl 2001; Mergel 2002; Landwehr 2003; Steinmetz 2007). The very question of which matters are defined as political in a certain historical situation is itself the object of negotiation and struggles of interpretation. And—even more fundamentally—what constitutes a collective political whole is not only historically variable, but has always been, in turn, the result of ascribing meanings. Polities, collective actors such as municipalities, churches, states, or nations have, in this respect, the character of guiding fictions. This is to say that they are called into existence through processes of representation. In this, representation is to be understood in both senses of the word: political units come about, on the one hand—by means of institutionalised procedures of attribution, by deputising. This is "political representation" in its narrower sense (Pitkin 1967; Morgan 1983; Göhler et al. 1997; Hofmann 2003). Someone acts in the name of the whole, which means his actions are looked upon as if they were actions of the whole and oblige all members of the whole. On the other hand, political units come about by symbolic representation and embodiment—for example, by political ceremonies and rituals,[2] or through symbolic objects such as flags, coats of arms, buildings, canonical scriptures, etc.

The "cultural history of the political" has given rise to a series of allegations, which, in my opinion, are based on misunderstandings. I would like to address a few here briefly in an attempt to dispel them.

2.1 First Misunderstanding: Cultural History is not Interested in Power

An old accusation states that a political history that regards itself as cultural history deals only with superficial phenomena and does not get at the "actual" matter of politics, namely power and interests as the basic anthropological constants of political action. It is allegedly concerned only with decorative appearances, which not only reveal nothing about the true essence of the political, but even worse, positively obscure it (Rödder 2006; Nicklas 2004; Kraus and Nicklas 2007). I do not dispute that this may apply to some works. The older approach of American research on "political culture" was still based on the assumption that it was possible to separate the representation and perception of the political from the "actual" structures of power and decision-making, thereby separating form from content (Almond 1963; Edelman 1964; Sarcinelli 1987). Representatives of a culturalist-oriented political history have expressly distanced themselves from such an understanding of their subject. They are much more concerned with breaking down oppositions precisely such as those between "symbolic" and "real" politics, appearance and reality, form and content, between interpretative systems on the one hand and structures of power, rule, and interests, on the other. The objective is, instead, to show the fundamental role played by symbolic practices and attributions already in the constitution of political institutions, categories, and, not least, claims to power. This, of course, is not to say that political actors never engage in strategic acts of staging that serve to obscure matters. But it is to say instead that there is no completely "naked", "unveiled" political reality that has not always been structured, in one way or another, by the ascription of meaning in the heads of all participants (not only in the heads of the "common people", but also of the political leaders themselves). The fact that power and authority cannot endure without collective imaginations and ascriptions was already remarked upon with great clarity by no less a personage than Thomas Hobbes, who said, "The reputation of power is power" (Hobbes 1839–1845).

---

[2] For ritual as a crucial form of symbolic representation in politics, cf. Kertzer, David J. (1988) *Ritual, Politics and Power*. New Haven/London: Yale University Press. – Bell, Caroline (1997) *Ritual. Perspectives and Dimensions*. New York/Oxford: Oxford University Press. – Althoff, Gerd (2003) *Die Macht der Rituale. Symbolik und Herrschaft im Mittelalter*. Darmstadt: Wissenschaftliche Buchgesellschaft. – Muir, Edward (1997) *Ritual in Early Modern Europe*, Cambridge: Cambridge University Press.

2.2 Second Misunderstanding: Cultural History is not Interested in Material Reality

A second and similar accusation states that cultural history ignores physical reality and the constraints of material needs; it is concerned "with nothing but meanings". Gadi Algazi, for example, has spoken polemically of the "culture cult". Cultural historians, so his accusation goes, have transferred hermeneutic methods that originated in the middle-class intellectual treatment of monuments of high culture on to culture in general, and have, as a result, reduced history to the arbitrary reading of texts from the past (Algazi 2000). In doing so, he claims, they have given everyday practices subtle and deeper meanings, which the historical actors were not at all aware of and which did not even matter to them, because they were "burdened by the constraints of everyday life and the urgency of their needs". I believe that this reproach is also based on a misunderstanding. For one thing, the objective of cultural historians is precisely to reconstruct symbol systems which, as a rule, served the historical actors in an unconscious and implicit way, much like a language. This does not argue against their relevance, quite the contrary. Moreover, cultural history by no means ignores the solid, material side of history. But it does not deal with physical reality per se—this is the task of e.g. the physicist—but rather as social reality, and here it is not possible to ignore the ascription of meaning. For only once it is conveyed through symbolic systems does material reality become social reality.

This can be demonstrated by an apparently purely material phenomenon like violence. Violence is, of course, first and foremost a physical reality. But this is not all. An act of violence—although this may sound strange—is always also an act of communication in that it tells something to the victim, but not only to the victim himself. Violence always has an effect upon not only those who suffer it physically, but also upon those who observe, imagine, remember, or expect it. In other words, violence also works symbolically and is an element of communication processes. If it is investigated as a social phenomenon, then the communicative dimension of violence cannot be ignored. In this context, the cultural turn opens up a fundamentally new way of access. It is no accident that precisely the history of the body has become an important branch of the new cultural history.

2.3 Third Misunderstanding: Cultural History Deals with "Cultures" (or "Civilisations") As If They were Closed Boxes.

It is a frequently justified reproach that "cultures"—in the plural—are often spoken of as if they were closed, opposing social units, apparently separated from one another by different cultural symbol systems (languages, religions, etc.). But the understanding of culture outlined above seeks precisely to counter this view. It is indeed possible to define and differentiate social communities in terms of their shared symbolic codes. But these symbolic codes are—as already mentioned above—by no means rigid forms with which the collective controls the individual, but always also flexible instruments that individuals use for their own ends and which can be changed. Individuals can participate in various codes simultaneously; different cultural symbolic languages are mutually permeable and can be translated into one another; their boundaries are fluid and can also constantly be readjusted through individual action. "Cultures" in the plural, in other words, are also social constructions, which can be perceived as such first through the cultural turn. This is why it was specifically the cultural turn that has opened up a new approach to the process of globalisation by putting the concept of entangled history on the agenda, arguing that we have to dissolve the image of distinct national histories and instead analyse the complex interactions between different—collective and individual—actors.

My interim summary is thus as follows: I see the cultural turn's achievement for history in general, and political history in particular, in two interrelated changes of perspective.

First: the cultural turn makes it possible to replace the description of substantial entities with the reconstruction of dynamic relations and processes. Thus, abstract institutions, structures, and so on dissolve—as if under a powerful magnifying-glass—into concrete individual processes of communication. Second, and related to the first: the cultural turn sharpens one's perception of the fact that, as a historian, one is always dealing with the ascription of meaning, and this is taking place on at least three different levels—on the level of the historical actor himself, which is no longer directly accessible to us, on the level of the sources that transmit these actions to us, and, finally, on the level of the historian him- or herself, who, in turn, performs his or her own ascriptions of meaning. This is essentially a hermeneutic truism, the root of which was already formulated at the end of the eighteenth century. But I believe the most essential achievement of the culturalist approach is to have re-imported, via the détour of ethnology, hermeneutics into the study of history. That is to say that the cultural turn has resuscitated the hermeneutic approach to history as indispensable (Daniel 2003). What characterises this perspective above all is, namely, that all phenomena are initially perceived as fundamentally requiring interpretation, that they are not to be taken for granted as self-evident and, as it were, "natural and inevitable". In other words, one regards the past from a stance of astonishment, similar to the way ethnologists regard foreign societies; one puts on the "glasses of the ethnologist".

3 The Symbolic Construction of Sovereignty

So what does the cultural turn mean for the history of the "sovereign state" as the traditional focus of political history, for that which Leopold von Ranke still referred to as "thoughts of God"? According to the classic master narrative, the process of European state-building has two sides, as is well known: the achievements of a sovereign supreme power and the juxtaposition of these sovereign actors on an independent and equal footing in their mutual relations. Obviously, these are two sides of the same coin.

As far as the history of internal state-building is concerned, I will not go into this further here to show the change of perspective according to the culturalist perspective—for example, the fact that one can describe the relations between authorities and subjects as a contingent process of "empowering interactions" (Blockmans, Holenstein and Mathieu 2009; Brakensiek and Wunder 2005; Asch and Freist 2005; Flüchter 2005; Kümin 2009).

I would like instead to devote my attention to the other side of the coin: the development of a European "system" of sovereign actors, and to do so based on a central moment, namely the Westphalian peace negotiations (1643–1648). In Anglo-Saxon scholarship, the system under international law of equal, sovereign states independent of one another is even called the "Westphalian System", implying, in other words, that such a system had its beginnings in Münster and Osnabrück in 1648; "Westphalian sovereignty" is literally a *terminus technicus* within political science.[3]

This raises the initial question: what does sovereignty even mean? To begin with, it is—as we all know—a theoretical concept shaped in the late sixteenth century to express the idea that a polity must have a unified, indivisible, highest or supreme power, from which all other powers are derived (Quaritsch 1986; Biersteker and Weber 1996). Jean Bodin famously defined the res publica essentially through the existence of this kind of supreme power. So much for theory. But what does this mean in practice? Here, things are much more complicated. The theory was meant, not least, to influence this heterogeneous and conflict-laden reality and to insure the assertion of that one, abstract *summa potestas* over a lot of competing actors.

In practice it was, firstly, not states that were sovereign but, at most, persons. And, secondly, among these persons—monarchs, potentates, princes—the question

---

[3] Cf. for a critical revision of the term: Duchhardt, Heinz (1999) "'Westphalian System'. Zur Problematik einer Denkfigur." *Historische Zeitschrift* 269: 305–315. – Krasner, Stephen D (1999) *Sovereignty: Organized Hypocrisy*. Princeton: Princeton University Press. – Osiander, Andreas (2001) "Sovereignty, International Relations, and the Westphalian Myth." In *International Organization* 55: 251–287. – For the Westphalian treaties, cf. Dickmann, Fritz (1972). *Der Westfälische Frieden*. 3rd edition. Münster: Aschendorff. – Duchhardt, Heinz, ed (1998). *Der Westfälische Friede. Diplomatie, politische Zäsur, kulturelles Umfeld, Rezeptionsgeschichte*. Munich: Oldenbourg. – Lesaffer, Randall, ed (2004). *Peace Treaties and International Law in European History*. New York: Cambridge University Press. – Asch, Ronald G., Wulf E. Voß, Martin Wrede, eds (2001). *Frieden und Krieg in der Frühen Neuzeit. Die europäische Staatenordnung und die außereuropäische Welt*. Munich: Fink. – Bély, Lucien, Isabelle Richefort, eds (2000). *L'Europe des traités de Westphalie. Esprit de la diplomatie et diplomatie de l'esprit*. Paris: Presses Universitaires de France. – Croxton, Derek and Anuschka Tischer, eds (2002). *The Peace of Westphalia: A Historical Dictionary*. Westport, CT/London: Greenwood Press. – Most recently: Wilson, Peter (2009). *The Thirty Years War. Europe's Tragedy*. London//Cambridge, MA: Harvard University Press: 751 – 779.

State and Political History in a Culturalist Perspective 51

of who was sovereign and who was not was by no means clear and undisputed (Thiessen and Windler 2010; Krischer 2010; Stollberg-Rilinger 2010). For this was a question not of a simple, objective reality, but of an ascription of social validity; to this end, having at one's disposal a minimum of the instruments of power was merely a necessary, but not a sufficient condition. The clear theoretical opposition—between the bearer of sovereignty and his subjects—by no means corresponded with the complex, overlapping, old European order of various kinds of rulers. In place of a dichotomous order, there was a broad range with fluid boundaries. On one side were indisputable sovereigns, such as the king of France, for example. But, contrastingly, there was also a great number of actors whose status was questionable. This included, for example, those potentates whose instruments of power were not entirely competitive, such as the electors and princes of the empire or the Italian princes. But it also included those actors who had no such lack of resources of power, but were probably lacking honour according to the standards of the princely society, such as the States-General of the Netherlands, not to mention the Swiss Confederation. And, finally, there were rebels whose status was completely in dispute, namely, the Portuguese, who were in rebellion against the Spanish crown, without it being clear as yet whether they would be successful. So, were they sovereign "states" or not? This was a question that, concretely and in practice, had to be settled in mutual interaction.

One place where this happened violently was on the seventeenth century's battlefields, but it also happened in symbolic form at the courts and congress cities. The central forum of these processes of negotiation was the Congress of Westphalia, and the most important medium in which this question was settled was the symbolic code of the legation ceremonial (Stollberg-Rilinger 2010; Roosen 1976; Müller 1976; Andretta 1975–1976; Bély and Richefort 1998; Bély 1990; Frigo 1999, 2000; Tischer 2005; Schilling 2007). In Westphalia, between 1643 and 1648, there occurred a situation without any procedural precedent. Almost all the European powers were represented; there were a total of 82 different delegations. Actors of totally different status and rank met with one another in a very small area—for here the stage of Europe had been constructed, on which all the actors who sought to be politically involved in the future had to readjust their relations to one another and assert their claims to validity.

It is common knowledge that the congress was burdened with ceremonial problems to an unprecedented degree.[4] This was true not only of the ceremonial

---

[4] For diplomatic ceremonial, cf. also Roosen, William (1980). "Early Modern Diplomatic Ceremonial: A Systems Approach." In *Journal of Modern History* 52: 452–476. – Giesey, Ralph E (1987). *Cérémonial et puissance souveraine. France XVᵉ-XVIIᵉ siècles*. Paris: Colin. – Bély, Lucien (1993). "Souveraineté et souverains. La question du cérémonial dans les relations internationales à l'époque moderne." In *Annuaire-Bulletin de la Société de l'Histoire de France*: 27–43. – Frigo, Daniela (1991). *Principe, ambasciatori e "jus gentium"*. Rome: Bulzoni (especially 269–281). – For the ceremonial conflicts in Münster and Osnabrück, see Dickmann (1972). *Der Westfälische Frieden*. op. cit.: 206 sqq. – Becker, Winfried (1973). *Der Kurfürstenrat. Grundzüge seiner Entwicklung in der Reichsverfassung und seine Stellung auf dem Westfläischen*

entries of the envoys at both of the congress locations, but also of all their public dealings with one another. Meetings between three or more envoys, let alone a plenary assembly, were out of the question owing to the unresolved conflicts of ceremonial. All the ceremonial details of official bilateral meetings required days of preparation, without any certainty that, in the end, there would not be a risk of conflict after all. The envoys' journals and correspondence weeks before and after such meetings are replete with the discussion of these kinds of questions, including even the most highly complicated details. Sometimes there was no alternative but to purposely arrange an apparently chance encounter while riding in the country in order to temporarily escape the burden of signs, something which was no doubt extremely unpleasant for all involved. All of this delayed negotiations terribly over the problems at hand and made it seem all the more a wonder of the world (in the words of the treaty's contemporaries) that, despite everything, in the end the treaties were signed which, in one single congress, settled "the matters of all of Christendom".

Modern observers confront cases like this uncomprehendingly. The huge commotion made about the ceremonial issues appears almost obscene when one considers what was at stake. For war was still raging in the empire, and in fact at this time more destructively than ever before. Just as astonishing was the envoys' great lavishness in terms of material expenditure at both congress locations, despite the heavy financial burden, particularly upon the emperor and the German princes because of the war. What they actually had the least of was time and money, and it was just these that they wasted extravagantly. These were apparently matters of pressure, which could not be simply disposed of. There must have been reasons for this, a logic to it, which did not lie in the hands of the individual actors. This logic is what can be reconstructed from a culturalist perspective.

As mentioned above, Münster and Osnabrück witnessed the assembling of envoys whose principals' political status not only differed greatly, but was also one of the reasons for the war that was being waged as they met. According to Hugo Grotius' classic work on international law, *De Jure Belli ac Pacis*, which had first appeared in 1625, strictly only the bearers of supreme power, thus sovereigns, were even entitled to dispatch representative envoys. Indeed this was the clearest sign of sovereignty (Grotius 1625; Wicquefort 1746). This meant, in other words, that if one delegation was recognised and treated as such by another, then this was proof that its principal was accepted into the circle of those with sovereign power.

Friedenskongress. Münster: Aschendorff – Repgen, Konrad (1997). "Friedensvermittlung und Friedensvermittler beim Westfälischen Frieden." In *Westfälische Zeitschrift* 147: 37–61, esp. 50 sqq. – Stiglic, Anja (1998). "Zeremoniell und Rangordnung auf der europäischen diplomatischen Bühne am Beispiel der Gesandteneinzüge in die Kongreßstadt Münster." In Bußmann, Klaus and Heinz Schilling, eds. *1648 – Krieg und Frieden in Europa. Politik, Religion, Recht und Gesellschaft*. Textband. Münster: Bruckmann: 391–396. – May, Niels Fabian (2006). *Le cérémonial diplomatique au XVIe siècle comme expression politique. Les différends pendant les négotiations de Westphalie (1643–1648)*, Maîtrise. Paris.

State and Political History in a Culturalist Perspective 53

The salient point here is that envoys in the full sense of the word, *ambassadeurs*, differed from other lower-ranking representatives or delegates, only and exclusively through the ceremonial treatment shown to them by others. Whether or not a ruler recognised another as a sovereign of equal standing could be quite precisely read from a standard set of ceremonial honours conferred upon his envoys, the so-called *honores regii*. (These consisted essentially of the address "Excellency", the granting of the "first visit", and entering a host's house first, the so-called "upper hand".) (Stollberg-Rilinger 2000, 2011; Krischer 2010, 2011; Becker 1973; Christ 1999) These very standards were established in practice in Münster and Osnabrück. For this reason, meetings between envoys were of the utmost political relevance—the reciprocal ceremonial treatment lent expression to how the powers recognised one another and which status they were prepared to grant each other. But these very questions of political status were among those that the peace negotiations were supposed to settle in the first place. Nearly every ceremonial gesture thus already amounted to a preliminary political decision concerning the central matter at hand. None less than Gottfried Wilhelm Leibniz recognised this in all its clarity. It is characteristic of the epoch after the Peace of Westphalia, he wrote, that formalities were held to be essentials ("formalia are now starting to be held *pro essentialibus*") (Leibniz 1678). This meant that the symbolic forms were quite simply inseparable from the political issue. It was a matter of reciprocal recognition as sovereigns and that meant it was a matter of establishing a new system of political and legal classification. This new order was not graduated but binary: sovereigns and subjects, rather than a hierarchy of various rulers. This was not a simple matter of fact, but a matter of the validity of facts, a matter of the collective ascription of meaning, and this meaning was negotiated in the medium of symbolic ceremonial forms.

For this reason, the envoys did not see themselves in a position to simply do without these forms from the outset, although they all groaned under the burden of the signs as well as constantly accusing each other of delaying the peace negotiations or sowing discord by their insistence on ceremonial details. No single actor could simply elude the logic of the ceremonial sign system, because this was the medium through which new boundaries were drawn and new criteria of order implemented. It was a matter of defining one's membership or non-membership in a circle whose circumference was in the process of being drawn, namely, the circle of sovereigns of equal status, independent of the respective potentate's social rank within the old European order. This was only possible through symbolic acts, for the claims to political validity on the part of all participants had to be visibly staked and reciprocally recognised even *before* the actual negotiations. The ceremonial code was thus not the chaos earlier historians believed it to be, but rather a system of basic geometric rationality. It could not be replaced by negotiation in the form of arguments, but was always one step ahead of them.

Now what is the example of the Peace of Westphalia supposed to demonstrate? Once again the question is: what kind of gains does the culturalist approach bring with it? For one thing, the cultural turn leads to precisely those phenomena formerly noted only as curiosities but which have become prominent objects of investigation; in this case, specifically, the very strange behaviour of the envoys among themselves. If the ceremonial conflicts are regarded not as mere externalities standing in the way of "actual" politics, then they themselves provide the key to the logic of the actors' political behaviour.

Secondly, the culturalist approach in this case makes clear in exemplary fashion that categories of order, which seem to be supratemporally and objectively factual, are in fact based upon reciprocal claims to and ascriptions of validity, here, the category of sovereignty. This becomes especially visible in the present case because these ascriptions were so controversial and precarious precisely at this historical moment, and for the first time the congress offered the opportunity for almost all European actors to register their mutual claims to status, since they were almost all involved in the war. The example shows that the culturalist view strips the political patterns of their self-evident quality, that it locates them instead as patterns of orientation in the heads of the actors, whose actions simultaneously help these patterns to achieve, in fact, an inter-subjective reality. This is even true, as the example shows, of the fundamental category of classical political history: the sovereign state as fictitious actor within an international system of states. To regard this through culturalist glasses is to dissolve the phenomenon which appears to be so thoroughly objective into a collective construct, which had to be adjusted and asserted by means of symbolic practices.

This sharpens one's view of the present as well. It is, of course, widely realized that, whether a collective actor is called a state or not, and its members treated as such or not, and whether a violent conflict is called a war or not, and its participants so treated or not, is not a matter of indifference. For those involved, the respective definitions have the most fundamental and also most tangible material consequences possible—this was recently made drastically clear to the public, for example, in the case of Guantánamo. The system of political and legal categories is also currently in a complete state of flux once again, similar in some respects to 1648. It is probable that precisely this present development is opening our eyes to the power of definitions and ascriptions of meaning.

What holds true for the understanding of the internal European phenomena that I have presented as an example here is even more true of the history of the interactions between Europe and other parts of the world. The cultural turn, with its roots in ethnology and the perception of the foreign, was imported into the study of European history in order to understand our own pre-modern European past anew, as if it was something unfamiliar. Now we are engaged in the task of, so to speak, re-exporting the "foreign view" and directing it outwards again in order to make it fruitful for the "entangled history" of globalisation.

I am quite confident that it is the cultural turn that helps us to find the way out of the Eurocentric impasse.

References

Algazi, Gadi. 2000. "Kulturkult und die Rekonstruktion von Handlungsrepertoires." *L'Homme* 11: 105–119.

Almond, Gabriel A. and Sidney Verba. 1963. *The Civic Culture: Political Attitudes and Democracy in Five Nations*, Princeton: Princeton University Press.

Althoff, Gerd. 2003. *Die Macht der Rituale. Symbolik und Herrschaft im Mittelalter*. Darmstadt: Wissenschaftliche Buchgesellschaft.

Andretta, Stefano. 1975–76. "La diplomazia veneziana e la pace die Vestfalia (1643–1648)." In *Annuario dell' istituto storico italiano per l'età moderna e contemporanea* 27–28: 3–128.

Asch, Ronald G. and Dagmar Freist, eds. 2005. *Staatsbildung als kultureller Prozess. Strukturwandel und Legitimation von Herrschaft in der Frühen Neuzeit*. Cologne, Weimar, Vienna: Böhlau.

Asch, Ronald G., Wulf E. Voß and Martin Wrede, eds. 2001. *Frieden und Krieg in der Frühen Neuzeit. Die europäische Staatenordnung und die außereuropäische Welt*. Munich: Fink.

Bachmann-Medick, Doris. 2009. *Cultural Turns. Neuorientierungen in den Kulturwissenschaften.* 3rd editionReinbek bei Hamburg: Rowohlt.

Becker, Winfried. 1973. *Der Kurfürstenrat. Grundzüge seiner Entwicklung in der Reichsverfassung und seine Stellung auf dem Westfälischen Friedenskongress.* Münster: Aschendorff.

Bell, Caroline. 1997. *Ritual. Perspectives and Dimensions*. New York, Oxford: Oxford University Press.

Bély, Lucien. 1990. *Espions et ambassadeurs au temps de Louis XIV*. Paris : Fayard.

Bély, Lucien. 1993. "Souveraineté et souverains. La question du cérémonial dans les relations internationales à l'époque moderne." In *Annuaire-Bulletin de la Société de l'Histoire de France* : 27–43.

Bély, Lucien and Isabelle Richefort, eds. 2000. *L'Europe des traités de Westphalie. Esprit de la diplomatie et diplomatie de l'esprit*. Paris: Presses Universitaires de France.

Bély, Lucien and Isabelle Richefort, eds. 1998. *L'Invention de la Diplomatie. Moyen âge – temps modernes.* Paris: Presses Universitaires de France.

Berger, Peter and Thomas Luckmann. 1979. *The Social Construction of Reality. A Treatise in the Sociology of Knowledge*. Harmondsworth: Penguin.

Biersteker, Thomas J., Cynthia Weber, eds. 1996. *State Sovereignty as Social Construct*. Cambridge: Cambridge University Press.

Blockmans, Wim, André Holenstein and Ion Mathieu, eds. 2009. *Empowering Interactions: Political cultures and the emergence of the state in Europe 1300–1900*. Farnham: Ashgate.

Bourdieu, Pierre. 1980. *Le sens pratique*. Paris: Minuit.

Brakensiek, Stefan and Heide Wunder, eds. 2005. *Ergebene Diener ihrer Herren? Herrschaftsvermittlung im alten Europa*. Köln/Weimar/Wien: Böhlau.

Cassirer, Ernst. 1953. *Philosophie der symbolischen Formen*. Darmstadt: Wissenschaftliche Buchgesellschaft.

Christ, Günter. 1999. "Der Exzellenz-Titel für die kurfürstlichen Gesandten auf dem Westfälischen Friedenskongreß." *Parliaments, Estates and Representation* 19: 89–102.

Croxton, Derek and Anuschka Tischer, eds. 2002. *The Peace of Westphalia: A Historical Dictionary*. Westport, CT/London: Greenwood Press.

Daniel, Ute. 2001. *Kompendium Kulturgeschichte. Theorien, Praxis, Schlüsselworte*. Frankfurt/Main: Suhrkamp.

Daniel, Ute. 2003. "Kulturgeschichte." In *Konzepte der Kulturwissenschaften. Theoretische Grundlagen – Ansätze – Perspektiven*, eds. Nünning, Ansgar and Vera Nünning. 186–204. Stuttgart/Weimar: Metzler.

Dickmann, Fritz. 1972. *Der Westfälische Frieden*. 3rd edition. Münster: Aschendorff.

Duchhardt, Heinz. 1999. "'Westphalian System'. Zur Problematik einer Denkfigur." *Historisches Zeitschrift* 269: 305–315.

Duchhardt, Heinz, ed. 1998. *Der Westfälische Friede. Diplomatie, politische Zäsur, kulturelles Umfeld, Rezeptionsgeschichte.* München: Oldenbourg.

Edelman, Murray J. 1964. *The Symbolic Uses of Politics.* Urbana: University of Illinois Press.

Flüchter, Antje. 2005. "Konfessionalisierung aus kulturalistischer Perspektive? Überlegungen am Beispiel der Herzogtümer Jülich-Berg." In *Was heißt Kulturgeschichte des Politischen?* ed. Barbara Stollberg-Rilinger. 225–252. Berlin: Duncker & Humblot.

Frigo, Daniela, ed. 1999. *Ambasciatori e nunzi. Figure delle diplomazia in età moderna.* Rome: Bulzoni.

Frigo, Daniela, ed. 2000. *Politics and Diplomacy in Early Modern Italy. The Structure of Diplomatic Practice 1450–1800.* Cambridge: Cambridge University Press.

Frigo, Daniela. 1991. *Principe, ambasciatori e "jus gentium".* Rome : Bulzoni.

Geertz, Clifford. 1973. "Thick Description: Toward an Interpretive Theory of Culture." In *The Interpretation of Cultures: Selected Essays,* 3–30. New York: Basic Books.

Giddens, Anthony. 1986. *The Constitution of Society. Outline of the Theory of Structuration.* Cambridge: Polity Press.

Giesey, Ralph E. 1987. *Cérémonial et puissance souveraine. France XVe-XVIIe siècles.* Paris : Colin.

Göhler, Gerhard et al. (eds.). 1997. *Institution – Macht – Repräsentation. Wofür politische Institutionen stehen und wie sie wirken,* Baden-Baden: Nomos.

Grotius, Hugo. 1625. *De jure belli ac pacis libri tres.* II, 18, 2–5. Paris: Buon.

Hobbes, Thomas. "Leviathan." In *The English Works of Thomas Hobbes of Malmesbury; Now First Collected and Edited by Sir William Molesworth.* 1839–45. 11 vols. Vol. 3. London: Bohn.

Hofmann, Hasso. 2003. *Repräsentation. Studien zur Wort- und Begriffsgeschichte von der Antike bis zum 19. Jahrhundert* (1st edition 1974). Berlin: Duncker & Humblot.

Hunt, Lynn (ed.). 1989. *The New Cultural History* (Studies on the History of Society and Culture, 6). Berkeley: University of California Press.

Kertzer, David J. 1988. *Ritual, Politics and Power.* New Haven/London: Yale University Press.

Krasner, Stephen D. 1999. *Sovereignty: Organized Hypocrisy.* Princeton: Princeton University Press.

Kraus, Hans-Christof and Thomas Nicklas, eds. 2007. *Geschichte der Politik. Alte und neue Wege* (Historische Zeitschrift, Beiheft 44). München: Oldenbourg.

Krischer, André. 2010. "Souveränität als sozialer Status. Zur Funktion des diplomatischen Zeremoniells in der Frühen Neuzeit." In *Diplomatische Praxis und Zeremoniell in Europa und dem Mittleren Osten in der Frühen Neuzeit,* ed. Jan-Paul Niederkorn et al. 1–32. Wien: Verlag der Österreichischen Akademie der Wissenschaften.

Krischer, André. 2011. "Das Gesandtschaftswesen und das vormoderne Völkerrecht." In Kintzinger, Martin and Michael Jucker, eds. 2011. *Rechtsformen internationaler Politik. Theorie, Norm und Praxis vom 12. bis zum 18. Jahrhundert.* Berlin: Duncker & Humblot 197–240.

Kümin, Beat. 2009. "Political Culture in the Holy Roman Empire." *German History* 27: 131–144.

Landwehr, Achim. 2003. "Diskurs – Macht – Wissen. Perspektiven einer Kulturgeschichte des Politischen." *Archiv für Kulturgeschichte* 85: 71–117.

Lehmkuhl, Ursula. 2001. "Die Diplomatiegeschichte als internationale Kulturgeschichte." *Geschichte und Gesellschaft* 27: 392–423.

Leibniz, Gottfried Wilhelm. 1678. "Germani Curiosi Admonitiones." In 1963. *Sämtliche Schriften und Briefe,* Vol. IV/2. 364–378, Berlin: Akademie-Verlag.

Lesaffer, Randall, ed. 2004. *Peace Treaties and International Law in European History.* New York: Cambridge University Press.

Luhmann, Niklas. 1995. "Kultur als historischer Begriff." In *Gesellschaftsstruktur und Semantik,* Niklas Luhmann, Vol. 4, 31–54. Frankfurt/Main: Suhrkamp.

May, Niels Fabian. 2006. *Le cérémonial diplomatique au XVIe siècle comme expression politique. Les différends pendant les négotiations de Westphalie (1643–1648),* Maîtrise (unpublished).

Mergel, Thomas. 2002. "Überlegungen zu einer Kulturgeschichte der Politik." *Geschichte und Gesellschaft* 28: 574–607.

Morgan, Edmund S. 1983. "Government by Fiction. The Idea of Representation." *The Yale Review* 72: 321–339.

Müller, Klaus. 1976. *Das kaiserliche Gesandtschaftswesen im Jahrhundert nach dem Westfälischen Frieden 1648–1740*. Bonn: Röhrscheid.

Muir, Edward. 1997. *Ritual in Early Modern Europe*, Cambridge: Cambridge University Press.

Nicklas, Thomas. 2004. "Macht – Politik – Diskurs. Möglichkeiten und Grenzen einer Politischen Kulturgeschichte." *Archiv für Kulturgeschichte* 86: 1–25.

Osiander, Andreas. 2001. "Sovereignty, International Relations, and the Westphalian Myth." *International Organization* 55: 251–287.

Pitkin, Hannah F. 1967. *The Concept of Representation*. Berkeley: University of California Press.

Quaritsch, Helmuth. 1986. *Souveränität Entstehung und Entwicklung des Begriffs in Frankreich und Deutschland vom 13 Jahrhundert bis 1806*. Berlin: Duncker & Humblot.

Rehberg, Karl-Siegbert. 2001. "Weltrepräsentanz und Verkörperung. Institutionelle Analyse und Symboltheorien – eine Einführung in systematischer Absicht." In *Institutionalität und Symbolisierung. Verstetigungen kultureller Ordnungsmuster in Vergangenheit und Gegenwart*, ed. Gert Melville, 3–49. Köln/Weimar/Wien: Böhlau.

Repgen, Konrad. 1997. "Friedensvermittlung und Friedensvermittler beim Westfälischen Frieden." *Westfälische Zeitschrift* 147: 37–61.

Rödder, Andreas. 2006. "Klios neue Kleider. Theoriedebatten um eine Kulturgeschichte der Politik in der Moderne." *Historische Zeitschrift* 283: 57–68.

Roosen, William. 1976. *The Age of Louis XIV. The Rise of Modern Diplomacy*, Cambridge, MA: Schenkman.

Roosen, William. 1980. "Early Modern Diplomatic Ceremonial: A Systems Approach." *Journal of Modern History* 52: 452–476.

Sarcinelli, Ulrich. 1987. *Symbolische Politik*. Opladen: Westdeutscher Verlag.

Schilling, Heinz. 2007. *Konfessionalisierung und Staatsinteressen 1559–1660* (Handbuch der Geschichte der Internationalen Beziehungen, Vol. 2). Paderborn: Schöningh.

Schütz, Alfred. 1975. *Strukturen der Lebenswelt*. 2 Vols. Neuwied: Luchterhand.

Schütz, Alfred. 1993. *Der sinnhafte Aufbau der sozialen Welt. Eine Einleitung in die verstehende Soziologie*. 6th edition. Frankfurt/Main: Suhrkamp.

Steinmetz, Willibald. 2007. "Neue Wege einer historischen Semantik des Politischen." In *„Politik". Situationen eines Wortgebrauchs im Europa der Neuzeit*, ed. Willibald Steinmetz Frankfurt/Main: Suhrkamp.

Stiglic, Anja. 1998. "Zeremoniell und Rangordnung auf der europäischen diplomatischen Bühne am Beispiel der Gesandteneinzüge in die Kongreßstadt Münster." In Bußmann, Klaus und Heinz Schilling, eds. *1648 – Krieg und Frieden in Europa. Politik, Religion, Recht und Gesellschaft*. Textband. Münster: Bruckmann: 391–396.

Stollberg-Rilinger, Barbara. 2004. "Symbolische Kommunikation in der Vormoderne. Begriffe – Thesen – Forschungsperspektiven." *Zeitschrift für historische Forschung* 31: 489–527.

Stollberg-Rilinger, Barbara. 2011. "Völkerrechtlicher Status und zeremonielle Praxis auf dem Westfälischen Friedenskongress." In Kintzinger, Martin and Michael Jucker, eds. *Rechtsformen internationaler Politik. Theorie, Norm und Praxis vom 12. bis zum 18. Jahrhundert*. Berlin: Duncker & Humblot: 147–164.

Stollberg-Rilinger, Barbara. 2000. "Honores regii. Die Königswürde im zeremoniellen Zeichensystem der Frühen Neuzeit." In *Dreihundert Jahre Preußische Königskrönung. Eine Tagungsdokumentation*, ed. Johannes Kunisch. Berlin: Duncker & Humbolt: 1–26.

Thiessen, Hillard von and Christian Windler, eds. 2010. *Akteure der Außenbeziehungen. Netzwerke und Interkulturalität im historischen Wandel*. Cologne, Weimar, Vienna: Böhlau.

Tischer, Anuschka. 2005. "Diplomatie." *Enzyklopädie der Neuzeit* Vol. 2. 1028–1041. Stuttgart/Weimar: Metzler.

Tschopp, Silvia Serena and Wolfgang E.J. Weber. 2007. *Grundfragen der Kulturgeschichte.* Darmstadt: Wissenschaftliche Buchgesellschaft.

Walz, Rainer. 2005. "Der Begriff der Kultur in der Systemtheorie." In *Was heißt Kulturgeschichte des Politischen?* ed. Barbara Stollberg-Rilinger, pp.97–114. Berlin: Duncker & Humblot.

Weber, Max. 1988. *Gesammelte Aufsätze zur Wissenschaftslehre.* Ed. Johannes Winckelmann, 7th edition. Tübingen: Mohr Siebeck.

Wicquefort, Abraham de. 1746. *L'Ambassadeur et ses fonctions,* 2 vols., p. 17. (1st edition 1676), Amsterdam: Honoré.

Wilson, Peter. 2009. *The Thirty Years War. Europe's Tragedy.* London, Cambridge, MA: Harvard University Press.

Part II
Case Studies: Knowledge

Pater patriae sinensis. The Discovery of Patriarchal Rule in China and Its Significance for German Theories of State in the Eighteenth Century

Susan Richter

1 Introduction

In his *Oratio de Sinarum philosophia practica*, delivered at the University of Halle's festive assembly on 12 June 1721, Christian Wolff (1679–1754) praised the "Weisheit der Chinesen seit den ältesten Zeiten und ihre geradezu außerordentliche Klugheit bei der Verwaltung des Staates". (Wolff 1985 [1726]: 13) (Wisdom of the Chinese since the earliest times and their extraordinary prudence in administering the state).[1] He ascribed this "extraordinary prudence" of the Chinese "in administering the state" primarily to their concept of rule: "Die alten Kaiser und Könige der Chinesen waren nämlich zugleich Philosophen: Was ist also daran verwunderlich, dass—gemäß dem Satz Platons—der Staat glückselig war, wo die Philosophen herrschten und die Könige philosophieren?" (Ibid.; Ho 1962; Lach 1953; Larrimore 2000). (The ancient Chinese kings and emperors were also philosophers: therefore it is not amazing that—according to Plato's phrase—it is a blissful state wherein philosophers rule and kings practise philosophy.)

To Wolff, the ideal ruler was the philosopher on the throne,[2] who played a decisive role in achieving a blissful state. Alongside this concept based on platonic-

---

[1] The translations of the German citations are by the author.

[2] The ancient idea of the philosopher-king is found in the works of Plato. Plato thought that the philosopher-king should be educated theoretically and practically, with equal time for both, before dealing with the idea of good, which was to complete the education. These philosopher-kings were supposed to divide their time between state business and scientific activities on a rational basis. (See Baicu 2006; Vonessen 2003) Marcus Aurelius is considered to be an example of such a philosopher on a throne. (Maier 1985) Immanuel Kant, however, criticised Plato's concept in his work "Zum ewigen Frieden" (On Perpetual Peace). A detailed comparison of the ancient and early modern European ideal of the "philosopher on a throne" with Asian ideas of the philosophical statesman is being prepared by Susan Richter.

S. Richter (✉)
Karl Jaspers Centre, University of Heidelberg, Voßstr. 2, 69115 Heidelberg, Germany
e-mail: richter@asia-europe.uni-heidelberg.de

A. Flüchter and S. Richter (eds.), *Structures on the Move*,
Transcultural Research – Heidelberg Studies on Asia and Europe in a Global Context,
DOI 10.1007/978-3-642-19288-3_4, © Springer-Verlag Berlin Heidelberg 2012

occidental traditions, he regards the philosophically-based empire in China as an ideal model for European rulers.[3] According to classical Chinese texts, the legendary First Emperor of China—*Fu Xi* (or *Fu-shi*)—founded the Chinese Empire in the year 2952 B.C.[4] He was, according to Wolff's "Anmerkungen zu seiner Rede" from 1726, a true "philosopher-sovereign", because, first and foremost, he regarded "das ganze Reich als eine einzige Familie" (the entire kingdom as one single family) and wanted to implement "zwischen Obrigkeit und Untergebenen dasselbe Verhältnis, wie es zwischen Eltern und Kindern besteht" (Wolff 1985 [1726]: 87) (the same relationship between state authorities and their subjects as exists between parents and their children).

Furthermore, according to Wolff, the state's welfare depended on peoples' virtue and reason in general, but especially on the person of the sovereign (Ibid.). In his *Oratio*, Wolff credited the Chinese Emperors with both these qualities and believed that, if one strives to attain higher virtues, one has to begin by schooling one's intellectual capacities. (Ibid.: 51)

He saw this realised primarily in the duality of the Chinese school of thought as described by Father François Noël (1651–1729).[5] (Ibid.: 11 and 199; Mungello 1988: 265 and 267) Each heir apparent in China received such an education; in the so-called "School of Minors" they learned about sensibility, as well as reverence towards their parents, elders and the emperor. (Wolff 1985 [1726]: 41) After this, future sovereigns went through the "School of Adults", gaining the ability for rational and philosophical thought. (Saine 1987: 177) "So waren die beiden Schulen beschaffen," so Wolff believed, "als der Staat im goldenen Zeitalter der Chinesen in höchster Blüte stand und die Herrschenden ebenso wie die Untertanen ihr Amt und ihre Pflicht erfüllten." (Wolff 1985 [1726]: 43) As an example "siehet man, daß die alten Regenten der Sineser [...] nicht allein über eine gute Regierung philosophiret, sondern ihre Scharfsinnigkeit auch in andern Dingen beübet haben." (Wolff 1981: 562)[6]

Thus was the nature of both these schools, during the golden age when the Chinese state was at its zenith and both the ruling class and the subjects fulfilled their function and their duties. [...] we see that the ancient rulers of the Chinese [...]

---

[3] Ancient Chinese rulers such as Fu Xi furnished historical evidence that it was not utopian to believe in a philosopher on the throne or at least in an understanding prince advised by philosophers.

[4] According to popular Chinese myths, Fu Xi was the first of three legendary emperors (*San-Huang*), a creator of deity in the shape of a double snake and the first regent of the cosmos. (Cf. Münke 1998: 71–75)

[5] François Noël's interpretation of Confucian teaching differs decisively from that of Philippe Couplet S.J. Couplet tried to interpret and present *Daxue* as "the learning of great men", because "great men" could be taken as referring to Chinese antiquity, making it comparable to Christianity. Although Couplet's work was better known than Noël's version, Wolff evidently favoured Noël's interpretation, which gives *Daxue* as "Adultorum schola" (the learning of adults) and *Xiaoxue* as "Parvulorum schola".

[6] Plato, too, describes a definite plan of education for the future philosopher-king, beginning in childhood and lasting many years.

Pater patriae sinensis

not only philosophised over the question of good governance, rather did they also use their wits in other matters.

Through Wolff's writings, this long-established ideal of government by a sovereign-philosopher re-entered the focus of contemporary discussion and advanced to an archetype of government adopted, propagated, and partially implemented, not only by Voltaire and many other political philosophers during the Age of Enlightenment, but also by monarchs such as Frederick II of Prussia. (Birtsch 1987)

In his recognition of the Chinese Empire as an existing model of state welfare, Wolff was not alone. From the mid-eighteenth century onwards, physiocrats and cameralists closely observed China's agricultural development. In 1758, the cameralist Johann Heinrich Gottlob Justi (1717–1771), influenced by Wolff's criterion of *Glückseligkeit* (happiness of the people), wrote in the second part of his book *Staatswirtschaft* (State Economy): "Wenn wir lernen wollen, wie der Boden eines Landes recht zu nutzen ist, so müssen wir nach Sina gehen." (Justi 1758: 162) (If we want to learn to make the best use of a country's soil, we must turn to China.)[7] Here again, first and foremost, it was the ruling class, primarily the sovereign, who was responsible for this success: a monarch who lived in accordance with the laws of nature, voluntarily complied with and respected them, and regarded the successful cultivation of the land as the most important criterion for the prosperity of the state. To illustrate these ideals Physiocrats no longer exclusively cited the well-known monarchs of antiquity or of Christianity to be found in European literature on sovereignty. Instead, they looked outside Europe to the Chinese Emperor, his capacities, rights and duties, as a role model for their ideal head of state. (Priddat 2001: 92)

In his *Vergleichungen der Europäischen mit den Asiatischen und andern vermeintlich barbarischen Regierungen* (Comparisons of the European governments to Asian and other supposedly barbarian governments) dating from 1762, Justi refers "to the preparations made by Chinese rulers preceding the cultivation of the land": "Jedes Frühjahr hat der Kaiser nach dem Exempel seiner ältesten Vorfahren die Gewohnheit, daß er unter gewissen Solennitäten einige Furchen höchst eigenhändig gräbet, um durch sein Exempel die Leuthe zum Ackerbau aufzumuntern." (Justi 1762: 300) (Each spring, the Chinese Emperor, in the exemplary tradition of his forefathers, is in the habit of ploughing several furrows himself, with accompanying solemnities, in order to encourage his people to cultivate the land.)

Justi interpreted the Emperor's ploughing by his own hand as a unique sign of regard and estimation of the peasant class by the country's ruler, who, at one and the same time, placed himself at the head of agriculture in a literal, as well as figurative way, thus furthering it. (Justi 1762: 305)[8] This action implied for Justi visible

---

[7] For Wolff's influence on Justi see Backhaus (2009).

[8] Long before physiocratic and cameralistic ideas appeared, agriculture was seen in Europe as the main factor in providing subsistence. Farmers therefore played a vital role as the *nourishing estate* of a country. In his *Institutio Traiani* Plutarch refers to farmers as the *feet* which support and carry

64 S. Richter

fatherly care on the part of the ruler for his subjects and the entire country, with food being provided by a functioning agricultural sector. For this reason, Justi enthusiastically states that China has a functioning patriarchal system of rule: "Dieses ist die Vorstellung von der unumschränkten Gewalt der Kaiser in Sina, und von denen vortrefflichen Triebfedern, wodurch diese Monarchen bewogen werden, diese Gewalt lediglich zu der Glückseligkeit ihrer Untertanen anzuwenden. (Justi 1762: 23) (This is the idea of the unlimited power of the Emperor in China, and of those admirable mainsprings that move these monarchs to apply this power purely for the felicity of their subjects.) Like the physiocrats in France, Justi's primary intention was to encourage European rulers, in particular, to advance agriculture; his message was well received by Europe's monarchs.[9] (Richter 2010a: 46)

The two examples given by Wolff and Justi, along with the physiocrats' ideas, show that, during the first and the second halves of the eighteenth century, different French and German schools of thought were discussing the theory of government prevalent in their own countries. In particular, they focused on the non-European concept of monarchy as seen in the Chinese Empire, and declared this to be exemplary. In the following, we will explain why the Chinese Empire was considered to be such a perfect model. Why was it that the Chinese emperors, of all rulers, provided such a good argument in favour of good rule?

I make the assumption that two fundamental phenomena in the perception of the Chinese monarchy played an important role. For one thing, from the German point of view there was a great similarity between their own concept of rule and the Chinese one, despite the geographical and cultural distance. For another, Wolff and Justi were also fascinated by the phenomenon of a certain simultaneity in these similarities. This permitted them to compare the two concepts directly and raised expectations of more direct application than was the case with examples from the ancient world.

The comparatist approach in the present study on the German perception of the Chinese *pater patriae sinensis*, consciously chosen, provides suitable equipment for explaining the transcultural meeting of similar Asiatic and European concepts of rule not as delimitation and differentiation, but as a unilateral process of acquisition. This, in turn, in the present case is not informed by the foreign nature of other cultures, or an alien nature of what is acquired, but rather by the compatibility of the concepts of rule. The present study will show that this compatibility enabled the

---

the entire *corpus reo publicae*. (Kloft and Kerner 1992: Fragment VII a, 74) As a result of this ancient ideal of the *farmer-statesman*, European rulers were not only responsible for directing agricultural matters centrally; they were also expected to promote agriculture in particular. Both the Mirrors of Princes and the entire patriarchal literature at the end of the seventeenth and throughout the eighteenth century called this to the attention of kings and princes alike. (Abel 1967: 201–208) However, the ruling classes ignored this for quite a long time, which encouraged the physiocrats and cameralists to look further for new, extra-European models.

[9] On 19 August of 1769, Emperor Joseph II himself actually worked the plough in the Moravian village of Slavkovitz. (Richter 2010a: 49)

examination of the efficacy of the concept of fatherly rule for German political theory, and helped in addition to confirm, and add new components to, this concept.

Wolff and Justi, of course, obtained their knowledge of the Chinese monarchy from various travelogues, and were confronted with reports which were not only not particularly uptodate, but also full of very subjective information on the part of these travel writers. Based on their intention to reveal European shortcomings in government by using non-European role models, and thus to instruct the ruling class, I intend to demonstrate how Wolff and Justi used the information at their disposal, and on which epistemological methods and procedures their model of government was constructed. This will be based on both historical and contemporary theories.

In doing this, it will be possible to see that European knowledge of the Chinese monarchy was not only quite vague and superficial, but despite this was considered assured with respect to the function of the monarchy, its status, its power, and the effective area of rule of the Emperor.

When one observes the early modern European discourses on the "state" and its formation, one can see, on the one hand, that school of thought that originated with Jean Bodin, and enquired about the sovereignty and the legal foundations or legitimation of the office of ruler. This is in contrast to the school of thought founded by the neo-Stoicist Justus Lipsius, which enquired primarily about forms of governability and good government of a country. This essay is intended to show that the authors Wolff and Justi, constructing their model in the eighteenth century, chose the Chinese ruler as a role model primarily because of the forms of good government and the practice of rule as a "philosopher on a throne", or as "first farmer of the state" in China.[10]

The exemplary government of the Chinese monarchs implied, however, complete sovereignty and legitimation of the power of the Chinese Emperor, which was described by all travellers as a father-children relationship. The Emperor, then, was clearly endowed with the corresponding power of command of a monarch, quite in the sense of Bodin's expressly named *patria potestas* or *puissance paternelle*, a power that was absolute, and formed the basis for the flowering of the community and the strength of the ruler. (Bodin 1981: I 124–138) Wolff and Justi found, in China, a functioning patriarchal kingdom, regarded by both in their works as a basic ideal of leadership and government of state communities, or of the German territories in the Holy Roman Empire, and which was seen as a foundation for the realisation of ideals of rule such as the "philosopher on a throne" or the "first farmer of the state".

---

[10] This term has been put forward by the author according to the contemporary German self-concept of "erster Diener des Staates" (Frederick II of Prussia). (See Richter 2010: 40)

2 Legal Prerequisites of Rank for Drawing on China as a Model

European forms of rule and their mutual legal recognition within Europe resulted from the fact that similar political structures were predominant in many European states, particularly in the monarchies, from the convergent intentions of their rulers and from their pan-European dynastic connections. As a result of the close relations of its royal families to one another,[11] Europe possessed a common political culture and was closely associated on a legal level. (Richter 2010b: 294; Mohnhaupt 2000) This meant that, in the early modern era, it was the monarchs above all who controlled and directed the community of nations, and who were the subjects of the laws of nations. Based on this assumption, foreign cultures and states were assessed and recognised under international law according to their established form of government and their monarch. (Richter 2010c: 28)

A key instrument in gauging the importance of a European or foreign potentate in the early modern era was the form of the so-called treatises of standing. They contained a catalogue of criteria by which the status of a monarch and his family within Europe's nobility could be discussed and defined. Aspects such as "das Altherthum der Monarchie oder Souveränität, die Macht, Potentatus oder Suprematus, die Vielheit der Königreiche, die Ehren = Titul, welche eine Majestät vor der anderen hat, die absolute Gewalt, die Würdigkeit der Vasallen, über welche eines Majestät herrschet" (Stieve 1723: 2; von Stosch 1677: 2) (the antiquity of the monarchy or sovereignty, its power, *Potentatus or Suprematus*, the multitude of its kingdoms, the honorary titles which one majesty holds above others, his absolute power, the dignity of the lieges whom his majesty commands) were taken into account. These criteria were also used in describing and understanding the Chinese monarchy. In 1585, the Augustinian Juan González de Mendoza wrote in his book *Historia de las cosas más notables, ritos y costumbres del gran reyno de la China* (translated and newly edited by Grießler, *Geschichte der höchst bemerkenswerten Dinge und Sitten im chinesischen Königreich*) (Contemporary English translation: The historie of the great and mightie kingdome of China, and the situation thereof (González de Mendoza 1853) that he intended to trace the succession of the Chinese Emperors, especially the founder of the Chinese "kingdom". (González de Mendoza 1992: 67; González de Mendoza 1853: 18) Mendoza's important message to Europeans was that China, just like the major European states or the smaller German territorial states, was ruled by a successful dynasty. It also could look back upon the magnificent personality of a founder who had unified the vast Empire and had laid the foundations for future prosperity and strength. It was exactly this type

---

[11] As a result, in this age of strong dynastically accentuated legal interaction between nations, the imperial cities and republics were much less involved in ceremonial interactions because of their lack of family ties, and first of all had to earn themselves status (in the sense of social acceptance) and forms of legal cooperation. To this end, they implemented the patterns which had already been established by the monarchies. (Cf. Krischer 2007: 3–11 and 19)

of founder-father that the ruling houses of Europe were searching for and what they indeed often built up for themselves around diverse myths and sagas. Written and illustrated genealogies appeared, recording the splendour of a particular house and describing the contribution made to it by each generation. Europeans discovered remarkable similarities in China: in the sixteenth and seventeenth centuries, Jesuits and similar learned Sinophiles produced genealogical and chronological lineages for former Chinese Emperors, listing an astonishing sequence of 86 monarchs in 2457 years. (Couplet i.e. 1686 and 1687; Grandi 1753: 712ff.; Paludan 1998) Christian Wolff had dealt with the genealogical and chronological lists of the Jesuit Philippe Couplet, and in detail, in the course of preparing his *Oratio de Sinarum philosophica practica*. Justi, too, recognised *in extenso* the long existence of the Chinese Empire and its laws, despite the dynastic changes. (Justi 1762: 454) The age of this foreign state—one of the most important criteria for equal standing—had been examined, verified, and attested by European authorities.

Travel literature of the period categorically refers to the Chinese monarch as "Emperor" or "King". This was derived from his original titles and appeared in translation in the travel literature, or resulted from the impression Europeans gained of the Chinese potentates having unrestricted power, plus the size of the area of influence under their rule. (Demel 1999: 63) Very often, the travel writers highly respectful esteem of the Chinese monarchs—for example, on the part of the Jesuits or members of the Dutch East India Company (VOC)—resulted from their wish to emphasise the importance of their own mission to such a remarkable court or country. (Richter 2010c: 29) Nevertheless, because of the age of the monarchy and the success of the dynasty, as well as the enormity of the empire, the title of Emperor seemed thoroughly appropriate. The French Jesuit Louis le Comte described the Emperor as an absolute ruler and the Empire as a person:

Cette profonde veneration est encore fondée sur l'interest que chacun a de luy faire sa cour. Dés qu'il a esté proclamé empereur, toute l'autorité de l'empire est réunie en sa personne, et il devient l'arbitre unique et absolu de la bonne ou de la mauvaise fortune de tous ses sujets.

Ce qui se passa dans une guerre que l'empereur eut il y a quelques années avec un roy tartare, prouve encore beaucoup mieux ce que j'ay dit de son pouvoir absolu. Il avoit envoyé une puissante armée sous le commandement de son frère, pour punir la témerité de ce petit roy qui avoit osé ravager les états de plusieurs alliez de l'empire. (Le Comte 1696: 7 and 11)[12]

(Interest is no small occasion of the respect which is shown him by his Subjects; for as soon as he is proclaimed Emperor, the whole Authority of the Empire is in his hand, and the good or ill Fortune of his Subjects is owing wholly to him.

You will have a plain proof of the absoluteness of the Emperors power from a passage which happened in a late war with one of the Kings of Tartary. The

---

[12] Constant came to the same result: the emperor is the absolute ruler above all and everything. (Cf. Constant 1791: 439)

Emperor sent a mighty Army under his Brothers Command, to punish the vanity and Rashness of that puny King, who had dared to make inroads into the Countries of several of the Allies of the Empire. (Contemporary English translation: Le Comte 1697: 244 and 247).

Descriptions taken from the missionaries' travel writings and historical essays were basing themselves on European international law treatises to give evidence of China's equality in terms of standing and esteem both as a political system and in the person of the Chinese Emperor. In his book *Absolutes Fürstenrecht* (1719), Wilhelm von Schroeder uses information taken from the Jesuit Louis le Comte when describing the "Sineser Monarchen Macht" as being "sehr absolute Iura majestatica" (powers of the Chinese monarch [as being] very absolute iura maiestatica), as an absolute and sublime majestic authority "Auctoritas illimitata legibus Sinensibus Principi conciliata & necessitas illi simul iniuncta eiusdem non temere usurpandae, duae illae columnae sunt, quae a tot saeculis grande aedificium Sinensis Monarchiae hucusque sustinent. Summa principis veneratio ad usque adorationis procedens, primus est sensus, quo subditi imbuuntur."[13] (von Schroeder 1719: 145–148)

From a European point of view, the Emperor was herewith afforded equal standing alongside the Holy Roman Emperor and the French and the Spanish Kings.[14] (Demel 1999: 75) At the same time, when classifying the Chinese ruler and his powers, these travel writers—together with Schroeder and other experts on international law—followed Bodin's concept of *maiestas* as *souveraineté*, as absolute power and authority held by the ruling class. (For the relation between Maiestas and Imperium cf. Scatolla 2000).

The rank of rulers and their territories under international law was reflected in the ceremonials, and thus in the science of ceremonial that was just coming into being at the start of the eighteenth century: in 1720, Johann Christian Lünig remarked in his *Theatrum ceremoniale* that there were also "unterschiedene mächtige Könige und Potentaten in Asia" (differently powerful kings and potentates in Asia). Among them were, in particular, the King of Persia, the Mogul Emperor, the Emperor of Japan, the Cham of the Tartars and also the Emperor of China, "denen Europäische Potentaten, so mit denselben zu negotiiren haben, Königen gehörige Ehren = Bezeugungen erweisen." (Lünig 1720: vol. 2, 1461) (to whom European potentates, in negotiating with the same, afford the same

---

[13] "The combined powers of the prince, unrestricted by Chinese law, thus making it unnecessary for him to fear these, are the two pillars on which the Chinese monarchy rests to the present day. The adoration of the prince goes as far as worshiping him; this is the first thought which most satisfies his subjects."

[14] The role of the Christian head of the Holy Roman Empire was not taken into account as a point of comparison or category in this classification. Only the reflection of standing and power in the title was of interest. Demel, for example, comes to the conclusion that the Chinese Emperor is frequently classified in travel reports as the wealthiest potentate in the world. (Demel et al. 1999: 75)

demonstrations of respect as to kings) Signs of respect, such as certain titles and forms of address, were part of the "ceremonial" according to Lünig, "eine unter souveränen, oder ihnen gleichgeltenden Personen [. . .] eingeführte Ordnung." (Ibid., I, 2) (a recognised code of behaviour among sovereigns or persons of equal standing) The European monarchs treated these non-European monarchs named by Lünig as equals and "colleagues" in the *société des princes* (Bély 1999). One pre-requisite for this recognition was a certain similarity in the structures of state governance and in their concept of sovereignty, which bore comparison to monarchic rule and emerging state structures in European monarchies, or which had even developed from traditions common to Europe and China.

This equal rank of the Chinese Emperor was also visible in diplomatic practice, such as the numerous legations and embassies continually sent to the Court at Peking by the Dutch, Portuguese, Russians and British throughout the eighteenth century to assert their commercial interests and to obtain trade privileges. The great respect shown by European rulers towards the Chinese Emperor was expressed in the diplomatic letters. The Bavarian Duke Maximilian I sent a letter to the Chinese Emperor in 1617, personally explaining Christian belief to him. In the introduction to this religious instruction, he expresses his great respect for the foreign monarch: "AD MAXIMVM POTENTISSIMVM ET PER OMNEM ORBEM CLARISSIMVM IMPERATOREM atque Sinensis regni Monarcham." (Greindl 2008: 158/159) (To the greatest, most powerful Emperor and monarch of China, famous all over the world)

Czar Peter the Great, to cite another example, called the Emperor *Votre Majesté, le bon ami*, signing this particular letter with *Pierre*. King George III of Great Britain, in his letter, went into detail about all the cultural virtues of China and the equal rank of the Chinese monarchy: "We have been [. . .] anxious to enquire into the arts and manners of countries where civilisation has been perfected by the wise ordinances and virtuous examples of their Sovereign thru [sic!] a long series of ages, and, above all, our ardent wish has been to become acquainted with those celebrated institutions of Your Majesty's populous and extensive Empire which have carried its prosperity to such a height as to be the admiration of all surrounding Nations. [. . .] We rely on Your Imperial Majesty's wisdom that You will please our Ambassador [. . .] to have the opportunity of contemplating the example of Your virtues and to obtain such information of Your celebrated institutions as will enable him to enlighten Our People on his return." The British King emphasised the equality in rank in his letter to the Qian Long Emperor: "We are Brethren in Sovereignty, so may a Brotherly affection ever subsist between us." He signed the letter with *Vester bonus frater et Amicus*. (Demel 1992: 145)

The acceptance of the equality in rank and position of the Chinese monarch displayed in the literature on the legal aspects of rank and diplomatic practice represented an important prerequisite for his suitability as a paragon and model, as the European potentates were supposed to orientate themselves according to his example in certain areas. This orientation was made easy in spite of the cultural and religious differences, in view of the fact that the role model chosen was verifiably "one of the select few".

70 S. Richter

3 Categories for Describing Rule

The use of ancient categories together with contemporary political vocabulary in describing Chinese rule suggested to the German reader that China was on a par with the Old World in every respect, for her Emperors possessed both *maiestas* and *summa potestas*, were committed as rulers to the ideal of *pater patriae*, and their governance was legitimated by a long ancestral lineage and their sacral duties. (Scatolla 2000: 31) In every respect, the state and its monarch seemed to be a comparable counterpart[15] to Europe, or especially to the Holy Roman Empire. This classification resulted primarily from the use of language and terms adopted from publications on philosophy or on empire, both by the travellers themselves and their recipients. Resorting to the ancient traditions they were familiar with, political and academic circles in Europe had developed abstract categorising mechanisms—the so-called *ars apodemica*—for use in the study and written description of foreign cultures. (Stagl 1980: 131–205; Stagl 1987) This describes a fifteenth- and sixteenth-century European method of systemisation, providing an abstract paradigm for categorising ethnographical knowledge against the background of domestic religious change, the beginning of the development of modern-era states, and the military confrontation with the Ottoman Empire. This paradigm was used by the political and academic European circles to attempt to comprehend an alien society by comparing it to their own. It described:

1. The power structure at court, in government, and in the military;
2. Customs and conventions;
3. Religion.[16]

Thus, a method of categorising came into general use which abstractly reflected European developments and permitted their description, and which could also be applied to non-European societies. Its theory was recorded by the Venetians in the *Relationes*, a handbook on how to communicate and interact with the Ottomans, and was adopted as standard practice throughout Europe. (Toscani 1980) So Europeans had at their disposal a scheme which could be used to analyse and describe alien cultures such as China.

The primacy of politics now becomes apparent. In the early modern era, people were alarmed by the changes taking place, and therefore directed their hopes and expectations towards those in power, who seemed to a certain degree able to guarantee peace, order and security, and who had emerged from rivalry among the elite by showing leadership qualities and the ability to govern. Monarchs and princes were not only judged according to their competence and abilities, but also

---

[15] Osterhammel discusses the highly-developed civilization as an antithesis of Europe, or, more precisely, the "Anti-Europe" (Cf. Osterhammel 1989: 4; Eun-Jeung 2003: 3)

[16] These principles have been used by Almut Höfert for the description of the Ottoman Empire (Cf. Höfert 2003: 29–31 and 313–316).

Pater patriae sinensis

by the mechanisms of their rise to power. As a rule, advancement was made possible to start with by a long lineage and corresponding laws of succession, as well as other means of securing one's socio-political position. In Europe these consisted, in practice, in implementing the Roman concept of *patria* to underline the patriarchal-pastoral character of rulers' governance, showing that gaining honour and a good reputation was the putative motivation for their actions, as well as being an outward display of their success. (Weber 1992: 173–182) Hence, when looking at China, the first and most important point in these categories had to be the analysis of both the power structure and of those in power. For this reason, the European focus was primarily on the Chinese Emperor, the form of government, court, and military machinery. The points of genealogy, of the person and life of the ruler, his morals, and also his behaviour towards his subjects, now stood—as the example of the Chinese Emperor now showed—at the centre of travel reports, and was to become a model in European publications on state theories.

4 Similarities in the Functions of Rule

In the German discourse on ruling, *Maiestas* was closely linked to the virtuousness of the ruling class and how they fulfilled their duties. (Scatolla 2000: 26f.) The European ideal of good government was that of the kindly father-figure and sovereign lord, emulating the omnipotence and endless benevolence of God's sublime rule, incorporating at the same time the common perception of the Roman concept of the patriarch. (Dreitzel 1980: 641–668; Alföldi 1971: 45; Frühsorge 1970: 74f.; Münch 1982; Wlosok 1978) The idea of this parallel role of both head of family and sovereign lord was common in a variety of literature: in early texts on economics, in literature on the ideal Christian patriarch, in Mirrors for Princes, in sermons based on Luther's Large Catechism, in his treatise "Temporal Authority—to what extent it should be obeyed" of 1523, and in Erasmus' humanistic recourse to the honorary title of the Roman Emperor as *Pater Patriae* in his *Institutio Principis Christiani*. The latter addresses the bearers of power and therefore explicitly the princely estates. (Frühsorge 1981: 211–215) Luther had derived sovereignty from the function and dignity parents used to have: he raised the ruler to the "status of a father" which he perceived as most widespread: "Denn hie ist nicht ein enzelner vater sondern soviel mal vater, soviel er landsessen, buerger oder unterthane hat. Denn Gott gibt und erhelt uns durch sie (als durch unsere eltern) narung, Haus und hoff, schutz und sicherheit."[17] (Münch 1981: 206)

---

[17] In his treatise *Von weltlicher Oberkeit* Martin Luther wrote: *Gleych wie eyn hauß vatter, ob er wol bestympte zeyt und maß der erbeyt* [sic!] *und speyße uber seyn gesind unnd* [sic!] *kinder setzt, muß er dennoch solch satzunge ynn seyner macht behallten, das ers endern odder nachlassen muge,* [...]. (Cf. Luther 1900: 272. For the concept of the father in the œuvre of Desiderius Erasmus cf. Erasmus and Gail 1968: 63, 77 ff. and 91).

(Because he is not one single father, but so many fathers as he hath barons, burghers or subjects. For God gives to us through their hand (as like to our parents) sustenance, house and land, protection and safe being.)

The idea of princely rule as fatherly rule continued to gain currency in German state and social discourse from the 1720s onward, far into the second half of the eighteenth century. Certainly, the small size of the territories in Germany played a role in this development. (Soerensen 1989: 199) On the other hand, the family and familial relations were returning to view at just this time.

Christian Wolff, in fact, emphasised the relationship between the household and the state in many of his works. In his *Vernünfftige*[n] *Gedanken von dem gesellschaftlichen Leben der Menschen* (Reasoned Thoughts on the Social Life of Man) of 1721, he wrote: "Regierende Personen verhalten sich zu Unterthanen wie Väter zu den Kindern [...] und danhero [sic!] werden auch die regierende Personen mit Recht Landes-Väter und Väter des Vaterlandes genennet." (Wolff 1975 [1721]: §264) (Persons who govern comport themselves to subjects like fathers to children and therefore those who govern are rightly called fathers of their country and fathers of the fatherland.) Wolff connected the image of the unlimited ruler, in particular, with that of the father: "Also dienet das Bild des Vaters die Beschaffenheit eines Regenten, hingegen das Bild der Kinder die Beschaffenheit der Unterthanen zu finden." (Wolff 1975 [1721]: §265) (Thus, the image of the father serves to describe the properties of a regent, the image of the children, on the other hand, those of the subjects.)

The cameralist Johann Heinrich Gottlob Justi, too, continued to see the ideal of princely rule represented by the Father of the Country, but could find the realisation of this ideal in very few princes of the territories of the Holy Roman Empire. (Justi 1762: 3) It was thus important to him to criticise the current conditions, and to point out repeatedly in his works that those maxims of state which bind the subjects to childish obedience oblige the monarchs to rule their subjects with fatherly care and tenderness. (Justi 1762: 45) For this reason, Justi wrote enthusiastically about the Chinese form of rule: "Ihre [the chinese] Herrschaftskunst beruht ganz allein auf diesem herrlichen Grundsatz, dass der Kaiser als der Vater seiner Untertanen, und Sina als eine grosse Familie zu betrachten sey." (Justi 1762: 29) (Their art of rule is based solely on this magnificent basic principle, that the Emperor is to be regarded as the father of his subjects, and Sina [China] as a great family.) With clear linguistic borrowing from his source, Louis Le Comte, he further remarked that "diejenigen, welche regieren, eigentlich die Väter des Volkes sind, nicht aber Herren, die man auf den Thron gesetzet, um von Sclaven bedienet zu werden. Daher nennet man von allen Zeiten her den Kaiser Ta-fou einen Großvater, und unter allen Ehrentiteln nimmt er diesen am liebsten an." (Justi 1762: 19) ([...] those who rule are actually the fathers of the people, but not masters set upon the throne to be served by slaves. That is why, from the most ancient times, the Emperor Ta-fou is called a grandfather, and of all honorary titles he accepts this one with the most pleasure.) As far as the European princes were concerned, he stated [...] "ihre Lüste und Leidenschaften statt der Gesetze und alles muß sich unter denselben auf eine sclavische Art schmiegen und biegen." (Justi 1762: 27) ([...] their lusts and passions instead of the laws, and

Pater patriae sinensis

everything must subject itself to these, being twisted in a slavish fashion.) From Justi's point of view then, China was not ruled by despotism;[18] rather, this was the case in the German territories: "Die Monarchie ist eine sehr einfache und ungekünstelte Regierungsform. Die wahren und guten Monarchien sind von dem Muster der Regierung eines Vaters übers eine Kinder und Familie hergenommen; und die mißgebrauchte Monarchie, oder die Despoterey, ist das Bild von der Herrschaft eines Herrn über seine Sclaven."(Justi 1762: 3) (Monarchy is a very simple, unaffected form of government. The true and good monarchies are patterned according to the governing of a child and family by the father; and the abused monarchy, or despotism, is the image of a master ruling his slaves.)

As already mentioned, Christian Wolff, according to his scholar Georg Bernhard Bilfinger and the translation of Philippe Couplet's Confucian Works, in 1687 had classified the Chinese Emperor's relationship to his subjects as familial, the monarch's fatherly relationship to his subjects being part of government by a philosopher on the throne. (Wolff 1985 [1726]: 87; Albrecht 1985: LXVII) Exactly as had Justi, Wolff also emphasised the patriarchal ethic of duty between monarch and subject in China, and particularly the similarities of the Christian ethic with that of Confucianism, since both placed the aspect of mutuality in the foreground and were intended to guide the actions of the rulers in Asia and Europe. (Zempliner 1962: 775)

The conferring of the ancient European category of *pater patriae* upon the Chinese Emperor was mostly correct, in view of the fact that—at least according to the Jesuit travel reports—the real Confucian state in China was based on the family or clans. The family in China was considered to be the origin of the state and a source of ethics. Within the family, people learned moral and ethical attitudes. The family was created by heaven and is a part of the world order. The patriarch in miniature is the ruler of a family or a clan, the Emperor is the ruler of all families. That is the world order of Tao.[19] Thus *state* (*guo jia*) in contemporary China was a

---

[18] Montesquieu in his work "Vom Geist der Gesetze" included China amongst the despotic states. Such a state was not good for a model: *Ehe ich diese Buch abschließe, möchte ich einem Einwand begegnen, den man gegen alles bisher Gesagte erheben könnte. Unsere Missionare berichten uns von dem weiten chinesischen Reiche als von einer ausgezeichneten Regierung, die in ihrem Prinzip die Furcht, Ehre und Tugend miteinander vereint. Allein ich weiß nicht, was für eine Ehre das ist, von der man bei Völkern spricht, die zu allem mit Stockschlägen getrieben werden müssen.* (Montesquieu 1992 I: 176–179)

[19] The Jesuits recognised an analogy between the European concept of the *patria postestas* and the Chinese concept of *hsiao*, filial duty. But this was only a surface analogy, because Le Comte and many other Jesuits had pointed out to their readers that there were serious differences, despite the seeming similarities. While in the European concept the *patria potestas* assumed the father's power over the family, the concept of *hsiao* emphasised the obedience of the children above all. In China, the *pater familias* did not possess the power of life and death over the members of his family, as had been the case in the ancient Roman context. The obedience of the children towards their parents or the Emperor was thus an essential basic commandment for family or social harmony. Not the power or force of the Emperor moved his subjects to be obedient, but his role between heaven and earth required loyalty and obedient subservience according to the precept of harmony, thus raising the Emperor to be father to all Chinese. A further error which established itself in German theories of state was the notion that the fatherly ruler in China was motivated by

74   S. Richter

compound: *guo* means land or territory, *jia* means the family or the clan. The coalition of all families is the building the state. State and family apart from their scale are structurally identical.[20] (Moritz 1990: 238)

Therefore Louis le Comte rightly identified the Chinese state (*état*) as an alliance of subjects, as the family of the Emperor:

> Premièrement les anciens legislateurs ont établi des le commencement de la monarchie, comme un premier principe du bon gouvernement, que ceux qui regnoient, estoient proprement les pères du peuple, et non pas des maistres établis sur le trône pour estre servis par esclaves. C'est pour cela que de tout temps on appelle l'empereur, le grand-père (Ta-fou), et parmi les titres d'honneur, il n'en reçoit aucun plus volontiers que celuy-là [...]. Leurs docteurs et leurs philosophes repétent continuellement dans leurs livres, que l' état est une famille, et que celuy qui sait gouverner sa famille particulière, est capable de gouverner l'état." (Le Comte 1696: 22)[21]
>
> (First, the old Lawgivers have from the first Foundation of the Government made this a standing Maxim, that Kings are properly the Fathers of their People, and not Masters placed in the Throne only to be served by Slaves. Wherefore it is that in all Ages their Emperor is called Grand-Father, and all of his Titles of Honour, there is none which he likes to be called by so well as this (Ta-fou) [...]. Their Teachers and their Philosophers constantly set forth in their Books that the State is but a large Family, and that he who knows how to Govern the one, is the capable of Ruling the other. (Le Comte 1697: 253)).

Hundred years later, in Winterbotham's *Historical, Geographical and Philosophical View of the Chinese Empire* of 1796, we find the Emperor described as a *pater patriae*: "For as it is the received opinion of the Chinese, that their monarch is the father of the whole empire". (Winterbotham 1796) The writers of travel reports had correctly interpreted the basic tenets of the patriarchal system of rule in China, although with a strongly Eurocentric view of the matter, and clearly they had recognised the similarities to Europe. These similarities lent themselves all the more to constructing ideals in the imperially-oriented journalism and theory of state

---

his love for his children. This agreed with the ideal of Christian and patriarchal rule. For this reason, an accordance with the Chinese concept of *hsiao* was seen, where none was. (Cf. Hamilton 1990: 84; Nylan 1996: 2)

   On the Jesuit reception of Confucianism cf. Rule 1986: 120 ff. Notably, the first French translation of Confucius was published as *Confucius Sinarum Philosophus* in 1687 in Paris. (Cf. Lundbaek 1991: 37)

[20] Max Weber found in the Chinese history three types of rule: feudalism, sultanism (the rule of eunuchs) and patrimonial rule. (Weber 1920: 330; see also Schluchter 1983) Stefan Breuer means that in the roman-legal sense the imperial rule in China is not a patrimonial rule, nor is it a subjective privilege of the holder of rule. (Breuer 1984: 73; Duan 1997) For Breuer it is another form of patrimonial government like the European type. That is true for Hamilton. (Hamilton 1990)

[21] The jurist Wilhelm von Schroeder also emphasised the fact that, according to the accounts of the French Jesuit Louis le Comte, the Chinese Emperor's rule was that of a *father to the fatherland.* (von Schroeder 1719: 145)

of the day, in view of the tenets mentioned having been realised in China, in contrast to Europe, with obvious success.

By conferring the ancient category and concept of *pater patriae* on the Chinese concept of sovereignty, it became possible to compare different structures of government. The result was all the more surprising, as this ideal concept of sovereignty was not only known in a state system outside Europe, but was even being implemented successfully.

If, due to their history and their apparently similar structures, the western Christian and oriental Chinese systems of monarchy could be directly compared with each other, then obvious shortcomings in either system would also have to become visible. In consequence, this comparison could also serve as a reflection and a guideline for one's own system. Both French and German political philosophers and writers at the beginning of the Age of Enlightenment recognised this fact, and elevated China and her monarchy to a hypothetical model to criticise and possibly correct the contemporary European understanding of governance. China's position changed from being recognised and described by explorers as equal in standing to Europe, to bring a purposely construed and stylised ideal state which could be used as a "target" and a legitimation for new concepts, and to initiate and implement reforms. China had become a role model for Europe.

5 Approaches to Epistemological Theory and Model Theory[22] in the Eighteenth Century

A model is either an "image" or a "paradigm" (example, pattern, or ideal). From a pragmatic point of view, the epistemological concept behind both terms reached new popularity during the Enlightenment. (Müller 1983: 30) Concepts of ideal models carry the mark of subjectivity, historical limitation, and intentionality. Both examples quoted earlier, the Chinese philosopher on the throne and the Emperor behind the plough, illustrate exactly this point. Because of the success of his administration, Christian Wolff and Johann Heinrich Gottlob Justi chose the Chinese monarch as a model character for their argumentation. They intended to provide improved knowledge of, and deeper insight into, adequate models by using new, contemporary extra-European sources. The conclusions drawn from these models were to provide concrete benefits in daily life, satisfying demand and meeting people's needs.

Christian Wolff expressly legitimated his concept with the help of past history, the long tradition of the Chinese monarchs and their philosophical studies, "[d]amit es nicht das Ansehen habe, als lehrete ich etwas, welches von der Ausübung

---

[22] The controversy over the contemporary understanding of patterns and models is an essential component of my habilitation (second book); in this essay it is only touched upon and will be discussed here in a very rudimentary way.

abgienge, und welches nur unter die Platonischen Begriffe zu rechnen, und mit dem Sonnenreich [Campanellas] zu verwerffen seye." (Wolff 1981 [1740]: 579) (that I do not appear to be teaching something which is impossible to put into practice, but is only reckoned among Plato's notions und may be dismissed in the same way as Campanella's utopian "City of the Sun".)

Justi also emphatically stresses that the models he is discussing are not mere utopias, but actual existing models: "Es ist also gar kein bloßes Schattenbild, das ich in den meisten Vergleichungen zum Muster vorstelle. Es sind wirklich in der Welt stattfindende Regierungsverfassungen, welche, wenn sie in der That vorzüglicher sind, als die unsrigen, dem sich so weise dünkenden Europa billig eine gewisse Schamröthe zuziehen sollten." (Justi 1762: Preface, 6) (These are no mere shadow-images I use as a model in most of these comparisons. Rather, they are genuine, existing constitutions of government, which, be they indeed better than ours, should lead this Europe, which thinks so highly of itself, to blush with shame.)

Exemplary models should be verifiable; they should be based on the realm of experience and not on utopia. At the same time, the "necessary" and the "desirable" were part of the criteria for such a model, intrinsic requirements which arose in analysing one's own failures and shortcomings.

Readers will find precisely this deficiency recognised and expressed in the historical context of these postulations and in Wolff's and Justi's justifications for turning to the Chinese system in search of solutions. Wolff called for a ruler who must be able to philosophise *von einigen Dingen*, a criticism aimed at the contemporary ruler Frederick Wilhelm I and his hostility towards academics. (Wolff 1981 [1740]: 561) Wolff wanted a monarch with philosophical abilities who would be able to understand the context of *ineinandergegründeten Wahrheiten* (interconnected truths). (Saine 1987: 177) Part of his call for a wise sovereign was aimed at implementing continuous philosophical counselling in political matters (Schneiders 1987: 41), "viel leichter und kürzer aber kan man durch eine richtig zusammenhangende Weltweisheit, zu den Begriffen eines guten Regiments kommen." (Wolff 1981 [1740]: 581f) ([...] for it is so much easier and quicker to reach a perception of good governance through a proper, coherent knowledge of the world.) He saw philosophical, political counselling as a combination of theoretical concepts and practical politics, and as a guarantor for the success of the latter.

In turning to China, Wolff and Justi took it for granted that their role model had proven successful in those fields in which their own country had deficiencies, i.e. that philosophical rule had actually been implemented in China, alongside the concept of rule by a farmer head of state.

But why did they come to the conclusion that it was possible for an ideal state to exist in another culture, but that this could not be achieved by their own culture? This was caused on the one hand by the similarity, discussed earlier in this paper, in the structures of power, which made it possible to compare and transfer conditions.

One part of the contemporary understanding of theoretical models was based on the phenomenon of *association*, the assumption of the identification of similarities.

For example, the acceptation of *association* is a very important element in the discussion of human understanding, especially David Hume's cybernetic scheme as set down in his *Philosophical essays concerning human understanding* of 1748. (Hume 1748) Hume assumed that sentiments and feelings provide important impressions. (Hume 1748: 4) Our powers of imagination use our thoughts and perceptions to produce associations. (Ibid.: 21ff.) In turn, these associations lead to three possible principles:

* either to the mental combination of two objects,
* to a re-orientation, or to an increase or
* reduction of contents. (Ibid.: 32)

Like many other political philosophers of their time, Wolff and Justi had combined, in their minds, the European and the Chinese state structure and political system to create a new reality. In doing so, they augmented and accentuated the positive aspects found in travel literature and historical descriptions and deliberately reduced, i.e. omitted, many negative aspects.

An examination of their work shows the accentuation of certain details from travel literature, where they were understandable and transferable to European reality. It has already been proven that Justi was familiar with Hume's œuvre and that this had a certain influence on Justi´s understanding about the theory of money in the year 1752: "Justi was also familiar with English and Scottish writers such as Hobbes, Temple, Bolingbroke, Mandeville, and Hume, whose Essays (1752) influenced his monetary theory." (Cf. Ulrich 2006: 54) We see this in Justi's work[23] in the single components of the Emperor's ploughing ritual, the public attendance at the ceremony, and the traditional actions involved. However, the religious components of the ritual were not transferable. It had to be secularised and completely reconstrued to fit into a European context, in other words, given a new meaning. The new meaning, in turn, resulted from the author's intentions. According to Hume, an association is followed first by the construction of a plan, then a resolution and the consequent realisation of one's aims. Justi and his colleagues intended to construct a new concept of governance, a counter-design to their own reality. This concept encompassed the extension of the monarch's role as head of state to include being the foremost patriot and farmer in the state.

Wolff and Justi intended to create a concept contrary to their own reality. In the context of contemporary requirements for such concepts, while those based on biblical origins or on ideals from antiquity were losing more and more ground to more recent concepts, whether these latter originated from near or far, China represented a real, complex and highly developed field of experience. Her model of state government could be verified by travel literature, and its similarity to

---

[23] Hume's "Essays" had already been anonymously into German in 1755, some 3 years prior to, when Justi's writings were published in French. Further translations from English into French soon followed and contributed to a wide knowledge of Hume on the continent. ([Anon.] 1755; Hume 1758; Id. 1761; Id. 1764; Id. and Jacob 1790)

Europe made it very convincing. This was supposed to influence princely readers in Europe and to bring about the last stage of the model, that is to say, action. (Müller 1980: 218)

Wolff himself had reflected on the ability of the mind to recognise similarities and included this as an important factor in his definition of wit (*ingenium*): "Man sieht aus den gegebenen Exempeln, dass man einen Fall in den anderen verkehret wegen der Ähnlichkeit, die sie miteinander gemein haben. Und gehöret demnach zu hurtigem Gebrauche des Grundes der Verkehrung, dass man die Ähnlichkeit leicht wahrnehmen kann. Wer hierzu aufgelegt ist, den nennet man sinnreich. Und die Leichtigkeit, die Ähnlichkeit wahrzunehmen, ist eigentlich dasjenige, was wir Witz heißen. Also gehöret außer der Kunst zu schließen zum Erfinden auch Witz, und man kann ohne diesen durch jene allein nicht zu rechte kommen."[24] (Wolff 1983 [1751]: 223) (We see from the given examples that we confuse one case with another because of the similarities they have in common. And this happens so easily, because we are able to notice these similarities without effort. We call people with this gift ingenious, and the ease with which the similarity is recognised is actually what we call wit. Therefore, apart from the art of deduction, we also need ingenuity to devise a thing; without the one, the other is of no help to us.)

Observation was an important step towards recognising evident similarities. Wolff claimed that genres and universally valid categories could be determined by their similarities, which in turn led to a better understanding and the ability to fulfil tasks more effectively.

Wolff obviously had realised that the fatherly rule is a phenomenon in China and Europe.[25] His wide knowledge of the relations between government in ancient and contemporary China led him to compare and recognise the similarities with his own contemporary patriarchal understanding of rule, established especially within the German territories, and the similarities with his own cultural past, with the archetypes of classical antiquity. The same was true of the idea of the philosopher on the throne. Wit (*ingenium*) was, for him, the cause of the creation of metaphors, allegories and tropes, all of which were based on the similarities among things, and also expressed this similarity. Similarities, in their turn, could bring about further associations and thus fulfil a heuristic function in aid of knowledge. Wolff thus used a demonstrative method of presenting well-known patterns in new situational contexts, which would necessarily make the similarities clear to the readers and audience of his *Oratio*.

Wolff drew an important conclusion from the recognised similarity and the successful realisation of patriarchal and philosophical rule in China. In China, he

---

[24] He continued: *Therefore, he who wishes to discover the similarity of two objects must also be able to differentiate everything, different components of one object and similarities in different objects and weigh them against each other; thus it will be proved whether they are the same or not and as a result, to what degree two things are similar.* (Wolff 1976: 204)

[25] A modern term in German is *eigenständige Parallelentwicklung* (independent parallel development).

saw the confirmation that the concept of rule was correct and could be made to work. This caused him to revive the ancient ideal of the *pater patriae* and the "philosopher on the throne", and to reintroduce it as a new model in the contemporary discussion on good government in Germany.

6 Conclusion

During the eighteenth century, these Chinese model rulers became an integral part of the discussion on new concepts of ruling and were used to criticise and reproach European monarchs. However, contemporary critics had already realised that they were a constructed reality, created by reducing or omitting certain content, or both, a point which was under discussion at the time. Especially those who had travelled to and personally experienced China protested against the instrumentalisation and over-stylisation of the country. In his report *Voyage aux Indes orientales et à la Chine, fait [...] depuis 1774 jusqu'en 1781*, the French naturalist Pierre Sonnerat condemned the physiocrats' exploitative use of the Emperor's ploughing ritual:

> Leurs relations paroissoient ensevelies dans l'oubli en même-tems que leur influence a été détruite, lorsque une classe d'hommes appellés en France les Economistes, occupés de calculs sur la subsistance des peuples, a fait revivre dans ses leçons agronomiques, les fables que les Jésuites avoient débitées sur le commerce & le gouvernement des Chinois. Le jour où l'Empereur descend de son trône jusqu'à la charrue, a été célébré dans tous leurs écrits; ils ont préconisé cette vaine cérémonie aussi frivole que le culte rendu par les Grecs à Cérès, & qui n'empêche pas que des milliers de Chinois ne meurent de faim, ou n'exposent leurs enfants, par l'impuissance où ils font de pourvoir à leur subsistance.
>
> Les Économistes se faisaient un titre de cette Comédie politique, pour blâmer les Souverains de l'Europe, qui partagent leur protection entre le commerce & l'agriculture. Ils demandent hardiment à quoi servent les colonies, le commerce maritime, les voyages lointains, & recueillent avidement les mensonges des voyageurs, quand ils favorisent tant soit peu leurs idées. (Sonnerat 1782: 3)
>
> (So now another society of people was created, the French Economists, who occupied themselves with calculations of the alimentation of the people; and these Economists have lately rehashed the fairy-tales which the Jesuits had spread earlier about China's trade and its form of government. In all their writings, they have trumpeted out the day on which the Emperor descends from his throne and steers the plough; they have praised and romanticised this childish spectacle at every turn, which is just as vain as the Greeks' worship of Ceres and which does not prevent the Chinese from dying in their thousands from hunger, nor from exposing their children and abandoning them to the wild animals, not being able to provide food for them. The Economists have made use of this political comedy to reproach the European monarchs. They brazenly have

called into question the benefits of founding new colonies, of maritime trade, or of journeys to far-away places, but have avidly gathered all those travel writers' lies that support their system.)

It becomes obvious that the model of the Emperor at the plough was a very subjective and one-sided picture in which certain matters were exaggerated to support a theoretical construct, and which did not necessarily have to coincide with reality.

It is also remarkable that the introduction of the Chinese model did not directly result in a rejection of traditional thinking or long-established role-models; on the contrary, it led to a renaissance of ancient traditions, such as Plato's philosopher on the throne or the ancient ideal of the statesman-farmer, among others. Indeed, it seemed to confirm these ideas and to allow elements from an extra-European cultural background to be incorporated into European tradition. This meant that the contents of the model of positive governance as proposed by Justi and Wolff were not entirely new, but rather had been enhanced by a new component in the form of the Chinese monarchy.

When constructing their models, it is evident that Justi and Wolff chose their examples from a non-European cultural background because of the fundamental similarities to their own European traditions, even if these had long since disappeared, and that their readers must also have noticed these similarities.

Some parts of the Chinese system of rule—which was regarded as extremely successful outside Europe—with its extra-European history, traditions and present-day characteristics, acted as a counterfoil for philosophers, political theorists and publishers from the different schools of thought, and as a counterfoil to their own system. This foreign model could be helpful in returning to traditional values and also in supplying substantial arguments for reform efforts by providing new, external perspectives. Owing to their obvious similarities to European traditions, both the model of the philosopher on the throne and of the Emperor at the plough allowed the continuing discussion of positive governance in a new context.

Both models subscribed to rather general, well-known ideals of ruling, but also reacted in some aspects to contemporary political requirements, such as the advancement of agriculture and the combination of sovereignty with philosophical concepts.

The reaction to their own shortcomings was combined with a search for solutions outside Europe. Because the sovereign played an important role in the foundation and the welfare of a state, and Europeans recognised a parallel to this principle in China, they used the Chinese Emperor as a role model.

This essay has attempted to show that Wolff and Justi succeeded in reviving old, hardly heeded European ideas of rule, such as the philosopher on the throne or the farming statesman, by integrating non-European, particularly Chinese, aspects of the understanding or practice of rule. This was especially successful when similarities between the foreign system and the one at home were obvious. The models constructed by Wolff and Justi purposefully produced interdependencies of their own ideal of rule with those of a foreign reality. By doing this, they expanded the ideals hitherto existing, which had been borrowed primarily from the Western past (the Bible, the Classical Age), in that they added the important components of the actual existence and the actual success to be observed in the Chinese past and the Chinese present. With this, Wolff and Justi brought the aforementioned ideals of rule into the realm of reality and implementation, from the regions of theory into the region of political practice. Two results can be observed as a consequence of Wolff's and Justi's models of good rule and their incorporation of non-European political elements: firstly, centuries-old ideas of rule were confirmed as apparently right, since they had been more strictly and successfully implemented elsewhere (China, to be specific), while rulers in Europe, especially in Germany, were increasingly ignoring these ideas. Secondly, the European contemporaries profited from the important realisation, besides the equality of China in rank and worth, that there was an obvious element of simultaneity and similarity in the concept of the practice of paternal monarchical rule in China and Germany.

In this perspective the interpretation of Chinese rule as a patriarchal system had firmly established itself since travellers' descriptions of the seventeenth century, and its transferral to the literature on the theory of state as well as to the journalism of the German Empire was complete by the end of the nineteenth century: the perception of the simultaneity of ideals of rule soon disappeared. An anonymous reviewer of Alexandre Messnier's *Essai sur l'histoire de l'esprit humain dans l'antiquité* of 1829–1830 determined, with some regret, in the *Göttingischen Gelehrten Anzeigen* of 1833 the "mistaken aberration from patriarchal rule" in China (die Abirrung von der patriarchalischen Herrschaft). "Wir sind gewohnt, die patriarchalische Herrschaft der Chinesen preisen zu hören, aber der Verfasser ist so ehrlich das "Aber" "einzugestehen und die Ausartung jener väterlichen Herrschaft in Tyrannei nicht zu verkennen." (Anonymous 1833: 1814) (We are used to hear the praises of the patriarchal government in China, but the author is honest enough to admit the "buts", and to recognise the degeneration of that fatherly rule into tyranny.)

References

Abel, Wilhelm. 1967. *Geschichte der deutschen Landwirtschaft vom frühen Mittelalter bis zum 19. Jahrhundert*. Deutsche Agrargeschichte II, 2nd edition. Stuttgart: Ulmer.
Albrecht, Michael. 1985. "Einleitung". Christian Wolff, Oratio de Sinarum philosophica practica. IX-LXXX. Hamburg: Felix Meiner.
Alföldi, Andreas. 1971. *Der Vater des Vaterlandes im römischen Denken*. Darmstadt: Wissenschaftliche Buchgesellschaft.
[Anon.]. 1755. *Philosophische Versuche über die menschliche Erkenntniß von David Hume, Ritter: Als dessen vermischter Schriften zweyter Theil. Nach der zweyten vermehrten Ausgabe aus dem Englischen übersetzt und mit Anmerkungen des Herausgebers begleitet.* Hamburg/ Leipzig: Bey G.C. Grund and A.H. Holle.
[Anon.]. 1833. Review of Alexandre Messnier. *Essai sur l'histoire de l'esprit humain dans l'antiquité*. 1829/1830. In Göttingische gelehrte Anzeigen unter Aufsicht der Königlichen Gesellschaft der Wissenschaften, 3, 14.11.1833, 182. Stück. Göttingen: Verlag Friedrich Ernst Huth.

82 S. Richter

Backhaus, Jürgen Georg. 2009. *The Beginnings of Political Economy. Johann Heinrich Gottlob von Justi.* (The European Heritage in Economics and the Social Sciences, 7). Heidelberg: Springer.

Baicu, Ovidiu. 2006. *Platons Lehre von der Philosophenherrschaft. Politisch-theologische Hintergründe seiner Lehre von der Politeia* (Deutsche Hochschuledition, Bd. 143), Neuried: Ars Una.

Bély, Lucien. 1999. *La société des princes. XVIe - XVIIIe siècle.* Paris: Fayard.

Birtsch, Günter. 1987. "Der Idealtyp des aufgeklärten Herrschers. Friedrich der Große, Karl Friedrich von Baden und Joseph II. im Vergleich". In *Der Idealtyp des aufgeklärten Herrschers*, ed. Birtsch, 9–47. Hamburg: Meiner.

Bodin, Jean. 1981.*Sechs Bücher über den Staat.* Buch I-III. Wimmer, Bernd (edited and translated). Munich: C.H. Beck.

Brandauer, Frederick P. (ed.). 1994. *Imperial rulership and cultural change in traditional China.* Seattle: University of Washington Press.

Breuer, Stefan. 1984. "Imperium und Rechtsordnung in China und Rom". In Stefan Breuer and Hubert Treiber (eds.): Zur Rechtssoziologie Max Webers. Interpretation, Kritik, Weiterentwicklung. Opladen: Westdeutscher Verlag.

Chang, Michael G. 2007. *A court on horseback: imperial touring & the construction of Qing rule, 1680 – 1785.* (Harvard East Asian monographs, 287). Cambridge, Mass.: Harvard University Asia Center.

Constant, Charles de 1791. *Terres de Chine. Nouvelle Compagnies des Indes 1789–1790.* Paris : Armine-Ediculture Edition.

Couplet, Philippe. 1686. *Tabula chronologica monarchiae sinicae juxta cyclos annorum LX. Ab anno post Christum primo, usque ad annum praesentis saeculi 1683.* Paris: Cramoisy.

Couplet, Philippe. 1687. *Tabula genealogica trium familiarum Imperialium Monarchiae Sinicae.* Paris : Apud *Danielem* Horthemels.

Demel, Walter. 1992. *Als Fremde in China. Das Reich der Mitte im Spiegel frühneuzeitlicher europäischer Reiseberichte*, Munich: Oldenbourg.

Demel, Walter. 1999. "Kaiser außerhalb Europas? Beobachtungen zur Titulatur außereuropäischer Herrscher zwischen "deskriptiver" Reiseliteratur und politischen Interessen". In *Beiträge der jüngeren Forschung. Festschrift anlässlich der Gründung der Forschungsstiftung für vergleichende europäische Überseegeschichte 1999 in Bamberg*, ed. Thomas Beck et al., Stuttgart: Steiner, 56–75.

Dreitzel, Horst. 1980. "Monarchiebegriffe in der Fürstengesellschaft". In *Semantik und Theorie der Einherrschaft in Deutschland von der Reformation bis zum Vormärz*, Vol. 2. Bielefeld (Diss.): Böhlau.

Duan, Lin. 1997. *Konfuzianische Ethik und Legitimation der Herrschaft im alten China. Eine Auseinandersetzung mit der vergleichenden Soziologie Max Webers.* Berlin: Duncker & Humblot.

Erasmus von Rotterdam and Anton Jakob Gail. 1968. "Fürstenerziehung. Institutio Principis Christiani (lat. u. dt.) Die Erziehung eines christlichen Fürsten", *Erasmus von Rotterdam.* Introduced, translated and edited by Anton J. Gail. Paderborn: Schöningh.

Eun-Jeung, Lee. 2003. *"Anti-Europa". Die Geschichte der Rezeption des Konfuzianismus und der konfuzianischen Gesellschaft seit der frühen Aufklärung* (Politica et Ars, Bd. 6). Münster/ Hamburg: Lit Verlag.

Frühsorge, Gotthardt. 1970. *Privatklugheit: zur Bedeutungsgeschichte des Politischen in der Hofliteratur des 17. Jahrhunderts in Deutschland und in den "politischen Romanen" Christian Weises.* Heidelberg (Diss.): J.B. Metzler.

Frühsorge, Gotthardt. 1981. "Oeconomie des Hofes". Zur politischen Funktion der Vaterrolle des Fürsten im Oeconomus prudens et legalis des Franz Philipp Florin. In August Buck et al (eds.): Europäische Hofkultur im 16. und 17. Jahrhundert II. Hamburg: Hauswedell, 211–215.

González de Mendoza, Juan. 1853. *The history of the great and mighty kingdom of China, and the situation thereof*, edited George T. Staunton. London: Hakluyt Society.

González de Mendoza, Juan. 1992. *Die "Geschichte der höchst bemerkenswerten Dinge und Sitten im chinesischen Königreich" des Juan González de Mendoza: ein Beitrag zur Kulturgeschichte des ming-zeitlichen China*, edited and translated with an introduction by Margareta Grießler. Sigmaringen: Thorbecke.

Grandi, Silvio. 1753. "Leben der Kayseren in China". In *Historischen Welt=Carten. Anfänge in italiänischer Sprach beschrieben/durch P. Antonio Foresti, 6. Theil*, edited D. Suarez and S. Grandi, 504–720. Wirzburg (= Würzburg), 504–720.

Greindl, Gabriele. 2008. "Die Briefe des bayerischen Herzogspaares 1618". In *Bayerisch-chinesische Beziehungen in der Frühen Neuzeit*. (Zeitschrift für Bayerische Landesgeschichte, Beiheft 34). In: Peter Claus Hartmann and Alois Schmid (eds). München: Beck. 119–158.

Ho, John. 1962. *Quellenuntersuchung zur Chinakenntnis bei Leibniz und Wolff*. Zürich/Hong Kong (Diss.): Lai Hing (Diss.).

Hamilton, Gary G. 1990. "Patriarchy, Patrimonialism, and Filial Piety: A Comparison of China and Western Europe Author(s)." *The British Journal of Sociology* 41/1. 77–104.

Höfert, Almut. 2003. *Den Feind beschreiben. "Türkengefahr" und europäisches Wissen über das Osmanische Reich 1450–1600*. Frankfurt am Main/New York: Campus-Verlag.

Hume, David. 1748. *Philosophical essays concerning human understanding. By the author of the Essays moral and political*. London: printed for A. Millar.

Hume, David. 1758. *Essais philosophiques sur l'entendement humain. Par Mr. Hume: Avec les quatre philosophes du même auteur, Traduit de l'Anglois*, Vol I. Amsterdam : Schneider.

Hume, David. 1761. *Oeuvres de Hume: traduits de l'anglois. Essais Philosophiques Sur L'Entendement Humain*, Vol. II., 2nd Edition. Amsterdam: Schneider.

Hume, David. 1764. *Oeuvres Philosophiques De M. D. Hume: Traduits De L'Anglois. Contenant les huits premiers essais sur l'entendement humain*, Vol. I., new edition. London: David Wilson.

Hume, David and Ludwig Heinrich von Jakob. 1790. *Über die menschliche Natur. Ueber den menschlichen Verstand, Enth. außerdem: Kritische Versuche über David Hume's erstes Buch der Abhandlung über die menschliche Natur*. Vol.1. Halle: Hemmerde & Schwetschke.

Justi, Johann Heinrich Gottlob. 1758. *Staatswirtschaft oder Systematische Abhandlung aller oeconomischen und Cameral=Wissenschaften, die zur Regierung eines Landes erfordert werden. 2 Theile*. Vol. 1. Leipzig: Breitkopf.

Justi, Johann Heinrich Gottlob von. 1762. *Vergleichungen der Europäischen mit den Asiatischen und andern vermeintlich barbarischen Regierungen, in drey Büchern verfasset von Johann Heinrich Gottlob von Justi*. Berlin/Stettin/Leipzig: Rüdiger.

Kloft, Hans and Maximilian Kerner (eds.). 1992. *Die Institutio Traiani. Ein pseudo-plutarchischer Text im Mittelalter. Text – Kommentar – Zeitgenössischer Hintergrund*. Stuttgart: Teubner.

Krischer, André. 2007. "Das diplomatische Zeremoniell der Reichsstädte, oder: Was heißt Stadtfreiheit in der Fürstengesellschaft?" *Historische Zeitschrift* 284 (2007): Oldenbourg-Wissenschaftsverlag, 1–30.

Lach, Donald F. 1953. "The Sinophilism of Christian Wolff (1679–1754)". *Journal of the History of Ideas* (1953): University of Pennsylvania Press, 561–574.

Larrimore, Mark. 2000. "Orientalism and Antivoluntarism in the History of Ethics: On Christian Wolff's 'Oratio de Sinarum Practica'". *The Journal of Religious Ethics* 28 (Summer 2000): 189–219.

Le Comte, Louis. 1696. *Nouveaux Mémoires sur l'état present de la Chine, par le P. Louis Le Comte de la Compagnie de Jésus, Mathématicien du Roy*, Vol. 2. Paris: Anisson.

Le Comte, Louis. 1697. *Memoires and observations [. . .] made in a late journey through the Empire of China*. London: Benjamin Tooke.

Lünig, Johann Christian. 1719/20. *Theatrum Ceremoniale Historico-Politicum , Oder Historisch- und Politischer Schau-Platz Aller Ceremonien, Welche bey Päbst- und Käyser-, auch Königlichen Wahlen und Crönungen [. . .] Ingleichen bey Grosser Herren und dero Gesandten Einholungen [. . .] beobachtet werden. 2 Volumes*. Leipzig: Weidmann.

84 S. Richter

Lundbaek, Knut. 1991. "First European Translations of Chinese Historical and Philosophical Works". In *China and Europe: Images and Influences in Sixteenth to Eighteenth centuries*, ed. Thomas H.C. Lee,. Hong Kong: Chinese University Press, 29–43. "

Luther, Martin. 1900. "Von weltlicher Oberkeit. Wie weit sich welltlich uberkeytt strecke". In *D. Martin Luthers Werke*, ed. Joachim K.F. Knaake, Vol. 11. Weimar: Böhlau.

Maier, Barbara. 1985. *Philosophie und römisches Kaisertum. Studien zu ihren wechselseitigen Beziehungen in d. Zeit von Caesar bis Marc Aurel*, Vienna: VWGÖ.

Mohnhaupt, Heinz. 2000. *Historische Vergleichung im Bereich von Staat und Recht. Gesammelte Aufsätze.* (Ius commune, Veröffentlichungen des MPI für Europäische Rechtsgeschichte, Frankfurt/M. Sonderhefte, Studien zur Europäischen Rechtsgeschichte, Bd. 134). Frankfurt am Main: Klostermann.

Montesquieu, Charles de. 1992. *Vom Geist der Gesetze*. Ernst Forsthoff ed. Vol. 1, Tübingen: Mohr.

Moritz, Ralf. 1990. *Die Philosophie im alten China*, Berlin: Deutscher Verlag der Wissenschaften.

Müller, Roland. 1980. "Zur Geschichte des Modellbegriffs und des Modelldenkens im Bezugsfeld der Pädagogik". In *Modelle und Modelldenken im Unterricht. Anwendungen der allgemeinen Modelltheorie auf die Unterrichtspraxis*, ed. Herbert Stachowiak. Bad Heilbrunn: Klinkhardt, 202–224.

Müller, Roland. 1983. "Zur Geschichte des Modelldenkens und des Modellbegriffs". In *Modelle – Konstruktion der Wirklichkeit*, ed. Herbert Stachowiak. München: Fink, 17–78.

Münch, Paul. 1981. "Haus und Regiment – Überlegungen zum Einfluß der alteuropäischen Ökonomie auf die fürstliche Regierungstheorie und -praxis während der frühen Neuzeit". In *Europäische Hofkultur im 16. und 17. Jahrhundert: Vorträge und Referate gehalten anläßlich des Kongresses des Wolfenbütteler Arbeitskreises für Renaissanceforschung und des Internationalen Arbeitskreises für Barockliteratur in der Herzog August Bibliothek Wolfenbüttel vom 4. bis 8. September 1979*, ed. August Buck et al. Vol. 2 (Wolfenbütteler Arbeiten zur Barockforschung, 8–10). Hamburg: Hauswedell, 205–210.,

Münch, Paul. 1982. "Die Obrigkeit im Vaterstand – Definition und Kritik des "Landesvaters" während der Frühen Neuzeit". In *Hof, Staat und Gesellschaft in der Literatur des 17. Jahrhunderts*, ed. Elger Blühm et al. Amsterdam: Rodopi, 15–40.

Münke, Wolfgang. 1998. *Mythologie der chinesischen Antike: mit Ausblick auf spätere Entwicklungen*. Frankfurt am Main/Berlin/Bern: Lang.

Mungello, David E.. 1988. "The Seventeenth Century Jesuit Translation Project of the Confucian Four Books". In *East Meets West: The Jesuits in China, 1582–1773*, ed. Charles E. Ronan. Chicago: Loyola University Press, 252–271.

Nylan, Michael. 1996. "Confucian Piety and Individualism in Han China." *Journal of the American Oriental Society* 116/1, 1–27.

Osterhammel, Jürgen. 1989. *China und die Weltgesellschaft. Vom 18. Jahrhundert bis in unsere Zeit*. Munich: C.H. Beck.

Paludan, Ann. 1998. *Chronicle of the Chinese emperors. The reign-by-reign record of the rulers of imperial China*. London: Thames & Hudson.

Priddat, Birger P. 2001. *Le concert universel. Die Physiokratie. Eine Transformationsphilosophie des 18. Jahrhunderts*. Marburg: Metropolis-Verlag.

Richter, Susan. 2010a. "Der Monarch am Pflug – Von der Erweiterung des Herrschafts-verständnisses als erstem Diener zum ersten Landwirt des Staates". *Das achtzehnte Jahrhundert* 34.1,. 40–64.

Richter, Susan. 2010 b. "Das Völkerrecht - Ein europäisches Phänomen? " *Zeitschrift der Savigny-Stiftung für Rechtsgeschichte. Germanistische Abteilung* 127, 293–300.

Richter, Susan. 2010 c. "Die Bewertung des chinesischen Kaisers in europäischen Druckwerken des 17./18. Jahrhunderts als Spiegel seiner völkerrechtlichen Gleichrangigkeit". *Staatliche Kunstsammlungen Dresden. Jahrbuch* 36, 27–39.

Rousselle, Erwin. 1934. "Zur Würdigung des Konfuzianischen Staatsgedankens". *Sinica. Zeitschrift für China-Kunde und China-Forschung* IX., 1–7.

Pater patriae sinensis

Rule, Paul A. 1986. *K'ungtzu or Confucius? The Jesuit Interpretation of Confucianism.* Sydney: Allen & Unwin.

Saine, Thomas P. 1987. *Von der Kopernikanischen bis zur Französischen Revolution. Die Auseinandersetzung der deutschen Frühaufklärung mit der neuen Zeit.* Berlin: Schmidt.

Scatolla, Merio. 2000. "Die Frage nach der politischen Ordnung: "Imperium", "maiestas", "summa potestas" in der politischen Lehre des frühen siebzehnten Jahrhunderts". In *Souveränitätskonzeptionen. Beiträge zur Analyse politischer Ordnungsvorstellungen im 17. bis zum 20. Jahrhundert* (Beiträge zur politischen Wissenschaft 119), ed. Martin Peters and Peter Schröder. Berlin: Duncker & Humblot, 13–39

Schluchter, Wolfgang. 1983. *Max Webers Studie über Konfuzianismus und Taoismus – Interpretation und Kritik.* Frankfurt: Suhrkamp.

Schneiders, Werner. 1987. "Die Philosophie des aufgeklärten Absolutismus. Zum Verhältnis von Philosophie und Politik, nicht nur im 18. Jahrhundert". In *Aufklärung als Politisierung – Politisierung der Aufklärung*, ed. Hans Erich Bödecker and Ulrich Herrmann. Hamburg: Meiner, , 32–52.

Schroeder, Wilhelm von. 1719. *Wilhelm FreyHerrn von Schrödern Disqvisitio politica vom absoluten Fürstenrecht mit noehtigen Anmerckungen versehen, welche derselben gefaehrliche Irzthuemer deutlich entdecken und solches praetendirte Recht gruendlich untersuchen.* Leipzig/Wolfenbüttel: Freytag.

Soerensen, Bengt Algot. 1989. "Die Vater-Herrschaft in der frühaufklärerischen Literatur". In *Tradition, Norm, Innovation. Soziales und literarisches Traditionsverhalten in der Blütezeit der deutschen Aufklärung*, ed. Wilfried Barner, München: Oldenbourg.

Sonnerat, Pierre. 1782. *Voyage aux Indes orientales et à la Chine, fait par ordre du roi, depuis 1774 jusqu'en 1781* [. . .], vol. 2, Paris : L'auteur.

Stagl, Justin. 1980. "Die Apodemik oder Reisekunst als Methodik der Sozialforschung vom Humanismus bis zur Aufklärung". In *Statistik und Staatsbeschreibung in der Neuzeit, vornehmlich im 16–18. Jahrhundert*, ed. Mohammed Rassem and Justin Stagl, Paderborn: Schöningh, 131–205.

Stagl, Justin. 1987. "Der wohl unterwiesene Passagier. Reisekunst und Gesellschaftsbeschreibung des 16. bis zum 18. Jahrhundert". In *Reisen und Reisebeschreibungen im 18. und 19. Jahrhundert als Quellen der Kulturbeziehungsforschungen*, ed. Gert Robel, Herbert Zeman and B. Krasnobaev. Essen, Hobbing, 353–384.

Stieve, Gottfried. 1723. *Europäisches Hof=Ceremoniel, in welchem Nachricht gegeben wird, was für eine Beschaffenheit es habe mit der Praerogativ und dem daraus fließendem Ceremoniel zwischen kayser und königl. Mayestäten*, 2nd edition. Leipzig: Gleditsch.

Stosch, Balthasar Sigismund von. 1677. *Von dem Praecedenz=Oder Vorder=Recht/aller Potentaten oder Republiquen in Europa.* Breßlau: Veit Jacob Treschern.

Toscani, Ignazio. 1980. "Etatisches Denken und erkenntnistheoretische Überlegungen in den venezianischen Relationen". In *Statistik und Staatsbeschreibung in der Neuzeit, vornehmlich im 16.-18. Jahrhundert. Bericht über ein interdisziplinäres Symposion in Wolfenbüttel, 25. - 27. September 1978* (= Quellen und Abhandlungen zur Staatsbeschreibung und Statistik, Bd.1), ed. Mohammed Rassem and Justin Stagl, Paderborn: Schöningh, 111–130.

Ulrich, Adam. 2006. *The Political Economy of J.H.G. Justi.* Oxford/Bern/Berlin: Lang.

Vonessen, Franz. 2003. "Platons Ideenlehre, Teil 2. Der Philosoph als König". (Die graue Reihe, Bd. 39), Kusterdingen: SFG-Servicecenter Fachverlage.

Weber, Max. 1920. *Gesammelte Aufsätze zur Religionssoziologie.* Vol. I: Konfuzianismus und Taoismus, p. Stuttgart: Union, 276–536.

Weber, Wolfgang. 1992. *Prudentia gubernatoria Studien zur Herrschaftslehre in der deutschen politischen Wissenschaft des 17 Jahrhunderts.* Tübingen: Niemeyer.

Winterbotham, William et al. 1796. *An Historical, Geographical and Philosophical View of the Chinese Empire* [. . .], *to which is added, a copious account of Lord Macartney's Embassy. Compiled from original communications. In two volumes.* Voll. II. London/Philadelphia: re-printed for R. Lee.

Wlosok, Antonie. 1978. "Vater- und Vatervorstellungen in der römischen Kultur". In *Das Vaterbild im Abendland*, ed. Hubertus Tellenbach, Vol. 1. Stuttgart: Kohlhammer, 18–54.

Wolff, Christian. 1975. "Vernünfftige Gedancken (Deutsche Politik). Von dem Gesellschaftlichen Leben der Menschen und Insonderheit dem gemeinen Wesen" (Reprint of the fourth edition. Frankfurt and Leipzig 1736), Preface. In *Gesammelte Werke*, ed. Jean École et al., 1. Abt., Deutsche Schriften. Vol. 5. Hildesheim/Zürich: Olms.

Wolff, Christian. 1976. "Vernünfftige Gedanken (Deutsche Ethik). Von der Menschen Thun und Lassen, zu Beförderung ihrer Glückseeligkeit". In *Gesammelte Werke, 1. Abt., Deutsche Schriften*, ed. Jean École et al. Vol.4. Hildesheim/Zürich: Olms.

Wolff, Christian. 1981. "Von den Regenten, die sich der Weltweisheit befleissigen, und von den Weltweisen, die das Regiment führen". In *Gesammelte kleine philosophische Schriften VI*, Reprint of the edition of Halle 1740. Hildesheim/Zürich: Olms.

Wolff, Christian. 1983. "Vernünfftige Gedanken von Gott, der Welt und der Seele des Menschen, auch allen Dingen überhaupt". In *Gesammelte Werke, 1. Abt. Deutsche Schriften*, ed. Jean Ecole et al., 1. Abt. Vol. 2 (Reprint of the eleventh edition of Halle 1751). Hildesheim/Zürich: Olms.

Wolff, Christian. 1985. *Oratio de Sinarum philosophia practica: Rede über die praktische Philosophie der Chinesen* [1721, 1726]. Translated, introduced and edited by Michael Albrecht. Hamburg: Felix Meiner.

Zempliner, Artur. 1962. "Die chinesische Philosophie und J.Ch. Wolff". In *Deutsche Zeitschrift für Philosophie* 10/1 (1962), 758–778. Berlin. Deutscher Verlag der Wissenschaften.

Survey the People

The Emergence of Population Statistics as Technology of Government in Early Twentieth-Century China

Nicolas Schillinger

Abbreviations

TK   *Tongji yuekan* 统计月刊 (The Statistical Monthly Magazine)
TB   *Tongji yuebao* 统计月报 (The Statistical Monthly)

Since the founding of the People's Republic of China in 1949, its political leaders have been greatly concerned with demographic developments and have looked for ways to govern the reproductive behaviour of the population (Greenhalgh and Winckler 2005). The logical consequence, to make a thorough register of the people and draw up census data as a basis for social-political decisions, was not a communist invention, but originated in the first half of the twentieth century. At that time, European and American scientific ideas of Malthusian-influenced demography, Social Darwinist race-biology, and statistics combined with older, late Imperial Chinese notions of collecting population numbers (Lee and Wang 1999; Dikötter 1995: 102–121).

Population statistics is nowadays an instrument used by governments and international organisations to accumulate knowledge about subjects or citizens, and divide this information into useful categories in order to improve the efficiency and effectiveness of administration. However, statistics are not simply an instrument for the collection of information, but a tool to produce and organise knowledge in the first place. It is one amongst a variety of technologies used by government which serve to translate certain rationalistic political discourses into action, but which, at the same time, also influence and interact with those rationalities. The term "technology of government" derives from the concept of "governmentality" developed by Michel Foucault. It describes the complex genealogy and totality of modern state government that had its origins in Early Modern Europe. The main focus of "governmentality" is the population. Instead of merely ruling a territory by divine

---

N. Schillinger (✉)
Karl Jaspers Centre, University of Heidelberg, Voßstr. 2, 69115 Heidelberg, Germany
e-mail: schillinger@asia-europe.uni-heidelberg.de

A. Flüchter and S. Richter (eds.), *Structures on the Move*,
Transcultural Research – Heidelberg Studies on Asia and Europe in a Global Context,
DOI 10.1007/978-3-642-19288-3_5, © Springer-Verlag Berlin Heidelberg 2012

authority and concentrating power on individual subjects, a newly emerging *raison d'état* urged state sovereigns to wield power over the people according to quantitative and rational aspects. Population statistics were seen as crucial for calculating social developments and identifying demographic relations. However, statistics was not only a tool, but ultimately created "population" as an object of reflection and rational government (Foucault 1991; Miller and Rose 1990; Dean 1999).

This article will examine how the concepts and practices of applying statistics for administrative purposes that emerged in Early Modern Europe contributed to make "population" a major political focus in twentieth-century China. It concentrates on sources published in the 1930s, notably the report on the census of 1927 and the official periodical *Statistical Monthly* (*Tongji yuebao* 统计月报, hereinafter TB) to show how specialists within the administration of the Nationalist Government invoked foreign models to promote the need for statistical population surveys.

Before analysing these sources, it is necessary to understand the emergence of population statistics in various European states and in the USA, and its adaptation in China during the first decade of the twentieth century. The first part of this article, therefore, briefly juxtaposes the formation of social statistics, and its administrative application in Europe since the seventeenth century, with practices of population registration in the Qing Empire (1644–1911). In the course of fundamental bureaucratic, political, educational and military reforms started in 1901, the Qing Government established statistical institutions according to European patterns. As Andrea Bréard shows, Qing officials sought to blend archetypes of inventory practices from Chinese antiquity with European models of statistical administration, notably the German *Staatswissenschaft* (Bréard 2008).

"Population" already emerged as a major category of statistical work during this period. Moreover, the Qing system of household monitoring was deemed to be inaccurate, static and totally unreliable, thus in 1908, the government started an empire-wide census to provide a new basis for governance and administration based on the "actual and true situation" (*shishi* 实事) of the empire.

The second part of the article will examine how this idea reappeared during the period of Nationalist rule, and how population statistics and demographic thinking increasingly gained importance. In the 1930s, specialist statisticians within the bureaucracy were aware of the latest developments of mathematical statistics and of the systematic use of social statistics by foreign administrations. They strongly advocated the significance of gathering demographic information in order to know everything about the population and to provide the state with what was considered indispensable data for government.

1 Population Statistics in Europe and America Since the Early Modern Era

While all kinds of inventories and enumerations had been conducted in Europe for several hundred years, the word "statistics" first emerged at the end of the sixteenth century in Italy and referred to political descriptions with numerical information, including population numbers and social classifications (Landwehr 2005). The German *Staatswissenschaft* used the term to describe the collection and investigation of any data concerning, and of concern to, the state. In an apparent reference to the mathematical background of statistics, the British statistician Maurice George Kendall, however, remarked that "[t]he true ancestor of modern statistics is not seventeenth-century statistics but Political Arithmetic" (Kendall 1960: 447). The adherents of "Political Arithmetic", such as John Graunt and William Petty, started to reason about their data, and tried to deduce regularities and abstract them for further predictions about society and its development. Both Graunt with his *Natural and Political Observations Made upon the Bills of Mortality* (1662) and Petty with his book *Political Arithmetic* (1690) provided basic groundwork for population statistics and census-taking, and were counted among the first demographers (Hacking 1975: 102–110).

During the eighteenth century, mathematical statistical methods were mainly used in the natural sciences, where the understanding of probability and statistical inference was elaborated. At the same time, however, Adam Smith, David Ricardo and Robert Malthus began to think and write about the development of population, thus giving birth to the science of demography, the statistical study of populations and their dynamics, reproductive and hygienic behaviour, and movements. Various Early Modern European governments made monitoring society and counting the population a priority. The doctrines of Mercantilism and Cameralism particularly in the German territories promulgated the growth of population, which was seen as imperative for economic development (Landwehr 2005: 212f.). "Population" increasingly was regarded not just as the sum of all subjects, but as a factor with very specific issues and attributes, such as birthrate, mortality, life expectancy, fertility, health, disease, nutrition and housing (Foucault 1998). Statistics provided the tool for rulers to collect, analyse and present population data—a tool which claimed to be objective and to represent the absolute truth. It was seen as crucial to collect population statistics frequently and systematically on a regular and standardised—and standardising—level, in order to enable comparability across time and space and deduce political action (Osterhammel 2009: 57–62; Stigler 1986).

Surveys on populations also began to make use of mathematical statistical methods when the Belgian astronomer and mathematician Adolphe Quetelet finally adapted them for the social sciences. In his work on social physics and public health he invented the "average man" (*l'homme moyen*), as well as the "body mass index". Quetelet contributed to the creation of statistics as a separate discipline and helped demographic thought to a hitherto unknown popularity (Hald 1998: 567–631; Stigler 1999; Yu 2009).

Although European governments in Iceland (1701), Sweden (1755) and Spain (1787), as well as in the USA (1790), had carried out comprehensive census surveys in the eighteenth century, the systematic establishment of institutions for gathering population data did not start before the early nineteenth century. By the 1870s, most European countries had set up a permanent central statistical department at national level. Additionally, the number of statistical offices at lower administrative levels, in cities and towns, increased rapidly in some states. These departments worked according to the latest verifiable scientific methods and their quality increased significantly during the century. They were closely connected to scientific and private organisations, which lobbied strongly for statistical work. In the 1830s and 1840s, Europe experienced a "wave of enthusiasms" in the field of statistics as private associations, specialists and journals increasingly provided governments with numerical information of all kinds, making population statistics one of various areas of surveying. International organisations emerged, for instance, the International Statistical Congress, which held meetings from 1853 to 1878. Its successor, the International Statistical Institute (ISI, founded in 1885) still exists in the twenty-first century, with the aim of improving and diffusing statistical methods and their application on the basis of international cooperation (Osterhammel 2009: 57–62; Dupâquier/Dupâquier 1985).

2 Population Control in the Late Imperial Period

Since the Ming dynasty (1368–1644), several different systems for registering at least parts of the populace had existed, which were much more accurate than anything before. These assessments concentrated on the male adult population and represented a predominant, and sometimes exclusive, interest in fiscal matters, in taxes related to land property and labour services. The yellow registers (*huangce* 黃冊) were established under the Hongwu Emperor (ruled 1368–98) to enumerate the households (*hu* 戶) and mouths (*kou* 口) of the entire empire. From the sixteenth century on, the *ding* (丁, literally a male adult) replaced the *hukou* as the most important figure for registration. The *ding* was supposed to represent a tax-paying adult male, but in reality it stood for a tax-paying unit, not a person (Ho 1959).

In the eighteenth century, the Qianlong Emperor (ruled 1735–1799) advocated closer monitoring of society and the populace and reinforced the *baojia* (保甲) system of mutual household surveillance. Population registration then became the primary function of the *baojia*-system, and lower administrative levels, like counties, were required to hand in population data (*hukou* enumerations which were regularly continued on the local level even after the introduction of the *ding*) to the Board of Revenue.[1] However, there was little demographic interest and knowledge on the part of local officials or the *baojia*-wards, and only in some cases did they provide information on birth and death rates, detailed age compositions, the sex ratio, or occupations. These wards, as well as local officials, were often deeply involved with local members of the gentry, who tried to avoid full and regular registration to avoid taxation. Others, such as "degraded" elements

---

[1] Interestingly, the *Hubu* (literally: Board of Households) is usually translated in English as *Board of Revenue* to indicate its actual function.

Survey the People 91

of society, or those of the servant class, as well as certain ethnic groups, for instance, often slipped through the net altogether (Jiang 1990; Hsiao 1967).[2]

To be sure, Imperial Chinese governments were aware of the populace and managed to produce enumerating inventory lists (Sigley 1996). But records, either of households and mouths or of land, were rather static documentations of size and property. The focus lay on fiscal matters, as well as on the control of behaviour according to social norms, with the family as the ethical model and instrument of policing through the *baojia*-system. Officials were little interested in the demographic development of the population and did not intervene in family matters, as long as no one acted against the norms (Dutton 1992). Similar to Foucault's notion of sovereignty as a mode of governance in Europe, legitimate power stemmed from a higher source, the classical writings, which demanded the observance of ritual (*li* 礼) and virtue (*de* 德) by the individual—at least within a normative discourse.[3]

Nineteenth century official-scholars like Wei Yuan 魏源, who advocated the wide collection of all kinds of data concerning the state, and Wang Shiduo 汪士铎, who promoted close control of subjects, as well as the increasing debate on European Malthusian thinking and Social-Darwinism, starting at the end of the century, all contributed to change (Kuhn 1995; Dikötter 1992). "Population" was given form as a concept and was increasingly understood as a resource, which the government had to manage for the greater good of the entire state. But it was administrative reforms and the use of European technologies of government, such as statistics, which provided the means to implement—and foster—such thinking. Imperial Chinese governments counted households, mouths, and *ding* to allocate resources, but the introduction of European-American statistics made "population" a major resource in itself, which could and should be measured and controlled.

3 The Adaptation of Statistics and the Emergence of "Population" in Twentieth-Century China

At the end of the nineteenth century, all kinds of scientific books from Europe, America and Japan were introduced to China, as officials and other elite members sought to adapt to a new global age and bring foreign sciences to the Qing Empire. Similarly, first translations of scholarly works on European mathematical and administrative statistics appeared and the government, using mostly Japanese textbooks, undertook attempts to educate specialists in the field.[4]

---

[2] Ho Ping-ti even states, that there was a "lack of even rudimentary demographic interest on the part of high officials". (Ho 1959: 38)

[3] See the references in the introductory part. For an overview on the many facets of Qing rule see Waley-Cohen (2004).

[4] For an overall account of the emergence of European–American statistics up to 1912, see the recent study of Andrea Bréard. This paper only outlines some aspects which show the increasing significance attributed to population statistics.

In 1903, Lin Zhuonan 林卓南 and Niu Yongjian 钮永建 translated a book by the influential Japanese statistician Yokohama Masao, which was entitled in Chinese *Tongji jianyi lu* 统计讲义录 (Record of Statistical Teaching Materials). The book was re-interpreted in 1908 by Meng Sen 孟森 and titled *Tongji tonglun* 统计通论 (An Outline of Statistics). This revised edition received great attention in China and was reprinted nine times. It described the history, theory, methodology, fields of application, schools of thought and latest developments of European and American statistics, and introduced the current German teachings on social statistics, represented by Georg von Mayr.[5] Like Mayr, Meng emphasised the fundamental importance of the use of statistics for society and the state in his translation (Li and Mo 1993: 227).

After the turn of the century, the Qing launched strongly contested structural reforms (*xinzheng* 新政) to recentralise imperial power and broaden governmental activities. The Qing government aimed to remodel the educational system, the empire's bureaucracy, the military, and even the political system, as it slowly prepared the introduction of a constitution.[6] It therefore established a Government Reform Commission (*Xianzheng biancha guan*宪政编查馆), which journeyed to various European states, the US and Japan to examine the respective constitutional systems of those countries. After the Commission's return, the Government created a Statistical Department (*Tongjiju* 统计局) to evaluate the Chinese electorate and thus prepare for a potentially upcoming election. In theory, it was responsible for all kinds of statistics and represented China's first central statistical institution on a national scale.

In 1907, the head of the Commission, Yikuang 奕劻 (Prince Qing), emphasised the great significance of statistics for "examining the country for its surpluses and shortcomings, its strength and weakness, [and] undertaking comparison to fix the direction of policy..." (Yikuang 1979a: 47). He demanded the adoption of the German as well as the Japanese systems of hierarchical, bottom–up separation of statistical work, in which every level of administration had a defined field of duty and was responsible to the next level (Yikuang 1979b: 51). As Andrea Bréard has shown in her recent study, it was in the context of these reforms that statistics as a scientific discipline and administrative tool in the European pattern was implemented and institutionalised. Officials, however, could not only draw on an apparently new European-American social science introduced via Japan, but also rhetorically and practically they were able ro refer to indigenous traditions of

---

[5] Mayr authored many books about population statistics, and was vice president and honorary member of the International Statistical Institute, honorary member of the Royal Statistical Society in London and the Société de Statistique in Paris, as well as president of the newly founded Deutsche Statistische Gesellschaft in 1911, see Neue Deutsche Biographie (1990).

[6] An overview is offered by Ichiko (1980: 375–415). A more recent assessment of the *Xinzheng*-Reforms, which emphasizes the significance of these reforms as the fundament of China's modern state, is Horowitz (2003), who systematically contrasts the difference between the established Qing bureaucracy and the European, American, and later Japanese ministerial governments. See also Strauss (1997, 2003) and Thompson (2003).

Survey the People 93

mathematical accounting, theoretically used within the administration for centuries (Bréard 2008).

In 1907, most of the new ministries, as well as the provinces, established statistical directorates (*tongjichu* 统计处, *diaochachu* 调查处) under the overall guidance of the new Statistical Department, which were required to collect and deliver data on foreign and domestic affairs, educational, military, legal and economic matters. The Qing government envisaged the implementation of a nationwide, hierarchical statistical system, but it is unclear how far it succeeded in organising statistical bureaus at the lower levels of administration (Li and Mo 1993: 218; Mou 2008: 53ff.).

The interest in "population" gained momentum in the following year, when the Qing government issued a Statute for Population Inspection (*Qingcha hukou tiaoli* 清查户口条例), which set out the framework for a state-wide census within four years. As in the case of the process of institutionalising statistical administration, foreign role models and global comparisons were invoked to emphasise the great significance of population statistics. On 1 January 1909, the Throne approved a bill brought by the Ministry of Civil Affairs (*Minzhengbu*民政部), called Regulations for Investigating the Population (*Diaocha hukou zhangzheng* 调查户口章程), which proclaimed: "In the East and the West, every country considers population (*hukou* 户口) a major aspect of internal administration" (quoted in Hou 2001: 21).

The Statistical Directorate of the Ministry was responsible for carrying out the census. It worked out a standard census formula, which was sent to the provincial authorities, and required them to enumerate both households and "mouth" numbers, according to sex, age, number of adults, and schoolchildren. Most provinces, however, only returned household numbers, and for many parts of the country population numbers had to be estimated. According to Ho, there was great resistance on the part of the people, who suspected the census of being used to raise taxes or enforce conscription. Many officials fabricated or purposely manipulated the numbers they reported to the central government authorities, because they either feared being punished or had been bribed. The census was completed in 1911, and the results were announced in 1912 by the Republican successor of the Ministry of Civil Affairs, the Ministry of the Interior (*Neiwubu* 内务部): the population of China at the time was given as 340 million people.[7]

Being aware of the many deficiencies of the census, the Republican Ministry of the Interior immediately ordered a new census for 1912, which was published little by little from 1916 on. The total population was then calculated to be about 405 million people, without any explanation of the huge increase as compared to the outcome of the previous census. This time, the Ministry was also interested in a more detailed survey of sex-ratio, occupation, age, status of marriage, and the rates of birth and death. Furthermore, the census-takers tried to distinguish between

---

[7] Another major point of criticism is that there was no exactly defined point of time for the survey. For the discussion of the census and its accuracy see Wang (1932/1933), Ho (1959: 76f.), Jiang (1993: 81ff.).

temporary and permanent residents. Again, some provinces did not report any numbers at all, and their population had to be estimated from the national mouth-per-household estimate (Jiang 1993: 93ff).

Despite tumultuous years between 1916 and 1928, and the lack of a national census, statistical work continued. The idea of its great importance was upheld by the Statistical Department,[8] which publicised statistical reports and numbers for different governments, as well as for the public. The most important of these reports was the Statistical Monthly Magazine (*Tongji yuekan* 统计月刊, from now on TK), published from 1918 to 1923. The magazine provided statistical tables in the different categories, including population statistics, as well as statistics from other states, for example import and export numbers from Britain, France and the US.[9]

Like the Qing officials some ten years earlier, the editors of the magazine still referred to the two models as "from antiquity" and from "Western states"; the latter were depicted as more progressive, and statistics was perceived as playing a much more decisive role than ever before in China. The foreword of the first volume stated that "in Western states statistics consisted of [nothing less than] politics (*xiguo tongji naiyu zhengzhi* 西国统计乃于政治)." Only a well-structured, thorough system of data-gathering in all areas of politics could obtain a general picture of the state (*kede dafan* 可得大凡). It was thus the objective of the magazine to edit the numerous statistical materials collected since the fall of the Qing dynasty and publish them for the good of everyone (TK 1918, 1: *Tongji yuekanxu*).

Whilst during the final decade of the Qing regime European administrative statistics had been introduced and the significance of population surveys was increasingly acknowledged, there were more and more detailed social investigations from the 1920s on. Besides academic research, the Communist party gave such investigations a high priority, and Mao even announced in 1930 that only detailed knowledge of the social-economic situation of the rural populace based on statistics would give the revolutionaries the "right to speak out" (*fayanquan* 发言权) (Mao 1982: 1). However, only after the formal re-unification and re-founding of the Republic of China were new attempts started to register the entire population and use these records for state governance.

---

[8] The original Statistical Department was closed down under President Yuan Shikai, who aimed to centralize the gathering of population statistics and other material under the aegis of his Political Bureau. It was reestablished in 1916 after Yuan's death. For this period see Wang (1986: 12–14), Li and Mo (1993: 232ff.).

[9] For a table of birth and death rates in Beijing over a period of six years, see the third issue. Altogether, the magazine was concerned more with economic and sociological, rather than population, statistics.

4 Statistics and "Population" in Guomindang China

Immediately after the *Guomindang* (Chinese Nationalist Party) formally claimed power over the whole of China, ending the so-called "warlord era" in 1927, it initiated a census for the whole country. This early census demonstrated the great significance the government and administration attributed to "population". The authors of the census report, which was only published in 1931, stated: "The state is built on the people. The people, in turn, depend on the state to survive. Prosperity or deterioration of the state depends upon the quality of government. [...] To govern the state, one must first know the situation of the people. To govern, one must first understand the needs of the people." One of the primary tasks of government, the report went on, is to "... investigate the population, which is acknowledged by all statisticians as the basic function of statistics" (*hukoutongji wei jiben tongji*户口统计为基本统计).[10] It concluded: "Every implementation of governmental standards depends in the beginning on population statistics as basis" (Minguo 1931: 2).

The census itself was organised and conducted by the Statistical Bureau of the Ministry of the Interior (*Neizhengbu tongjisi* 內政部统计司) of the Guomindang government, which was also responsible for the report. In mid-1928, the Ministry repeatedly ordered the provinces to take part in the census, issuing strict regulations concerning the procedure, and form sheets for the provincial officials. The government had to rely on provincial and local authorities for the census, as there was no centrally operated, state-wide police system. Based on the regulations for population survey and statistics (*Hukou diaocha tongji guize* 户口调查统计规则), proclaimed on 19 July 1928, the Statistical Bureau had carefully planned to draw up a broad variety of statistics, for instance information on the name, sex, relation to the head of household, marriage status, children (per woman), exact age and date of birth, place of origin, membership in the Nationalist Party, length of residence at the current home, occupation, level of education, religion and disabilities of every single person. Additionally, it grouped the households in four categories: regular households, boat households, public households (e.g. members of the military), and monastery/temple households (Minguo 1931: 1–35).

Until its official end in 1930, only 16 of 28 provinces and five special municipalities (Nanjing, Shanghai, Beiping, Hankou, and Tianjin) participated in the census and sent back the requested data. In the case of three provinces, not all counties reported back to the Ministry. Finally, it received only the total numbers of the households, as well as of males and females, and could thus only provide a total population number, an average number of people living in a household, the

---

[10] *Minguo shiqinian geshengshi hukou diaocha tongji baogao* 1931: *bianyan* 1. From now on Minguo (1931).

female–male ratio, and some numbers on age composition.[11] As there were many provinces and counties which did not report anything to the Ministry, the missing data had to be estimated. The total population of 474, 787, 386 was an estimate, albeit based on sophisticated mathematical methods (Minguo 1931: *bianyan* 弁言 2 and 623f.).

The Ministry officials were not satisfied with the 1928 census and were fully aware of its many shortcomings. For instance, the fact that there had been no exactly defined, appropriate time frame for performing the data collection, or the lack of qualified personnel on the ground were seen as major insufficiencies. The report demanded the implementation of a system of regional statistical institutions in China, the consideration of European and American models, and making clear the great importance of population investigations to everyone, even to schoolchildren, as was the case in Switzerland, France and other countries (Minguo 1931: 611f.).[12]

The significance the report attributed to the census was not just self-aggrandisement, but part of the attempt to develop a thoroughly institutionalised application of population and other statistics by the bureaucracy. Apart from the Statistical Bureau of the Ministry of the Interior, most state ministries possessed some kind of statistical department by 1928. The *Lifa Yuan* 立法院, the legislative branch of the Guomindang government, established a Statistical Directorate (*Tongjichu* 统计处) with relatively great authority, which was supposed to collect statistical information in the fields of the judiciary, politics, economy and society, and to publish a statistical yearbook. However, it had no superiority over other statistical departments, not even nominally.

Acknowledging the great importance of statistics and bureaucratic technocracy, the Republican Government eventually founded the General-Directorate of Budget, Accounts and Statistics (*Zhujichu* 主计处) on 1 April 1931. The Statistical Directorate of the *Lifa Yuan* became one of the three departments of the General Directorate, which was directly subordinate to the Republican Government.[13] It was in charge of leading, supervising and organising every governmental

---

[11] The report included statistics on children, the working population, and able-bodied men, who could be subject to conscription (*zhuangding*).

[12] For the census, a contemporary introduction to the preceding (late Qing) and the later population investigations, registration efforts, and the respective regulations and laws of the government, as well as surveys of non-governmental organization, see Wen Yonggou. *Wo guo lilai zhi renkou diaocha* (Population Surveys in the History of China), TB (1934, 26:1–14). The population total was subject to discussion and recalculated several times. See also Jiang (1993: 105).

[13] The Statistical Directorate now had the rank of a department (*ju*). As the ministry itself translated both *chu* and *ju* as *directorate* (in the cases of *Zhujichu* and its subordinate *Tongjiju*), the English rendering of the institution as Statistical Directorate will be retained. The hierarchy in Chinese at the time, generally but not always, was *bu* (ministry), *chu* (directorate), *ju* (department), *ke* (bureau), *si* (office). The *Zhujiju* became a full ministry in 1948 and was renamed *Zhujibu* (in English it was then named Ministry of Budget, Accounts, and Statistics). It was renamed one year later, but still had the rank of Ministry. See the editorial note in the *Tongji yuebao*.

department and institution which had anything to do with the compilation of statistics. It was supposed to standardise the appropriate statistical methods and define the format of statistical tables, plan and coordinate the scope and area of surveys, and draw up fundamental statistics itself. Furthermore, it was obligated to examine mistakes and deficits of any statistical survey, as well as to work out ways to improve the utilisation of statistics on every administrative level, and manage and train specialised personnel. Initially, it was headed by Liu Dadiao 刘大钧 as director and Wu Dadiao 吴大钧 as vice-director, and consisted of five divisions or bureaus (*ke* 科), including one especially for population and social statistics (*renkou ji shehui tongji* 人口及社会统计).[14]

The Statistical Directorate not only managed to increase the density of statistical institutions and broaden the number of statistical surveys in many fields on all administrative levels,[15] but its staff also stayed in close contact with the latest global and national scientific developments. In February 1930, the Statistical Study Society of China (*Zhongguo tongji xueshe* 中国统计学社) was founded at Nanjing Zhongyang University by the members of various governmental statistical institutions. It was supposed to improve research and contribute to the standardisation of statistical methods used by the academic community in universities, as well as by the bureaucracy. Both Liu Dadiao and Wu Dadiao, as well as Jin Guobao 金国宝, Chen Da 陈达 and Zhu Junyi 朱君毅, who were authors of influential scientific books, were senior members. Liu and Wu also contributed regularly to the major publication of the society, the Statistical Anthology (*Tongji luncong* 统计论丛), first published in 1934 (Li and Mo 1993: 276f.).[16]

In the 1930s, the focus of scientists shifted to American–British mathematical theories, and statistics was more or less acknowledged as a separate scientific discipline. Although there was a clear emphasis on translating and reproducing foreign methods and theories, Chinese authors produced some independent works on the application of statistics in China, and promoted particularly the utilisation of population or social statistics in the realm of politics and state administration (Wang 1998: 57f.; Yuan et al. 2004: 56f.; Li and Mo 1993: 272). Jin Guobao 金国宝, for

---

[14] The others were: Statistics concerning Agriculture and other Extractive Industries (*chanye tongji*); Economic and Financial Statistics (*jingji ji caizheng tongji*); Political, Educational and International Statistics (*zhengzhi ji guoji tongji*); General Affairs and Personnel Statistics (*zongwu ji renshi tongji*). In 1947 two additional bureaus were established, which primarily managed statistics on the work of the whole Republican administration. On the tasks of the Statistical Directorate see Wu Dayao. *Zhujichu tongjiju zhizu zhi jiqi shiye* (The Organization and Activities of the Statistical Directorate of the General Directorate), TB (1935, 1: 1–14). Wu was then director. Note that all translations here are given by the *Tongji yuebao* itself. On the *Zhujiju* see also Ren (2008: 25ff.).

[15] Wang reports of eight larger statistical departments and over 600 smaller sub-units with hundreds of employees in the 1930s, and even more in the 1940s under the overall direction of the *Zhujichu*. See Wang (1986: 15f.) and Li and Mo (1993: 236ff.).

[16] Another publication was the Journal of the Statistical Study Society of China (*Zhongguo tongji xueshe xuebao*).

instance, regarded social policy and public hygiene as two of the most important areas where statistics should be implemented. The author of *Tongjixue dagan* 统计学大纲 (An Outline of Statistical Studies) explained "... if one wants to understand the reason [for social diseases] the application of statistics must not be neglected. [...] Death numbers of population diseases and public hygiene are closely connected. The only references for the authorities responsible for hygiene are statistics" (Jin 1934: 2).

The publication of population, social and medical statistics for both the public and the government was indeed one of the most important assignments of the official Statistical Directorate. It issued a Full Statistical Report (*Tongji zongbaogao* 统计总报告) for the Republican Government on an irregular basis, a public Statistical Synopsis (*Tongji tiyao* 统计提要) of these reports, and a Statistical Yearbook (*Tongji nianjian* 统计年鉴).[17]

The most important publication that invoked foreign role models of statistical administration and the significance foreign governments attributed to *population* was the Statistical Monthly (*Tongji yuebao* 统计月报), which was published between 1931 and 1948.[18] The first issue of the Statistical Monthly introduced the aim of the magazine and the Statistical Directorate, repeating more or less the foreword of its forerunner, the Statistical Monthly Magazine (*Tongji yuekan* 统计月刊): "To scrutinise the statistical organisation of other countries [and] publicise all kinds of statistics to improve the situation of the country" (TB 1931: 1). The second issue was a special edition about the International Statistical Institute (*Guoji tongji huiyi* 国际统计会议) and the global exchange among statistical experts. It introduced the history of international statistical organisations, including the first meeting of the International Statistical Congress presided over by Adolphe Quetelet (TB 1931: 2), and reported on the 19th Conference of the ISI held in Tokyo in 1930. The majority of the papers presented there in three sections (population, economy, society) were about demography or population statistics (TB 1931, 2: 3–18). Director Liu Dadiao had attended the Conference and presented a paper about the Census of 1912, which was printed in this issue (TB 1931, 2: 19–38). He also took part in the Conference the following year in Madrid and had attended the International Congress for the Study of Population in Rome. Afterwards he visited six other states to "investigate the organisation of the statistical system of these states" (TB 1931, 2: 47–76). Liu described how impressed he was by the existence of central statistical agencies in the Netherlands, Russia and Germany, and especially praised the dense, hierarchical German system. Although France, Italy, Spain and Belgium possessed central statistical departments, he wrote, these only managed a

---

[17] These are only some of the major governmental publications. Altogether, there existed over one hundred statistical publications by the central government, provinces, and private organizations (including academic institutions), demonstrating the immense increase of statistical surveys in every imaginable field, especially after 1930.

[18] In 1935, it was re-launched and changed its name to Statistical Quarterly (*Tongji jibao*) but returned to the old name at the end of 1936.

Survey the People

few sectors where statistics were produced. However, as in Japan and the USA, which he had visited earlier, population statistics was always the most important area in each of those European states (*yi hukou tongji zui wei zhongyao* 以户口统计最为重要). Liu closely examined the work, tasks and function of the central governmental statistical institutions[19] and the procedure of census surveys. He admired the German system and emphasised the hierarchical relationship between central, regional and local statistical state institutions, its density, and the wide scope of statistical work, as well as the close connection of the administration to the academic community.

Not only this issue, but the whole magazine had a global orientation and regularly reported about the organisation of statistical research in other states, and presented tables, for instance import and export indices, of and from other countries. Although the focus was on states such as Britain and Germany, which were regarded as rather important, the Statistical Monthly also reported on the utilisation of statistics in less powerful countries. A census in Poland was as much a topic as the establishment of a central statistical department in Mexico (TB 1934, 15: 120 and 131). Population and demographic statistics in China and abroad were one major focus of the periodical, demonstrating the huge interest of the bureaucracy and the government of Republican China in the matter.[20] Interestingly, there were no more references to any alleged Chinese tradition of collecting statistics or population registration.

To sum up, in the period between 1927 and the late 1940s population statistics received ever more attention. Statistics developed into a professional scientific discipline, specialists within the bureaucracy promoted its administrative application, and the importance officials ascribed to the notion of "population" turned census-taking into a major issue of state government.

5 Conclusion

Early twentieth-century Chinese officials, scholars and politicians drew on ancient indigenous role models of population registration and, increasingly, on foreign models of scientific statistical administration and population surveys. First, foreign examples served more as authorities than as actual sources of new methods. But, as

---

[19] He mentioned, for instance, the *Statistische Reichsamt*, the *Statistique General de la France* [sic], the *Divisione di Statistica Generale* [sic], and the *Direccion General del Instituto Geografino Cadastral y pe Statistica* [sic].

[20] See, for instance, TB (1933, 14), which exclusively dealt with population investigation. In his analysis of the census of 1928, Huang Zhong uses German terminology like *Stichtag* (cut-off date, *diaocha riqi*) to emphasize his criticism and again demonstrate the transnational character of statistics as a scientific subject. Huang Zhong. *Ping Minguo shiqinian woguo quanguo renkou diaocha de fangfa* (Criticism of the Methods of the 1928 National Census), TB (1933, 14: 76).

in Europe and the USA, governance was more and more influenced by a modernist positivist science, which was characterised by a spirit of representing or searching for an objective truth and impartial facts.

Drawing up statistics as the basis and justification of political action was globally acknowledged to be an important instrument of modern government. While, at least in the Chinese case, the political rhetoric usually used the term "people", implying some kind of citizenship and participation, "population" was the anonymous technical term of bureaucratic governance. Ideology certainly transformed policy in twentieth-century China, but bureaucracy had a huge part in reshaping state government, and contributed to the transition from empire to nation-state. The "governmentality" of the modern administrative state focused on "population".

While Chinese specialist statisticians regarded "population" as the most important field of their work, the political interest in demography was facilitated by the development of statistics into a scientific discipline and its administrative utilisation from the early twentieth-century. Although population statistics were not translated into a thorough policy of demographic control during that time, "population" was increasingly regarded as major concern of the government.

We have to be very careful when applying Foucault's concept of "governmentality", which was developed in connection with Modern European history, to Late Qing and Early Republican China. The massive amounts of demographic data statisticians accumulated during the Republican period, on birth and death rates, pregnancy rates, causes of death of infants, and hygiene, had not yet been transformed into a full governmental agenda.[21] However, the political rationality began to shift during this period. Political legitimacy increasingly derived from rational governance that ultimately centred on "population", which became a category of knowledge any regime increasingly had to deal with. Statistics functioned as a governmental technology of state formation as it had done in Europe since the middle of the eighteenth century.

As one of the most important objects of modern government, population and its management played a crucial role in the formation of the modern Chinese state. State formation, in this context, cannot be simply viewed as a process initiated from above or below, but as a much more complex political process, which included new knowledge and ideologies as well as changing discourses, practices and institutions. Governance and administration had to accommodate to socially dominant discourses, requirements of certain groups, and rational scientific arguments.

---

[21] After 1934, the Guomindang reintroduced the *baojia*-system in parts of the country. This was no step backward, but an expression of the importance the government attached to the registration and control of population. Even during the wars with the Japanese, and then with the Communists, this interest did not cease. In 1947, the government again planned to conduct a new census to be performed by the newly formed Department of Population (*Hukouju*). The census was carried out under the Communist Party, which also inherited the idea of governing the *population*. See Jiang (1993: 108).

Neither the use of statistics nor the focus on population nor any other technology of government were simply acts of central state-building from above. Grass-root demands and movements, for instance, interacted with central political action, changed in the course of these interactions and produced new meanings, ideas and technologies.

Census surveys and registration efforts stabilised old categories of social perception, such as the household (*hu*) as the foundation of social organisation, and introduced new ones, such as the able-bodied, adult male liable to military service. While in Europe governmental technologies, which put population at the centre of governmental focus, also caused individualisation and a devaluation of the familial, the family remained the basic, but increasingly disruptive, category by means of which Chinese regimes governed—at least until the beginning of the Communist period. However, the propositions totally changed as new kinds of statistical data influenced political rationality and enabled different kinds of policy-making. For instance, only the knowledge and production of death tables could make possible health and hygiene policies (Yip 1995), as well as the governing of bodies and the reproductive behaviour of the population. Through their activity as scientific experts, the administrative personnel in the statistical organisations of Republican China obtained information and created knowledge which helped them to influence political decision-making and to turn the attention of politicians to demography. Governing China's population, however, was not fully acknowledged and accomplished before the founding of the People's Republic, when sweeping programmes, such as the one-child policy to control the quality and quantity of the population, were implemented.

Bibliography

Bréard, Andrea. 2008. *Reform, Bureaucratic Expansion and Production of Numbers: Statistics in Early 20th century China*. Berlin: Technische Universität. Habilitation.

Dean, Mitchell. 1999. *Governmentality: Power and Rule in Modern Society*. London: Sage Publications.

Dikötter, Frank. 1992. The Limits of Benevolence: Wang Shiduo (1802–1899) and Population Control. *Bulletin of the School of Oriental and African Studies* 55.1: 110–115.

Dikötter, Frank. 1995. *Sex, Culture, and Modernity in China: Medical Science and the Construction of Sexual Identities in the Early Republican Period*. London: Hurst.

Dutton, Michael. 1992. *Policing and Punishment in China: From Patriarchy to "the People"*. Cambridge: Cambridge University Press.

Dupâquier, Jacques and Michel Dupâquier. 1985. *Histoire de la Démographie. La Statistique de la Population des Origines à 1914*. Paris: PUF.

Foucault, Michel. 1991. Governmentality. In *The Foucault Effect: Studies in Governmentality*, ed. Graham Burchell et al., 87–104. Chicago et al.: Harvester Wheatsheaf.

Foucault, Michel. 1998. *The History of Sexuality. Volume 1: The Will to Knowledge*. London: Penguin Books.

Greenhalgh, Susan and Edwin A. Winckler. 2005. *Governing China's Population: From Leninist to Neoliberal Biopolitics*. Stanford: Stanford University Press.

Hacking, Ian. 1975. *The Emergence of Probability: A Philosophical Study of Early Ideas About Probability, Induction and Statistical Inference*. Cambridge: Cambridge University Press.

Hald, Anders. 1998. *A History of Mathematical Statistics From 1750 to 1930*. New York et al.: Wiley.

Ho, Ping-ti. 1959. *Studies on the Population of China. 1368–1953*. Cambridge: Harvard University Press.

Horowitz, Richard S. 2003. Breaking the Bonds of Precedent: The 1905–6 Government Reform Commission and the Remaking of the Qing Central State, *Modern Asian Studies* 37.4: 775–797.

Hou, Yangfang 侯杨方. 2001. *Zhongguo renkoushi 中国人口史 (History of the Population of China). Volume 6. 1910–1953*. Shanghai: Fudan Daxue Chubanshe.

Hsiao, Kun-chuan. 1967. *Imperial Control in the Nineteenth Century*. Seattle: University of Washington Press.

Ichiko, Chuzo. 1980. Political and Institutional Reforms 1901–1911. In *Cambridge History of China Volume 11, Part 2*, ed. John K. Fairbank and Kwang-ching Liu, 375–415. Cambridge: Cambridge University Press.

Jiang, Tao (姜涛). 1990. Qingdai renkou tongji zhidu yu 1741–1851 nianjian de zhongguo renkou 清代人口统计制度与1741–1851 年间的中国人口 (The System of Population Statistics in the Qing period and the Population of China between 1741–1851). *Jindaishi yanjiu 近代史研究* 5: 26–50.

Jiang, Tao (姜涛). 1993. *Zhongguo jindai renkoushi 中国近代人口史 (The History of Modern China's Population)*. Hangzhou: Zhejiang Renmin Chubanshe.

Jin, Guobao 金国宝.1934 (1992). *Tongjixue dagang 统计学大纲*. Shanghai: Shanghai Shudian (1992).

Kendall, Maurice George. 1960. Studies in the History of Probability and Statistics: Where Shall the History of Statistics Begin? *Biometrika* 47.: 447–449.

Kuhn, Philip. 1995. Ideas Behind China's Modern State. *Harvard Journal of Asiatic Studies* 55.2: 295–337.

Landwehr, Achim. 2005. Das gezählte Volk: Bevölkerung als Gegenstand einer Kulturgeschichte des Politischen. *Zeitschrift für Historische Forschung* 35: 207–224.

Lee, James Z. and Feng Wang. 1999. *One Quarter of Humanity: Malthusian Mythology and Chinese Reality 1700–2000*. Cambridge: Harvard University Press.

Li, Huicun 李惠村 and Yueda Mo 莫曰达. 1993. *Zhongguo tongjishi 中国统计史 (The History of Statistics in China)*. Beijing: Zhongguo Tongji Chubanshe.

Mao, Zedong. 1982 (1930). Fandui benbenzhuyi 反对本本主义 (Against Bookishness). In *Mao Zedong nongcun diaocha wenji 毛泽东农村调查文集 (Collected Writings of Mao Zedong on Rural Surveys)*. Beijing: Renmin Chubanshe.

Miller, Peter and Nikolas Rose. 1990. Governing Economic life. *Economy and Society* 19.1: 1–31.

Minguo shiqinian geshengshi hukou diaocha tongji baogao 民国十七年各省市户口调查统计报告 (Statistical Report of the Population Investigation in every Province and City in the 17th year of the Republic) 1931. Published by the *Neiwubu zongwusi* 内务部总务司 (General Service Department of the Ministry of the Interior). Edited by the *Neiwubu tongjisi* 内务部统计司 (Statistical Department of the Ministry of the Interior). Nanjing.

Mou, Yongru 牟永如. 2008. *Qingmo shehui diaocha yanjiu 清末社会调查研究 (Social Investigation in Late Qing China)*. Wuhan: Unpublished master thesis. Central China Normal University.

Neue Deutsche Bibliographie, Volume 16. 1990. Ed. Historische Kommission bei der Bayrischen Akademie der Wissenschaften. Berlin.

Osterhammel, Jürgen. 2009. *Die Verwandlung der Welt: Eine Geschichte des 19. Jahrhunderts*. München: C.H. Beck.

Ren, Weiei 任伟伟. 2008. *Nanjing guomin zhengfu shehui diaocha yanjiu 1927–1937 南京国民政府社会调查研究 (A Study on the Social Investigation of the Nanjing National Government)*. Jinan: Unpublished master thesis. Shandong Normal University.

Sigley, Gary. 1996. Governing Chinese Bodies: The Significance of Studies in the Concept of Governmentality for the Analysis of Government in China. *Economy and Society* 25.4: 457–482.

Stigler, Stephen M. 1986. *The History of Statistics: The Measurement of Uncertainty before 1900*. Cambridge: Belknap Press of Harvard University.

Stigler, Stephen M. 1999. *Statistics on the Table: The History of Statistical Concepts and Methods*. Cambridge: Harvard University Press.

Strauss, Julia C.1997. The Evolution of Republican Government. *The China Quarterly* 150: 329–351.

Strauss, Julia C. 2003. Creating "Virtuous and Talented" Officials for the Twentieth Century: Discourse and Practice in Xinzheng China. *Modern Asian Studies* 37.4: 831–850.

Thompson, Richard. 2003. The Lessons of Defeat: Transforming the Qing State after the Boxer War. *Modern Asian Studies* 37.4: 769–773.

Tongji yuebao 统计月报 (The Statistical Monthly). 1931–1948. Published by Guomin zhengfu zhujichu tongjiju 国民政府主计处统计局 (Statistical Directorate of the General-Directorate of Budget, Accounts and Statistics, National Government of China). Nanjing and Chongqing.

Tongji yuekan 统计月刊 (The Statistical Monthly Magazine). 1918–1923. Published by Guowuyuan tongjiju 国务院统计局 (Department of Statistics of the State Cabinet). Beijing.

Waley-Cohen, Joanna. 2004. New Qing History. *Radical History Review* 88: 193–206.

Wang, Huting 汪琥庭. 1998. Zhongguo tongji jiaocun bianxue fazhanshi 中国统计教村编写发展史 (History of the Development of the Compilation of Statistical Teaching Materials). *Gaodeng jiaoyu yanjiu* 高等教育研究 2: 57–59.

Wang, Shida 王士达. 1932/1933. Minzhengbu hukoudiaocha ji gejia guji 民政部户口调查及各家估计 (The Population Investigation and Calculation of the Ministry of Civil Affairs). *Shehui kexue zazhi* 社会科学杂志 3.3/4.1.

Wang, Yifu 王一夫. 1986. *Xin zhongguo tongji shigao* 新中国统计史稿 *(A Draft History of Statistics in Communist China)*. Beijing: Zhongguo tongji chunbanshe.

Yikuang 奕劻 et al. (ed.). 1979a (1907). Xianzheng bianchaguan daju Yikuang deng nicheng xianzheng bianchaguan banshi zhangchengzhe 宪政编查管大臣奕劻等拟呈宪政编查管办事章程折 (Memorial of Yikuang and others in the Government Reform Commission on the Draft for Responsibilities of the Government Reform Commission). In *Qingmo choubei lixian dangan shiliao* 清末筹备立宪档案史料 *(Historical Documents on the Preparation of Constitutionalism at the End of the Qing Dynasty)*, ed. Gugong danganguan Ming Qing danganbu 故宫档案馆明清档案部 (Ming-Qing Archive Department of the Palace Archive). Beijing: Zhonghua shuju.

Yikuang 奕劻 et al. (ed.). 1979b (1907). Xianzheng bianchaguan daju Yikuang deng qingchi gesheng sheli diaochajuzhe 宪政编查管大臣奕劻等清饬各省调立调查局折 (Memorial of Yikuang and others in the Government Reform Commission for the Establishment of Survey Departments in the Provinces). In *Qingmo choubei lixian dangan shiliao* 清末筹备立宪档案史料 *(Historical Documents on the Preparation of Constitutionalism at the End of the Qing Dynasty)*, ed. Gugong danganguan Ming Qing danganbu 故宫档案馆明清档案部 (Ming-Qing Archive Department of the Palace Archive). Beijing: Zhonghua shuju.

Yip, Ka-che. 1995. *Health and National Reconstruction in Nationalist China: The Development of Modern Health Services 1928–1937*. Ann Arbor: Association for Asian Studies.

Yu, Zhongyi 于忠义. 2009. Jianming tongji xueshushi gangyao 简明统计学学术纲要 (A Brief Outline of the History of Statistics). *Statistical Research (Tongji yanjiu* 统计研究*)* 26.6: 102–111.

Yuan, Wei 袁卫; Liu, Chang 刘畅; Zhang, Yun 张云. 2004. Woguo tongji jiaocun jianshe de lishi huigu yu xianshi sikao 我国统计教村建设的历史回顾与现实思考 (Historical Retrospective of the Introduction of Statistical Teaching Materials in China and Thoughts on the Current Situation). *Statistical Research (Tongji yanjiu* 设计研究*)* 6: 55–60.

China and Constitutional Monarchy: Four Short Encounters Around 1900

Guido Mühlemann

1 Introduction

For many centuries, China with its deep-rooted and ancient culture was one of the most advanced civilisations on our Earth and usually far ahead of its counterparts on the European continent. As a matter of fact, before the beginning of the Modern Era in about 1500 A.D., only the Roman Empire at its height in the first two centuries A.D. was able to measure up to its Chinese counterpart (then the Eastern Han 東漢 Dynasty, 25–220 A.D.) by virtue of its population (more than 50 million people), territorial extension, military strength, technological level and economic exchange. Although the Eastern Han Dynasty collapsed two centuries earlier than the (Western) Roman Empire whose last Emperor, Romulus Augustulus, was forced to abdicate in 476, China saw the establishment of a series of big, centralised empires—starting with the Jin 晉 Dynasty which lasted from 265 to 420—whereas the European continent remained fragmented (with the exception of the Napoleonic Empire in 1804–1814/15). Also, even though China itself was, during the last two millennia, divided into a series of smaller states many times adding up to several centuries in total, it never faced the same kind of cultural decline as Europe did just after the collapse of the Western Roman Empire. In fact, the periods when China was fragmented into smaller states became shorter with time, whereas the times when it was unified under a central government became longer. Also, the area of the empires ruling China had the tendency to grow larger after each reunification. Huge increases in area occurred during the Mongol Yuan 元 Dynasty (1279–1368) and the last dynasty, the Qing 清.

G. Mühlemann
Bergstrasse 4, 8200 Schaffhausen, Switzerland

A. Flüchter and S. Richter (eds.), *Structures on the Move*,
Transcultural Research – Heidelberg Studies on Asia and Europe in a Global Context,
DOI 10.1007/978-3-642-19288-3_6, © Springer-Verlag Berlin Heidelberg 2012

Dynasty (1636/1644–1912), which was originally founded in Manchuria[1] in 1636.

It was under this Qing Dynasty that imperial China witnessed its last golden age which spanned the whole eighteenth century: not only was the territory ruled by this dynasty 20% larger than today's People's Republic of China (11.5 billion square kilometres in comparison to the PRC's 9.5 billion), but Qing China was also at that time by far the largest economy in the world (Mühlemann 2006: 86–88; Jacques 2009: 29ff.). Thanks to the rather peaceful times—with the exception of some smaller rebellions, especially in areas of today's southwest China, the major military operations were concentrated on far-away border regions, like Xinjiang 新疆 and Tibet 西藏—the population was beginning to increase massively in the 18th century. If for 1741 the population of China is estimated as being 141 million people, the number of inhabitants more than doubled 50 years later, so that in 1794 there were about 313 million people living in China; at the start of the Taiping 太平 Rebellion in 1850—which would cause a loss of nearly 30 million lives during the next 14 years—the number of inhabitants had almost trebled to about 430 million people (Gernet 1989: 409). Other than the peaceful political environment, the increase in population resulted mainly from the high accomplishments of Chinese agriculture, as well as from the successful introduction since the Ming 明 Dynasty (1368–1644) of new crops from the Americas such as the sweet potato and maize (Mühlemann 2006: 88). Also, the golden age of the Qing Dynasty in the eighteenth century was characterised by a state-of-the-art manufacture of products whose quantity[2] would only be topped in fully-industrialised countries several decades later, and whose quality[3] in many instances remains unmatched. Finally, the subjects of the Qing Empire were ruled by a small, but efficient bureaucracy which was itself in a large part recruited by way of a series of different examinations which were—at least in theory—open to virtually every male Chinese.[4]

---

[1] Today "Manchuria" consists of the three "northeastern" (東北 dongbei) provinces of Heilongjiang 黑龍江, Jilin吉林 and Liaoning 遼寧 as well as the northernmost parts of the Inner Mongolian Autonomous Region (內蒙古自治區 Nei Menggu Zizhiqu).

[2] In China, certain products were already being produced on a quasi-industrial scale. In this context, it is interesting to note that, for example, in the eighteenth century the porcelain kilns of Jingdezhen 景德鎮 employed at least 100,000 people, cf. Seitz (2000: 80). However, Friedrich Reichel advances an estimated figure of "one million people, that earned their living [in 1720] in a direct or indirect way from the fabrication of porcelain", cf. Reichel (1993: 12). However, the manufacture of products on a pre-industrial level in China is not restricted to the era of the Qing 清 Dynasty; as a matter of fact, already in 1100 A.D. during the Song 宋 Dynasty (960–1279), China's steel foundries produced annually about 150,000 metric tons of iron and steel, a figure which in Europe was not achieved before the eighteenth century, cf. Cerutti (1986: 15).

[3] This is especially true for the porcelain produced for the Imperial court at the kilns of Jingdezhen 景德鎮 in present-day Jiangxi 江西 province or for the dragon robes and other silk products produced in the Jiangnan 江南 region.

[4] For more information regarding social mobility by way of passing imperial examinations (Chinese: keju 科舉), cf. Ho 何 (1962: especially 87), where Ho 何 mentions a number of Chinese

For all these reasons it is not surprising that the Chinese found their idea of China being at the "centre of the world" confirmed in many ways and were thus very sceptical towards foreign influence, especially as far as it concerned the ideological and philosophical framework of state and society. In the eyes of China's elite, there was no need for any change.

However, things changed dramatically during the nineteenth century. First of all, China was the victim of its own success: because of the massive increase in population in the period from the beginning of the eighteenth century to the middle of the nineteenth, large numbers of China's population became impoverished because agricultural production could not keep up with the increasing demands of the rising population.[5] Furthermore, following an increase in corruption, but also because of the freezing of the level of taxation during the reign (1661–1722) of the Kangxi 康熙.

Emperor (Spence 2001: 102–106)—a level which remained basically in place until the end of the Empire in 1912 and was not adapted to the growing population—large parts of the Empire's infrastructure such as dykes, streets and waterways fell into disrepair, which increased the consequences of natural catastrophes and was also a hindrance to the swift transportation of goods.

This impoverishment of the state as well as of large parts of the population was exacerbated by the steep rise in opium imports (mainly from British traders) which not only led successively to the addiction of many people in China[6] but also further strained the Empire's financial situation, as the balance sheet of its international trade turned negative around 1820–1825 so that the silver reserves the state had managed to accumulate during the eighteenth century completely vanished.[7]

As a consequence of these financial strains, the Qing Empire was faced with an increasing number of upheavals and large-scale rebellions,[8] which in some cases caused enormous damage to China's society and economy, thus further weakening the Empire. When foreign powers started to encroach upon China's sovereignty—

---

from the most modest backgrounds who managed to pass imperial examinations and thus raise their social status considerably.

[5] A similar, fateful development was to occur on the African continent in the second half of the twentieth century: according to Meredith (2006: 289ff.), "from a little over 200 million in 1960, the population by 1990 had reached 450 million. [...] The rate of population growth added to pressures on agricultural production, on urban growth and on government spending."

[6] According to Hibbert (1989: 152), there were about two million opium addicts in China in the year 1835.

[7] According to Flessel (1988: 111), starting in 1834, China each year had to use 2,000 t of its silver reserves in order to pay for opium, as the earnings from the export of tea and silk proved insufficient to cover the expenses of rising opium imports.

[8] The biggest rebellion was the Taiping 太平 Rebellion from 1850 to 1864, which not only resulted in the deaths of nearly 30 million people, but also the large-scale destruction of China's economic powerhouse region of Jiangnan 江南 (which encompasses the regions on the shores of the Yangzi river 揚子江 of today's provinces of Anhui 安徽, Jiangsu 江蘇, Jiangxi 江西, Zhejiang 浙江 as well as the Shanghai municipality 上海市). According to Gernet (1989: 469), even 50 years after the end of the Taiping Rebellion the scars of the destruction were still very visible in this region.

the first serious act of this kind being the First Opium War of 1839–1842—the country could ill defend itself. Each time China was attacked by foreign powers, it did not only sustain severe damage but had, moreover, to pay heavy indemnities to its aggressors and make numerous other concessions, all of which further aggravated its situation. This caused a larger proportion of China's political and literati elite to be worried about the future of their country. If, soon after the First Opium War, some forward-looking statesmen proposed the adoption of Western science and technological knowledge in order to improve China's defence while at the same time leaving China's traditional thoughts unaffected, the crushing defeat of the Qing Empire by its former tributary state Japan in the war of 1894/95 demonstrated that this concept was inadequate, increasing the pressure on the political elite to study the political structures in foreign countries.

As most of the more powerful and advanced countries[9] on the globe around 1900 (with the notable exceptions of the republican[10] democracies in the United States of America, France and Switzerland, and the autocratic monarchy in Czarist Russia) were ruled by constitutional monarchs, it is not a surprise that the elites of the Qing Empire focused their attention on this kind of government model, which—at least at the time—was considered to be especially successful.[11]

2 The Concept of Constitutional Monarchy

The main feature of a constitutional monarchy is the limitation of the power of the ruler by legal provisions, typically written in a formal constitutional text where the duties and rights of the sovereign as well as of the subjects are clearly defined. Depending on the epoch and the historical circumstances of the enactment of the constitution, the number of subjects being able to participate in political affairs was

---

[9] This applies especially to the kingdoms of the United Kingdom, Belgium, Italy and the Netherlands, as well as to the Empires of Germany and Japan.

[10] In this paper, "republican" is understood as being of "non-monarchic" nature.

[11] With hindsight, even in the first half of the twenty-first century, where the most widespread forms of government are various kinds of democracies in republican systems, it is still possible to recognise some of the advantages inherent to a constitutional monarchy: as the example of Belgium illustrates, the fact of having a constitutional monarch from a hereditary royal family at the summit of the state can be very effective in keeping different ethnic groups (in this case French-speaking Walloons, Dutch-speaking Flemish and Germans) together within the same multi-ethnic state. Cf. for example, Israel (2010: 5). For more information on the Kings of the Belgians, cf. Roegiers (2007). Another interesting example of a country that has strongly benefited from a (past) constitutional monarchy is Brazil: as a matter of fact, the Brazilian Empire of 1822–1889 under its able Emperors Pedro I and especially Pedro II played a crucial role in uniting and modernising this huge country and providing it with a national identity. For more information on this Empire as well as its rulers, cf. Kienzl (1942), Barman (1999) and Schwarcz (2004).

China and Constitutional Monarchy: Four Short Encounters Around 1900

smaller or greater, ranging from a very restricted number of peers to a full-scale democracy.

The origin of this form of government is closely linked to measures undertaken to restrain the power of the monarchs in the Kingdom of England, and later in the United Kingdom. A first but important step to limit the power of the King was the writing of the *Magna Charta Libertatum* in 1215, whose clause 61 stipulated that a college composed of 25 barons was to survey the implementation of certain fundamental rights[12] that had been guaranteed the barons in the same Charter. During the seventeenth century, the power of the monarchs of the United Kingdom was further curtailed by important acts such as the *Petition of Rights* of 1628, the *Habeas Corpus Act* of 1679 and—after the Glorious Revolution of 1688—the *Declaration of Rights* of 1689. Yet it is interesting to note that while the United Kingdom might be considered as being the initiator of the constitutional form of monarchy, it is today one of the very few countries in the world that lacks a formal constitution (Willoweit 2005: 157; Haller et al. 2008: 102f.).

The first case of a monarch having his power circumscribed by a formal constitutional text was that of Louis XVI of France. Although he had already lost many of his powers soon after the start of the French Revolution on 14 July 1789, it was not until 3 September 1791 that his duties[13] were circumscribed by the (first) French constitution (which was itself heavily influenced by the United States' Constitution of 17 September 1787). However, since during the radical phase of the French Revolution the monarchy was abolished on 21 September 1792,[14] it was only after Napoleon had himself proclaimed constitutional Emperor on 18 May 1804 that constitutional monarchy was to see a rapid expansion in Europe, especially after Napoleon's conquest of large portions of the European continent in the following years up until his ill-fated campaign in Russia in 1812.

Looking more closely at Napoleon's "constitution"[15] and contrasting it with the first French constitution of 3 September 1791, it is interesting to note that Napoleon

---

[12] E.g. according to clause 21, earls and barons should only be judged by their peers.

[13] According to Article 4 of Chapter II of the French Constitution, the main function of the French King was to maintain the Constitution and to ensure laws were kept to: "Le roi, à son avènement au trône, ou dès qu'il aura atteint sa majorité, prêtera à la Nation, en présence du Corps législatif, le serment d'être fidèle à la Nation et à la loi, d'employer tout le pouvoir qui lui est délégué, à maintenir la Constitution décrétée par l'Assemblée nationale constituante, aux années 1789, 1790 et 1791, et à faire exécuter les lois.—Si le corps législatif n'est pas assemblé, le roi fera publier une proclamation, dans laquelle seront exprimés ce serment et la promesse de la réitérer aussitôt que le Corps législatif sera réuni." Perhaps the most patent innovation in relation to the new form of a constitutional monarchy is Article 3 of Chapter II which states that law—and not the monarch—is the highest authority in France: "Il n'y a point en France d'autorité supérieure à celle de la loi. Le roi ne règne que par elle, et ce n'est qu'au nom de la loi qu'il peut exiger l'obéissance."

[14] Actually, the power of the French King had already been "suspended" on 10 August 1792. Cf. Kuhn (2003: 89).

[15] The "constitutional" law for the First Empire of France was in fact the "Senatus-consulte organique du 28 floréal an XII", which was declared on 18 May 1804. The terminology of this basic law takes its inspiration from Republican Rome, cf. Jörs et al. (1987: 15f.)

enjoyed much more power than did Louis XVI.[16] The fact that there are sometimes huge differences in the scope of power of rulers in constitutional monarchies is very important for the understanding of this concept of government. For example, there are constitutional monarchies that would in fact be better characterised as "democracies with a crowned head of state". This is the case in the modern monarchies of Belgium, Denmark, the Netherlands, Norway, Spain, Sweden and the United Kingdom.[17]

In Thailand, however, matters are getting much more complicated. Although, according to the Thai constitution, the political role of the monarch is rather limited,[18] nowadays the authority of King Bhumibol Adulyadej ภูมิพลอดุลยเดช—who has reigned over Thailand since 1946 and played an important role as a mediator in several political crises—has grown so great within the Thai population that the Thai monarchy is a political force to be reckoned with.[19]

Another very interesting variant of a constitutional monarchy is to be seen in the Brazilian Empire of 1822–1889, in whose Constitution of 25 March 1824 we find not only the typical division of power in a legislative, executive, and judicial branch, but moreover, in article 98, a "moderating power" which was "the key of the whole political organization" and was "exclusively delegated to the emperor as

---

[16] The enhanced position of the French Emperor in comparison to the reduced role of Louis XVI after the proclamation of the first French constitution can be seen both in the absence of an article putting the law above the Emperor and in the absence of a clear-cut separation of the legislative, executive and judicial powers in Napoleon's imperial "constitution". Indeed, the Emperor of the French could appoint many key people, among them the president of the Senate (Title VIII, Art. 58 Senatus-consulte organique du 28 floréal an XII) and the presidents of the Courts of cassation, appeal and criminal justice (Title XIV, Art. 135). Concerning the Emperor's authority over judicial matters, see also Art. 1 under Title I of this Senatus-consulte: "Le Gouvernement de la République est confié à un Empereur, qui prend le titre d'Empereur des Français. La justice se rend, au nom de l'Empereur, par les officiers qu'il institue". Nevertheless, it is possible to recognise the constitutional character of the First Empire in France in the oath the Emperor had to take: "Le serment de l'Empereur est ainsi conçu: 'Je jure de maintenir l'intégrité du territoire de la République, de respecter et de faire les lois du concordat et la liberté des cultes; de respecter et faire respecter l'égalité des droits, la liberté politique et civile, l'irrévocabilité des ventes des biens nationaux; de ne lever aucun impôt, de n'établir aucune taxe qu'en vertu de la loi; de maintenir l'institution de la Légion d'honneur; de gouverner dans la seule vue de l'intérêt, du bonheur et de la gloire du peuple français." (Title VII, Art. 53).

[17] As the British monarch—currently Queen Elizabeth II—is also the sovereign of Canada, Australia, New Zealand, Jamaica, Barbados, the Bahamas, Grenada, Papua New Guinea, the Solomon Islands, Tuvalu, Saint Lucia, Saint Vincent and the Grenadines, Belize, Antigua and Barbuda as well as Saint Kitts and Nevis, and holds each crown separately but equally shared in a monarchy, this applies, of course, also to all these countries.

[18] Cf. Section 3 of chapter I of the Thai Constitution of 26 April 2007: "Sovereign power belongs to the Thai people. The King as head of the state shall exercise such power through the National Legislative Assembly, Council of Ministers, courts, other constitutional organizations and state agencies in accordance with the rule of law."

[19] For a detailed analysis of how Thailand's King Bhumibol was able to enhance his power incrementally during his long reign, cf. Handley (2006).

supreme chief of the nation, and its highest representative, so that he may constantly keep watch to maintain the independence balance, and harmony of the other political powers" (Schwarcz 2004: 25–27). Thanks to this fourth power, and the fact that, according to article 99 of the Constitution, "The person of the emperor is inviolate and sacred. He is not subject to any kind of responsibility", the Brazilian Emperor's[20] position was, in fact, the most powerful in his huge Empire. This was because his position was further enhanced by the fact that according to article 101 of the Brazilian constitution he "could nominate senators, call an Extraordinary General Assembly, sanction its decrees and resolutions, temporarily suspend resolutions of the provincial councils, prorogue or delay general assemblies, dissolve the Chamber of Deputies, freely name ministers of state, suspend magistrates, and give amnesties in urgent cases" (Schwarcz 2004: 27).

Even more autocratic were the constitutions of Prussia[21] and—after the reunification of the German states under Prussian leadership—of the German Empire of 1871–1918, whose constitution[22] itself directly influenced (Marquardt 2009: 483; Hall 1997: 289–293) the Japanese one of 1889 (Bix 2001: 7f.) which in turn would have a great impact on China's later constitutional reforms, especially on the *Outlines of the Constitution by Imperial Order* (*Qinding Xianfa Dagang* 欽定憲法大綱) of 27 August 1908.[23]

3 Excursus: Japan and the Elaboration of its 1889 Constitution

Because the Constitution of the Japanese Empire of 11 February 1889 was not only to exert great influence on many Chinese officials and scholars who would try to introduce a constitutional monarchy in China, but was in itself an illustration of how a Far Eastern Empire answered the new challenges of the imperial powers of the West, it is therefore worth briefly relating its genesis.

Not unlike China under the Qing 清 Dynasty, Japan under the Tokugawa 德川氏 Shogunate (1603–1867) was a culturally very advanced society with a successful economy (Jacques 2009: 24f.) that was rather isolated from foreign influence. However, and again like China, in the first half of the nineteenth century Japan

---

[20] According to article 100 of the constitution of the Brazilian Empire his title was "Constitutional Emperor and Perpetual Defender of Brazil". Cf. Schwarcz (2004: 27).

[21] The Constitution of the Prussian State was proclaimed on 5 December 1848 and revised on 31 January 1850 and remained in force thereafter until the collapse of the German Empire in 1918. The main focus of the Constitution's revision in 1850 was to divide the population into three tax-classes. As each tax-class chose one third of the electors, this meant in fact a massive increase in power and influence for the wealthy classes, thus pushing back the democratic element. Cf. article 71 of the revised Prussian Constitution.

[22] A reprint of the constitution of the German Empire of 16 April 1871 is to be found in Willoweit and Seif (2003: 589–609).

[23] Cf. Sect. 4.2.2.

had to face a rising number of social and economical problems, which were partly related to a sudden and drastic rise in the population since the eighteenth century (Hall 1997: 198–200). When in 1853 American steamers and sailors under the command of Commodore Matthew C. Perry entered the bay of Tokyo 東京, the Japanese were still far from having resolved these problems. However, this intrusion of unknown—but obviously very powerful—American ships so close to the seat of the Shogun's government in Edo 江戸 (present-day Tokyo) was to prove a catalyst for Japanese reforms. An additional important factor in speeding up the pace of reforms in Japan was the fact that the Japanese were very well aware of the defeat China had sustained against the British invaders during the First Opium War in 1839–1942 (Hall 1997: 245; Jacques 2009: 53). In fact, it is likely that the Japanese would have had to face a real challenge[24] by the Western colonial powers much earlier than 1853 if the British had not chosen to focus on the "opening up" of the Chinese market for the opium trade and then gone to war against China (Hall 1997: 244).

With Japan having first to sign several unequal treaties in 1858 opening up the country to foreign powers,[25] and, in 1859, lifting the ban on Christianity imposed some 300 years earlier (Jacques 2009: 52), the pressure on the Shogunate's regime grew in the years immediately following, culminating in the overthrow of the Shogunate in 1868 and the restoration to power of the Emperor (Hall 1997: 247–266; Jacques 2009: 52). The restoration of the Meiji Emperor 明治天皇 was accompanied by a thorough-going modernisation (or rather: Westernisation) of many aspects of Japanese life and society—among them the reorganisation of the state and the enacting of new laws.[26] The promulgation of the Constitution of the Japanese Empire 大日本帝國憲法 of 11 February 1889 is closely tied to Ito Hirobumi 伊藤博文 (1841–1909)—a leading Japanese politician who served four times as prime minister of Japan. Ito—who had already been abroad in 1868 (Hall 1997: 263) and was also a member of the Japanese Iwakura 岩倉 mission despatched to the United States of America and Europe in 1872/3 (Hall 1997: 280)—came to the conclusion that Japan needed to modernise its form of government and announced in 1881 that, within 10 years' time, the Japanese government would put into practice a modern constitution. Not surprisingly, in reorganising their government the Japanese wanted to emulate the countries they perceived as the strongest in the world and thus hesitated between the British model of a liberal,

---

[24] In fact, before the arrival of Commodore Perry's fleet, there had been several encounters with Western powers, especially with Russia, but also with the United Kingdom and the United States of America. However, until 1853, the Japanese managed to keep every foreign power at a distance. Cf. Hall (1997: 242–244)

[25] I.e. to the United States of America, England, France, Russia and the Netherlands; cf. Choi (2011: 97–108).

[26] For more information about the Western influence on Japanese laws, cf. Choi (2011: 97–108).

China and Constitutional Monarchy: Four Short Encounters Around 1900   113

parliamentarian democracy and the more authoritarian Prussian monarchy.[27] Finally, they decided to form a constitution based on the more authoritarian Prussian model (Marquardt 2009: 483) where the monarch held much more power than in Britain. With the assistance of a judge from Berlin, Albert Mosse (1846–1925) (Hall 1997: 280), the Japanese government finally proclaimed its new constitution on 11 February 1889 and put it in force on 29 November 1890.

4 China's Experiments with Constitutional Monarchy

4.1 Constitutional-Like Elements in Imperial China

Whilst in Europe, from the time of Montesquieu at the latest, prejudices dominated the perception of the traditional Chinese government in the sense that imperial China was considered a succession of despotic regimes,[28] the reality was, in fact, much more complicated. Even though the different ruling dynasties in China lacked a written constitution in the modern sense until the very end of the Qing 清 Dynasty, the power of the Emperors was regularly restrained, contrary to what was thought prejudicially in the West. First of all, in accordance with Confucian teachings, it was expected of the rulers that they rule for the benefit of the people.[29] If they did not, especially if they oppressed the people and were lacking in morals, then they could lose the "Mandate of Heaven" (*tianming*天命) and could be deposed, thus paving the way for a new dynasty under a ruler who cared for the people and adhered to the moral principles as they can be found in the so-called "Confucian Classics" (*Sishu Wujing* 四書五經). Apart from these classics, the Emperors could

---

[27] France having been defeated by the Prussians in the Franco-Prussian War of 1870 and the United States of America being somewhat weakened because of the devastations of the War of Secession (1861–1865) might explain to some extent why these two countries did not serve as possible models for the reorganisation of the Japanese form of government.

[28] Cf. Montesquieu [1748]: book VIII, chapter XXI, 260f.: "La Chine est donc un État despotique, dont le principe est la crainte. Peut-être que dans les premières dynasties, l'empire n'étant pas si étendu, le gouvernement déclinait un peu de cet esprit. Mais aujourd'hui, cela n'est pas." Such prejudices against Asian countries and their culture are typical examples of what has been dubbed "Orientalism" since Edward W. Said's book of the same name. Cf. Said (2003) and Sardar (2002).

[29] The idea that China's rulers ought to reign for the benefit of their people is also called "*minben* 民本"-thought. Cf. Müller (1997: 43–48). The origin of the term "*minben*" (which could also be translated as "the people are the fundaments [of society]") derives from ideas and ideals of Mencius 孟子 (the second most influential Confucian philosopher after Confucius himself), a typical expression of his on this subject being the following: "Mencius said, 'The people are of supreme importance; the altars of the gods of earth and grain come next; last comes the ruler. That is why he who gains the confidence of the multitudinous people will be Emperor. [...]'" cf. Meng Zi 孟子 1979, Mencius, vol. II, book 7, part B, section 14, 290f. (original Chinese text: 孟子曰: 《民爲貴,社稷次之, 君爲輕。是故得乎丘民而爲天子。……》)

find more detailed norms for behaviour expected and information on the principles of government in the "Institutions of the Forebears". They consisted generally of edicts which had usually been issued by Emperors founding a new dynasty and contained key data about the structure and functioning of the state; furthermore, they also included the "Collected Institutions" (*huidian* 會典), which contained detailed data about the institutions of the state as well as a collection of precedents.[30] Owing to their content, these "Institutions of the Forebears" appear somewhat similar to constitutional texts like the ones restraining the power of the British monarchs.

Yet it should be remembered that in China the Emperors retained much more power than was left to the British monarchs after the latter had seen their power curtailed in the second half of the seventeenth century. Also, because of the critical stance of Confucianism towards law in general and formal written law in particular—for Confucians, the fact that a court had to be involved in the resolution of a dispute was tantamount to a failure of the morals of society[31]—written laws in Imperial China never enjoyed the same prestige and authority as in the Western countries. In Confucian[32] China, the aim[33] was that everybody would be able to achieve moral perfection so that there would be peace and harmony within society, meaning that there would be no disputes any more. The achievement of these lofty moral ideals concerned above all the person of the Emperor himself of whom it was expected that he should be an example of good and benevolent behaviour towards the whole people. This explains the creation of an interesting institution in Imperial China: the Censorate. Although the roots of the censorial system can be traced back to the Zhou 周 Dynasty (1122–249 B.C.), it was only during the first imperial

---

[30] During the last Imperial dynasty in China, the Qing 清, the edicts of the (founding) Emperors were called "*shengxun* 聲訊" ("Sage Commands") whereas the "Collected Institutions" were called "Collected Institutions of the Qing Dynasty" (Chinese: *Da Qing huidian* 大清會典). According to Simon (2007: footnote 72 on p. 39), when the "Collected Institutions of the Qing Dynasty" were revised the last time, in 1904, they comprised 100 books containing regulations and describing the imperial institutions of the state as well as 1220 volumes full of precedents.

[31] A good example of this attitude can be seen in the following expression of Confucius 孔子: "*The Master said: 'Listening to the divergent positions of litigating parties is something I can do as well as anybody else. But what one should really achieve is to let no disputes arise.'*" (original Chinese version: 子曰:≪聽訟, 吾猶人也。必也是無訟乎!≫), for a German translation, cf. Kong Zi 孔子 (1998, chapter XII, part 13, 75).

[32] Although there were many other important philosophies in traditional China, e.g. Legism (*Fa Jia* 法家), Daoism (*Dao Jia* 道家), Mohism (*Mo Jia* 墨家) and Buddhism (*Fo Jiao* 佛教), starting with the Han 漢 Dynasty, Confucianism (*Ru Jia* 儒家) was the dominant philosophy throughout the greater part of the history of Imperial China. However, as far as law is concerned, the Confucian lawmakers of the Han Dynasty as well as those of succeeding dynasties were heavily inspired by Legism. Cf. Heuser (2002: 93f). For more information concerning these traditional Chinese philosophies (apart from Buddhism which originated in present-day India and Nepal), cf. Mühlemann (2006: 25–59).

[33] The Confucian philosophers were realistic enough to know that the fulfilment of this aim was very hard to achieve if not outright utopian.

China and Constitutional Monarchy: Four Short Encounters Around 1900

dynasty in China, the Qin 秦 Dynasty (221–206 B.C.), that this institution evolved into a state organ for the control of the imperial administration.[34] Since the times of the Song 宋 Dynasty (960–1279 A.D.), the censors were also empowered to criticise personal shortcomings as well as mistakes made by the Emperor in the administration of the country (Lui 呂 1978: 4). In their criticisms, the censors based themselves on the traditional Confucian morals as well as on the "Institutions of the Forebears",[35] thus exercising a kind of constitutional control. However, such criticisms always remained a risky undertaking, for in many cases where criticised Emperors felt offended, the censors were severely punished, sometimes even put to death. Therefore, the success or failure of this kind of constitutional control was directly linked to the personality of the Emperor himself, especially to his willingness to accept criticism and his readiness to implement the suggestions of the censors. In consequence, it can be said that the position of the Emperor, though not unlimited in scope—there were many written and unwritten (moral) rules he had to adhere to—remained much stronger than what can usually be expected in a system of constitutional monarchy (Mühlemann 2008: 357).

4.2 Chinese Attempts to Introduce a Constitutional Monarchy

4.2.1 The 1898 Reform Movement and its Aftermath

Whilst, as early as in the mid-nineteenth century, some thinkers such as Wei Yuan 魏源 and Feng Guifen 馮桂芬 were in favour of strengthening the monarchy by enhancing its legitimacy through letting more people (especially from among the literate classes) participate in the affairs of the country (Klein 2007: 94), it was not until China's defeat in the Sino-Japanese War of 1894/95 that calls for installing a constitutional monarchy in China gained momentum. The main proponents of this new form of government were the famous philosophers Kang Youwei 康有爲[36] (1858–1927) and his disciple Liang Qichao 梁啟超 (1873–1929). Both were to have an important influence on the reform movement of 1898.

---

[34] Cf. Lui 呂 (1978, 1f.)—for more information on the Censorate in Imperial China, see also Hucker (1966).

[35] For an example of actions by the Censorate based on the "Institutions of the Forebears"—in this case those of the Ming 明 Dynasty (*Da Ming huidian* 大明會典)—cf. Will (2007: 148–154).

[36] Whilst Kang Youwei 康有爲 is well known for his stance in favour of constitutional monarchy, it is interesting to see that according to his utopian vision of the world as described in his posthumously published "Book on the Great Unity" (*Da Tong Shu* 大同書), his real aim was a worldwide democratic republican system, somewhat similar to the federal government systems of the United States or Switzerland. Cf. Kang 康 (2002: 105) (Chinese text) or Kang 康 (1974: 83f.) (German translation). Once this stage had been achieved, there would be no place for ruling monarchies, cf. Kang 康 (2002: 106) (Chinese text) or Kang 康 (1974: 85f.) (German translation).

Kang—a prominent scholar and philosopher who remained a loyal adept of the Qing Dynasty all his life—was deeply worried about the weakness of China in comparison to foreign powers and tried to get the attention of the imperial government by writing petitions with suggestions on how to strengthen China by carrying out modernisations, the first being written in 1888 and the second—co-signed by 603 candidates of the highest imperial examinations—in 1895. In his second petition he implored the Emperor to promulgate an edict which would contain many profound reforms, such as a relocation of the capital city, reforms in the army, and reforms in the Imperial government.[37] As far as government reforms were concerned, Kang advised the Emperor to involve the population when having to make crucial decisions, as was apparently done in the past.[38] Kang saw his dream of being listened to by the Emperor fulfilled in 1898, when during the so-called "Reforms of the 100 days", the Guangxu 光緒 Emperor—who had received Kang Youwei in a 5-h audience on 16 June 1898—issued some 40-odd edicts containing reforms of the administration, commerce and trade, the industrial as well as the legal sector (Hsü 2000: 375). However, when the Emperor reshuffled important administrative offices such as the posts of governor, and started to reorganise the educational sector, he aroused the ire of conservative elites which ultimately resulted in the coup of 21 September 1898 that saw the Emperor put under house arrest and power handed back to the Empress Dowager Ci Xi 慈禧太后, thus putting an end to these accelerated reforms after exactly 103 days. In the days following the coup, six leading proponents[39] of these reforms were beheaded while Kang Youwei and his disciple Liang Qichao only just managed to escape abroad. Because both were sentenced to death in absentia and therefore had to stay in exile, they lost all possibility of influencing the affairs of the Dynasty until its collapse in 1912. This dramatic turn of events also meant that any attempt the Guangxu Emperor might have envisioned in installing a constitutional monarchy along the

---

[37] Cf. Kang 康 (1996: 194): 伏乞皇上下詔鼓天下之氣, 遷都定天下之本, 練兵強天下之勢, 變法成天下之治而已。(We implore His Imperial Majesty to proclaim an edict that would mobilise the energies of the Empire, that would move the capital in order to stabilise the foundations of the Empire, that would train the army in order to strengthen the power of the Empire, and, finally, that would complete the reforms of the government of the Empire.)

[38] Cf. e.g. Kang (1996: 171): 夫先王之治天下, 與民共之, ≪洪範≫ 之大疑大事, 謀及庶人愛大同。≪孟子≫ 稱進賢、 殺人 待於國人之皆可。(When the ancient Kings governed the Empire, they did it together with the people. "The Great Rule" said that in case of doubts or important events, the population had to be consulted because the multitudes loved the "Big Unity". According to "Mencius", the ruler waited upon knowing the opinion of the population before appointing high officials or pronouncing death sentences.) While Kang 康 did often refer to ancient Confucian sources in order to legitimate reforms, he sometimes went as far as manipulating these texts. In one example he exchanged one character for another that was invented entirely by himself, thus trying to "legitimate" more freedom for women. cf. Senger (2000: 366f.)

[39] Among those executed were Kang Youwei's 康有爲 own brother, Kang Guangren 康廣仁, and the famous thinker Tan Sitong 譚嗣同.

lines of Kang's suggestions was deferred indefinitely.[40] However, this setback did not change Kang's pro-monarchy stance in the slightest: having been deeply impressed (Spence 1992: 29) by the young Emperor's willingness to reform the country, Kang founded the "Protect the Emperor Society" (Chinese: *Bao Huang Hui* 保皇會) in Canada in 1899. Its aim was for power to be handed back to the Guangxu Emperor so that the reform process could ultimately be resumed and the monarchy saved by being converted into a constitutional form. Even after the collapse of the Qing Dynasty in 1912, Kang remained loyal to this dynasty and continued to act in favour of the restoration of the monarchy in China. When on 1 July 1917, the so-called "Pig-tailed General",[41] Zhang Xun 張勳, restored to power the last Emperor of the Qing Dynasty, Aisin-Gioro Puyi 愛新覺羅溥儀, Kang was at first enthusiastic about this new development and expected a constitutional monarchy to be at last installed in China (Spence 1992, 115). However, when on 12 July Zhang Xun was driven out of Beijing 北京 by warlord Duan Qirui 段祺瑞 and the Emperor was dethroned again, nothing came of it.[42]

Whereas Kang Youwei outwardly remained a staunch monarchist till the end of his life in 1927, his former disciple Liang Qichao was to change his stance on the monarchy several times. In the beginning—under the influence of Kang—he was in favour of constitutional monarchy, but after the coup of 1898 he read many Japanese translations of Western political literature and became a supporter of Republicanism. However, after being deeply disappointed by the Republican form of government during a trip to the United States of America in 1903, he moved once more to being in favour of a constitutional monarchy (Nathan 1986: 59–63). When in 1906 the Qing government under Empress Dowager Ci Xi began its preparations for setting up a constitutional government, Liang 梁 approved these steps in articles he published in exile. Even so, after the collapse of the Qing Dynasty, he changed his mind on this issue yet again and finally remained a fierce adherent of Republicanism until his death in 1929, thereby also falling out with his former mentor, Kang Youwei (Mühlemann 2006: 151f.).

4.2.2   The Qing Government's Reforms (1901–1912)

If the conservative faction in the Qing 清 government managed to suppress the reformist ambitions of the Guangxu 光緒 Emperor in the coup of 1898, doing this did not mean resolving any of the huge problems China was facing. On the contrary, poor judgement on the part of the conservative faction ultimately led to the invasion

---

[40] According to Klein (2007: 95), without the coup of the conservatives, the Reform movement of 1898 would have "without any doubt" resulted in a constitutional monarchy in China.

[41] This nickname was due to the fact that unlike most people in the Republic of China, General Zhang Xun 張勳 (as well as his troops) kept their hair plaited in a pigtail, a sign of allegiance to the defunct Qing 清 Dynasty.

[42] Cf. Sect. 4.2.4.

of Beijing by the "Eight Allied Armies" in 1900 in the wake of the Boxer Rebellion. Once more, China sustained heavy damage and had to pay a huge war indemnity.

When, in the war of 1904/5, autocratic Czarist Russia was defeated by the constitutional monarchy of Japan, many members of the political elite in China[43] became convinced that a constitutional monarchy was superior to an autocratic monarchy, seeing in its broader legitimacy in the population a means to strengthen the state.[44] For this reason, in 1905/6 the Qing government sent two missions abroad in order to study foreign government structures.[45] The first, led by prince Zaize 載澤, went to Japan, the United States, England, France and Belgium. The second mission, led by the officials Dai Hongci 戴鴻慈 and Duanfang 端方, visited Japan, the United States and 12 European countries (Austria, Belgium, Denmark, France, Germany, the Netherlands, Hungary, Italy, Norway, Russia, Sweden and Switzerland) (Meienberger 1980: 29). As soon as both delegations returned to China in the middle of 1906, they were received in audience by the court. Following this Dai Hongci and Duanfang wrote a *Report about the Essentials of Political Administration in Europe and America* (*Ou-Mei Zhengzhi Yao Yi* 歐美政治要義), in which—among others—the following aspects of a constitutional monarchy were described: the statutes of the Imperial house, the drawing up of a constitution, the division between the Imperial court and the government, the power of monarchs in constitutional systems, the highest advisors of the ruler, the government and the responsibility of the cabinet, the introduction of a national assembly, laws and regulations, the division of the executive and the judiciary, and the relationship between central and local governments (Meienberger 1980: 33f.). In their report, Dai Hongci and Duanfang came to the conclusion that constitutional government would indeed provide many advantages.[46]

---

[43] Obviously, the Russian people seemed to come to a similar conclusion: in Russia, the sinking of the Czar's Baltic fleet and the defeat of his land forces in the Russo-Japanese War of 1904/5 led to the Russian Revolution of 1905 with its calls for more participation from the people. Under such heavy pressure, Czar Nicholas (Николай) II agreed to the establishment of a parliament (the Duma Дýма) and to the first Russian constitution of 23 April 1906.

[44] Cf. Hsü (2000: 412). In this context, the famous scholar and politician Zhang Jian 張謇 exclaimed "triumphantly": "The victory of Japan and the defeat of Russia are the victory of constitutionalism and the defeat of monarchism" (Hsü 2000: ibid.).

[45] As a matter of fact, in the decades preceding there had already been several important Chinese missions abroad, tasked with studying the society and culture of advanced (mostly Western) nations. Here one should especially mention the missions of Zhang Deyi 張德彝 (1847–1919) to America and Europe (particularly France) in the years 1866–1871 as well as the diplomatic tour of Li Hongzhang 李鴻章 (1823–1901)—one of China's most influential statesmen at the end of the Qing 清 Dynasty—to Russia, Germany, the Netherlands, Belgium, France, the United States and Canada. Undertaken just after China's defeat in the Sino-Japanese War of 1894/95, the principal aim of Li's 李 mission consisted in forging alliances—especially with Russia—in order to counter Japan's growing influence in East Asia.

[46] For more details, cf. Mühlemann (2006: 155).

China and Constitutional Monarchy: Four Short Encounters Around 1900 119

On the basis of this report, Empress Dowager Ci Xi finally decreed the introduction of a constitutional monarchy in an edict of 1 September 1906.[47]

After having taken this decision, the Qing government had to decide which country's constitution should serve as a model for the planned Chinese constitution. Although it seems that "the decision to pattern China's constitutional government after that of Japan was made before 1907",[48] the influence of those opposed to this solution was obviously still strong enough that on 9 September 1907 three more delegations were sent abroad in order to investigate, once again, the constitutional form of government of the three monarchies that were of the greatest interest at the Qing court: Wang Daxie 汪大燮, a vice-president of the Ministry of Foreign Affairs, was sent to the United Kingdom; Yu Shimei 于式枚, a vice-president of the Ministry of Post and Communications, was sent to Germany; and Da Shou 達壽, a vice-president of the Ministry of Education, was sent to Japan (Meienberger 1980: 57).

Since the Japanese constitution of 1889 was issued by the Emperor without having to be approved by parliament and thereby invested him with a lot of power, leading officials in the Qing court pronounced themselves in favour of this autocratic Japanese model.[49] It is, therefore, not surprising that the content of the first two articles of the *Outlines of the Constitution by Imperial Order* (*Qinding Xianfa Dagang* 欽定憲法大綱) of 27 August 1908 was more or less the same as in the Japanese constitution of 1889:

1. The Emperor of the Great Qing [Dynasty] will rule supreme over the Great Qing Empire for 10,000 generations in succession and be honoured forever.[50]
2. The sacred Majesty of the Sovereign must be earnestly revered and must not be offended.[51]

Subsequent articles gave an outline of the vast powers of the Chinese monarchs and of the—rather limited—rights and duties of the "people", making it probably the most autocratic (Hsü 2000: 416) form of a "constitutional" monarchy known to this day.[52] On the same day in 1908 a "9 Year Programme of Constitutional

---

[47] This edict is translated into English in Meienberger (1980: 42–44).

[48] Cf. Meienberger (1980: footnote 8 on 58).

[49] Cf. Meienberger (1980: footnote 8 on p. 58) and Klein (2007: 95). Because the Chinese decided on a written constitution, they ruled out the British model.

[50] Original Chinese text: 一、大清皇帝統治大清國,萬世一係,永永尊載。Article 1 of Chapter I of the Japanese constitution of 11 February 1889 states the following: "The Japanese State will be ruled forever by an uninterrupted succession of Emperors."

[51] Original Chinese text: 二、君上神聖尊嚴,不可侵犯。This compares with article 3 of Chapter I of the Japanese Constitution of 11 February 1889: "The person of the Emperor is holy and inviolable".

[52] A full translation of these "Outlines" is to be found in Meienberger (1980: 91–93). The autocratic nature of the planned constitutional monarchy can be seen especially in article 1 of the "Outlines of the Parliamentary Law" which was also approved on 27 August 1908: "The parliament has only deliberative powers. It has no executive power. Measures which have been

Preparation" was approved by the court. This was an outline on how to introduce a constitutional form of government into China within a 9 year[53] period which would have meant that by 1917 the transformation of the Qing monarchy would have been accomplished. Among the planned measures was the convening of a national assembly in 1910, in which half of the delegates would be nominated by the throne while the other half would be chosen from provincial assemblies (*ziyiju* 資議局).[54] Afterwards, it was expected that the national assembly as well as the provincial assemblies would conduct further reforms, especially in the fields of decentralisation and local autonomy. However, with the abdication of the Regent (Empress Dowager Longyu 隆裕太后) in the name of the last Emperor of China on 12 February 1912, this experiment was abruptly ended.

It is nevertheless more than doubtful whether these reforms would have proved enough to ensure the survival of a dynasty that found itself under increasing criticism by a rapidly growing number of the population. After all, as it has already been shown in the first two articles of the *Outlines of the Constitution*, the court was not ready to relinquish much power. Also, according to the second of the *Guidelines for the Electoral Law*—which were also published on 27 August 1908—, many people such as illiterates, criminals, opium addicts and people with "bad behaviour", were excluded from the elections of the National Assembly, the consequence being that during the first elections of deputies to the national assembly, which were held in 1909, only 1.7 million people (or 0.4% of the whole population) could take part. Of these 1.7 million, only one million did actually participate in the elections (Fincher 1981: 111f.). Never before in China had so many people been able to participate in the political process. But even if all of them made use of this opportunity, the monarchy would still have been faced with so many problems that this could have spelt its end.

4.2.3 Yuan Shikai's Attempt to Reinstate a Monarchy in 1915/16

Perhaps the most notable attempt to introduce a constitutional monarchy—at least outwardly—was the one by Marshal Yuan Shikai 袁世凱 at the end of 1915. Even though, when appointed president of the Republic of China in March 1912, Yuan did swear that "never shall we allow the monarchical system to reappear in China",[55] it is probable that from the start Yuan envisioned a restoration of the

---

decided upon by parliament shall not be carried out by the Government until after the imperial sanction has been obtained." Cf. Meienberger (1980: 93).

[53] The reason why a 9 year period was chosen for the planned implementation of a constitutional form of government in China is probably to be explained by the fact that in Japan the Constitution came into force [on 29 November 1890] exactly nine years after the announcement made by the government in 1881 to establish a Constitution "within the next 10 years"; cf. Meienberger (1980: 82) and Sect. 6.3.

[54] These had already been established in the years 1907 and 1908.

[55] Hsü (2000: 474). This pledge was repeated by Yuan 袁 in 1913, cf. Ch'en (1961: 201).

China and Constitutional Monarchy: Four Short Encounters Around 1900   121

Empire with himself as emperor. This would explain to some extent the more than favourable conditions Yuan accorded to the abdicated Emperor in the "Articles of Favourable Treatment of the Emperor of the Great Qing after his Abdication" (*Qing Di tuiwei youdai tiaojian* 清帝退位優待條件),[56] as well as the fact that the highest order of the early Republic of China, the "Grand Order" (*Da Xunzhang* 大勳章), was, in design and rank, identical to the highest order at the end of the Empire, the "Great Order of the Throne" (*Da Bao Zhang* 大寶章).[57] However, in the summer of 1915 Yuan began to contact foreign governments in order to ascertain whether they would be supportive of the restoration of monarchy in China. Furthermore, he asked an American scholar, Professor Johnson Goodnow, a former president of Johns Hopkins University, to write an expert report on the form of government that best suited China. Not unexpectedly, Goodnow came to the conclusion that monarchy suited China best (Young 1977: 221; Aisin-Gioro Puyi 愛新覺羅溥儀 1987: 109f.). In accordance with this "suggestion", Yuan acted swiftly to proclaim himself Emperor of an "Empire of China" (*Zhonghua Diguo* 中華帝國).

In November and December 1915, he managed to be elected as constitutional monarch in two rounds of votes by 1993 members of a "National Congress of Representatives". On 1 January 1916, the new era's name "*Hongxian* 洪憲"— which means "Great Constitution"—was used in official documents, thus clearly demonstrating that the new Empire of China was meant to be a constitutional monarchy. However, as soon as Yuan had got himself proclaimed Emperor, most of the regional military rulers—among them Qing loyalist Zhang Xun 張勳— opposed Yuan's move, so that on 22 March 1916 he had to rescind his monarchical plans. This meant also that there was not enough time for a constitution for Yuan's "Empire of China" to be laid out. But despite all the claims of constitutionality, it remains highly doubtful whether Yuan in reality intended to rule merely as a constitutional Emperor, for his presidency in the years 1912–1915 was characterised by an increased muzzling of parliament as well as of the press (Mühlemann 2009: 229) and the disbanding of opposition parties.

4.2.4   Zhang Xun's Brief Restoration of Monarchy in July 1917

The last[58] attempt to restore the monarchy in China occurred in July 1917, when General Zhang Xun 張勳 handed power back to the last Emperor of the Qing Dynasty, Aisin-Gioro Puyi 愛新覺羅溥儀. As this attempt lasted only 12 days,

---

[56] The full text of these Articles is rendered in its Chinese original and in an English translation in Mühlemann (2006: 359–361).

[57] Cf. Tammann (1999) and Kua (1998).

[58] Because the establishment in 1934 of the Empire of Manzhouguo 滿州國 with the last Emperor of China, Aisin-Gioro Puyi 愛新覺羅溥儀, as ruler, by the Japanese militarists was not designed by them as a resuscitation of the old Qing 清 Empire, but merely as a tool for carving up China by creating several states in its former area, this monarchy will not be further discussed in this paper.

there was, of course, no way to introduce any kind of constitutional monarchy, even if this had really been the aim of General Zhang Xun and the Qing court of 1917. However, according to the little information available about this brief episode of Chinese history, it remains highly doubtful that Zhang Xun would have been ready to limit the power of the restored Emperor and bind him to a constitutional act (Spence 1992: 115; Aisin-Gioro Puyi 愛新覺羅溥儀 1987: 112–129).

5 Conclusion

At the turn of the twentieth century, there were four separate attempts to introduce some form of constitutional monarchy in China. As all of them were interrupted before they could be fully implemented, it is not possible to say whether they would have been successful in the sense that they would have brought lasting political stability to China and thus ensured the survival of the Qing 清 Dynasty, or, in the case of Yuan Shikai 袁世凱, of Yuan's 袁 own dynasty. In consideration of the fact that (perhaps with the exception of the 1898 reforms) all these attempts would have concentrated most of the power in the hands of the rulers, whether they could have ensured the political survival of the monarchy, even if these experiments could have been completed, remains doubtful at best. Also, with the exception of some constitutional-like elements, such as the "Institutions of the Forebears" or the Censorate (cf. Sect. 4.1), the concept of constitutional monarchy is not rooted within Chinese culture. Neither Confucianism, nor Legism, Mohism, or Daoism support the idea that the power of the rulers should be circumscribed and tied to a formal, written constitution. As far as the future is concerned, after almost a century without a monarch, the prospects remain dim that one day monarchy will be restored in China with a constitutional Emperor as ruler. Although a potential "pretender to the throne" still exists in the person of Aisin-Gioro Hengzhen 愛新覺羅恆鎮[59] and despite the fact that a rather obscure pro-monarchy group[60] has even been created recently, a restoration of monarchy in China remains highly unlikely.

---

[59] In his research into the question of a possible pretender to China's Dragon Throne, Tony Scotland found that Aisin-Gioro Yuyan 愛新覺羅毓嵒 would have been most entitled to this position. Cf. Scotland (1994: 180). However, as Yuyan 毓嵒 passed away in 1997, this position would now belong to his son, Aisin-Gioro Hengzhen 愛新覺羅恆鎮.

[60] Cf. the "official website" of the Qing Restoration Organization: http://sites.google.com/site/monarchyrevival/.

Bibliography

Aisin-Gioro Puyi 愛新覺羅溥儀. 1987. *Der letzte Kaiser von China. Eine Autobiographie* (3rd ed.). Vol. I. Beijing: Verlag für Fremdsprachige Literatur.

Barman, Roderick J. 1999. Citizen Emperor. Pedro II and the Making of Brazil, 1825–91. Stanford: Stanford University Press.

Bix, Herbert P. 2001. *Hirohito and the Making of Modern Japan*. New York: Perennial.

Cerutti, Herbert. 1996. "Technische Glanzleistungen im alten China. Sorgfältige Experimente statt grauer Theorie". In *China – Wo das Pulver erfunden wurde. Naturwissenschaft, Medizin und Technik in China*, ed. Herbert Cerutti, 2. A., 9–22. Zürich: Verlag NZZ.

Ch'en, Jerome. 1961. *Yuan Shih-K'ai 1859–1916. Brutus Assumes the Purple*. London: George Allen & Unwin.

Choi, Chongko. "East Asian Encounters with Western Law and the Emergence of East Asian Jurisprudence". In *Interpretation of Law in China – Roots and Perspectives*, ed. Michal Tomášek and Guido Mühlemann, Prague: Charles University in Prague, Karolinum Press, 2011, 97–108.

Fincher, John H. 1981. *Chinese Democracy. The Self-Government Movement in Local, Provincial and National Politics, 1905–1914*. London/Canberra: Croom Helm (London)/Australian University Press (Canberra).

Flessel, K. 1988. "Geschichte". In *Das Alte China. Geschichte und Kultur des Reiches der Mitte*, ed. Roger Goepper,. Munich: C. Bertelsmann Verlag, 47–111.

Gernet, Jacques. 1989. *Die chinesische Welt* (6th ed.). Frankfurt a.M.: Insel Verlag.

Hall, John W. 1997. *Das Japanische Kaiserreich*. [1st ed. 1966], (Fischer Weltgeschichte Vol. 20) Frankfurt a. M.: Fischer Bücherei.

Haller, Walter, Alfred Kölz and Thomas Gächter. 2008. *Allgemeines Staatsrecht*. (4th ed.). Basel/Genf/München: Helbing & Lichtenhahn.

Handley, Paul M. 2006. *The King Never Smiles. A Biography of Thailand's Bhumibol Adulyadej*. New Haven/London: Yale University Press.

Heuser, Robert. 2002. *Einführung in die Chinesische Rechtskultur* (2nd ed.). Hamburg: Mitteilungen des Institutes für Asienkunde (Vol. 315).

Hibbert, Christopher. 1989. *Die Kaiser von China*. (Part of the series: Schatzkammern und Herrscherhäuser der Welt) Herrsching: Manfred Pawlak Verlag.

Ho Ping-ti 何炳棣 (in Pinyin: He Bingdi). 1962. *The Ladder of Success in Imperial China. Aspects of Social Mobility, 1368–1911*. New York/London: Columbia University Press.

Hsü, Immanuel. 2000. *The Rise of Modern China* (6th ed.). New York/Oxford: Oxford University Press.

Hucker, Charles O. 1966. *The Censorial System of Ming China*. Stanford: Stanford University Press.

Israel, Stephan. 2010. "In der Krise schlägt die Stunde des letzten Belgiers. Belgiens Schicksal liegt in der Hand von König Albert II. Nur er kann noch Brücken über die tiefen Gräben zwischen Flamen und Wallonen bauen". In: *Der Bund*, 28 April 2010, 5.

Jacques, Martin. 2009. *When China Rules the World. The Rise of the Middle Kingdom and the End of the Western World*. New York: Allen Lane.

Jörs, Paul, Wolfgang Kunkel and Leopold Wenger (in new edition by Honsell Heinrich, Theo Mayer-Maly & Walter Selb). 1987. *Römisches Recht* (4th ed.). Berlin/Heidelberg/New York et al.: Springer.

K'ang, Yu-wei (Kang Youwei 康有爲). 1974. *Ta T'ung Shu. Das Buch der Grossen Gemeinschaft*. Ed. Wolfgang Bauer, Düsseldorf/Cologne: Eugen Diederichs.

Kang Youwei 康有爲. 2002. *Da Tong Shu* 大同書. Beijing 北京: Huaxia Chubanshe 華夏出版社.

Kang Youwei 康有爲. 1996. *Manifeste à l'Empereur. Adressé par les Candidats au Doctorat* (上清帝第二書). Paris: Editions You-Feng.

Kienzl, Florian. 1942. *Kaiser von Brasilien. Herrschaft und Sturz Pedros I. und Pedros II*. Berlin: Propyläen.

Klein, Thorald. 2007. *Geschichte Chinas. Von 1800 bis zur Gegenwart.* Paderborn/München/Vienna/Zürich: Schöningh.

Kong Zi 孔子 (Confucius). 1998. *Gespräche (Lun-yu* 論語). Translated & edited by Ralf Moritz, Leipzig: Reclam Verlag.

Kong Zi 孔子 (Confucius). 2002. *Lunyu* 論語, Qufu 曲阜: Shandong Youyi Chubanshe山東友誼出版社.

Kua, Paul L.T. 1998. "Two Rare Orders of the Early Republic of China". *The Journal of the Orders and Medals Society of America (JOMSA)*, Vol. 49, No. 3 (May-June), 9–16.

Kuhn, Axel. 2003. *Die Französische Revolution.* Stuttgart: Reclam.

Lui, Adam Y.C. 呂元驄. 1978. *Chinese Censors and the Alien Emperor 1644–1660.* Hong Kong: Centre of Asian Studies, University of Hong Kong.

Marquardt, Bernd. 2009. *Universalgeschichte des Staates. Von der vorstaatlichen Gesellschaft zum Staat der Industriegesellschaft* (Der Europäische Sonderweg, 3), Vienna/Berlin: Lit-Verlag.

Meienberger, Norbert. 1980. *The Emergence of Constitutional Government in China (1905–1908). The Concept Sanctioned by the Empress Dowager Tz'u-Hsi.* Bern: Peter Lang Verlag.

Meng Zi 孟子 (Mencius). 1979. Mencius. Vol. II, trans. by D.C. Lau. Hong Kong: The Chinese University Press. [reprint of 1984].

Meredith, Martin. 2006. *The State of Africa. A History of Fifty Years of Independence.* London/New York/Sydney/Toronto: The Free Press.

Montesquieu, Charles-Louis Secondat, Baron de la Brède et de. 1979 [1748]. *De l'esprit des lois.*, Vol. I, Paris: Garnier-Flammarion.

Mühlemann, Guido. 2006. *Chinas Experimente mit westlichen Staatsideen. Eine rechtshistorische und zeitgeschichtliche Untersuchung zur chinesischen Rezeption europäischer Staatsideen.* Zürich/Basel/Genf: Schulthess.

Mühlemann, G. 2008. "Sind die Chinesen fähig zur Demokratie? Eine Darstellung von demokratischen Elementen im traditionellen China". In *Freiheit ohne Grenzen – Grenzen der Freiheit. Eine rechtshistorische und zeitgeschichtliche Untersuchung zur chinesischen Rezeption europäischer Staatsideen.* ed. Guido Mühlemann & Annja Mannhart. Zürich/St. Gallen: Dike, 337–370.

Mühlemann, G. 2009. "Printmedien und Zensur in China. Von den Anfängen in der Kaiserzeit bis zur Gegenwart". In *Brennpunkt Medienrecht. Das mediale Zeitalter als juristische Herausforderung*, ed. Julia Hänni & Daniela Kühne. Zürich/St. Gallen: Dike, 211–244.

Müller, Sven-Uwe. 1997. *Konzeptionen der Menschenrechte im China des 20. Jahrhunderts.* Hamburg: Mitteilungen des Instituts für Asienkunde (vol. 274).

Nathan, Andrew J. 1986. *Chinese Democracy.* London: I.B. Tauris .

Reichel, Friedrich. 1993. *Die Porzellansammlung Augusts des Starken. Porzellankunst aus China. Die Rosa Familie.* Dresden: Staatliche Kunstsammlung Dresden – Porzellansammlung.

Roegiers, Patrick. 2007. *La spectaculaire histoire des rois des Belges.* Paris: Perrin.

Said, Edward W. 2003 (25th anniversary edition) [1978]. *Orientalism.* New York: Vintage Books.

Sardar, Ziauddin. 2002. *Der fremde Orient. Geschichte eines Vorurteils.* Berlin: Wagenbach.

Schwarcz, Lilia Moritz. 2004. *The Emperor's Beard. Dom Pedro II and the Tropical Monarchy of Brazil.* New York: Hill and Wang.

Scotland, Tony. 1994. *The Empty Throne. The Quest for an Imperial Heir in the People's Republic of China.* London: Penguin Books.

Seitz, Konrad. 2000. *China. Eine Weltmacht kehrt zurück.* Berlin: Siedler Verlag.

Senger, Harro von. 2000. *Strategeme. Lebens- und Überlebenslisten aus drei Jahrtausenden.*, Vol. 2 (stratagems 19–36), Bern/Munich/Vienna: Scherz Verlag.

Simon, O. 2007. "Pandektensystematik oder Code Civil? Eine Abhandlung aus dem Jahre 1907" Über die zukünftige Kodifikation eines Zivilrechts in China" von Qin Lianyuan". *Zeitschrift für Chinesisches Recht (ZChinR)*, 1/2007, 27–46.

Spence, Jonathan D. 1992. *Das Tor des Himmlischen Friedens. Die Chinesen und ihre Revolution 1895–1980.* München: Deutscher Taschenbuch Verlag.

China and Constitutional Monarchy: Four Short Encounters Around 1900

Spence, Jonathan D. 2001. *Chinas Weg in die Moderne*. (2nd, actualised and expanded edition) München: Deutscher Taschenbuch Verlag.

Tammann, Gustav-Andrea. 1999. *The Five Last Imperial Orders of China and the First Orders of the Republic of China*. (unpublished manuscript; October 1999).

Will, P. 2007. "Le contrôle de l'excès du pouvoir sous la dynastie des Ming". In *La Chine et la démocratie*, ed. Mireille Delmas-Marty & Pierre-Étienne Will. Paris: Fayard, 111–156.

Willoweit, Dietmar. 2005. *Deutsche Verfassungsgeschichte. Vom Frankenreich bis zur Wiedervereinigung Deutschlands* (5th ed.). Munich: C.H. Beck.

Willoweit, Dietmar and Ulrike Seif. 2003. *Europäische Verfassungsgeschichte*. Munich: C.H. Beck.

Young, Ernest P. 1977. *The Presidency of Yuan Shih-k'ai*. Ann Arbor: University of Michigan Press.

Legal Documents

Brazil: Constitution of the Brazilian Empire of 25 March 1824

China: "Outlines of the Constitution by Imperial Order" (*Qinding Xianfa Dagang* 欽定憲法大綱) of 27 August 1908

"Articles of Favourable Treatment of the Emperor of the Great Qing after his Abdication" (*Qing Di tuiwei youdai tiaojian* 清帝退位優待條件) of 12 February 1912

France: French Constitution of 3 September 1791

Senatus-consulte organique du 28 floréal an XII (= 18 May 1804)

Germany: Constitution of the Prussian State of 5 December 1848

Constitution of the German Empire of 16 April 1871

Japan: Constitution of the Empire of Japan 大日本帝國憲法 of 11 February 1889

Thailand: Thai Constitution of 26 April 2007

United Kingdom: Magna Carta Libertatum [1215]

Europe–Mughal India–Muslim Asia: Circulation of Political Ideas and Instruments in Early Modern Times

Corinne Lefèvre

1 Introduction

The purpose of this essay is to consider Mughal state-building and ideology in a wider geopolitical context than has generally been the case. By wider geopolitical context, I mean not only Europe, but also what I would call the Asian-Islamicate ecumene—a region that stretched from Istanbul to Aceh and housed a number of powerful polities in early modern times—for it is my contention that the processes of political and cultural transfer that took place between Asia and Europe in the sixteenth-eighteenth centuries should be examined side by side with those transfers that took place within Asia *and* within Europe, in order to provide a fuller and more balanced picture of the issue. From the restricted point of view of the Mughal empire, which is my area of expertise, this means tackling a number of questions, such as: what was the political horizon of the Mughals, what did they know about the political experiments that were carried out in early modern Europe and Muslim Asia, and what were the elements of these experiments, if any, that were deemed adaptable in the Indian context? Conversely: what were the perceptions of the Mughal polity in early modern Europe and Asia, and to what extent and to which states did it act as a model or, on the contrary, as a foil? Because of space limitations, I will focus here on the first set of questions.

These first questions are all the more interesting because they point to a significant and lasting feature of the historiography of the Mughal state, i.e. its presentation as an exclusively Indian phenomenon. Contrary to what this "Indocentric" view suggests, the empire founded by Bābur (ruled 1526–1530) cannot be reduced to an extractive machine feeding itself with agrarian surplus and working in quasi-complete isolation from the rest of the early modern world. Quite the opposite: the

---

C. Lefèvre (✉)
Centre d'Études de l'Indes et de l'Asie du Sud, École des Hautes Études en Sciences Sociales, 190-198 avenue de France, 75244 Paris Cedex 13, France
e-mail: co.lefevre@gmail.com

A. Flüchter and S. Richter (eds.), *Structures on the Move*,
Transcultural Research – Heidelberg Studies on Asia and Europe in a Global Context,
DOI 10.1007/978-3-642-19288-3_7, © Springer-Verlag Berlin Heidelberg 2012

seventeenth century whose beginning roughly coincided with the accession to the throne of Jahāngīr (ruled 1605–1627), witnessed the development and diversification of the European presence in the subcontinent on an unprecedented scale, as well as a significant increase in exchanges with the West. Concurrently, and as may be seen, for instance, from the multi-ethnic composition of the Mughal nobility, the empire attracted elites in search of employment from all over the Asian-Islamicate ecumene. And yet, the impact of those multi-directional exchanges on the political genesis and evolution of the Mughal state has not, until now, received the attention it deserves.

This holds particularly true for the question of the political-cum-cultural impact of the European presence on the Mughal elite, most authors concentrating on the economic changes brought by the Western trade companies (Das Gupta 1979; Prakash 1985) or on Said-inspired analyses of European writings on Mughal India (Teltscher 1995). The reason often advanced for this cursory treatment is the scarcity of Indo-Persian texts dealing with Europeans—this very scarcity being usually interpreted as "the" sign of the Mughals' lack of interest for things Western (Pearson 1987: 53). While Mughal writings on the West can hardly be compared in quantity to the massive European production documenting the encounter with the empire, there are nevertheless—as pointed out more recently by a number of historians and art historians (see below for references)—a number of texts, as well as iconographic materials that shed some light on the politico-cultural impact of the European presence and on some interesting cases of circulation and transfer in this domain.

Even though the relation between pre-colonial India and European powers is a research topic that is today far from being exhausted and needs to be pursued, the great importance it has been given since colonial times has led to the neglect of the relations connecting the Mughals with another set of polities geographically and culturally far closer to them (Ottomans, Safavids, Uzbeks, sultans of Aceh). As a matter of fact, the historiography dealing with these relations has been largely confined to diplomatic studies of traditional workmanship (Islam 1970; Farooqi 1989), and to a handful of structuralist comparisons informed by the old orientalist paradigm (Ali 1992; Moosvi 2002). Besides, on the margins of Mughal historiography proper, a number of scholars have dealt with the circulation of elites and analysed their role in the transmission of political ideas within the Asian-Islamicate ecumene (Subrahmanyam 1992; Wormser 2009). Finally, the last two decades have seen the publication of quite a few essays examining jointly the ideological discourses produced by different dynasties of Muslim Asia (Dale 1998; Necipoğlu 1993; Moin 2010).

As shown by this brief survey, research connecting the political and cultural history of the Mughal empire with that of the contemporary states of Europe and Muslim Asia has, until quite recently, remained largely fragmentary. And yet, as advocated by the editors of this volume and a number of other scholars, the histories of the various components of the early modern world have a lot to learn from each other, the early modern times being a period of increased contact between the four parts of the world, as well as a moment of intense political rivalry both within Europe and Muslim Asia and between them. In this highly competitive context, the solutions worked out by a dynasty in such important fields as taxation, relations between ruler and nobility, or management of religious plurality came to constitute

Europe–Mughal India–Muslim Asia 129

as many models, which could possibly influence the choices made by one or more of its rivals. However, not every route that ran across the political space of early modern Europe and Muslim Asia was equally busy: as this essay will demonstrate, some of them proved dead ends, while others developed into highways.

2 European Political Culture and History in Mughal India

I will start, then, with a re-examination of contemporary primary sources (mostly from the seventeenth century) documenting Mughal interest for things Western in the politico-cultural sphere. If one turns first to the European writings and records of the time, one comes across a series of passages showing Mughal monarchs and *amīrs* enquiring about the political situation of one or more European countries. One of the most interesting comes from the pen of Edward Terry, chaplain to Sir Thomas Roe, the first English ambassador sent to the Mughal court in the mid-1610s. In the course of his *Voyage to East-India*, Terry describes the reaction of Jahāngīr to Mercator's *Atlas* in the following way: "The Mogul feeds and feasts himself with this conceit, that he is Conqueror of the World; and therefore I conceive that he was troubled upon a time, when my Lord Ambassador presented him with Mercator's great book of Cosmography that described the four parts of the world. The Mogul at first seemed very much taken with it, desiring presently to see his own territories, which were immediately shown to him; and then [. . .], finding no more to fall to his share, [. . .] seemed to be a little troubled, yet civilly told the Ambassador, that neither himself, nor any of his people, did understand the language in which that book was written, and therefore returned it unto him again" (Terry 1777: 350–351).

These few lines are particularly interesting because they clearly associate geographical knowledge with political power. Following this is the idea that the monarch's limited interest in the *Atlas*, i.e. in the world beyond his kingdom, derived from a denial of the supposed objective geographical reality it depicted: in other words, Jahāngīr sent the *Atlas* back because he refused to be confronted with the relativity of his power and to revise his claims accordingly. Although the bias underlying such an explanation is quite obvious, these lines, as well as Roe's account of the same event, have often been used by modern scholars as a proof of Mughal indifference to the wide world in general, and to Europe more specifically. However, as argued by Ahsan Qaisar three decades ago (Qaisar 1982: 148–149), Roe and Terry may be contrasted on this subject with other contemporary European writings showing that geographical artefacts such as globes, maps and atlases were actually in demand at the Mughal court. Pointing towards the same direction is the existence of a mid-seventeenth century atlas (Habib 1980), as well as the specific role terrestrial globes of European inspiration came to play in imperial allegorical painting.

Reference here is to the works of Ebba Koch and Sumathi Ramaswamy who have shown how, starting with Jahāngīr, the terrestrial globe penetrated the allegorical portraits of the monarch, where it came to stand as an exclusive imperial attribute and a symbol of world domination (Koch 1997: 139–141; 2009: 330–333; Ramaswamy 2007). This was not, however, a case of straightforward adoption: having fully grasped the potentialities of this imported cartographic language, the Mughal artists deployed the globe-form in support of the agenda of their patron, subverting at the same time the Europe-centred mapping of the Earth that originally underlay it. As a matter of fact, a remarkable feature of these Mughalised globes is that they centred on India, which also assumed larger dimensions than in their European counterparts. The specific example of the globe points more generally to an area where the European impact on Mughal political culture can hardly be denied, i.e. the visual propaganda in the service of the empire. As shown by a number of art historians such as Gauvin Bailey and Ebba Koch (Bailey 1998; Koch 2001), Mughal borrowings were particularly important in this domain, ranging from the appropriation of a whole visual language (the allegorical manner) to that of isolated motifs (*putti*, portraits of Jesus and Mary, etc.). As in the case of the globe, however, the European-Christian elements were extracted from their original context of production and given a new garb or meaning that best fitted their redeployment as instruments of the Mughals' legitimacy. While the Mughals were themselves heirs to a Tīmūrid tradition that particularly valued the visual representations of power, the European visual strategies they encountered significantly influenced the political vocabulary they elaborated to depict themselves and their achievements.

In contrast to the evidence of transmission provided by the pictorial records of the imperial atelier stands the relative dearth of actual references to Europe, particularly to its political history and culture, in the Indo-Persian writings produced before the mid-eighteenth century. In the last decade, however, two publications by Simon Digby and Sanjay Subrahmanyam have qualified this scarcity through the analysis of texts that had so far escaped the attention of historians, possibly because of their too-heavy reliance on official court chronicles (Digby 1999; Subrahmanyam 2005). However, the conclusions they draw from these materials differ rather substantially. Digby focuses, for his part, on two texts in which Europe is seen either through the lens of older and obsolete Arabo-Persian geographical lore or as a reservoir of exotic marvels—the two perspectives sometimes coexisting, as in the case of the *Ma'lūmāt-ul-āfāq* (*Knowledge of the horizons*) written by the Mughal official Amīn-ud-dīn K͟hān in the second half of the seventeenth century. This leads Digby to conclude that Mughal elites generally had no curiosity about the outside world and were unable to grasp contemporary information about it in the few geographical works they produced. Whilst acknowledging the existence of fanciful accounts of Europe such as those presented by Digby, Subrahmanyam underlines the fact that these partook of a shared early modern attraction to wonders—referred to as *'ajā'ib-u-g͟harā'ib* in Persian and as *mirabilia* in Latin, an attraction which surfaces as well in contemporary accounts of the East and West Indies. Furthermore, "just as is the case with the Europeans, the presence of a register of "wonders" in the Indo-Persian corpus does not in fact preclude the simultaneous accumulation of political, economic and other materials

Europe–Mughal India–Muslim Asia

in a far more matter-of-fact tone" (Subrahmanyam 2005: 80). As an illustration of this point, he calls attention to a little-known work completed in 1606 by another Mughal official by the name of Ṭāhir Muḥammad. Entitled *Rauẓat-uṭ-ṭāhirīn* (*The garden of the immaculate*), the text is a general history of the oriental Muslim world and has a chapter devoted to "the wonders and curiosities of the ports and islands" surrounding Bengal, in which may be found a description of Portugal. True to the general title of the section, wondrous tales are well represented in the account, but they appear side by side with much more reliable information about contemporary events which, the author writes, he had gathered during his mission to Goa at the end of the 1570s. Among such information, pride of place is given to the fateful campaign of the Portuguese monarch Dom Sebastião (ruled 1557–1578) against the kingdom of Morocco, the account of which, notwithstanding some inaccuracies and an underlying Muslim bias, perfectly matches the criteria of political report, and clearly does not belong to the repertoire of wonders.

The corpus brought to light by Digby and Subrahmanyam certainly gives a better idea of the dual regime (wondrous/factual) that underlay the recording of the Mughal perceptions of Europe; yet, it does not say much about the central question raised at the beginning of this essay. In this perspective, I would like to draw attention to a couple of works composed by two eminent figures who flourished during the reigns of Akbar (ruled 1556–1605) and Jahāngīr. The first and best known of them is the Jesuit Spaniard Jerónimo Xavier (d. 1617), who headed the third Jesuit mission to the Mughal court from 1595 to 1615; the second is the Mughal courtier and scholar 'Abd-us-Sattār ibn Qāsim Lāhaurī (d. after 1619). Under the instructions of emperor Akbar, the two men came to constitute some kind of a translation team whose task was to familiarise the Mughal elite with the Greco-Roman and Christian foundations of contemporary European culture. This implied an intensive linguistic training, to which both men submitted: in their writings, they indicate how they respectively learnt how to read and write Persian (for Xavier) and Latin (for Sattār).

The best known results of this collaboration are a series of catechistic works written in Persian and including Lives of Jesus (*Mir'āt-ul-quds* or *Mirror of Holiness*, 1602) and of the Apostles (*Dāstān-i aḥwāl-i hawāriyyān* or *Account of the Life Episodes of the Apostles*, 1605–1607). While these texts have long been objects of interest for specialists of Jesuit studies (Maclagan 1932; Camps 1957), the recent publication of a hitherto unknown chronicle by Sattār—the *Majālis-i Jahāngīrī* (1608–1611), which, among other things, documents the Mughal view-point on the religious debates held at court ('Abd-us-Sattār 2006)—has led to a reconsideration of contemporary Muslim-Christian discussions, as well as of the exact nature of the collaboration between Sattār and Xavier (Alam and Subrahmanyam 2009). Much more relevant for the present purpose is, however, the production of two other works whose ambition was much more secular in nature. Completed in 1603 by Sattār, the earliest one is a history of the great kings and philosophers of Antiquity entitled <u>*Samarat-ul-falāsifa*</u> (*The fruit of philosophers*); the second—the *Ādāb-us-salṭanat* (*The duties of kingship*)—is a mirror for princes dedicated by Xavier to Jahāngīr in 1609. Neither of these texts

132 C. Lefèvre

has been edited so far, and the following analysis is based on a preliminary survey of two manuscript copies preserved in London.[1]

In the preface to their respective works, both authors underscore the originality, within the Indian context, of the information they are about to reveal to their readers, highlighting by the same token their own role as cultural brokers. In the first pages of the *Samarat-ul-falāsifa*, Sattār thus writes that he was ordered by Akbar "to learn the European language (*zabān-i firangī*), to inquire the secrets of this people and the affairs of the sultans of this group as well as to render into Persian what Greek and Latin philosophers (*ḥukamā-yi yūnān-zamīn wa latin*) had said in their books, in order to reveal what had so far remained hidden because of the foreignness of the language, the unavailability of a translator and the distance [between Europe and India]" (BL, MS. Or. 5893: 5).

He then goes on to explain how he learnt Latin in six months with the help of Jerónimo Xavier. In his own preface, the latter similarly underlines the scarcity of Western books in India and the difficulty of accessing them for the Persian-speaking community; this is in contrast to his own knowledge of both Western literature and the Persian language, which allows him to present Jahāngīr with the gist of European political wisdom (SOAS, MS. 7030, 4r-v). While Xavier openly boasts here of his achievement and implicitly compares it to the advice offered by Aristotle to Alexander or by Seneca to Nero (*ibid.*: 3v), the preface to his *Mir'āt-ul-quds* shows that he was actually aware that his was only a contribution to the much more ambitious project of cultural "translation" undertaken by the Mughals ('Abd-us-Sattār 2006: xl)—a project that also included the rendition in Persian of Sanskrit texts such as the *Mahābhārata*, and whose universal scope was equally noted by Sattār, who mentioned Akbar's urge to know "the secrets of the religions and the affairs of the monarchs of every country" (BL, MS. 5893: 4). The results of both these enterprises of knowledge transfer from Europe to Mughal India are, as could be expected, texts endowed with a fair degree of hybridity when language, form and contents are considered together. This comes out rather clearly when one examines their general structure or the diversity of the traditions they drew upon.

The *Samarat-ul-falāsifa* is structured along both chronological and biographical lines. It has three main parts which successively deal with the Roman kingdom (753–509 B.C.), Ancient Greece until the reign of Alexander the Great (356–323 B.C.), and the time period surrounding the birth of Jesus; this general progression is, however, broken at several points by temporal or spatial leaps, an example of

---

[1] The British Library has a nineteenth-century copy of the work of Sattār (hereafter BL, MS. Or. 5893), which bears the slightly different title of *Samarat-ul-falāsifa* or *Evening story of the philosophers*. Of the six other known manuscripts of the text (sometime also entitled *Aḥwāl-i Firangistān* or *Events of the land of the Franks*), three are preserved in India, two in the United Kingdom, and one in Iran. The copy of the *Ādāb-us-salṭanat* preserved in the School of Oriental and African Studies (hereafter SOAS, MS. 7030) dates from 1609; the Casanatense Library of Rome holds the only other known copy, which was similarly completed in 1609. For two recent overviews of these works, see Alam and Subrahmanyam (2009: 472–475) and Sidarus (2010). I am grateful to the latter for having given me access to his paper before publication.

Europe–Mughal India–Muslim Asia 133

which will be examined below. Within each of the chapters are included biographical accounts of the great men of the age (legislators, philosophers, poets, etc.) along with some of their sayings. This is in perfect consonance with Sattār's main source for his work, which he mentions in the preface (BL, MS. 5893: 7): the chronicles or *Summa Historialis* of Saint Antoninus of Florence (1389–1459), of which Akbar actually owned a copy (Bailey 2000: 385). In this respect, the Dominican archbishop was himself following the model initiated by his coreligionist Vincent of Beauvais (approx. 1190–1264), who was the first universal chronicler of medieval Europe to mix historical discourse with bio-hagiographies and anthologies in his *Speculum Historiale* (Walker 1933: 107–108; Paulmier-Foucart 2004: 84–92). The adoption by Sattār of such a structure must have been all the more easy since it echoed that of many Indo-Persian chronicles which bore the simultaneous imprint of the two classical genres of *tārīkh* (history) and *tazkira* (biography). The general organization of the *Samarat* calls for two further remarks. One is about the quasi-complete absence of the high Roman Empire, which is only touched upon in relation to the events surrounding the birth of the Christ. The other concerns the organisation and contents of the second part: while its title promises the reader all the truth about Greece (*Krisiyya*), the chapter actually proceeds with an account of the Achaemenid empire, starting with its founder Cyrus the Great (approx. 559–529 B.C.) and ending with Artaxerxes III (approx. 425–338 B.C.), at which point Alexander—and, beyond him, Greece—becomes the focus of the story. This is not to say that the second part does not deal with Greece at all, since each sub-heading contains biographical notices of men such as Thales, Solon, Democritus, or Aristotle, which, in the latter's case, actually constitutes almost the whole of the account of Artaxerxes. Even though the choice by Sattār of the Achaemenid prism certainly derives from his adherence to the Western scheme of the succession of empires as exemplified in the *Summa Historialis*,[2] it takes on an additional dimension when one considers the identity of his patron, for whom the Achaemenids clearly constituted an imperial model.

If one now turns to the general structure of the *Ādāb-us-salṭanat*, what is most striking at first glance is its outward resemblance to that of Tīmūrid and contemporary Mughal mirrors for princes. It typically opens with a chapter in praise of God, the Lord of all, and on the importance of divine worship ("on the respect due to God")—a chapter whose length is, however, greater than is usually the case (SOAS, MS. 7030: 9v–61a). This is followed by two chapters devoted to "the reformation of the emperor (*iṣlāḥ-i bādshāh*)" and to "the guidance and instruction of officers (*hidāyat wa tarbiyat-i 'uhdadārān*)". This successive focus on the person of the emperor and his relations with the political elite is also traditional, and may be found only a couple of years later in the *Mau'iza-i Jahāngīrī* or *Admonition to Jahāngīr*. Dedicated to the monarch by the Iranian *émigré* Bāqir Khān in 1611, the text is composed of two parts dealing with "the exhortation of the emperors" and

---

[2] For the origins of this scheme in Greek historiography, see Momigliano (1982).

"the admonition of subordinates and peers" (Bāqir Khān 1989). Finally, the central topic of the fourth and last chapter of the *Ādāb-us-salṭanat*—the love and protection due to the subjects—echoes another common preoccupation of the Indo-Persian authors of mirrors for princes. Its best known symbol is probably the "circle of justice", according to which the prosperity of the king and the kingdom ultimately derives from the prosperity of the subjects. If the structure of Xavier's mirror is then very much akin to that of Mughal treatises of government, the origin and nature of the numerous anecdotes the Jesuit uses to illustrate his general principles differ to a great extent from what is usually found in the latter texts. Whereas the repertoire of Indo-Persian authors traditionally included stories taken from Sassanid and classical Islamic history and, less frequently, from the more recent Indo-Muslim past, Xavier's anecdotes derive for the most part from Biblical and Classical history—a point that leads me to the more general question of the sources used by Sattār and Xavier in their works.

Sattār is probably the most explicit in this regard: besides the *Summa Historialis* of Antoninus already mentioned, he refers in his preface to his use of the Bible (*injīl*) and other books without, unfortunately, providing further details about them. Although Xavier does not specify the materials on which he relied for his work, they most certainly included the ones indicated by Sattār. Moreover, as he himself points out, he benefited from the knowledge acquired during a life dedicated to "the study of the books of prophets and scholars of the past (*muṭāla'a-i ṣuhuf-i paighāmbarān wa dānishwārān-i pishīn*)". There is a hint here of the extensive scholastic culture every Jesuit was supposed to possess and of which the *Summa Theologica* by Thomas Aquinas (approx. 1225–1274)—who is referred to in the same folio (SOAS, MS. 7030: 4r)—was one of the masterpieces. Finally, there is one part of the *Ādāb* for which Xavier explicitly indicates his source: the conclusion of the book, he writes at different points in the text (*ibid.*: 9r, 274v, 275v, 286r), is an abridgement of the advice given by Maecenas (70–8 B.C.) to the first emperor of Rome, Caesar Augustus (ruled 27 B.C.–14 A.D.). Although no author's name or title is given, the reference is clearly to the 52nd book of Cassius Dio's (d. after 229) *Roman History*, which is almost entirely taken up by the aforementioned advice.

If both the *Samarat-ul-falāsifa* and the *Ādāb-us-salṭanat* were, then, mostly the result of the transmission of multilayered Western lore into Mughal India, there is interesting evidence in the former work that this process of translation was not carried out without raising a number of questions on the receiving side. This is evident from the few pages Sattār devotes to some episodes of the history of Spain (BL, MS. 5893: 48–56), which is here not referred to as such, but as "the peninsula of al-Andalus (*jazira-i ūndalus*)". Perhaps prompted by a discussion with Xavier about his homeland, the Spanish digression is inserted at the beginning of the section on Greece and may be divided into two parts. Relying mostly on medieval Arab geographers,[3] the first starts with the Greek colonisation of the peninsula

---

[3] For the pre-Islamic history of Spain as seen by Arab geographers and historians, see Picard (2003).

Europe–Mughal India–Muslim Asia 135

under Alexander the Great and ends with the Muslim conquest of Toledo at the time of the Visigothic (*wisiq*) king Roderic, in 711; the crux of the story here is Roderic's seizure of the famous Table of Solomon, whose power had until then protected the kingdom from foreign invaders.[4] At this point in the account, Sattār stops and writes that the European priest (*pādrī-yi firang*, i.e. Jerónimo Xavier) gave him another version of the story, which constitutes the second part of the Spanish digression. In contrast to the first, this provides dates according to the Christian rather than to the Hijri calendar, as well as transliterations of the exact names of the European protagonists. It starts with the traditional explanation of the loss of Toledo as recorded in Western medieval sources: as Xavier himself explains in his *Ādāb* (SOAS, MS. 7030: 140v–141v), it was all because of the treason of Julian, count of Ceuta, who avenged himself for Roderic's insult (he had seduced Julian's daughter) by giving the Muslims considerable help. The account that follows of the eleventh-century *reconquista* of Toledo at the hands of Alphonse VI of León and Castile (1085) similarly derives from European materials. It is Sattār, however, who has the last word: since this time, he laments, not a single Muslim may be found in the country. Sattār's Spanish digression is particularly interesting for two reasons. First, in contrast to the "translation" logic that lay at the root of the *Samarat*, he here juxtaposes side by side Arabo-Muslim and European-Christian versions of the same event, while refraining from openly favouring one over the other (probably because both put the blame on Roderic, although for different reasons). Second, these pages constitute one of the very few glimpses the *Samarat* gives its reader into more recent Western history. The only other one is situated at the end of the preface where Sattār provides a very brief geopolitical sketch of contemporary Europe: Italy, Spain, France, Germany and Castile are mentioned in turn without, however, further details (BL, MS. 5893: 9).

This brings me to the more general question of the presence and role of contemporary Europe in the two works under analysis. As has just been mentioned, it was minimal in the case of the *Samarat*, where contemporary Europe was first and foremost a reservoir to be tapped for information on Western ancient history and lore—the actual focus of the work. Still one may wonder why, so far as is known, the Mughals' universal curiosity did not prompt them to commission some kind of continuation to the *Samarat*, or why the Jesuits did not think it necessary for them to have one. A closer look at the *Ādāb-us-salṭanat*, and more specifically at the anecdotes it includes, certainly helps to clarify the last point to some extent. In this perspective, the brief piece of advice Xavier gives to the reader in the final lines of the preface is particularly illuminating: because the people mentioned in his book do not hail from India, he writes, he decided to remove their names from the body of the text (*matn*) in order to facilitate the comprehension of its general principles, and to indicate them instead in the margin (*ḥāshiya*) so that the credibility of their words

---

[4] BL, MS. 5893: 49–51. For a similar account by a fifteenth-century North African geographer, who was himself relying on a number of predecessors such as al-Idrīsī (d. approx. 1165), see al-Ḥimyarī (1938: 10–11, 157–159).

might not be doubted (SOAS, MS. 7030: 9r-v). In other words, the true objective of the *Ādāb* seems to have been primarily to arouse Jahāngīr's interest in the moral principles of Christianity as applied to politics, and secondarily only to inform him about contemporary Europe.

For all that, it is nonetheless significant that among the great men mentioned by Xavier as *exempla*, figures from Biblical and Classical history are far better represented than personalities of late medieval or early modern times. While the possible reliance of the Jesuit on the *Summa Historialis* of Antoninus may partly account for this imbalance, his own Navarrean origins and his close relationship with Goa explain to a large extent the Iberian identity of the vast majority of the most recent political figures he refers to. Taking the sixteenth century as an example, the only exception to this scheme is the French Valois king Francis I (ruled 1515–1547), Philip II of Spain (ruled 1556–1598) being by far the most often mentioned. Because Philip II is also the European monarch with whom the Mughals had, by that time, established the closest relations, it is worth pausing for a while on the aspects of his personality and policy Xavier thought fit to publicise in the eyes of his Indian audience.

So far, I have been able to identify six anecdotes relating to the dispensation of the Habsburg who, in the Persian text, is generally referred to as "the emperor of Spain" (*bādshāh-i ispāniyya*). These anecdotes are unequally distributed across the *Ādāb*, all of them being found in the third and fourth chapters (SOAS, MS. 7030: 198v–199r, 204v, 229v, 248r-v, 259r, 265v–266r). All in all they illustrate two characteristics of Philip II's government as seen by Xavier. First, the ability of the monarch to gather information on every possible individual: such knowledge endows him with the necessary foresight to pick up the right men for advice and administration as well as to anticipate his enemies' moves. Second, Philip II is portrayed as a ruler deeply devoted to the well-being of his subjects: magnanimous and just, he constantly favours peaceful solutions over war. Moving from the universal principles of good government illustrated by these anecdotes to what may be called their historical "traceability", the analysis takes an interesting turn. In this respect, it should first be noted that only two of these anecdotes name historical characters other than the Habsburg. Interestingly enough, both of them pertain to the Iberian union that followed the death of the Portuguese cardinal-king Dom Henrique (ruled 1578–1580) in 1580.

The shortest one narrates how Philip II gained sovereignty over Portugal through the decision of an assembly (*arish*)—probably a reference to the *Cortes* of Tomar of 1581—and how, fearing resistance from his new subjects, he entrusted the Duke of Alba (d. 1587) with taking over the kingdom. To such a request, the latter replied that if he could easily bring the kingdom and its inhabitants to submission, the conquest of their hearts was beyond his capacity, and eventually rested with the monarch himself. His words met with Philip II's approbation who, after the effective conquest of Portugal, decided to visit his new possessions personally: there, he quickly won the affection of his subjects through his benevolence. While the distortion of historical events is here minimal—the *Cortes* of Tomar did not precede but follow the Spanish demonstration of force—it grows out of proportion in the second anecdote referring to the Iberian union. This focuses on Martim Gonçalves da Câmara (1539–1613) who receives here unconditional praise as the faithful minister of two successive Portuguese monarchs, as well as Philip II of Spain after Portugal had come into his possession. Although neither of the Portuguese kings is named, the identity of who Xavier had in mind leaves little doubt. The first, after whose death a very young monarch is said to have ascended the throne, can only be Dom João III (ruled 1521–1557). As to his heir, it is of course the ill-fated Dom Sebastião whose personal reign and demise are duly but very briefly mentioned. Nothing, however, is said of his successor Dom Henrique, Xavier jumping directly to Philip II. Like his Portuguese predecessors, the latter decided to entrust Martim Gonçalves with the affairs of the kingdom, but only after a thorough investigation had convinced him of the man's exceptional qualities and probity.

Such a narrative raises, however, a number of issues when compared to what is known otherwise of the figure of Martim Gonçalves da Câmara, for, if he did indeed wield enormous power and influence during the first part of Dom Sebastião's reign, he was disgraced by that same monarch in 1576. In addition, he is not known to have played any significant political role under Dom João III nor under Philip II. On the contrary: dated April 1580, a letter by Cristóvão de Moura (1538–1613), Philip's agent in Portugal, describes him as one of the king of Spain's worst enemies (Paiva 2006: 14–15). One is therefore left to wonder why Xavier chose to inflate Martim Gonçalves's profile to the point of making it necessary to revise the latter's career so extensively. True, Martim was himself a secular priest closely connected with the Jesuit milieu (on his brother Luís Gonçalves, a Jesuit who served Dom Sebastião as tutor and confessor, see Alden 1996: 81–84) but, as this piece of information surfaces nowhere in the *Ādāb*, it is hard to believe that Xavier's distortion was meant to highlight the Jesuits' qualities as kingly advisers. Be that as it may, the treatment Martim Gonçalves received at the hands of Xavier is very instructive where the transmission of Western political history to the Mughal court is concerned. Indeed, it shows that the transformations entailed by such a process did not solely derive from the requirements of translation but may have followed a different logic that is sometimes difficult to grasp.

All in all, Xavier's mirror for princes was hardly the place for the Mughals to find a discussion about the latest developments of Western political history and thinking; it was unlikely, therefore, to act as a source of inspiration in this domain. Besides, the scarcity of the surviving manuscripts as well as their exclusively European location (see *supra*: n. 1) point to the rather limited success of the *Ādāb-us-salṭanat* in India, particularly as compared to the *Samarat-ul-falāsifa*. On the basis of the present survey, and pending further research on the subject, it may therefore be safe to conclude that early modern Europe was not among the role models the Mughals referred to in matters of state building or technologies of governance. Why exactly such was not the case is, however, a question that remains to be thoroughly examined.

3 Mughal India and Safavid Iran: Political Transfers in Muslim Asia

In this respect, and in contrast to the situation described above, one stands on firmer ground when moving into what I have called the Asian-Islamicate ecumene. As indicated in the introduction, recent scholarship has called attention to the circulation of elites and their contribution to the dissemination of political models within this space. If a number of studies have brought to light interesting cases of sometimes multilateral ideological influences, fewer have addressed the question of governmental technologies as part of politico-cultural transfers. The second part of the present essay will focus on such a case of transfer through the analysis of Mughal emulation of the Safavid mercantilist policy inaugurated by Shāh Abbās I (ruled 1587–1629).[5]

Before presenting the main characteristics of the latter, it is important to note the existence among the Tājik elites of Iran of a long tradition combining political and commercial participation and embodied by the figure of the *tājir* (pl. *tujjār*) or merchant (Calmard 1988). From the fifteenth century onwards, a number of them chose to settle in South and South-East Asia, sometimes responding to the invitation of newly-created dynasties. This holds particularly true for the Deccan, where Bahmanid sultans (1387–1489) and their successors in Bijapur, Ahmadnagar, and Golconda encouraged the migration of Iranians to their territories and gave pride of place to individuals with dual administrative and commercial expertise (Subrahmanyam 1992). For all that, it was not to the Tājik *tujjār*—among whom many Sayyids were also to be found—that Shāh 'Abbās turned for the implementation of his centralising reforms, of which the new mercantilist orientation was only a part. On the contrary, he treated them with greater hostility than his predecessors, being suspicious of the socio-religious prestige of the Sayyids, and, more generally, of their propensity to invest both in land property and in commercial activities. The Safavid therefore chose to rely on two groups—a corps of slaves and the Armenian merchant community—who were more amenable to his wishes than the Tājik merchant-administrators. The Armenian support was especially important for the development of 'Abbās' new commercial policy which aimed primarily at increasing the silver reserves of the state.[6] In order to do so, the monarch resorted to a number of measures, including an import-substitution policy for cotton cloth, a ban on gold and silver exports, and, most famously, the instauration of a state monopoly on silk exports (1619). Silk was Iran's most valuable export product and the newly created monopoly guaranteed the state the major part of the benefits accruing from its trade by compelling foreign merchants—mostly representatives of the East India Company (EIC) and the Verenigde Oostindische Compagnie (VOC)—to deal

---

[5] For an extended version of this point and a larger discussion of reciprocal Mughal and Safavid influences, see Lefèvre (2010).

[6] The following presentation of 'Abbās's mercantilist policy is based on Matthee (1999: 61–118).

exclusively with state-appointed intermediaries. Besides, 'Abbās worked hard to provide Iran with a commercial outlet that would be safe from Ottoman and Portuguese appetites. To this end, he simultaneously explored the possibilities offered by the Northern land route (via Russia) and the Southern maritime axis (via the Persian Gulf). Thanks to the expulsion of the Portuguese from Hormuz in 1622, the latter solution finally prevailed: the port of Bandar 'Abbās was founded on the site of ancient Gombroon and soon became a major commercial hub.

In contrast to the mercantilist model elaborated by Shāh 'Abbās, Mughal participation in trade appears far more limited at first sight. Just as their Afghan predecessors and their Uzbek and Safavid contemporaries, Akbar and Jahāngīr certainly considered the protection of merchants and the maintenance of a decent road network a part of their kingly duty. Besides, trade represented a significant source of income for the state, especially after the conquest of the two maritime sultanates of Gujarat and Bengal in the 1570s, even though the revenues deriving from this lagged behind those accruing from agricultural production. Even so, beyond this traditional relationship of protection and taxation, a number of elements point to the greater involvement of the Mughals in commercial activities from the first quarter of the seventeenth century onwards.

The first element is undoubtedly the growing participation of the imperial family and the Mughal elite in maritime trade. This is borne out by a series of documents such as the registers of the Estado da Índia (Flores 2005: 261–264), the correspondence of English and Dutch merchants with the EIC and the VOC (Chandra 1959: 93–94) and a collection of Mughal administrative papers concerning the port of Surat (Hasan 1989–1990; Moosvi 1990). All testify to the fact that Mughal monarchs and members of their family (including women) were the owners of ships conveying their goods (textiles, indigo, tobacco) to the great ports of the Persian Gulf, the Red Sea and South-East Asia. As shown by the nature of the evidence gathered here, the mercantilist evolution of the dynasty failed, however, to be integrated on the ideological level. The same holds true for administrative elites who, from the 1600s on, increasingly engaged in sea trade. The more active among them were the officials posted in the maritime provinces of the empire, such as Gujarat (Flores 2011; Hasan 2004: 31–51), along with the many Iranian migrants who gained predominance in the Mughal nobility precisely around this time. Particularly significant is, in this last respect, a remark by the Dutch factor Francisco Pelsaert, who blamed the Iranians as much for trusting the higher levels of Mughal administration as for their excessive intervention in the economy (Pelsaert 1957: 92).

The successive stages of the Iranian rise to power in the Mughal state apparatus are well known: initiated by Humāyūn (ruled 1530–1540; 1555–1556), vigorously pursued by Akbar, the recruitment of Iranians further intensified in the time of Jahāngīr, during whose reign they achieved first rank in the nobility in respect both to numbers and positions. Symbolised by the ascendancy of Nūr Jahān's family (the favourite queen, herself of Iranian origin), the migration flow continued unabated throughout the seventeenth century even though, from the 1650s on, Iranians increasingly had to compete with other groups (Indian Muslims, Rājpūts) for state patronage. In their attempt to explain Mughal "Iranophily", historians have generally emphasised the push factors lying behind it, including Safavid religious intolerance and the limited career prospects offered by Iran as compared to India. While it cannot be denied that such factors did play a substantial role, this line of explanation is marred by its portraying of the Mughals as totally passive in the process. As rightly suggested by Sanjay Subrahmanyam (1992), the profile of those Iranians who reached the highest levels of Mughal state apparatus, as well as the nature of the positions they held, rather point to the fact that Indian monarchs valued these individuals for very specific competences.

The case of Nūr Jahān's family appears particularly significant in this respect (Habib 1969). Of her grandfather Khwāja Muhammad Sharīf, a Tājik from Tehran, we know that he held an important position in the Safavid fiscal administration under Shāh Ṭahmāsp (ruled 1524–1576) and was associated with the renowned and powerful family of Āqā Muhammad Dawatdār through matrimonial alliance. His son I'timād-ud-daula chose to settle in India, where his expertise in fiscal matters enabled him to hold the combined offices of *wazīr* and *wakīl* from 1611 until his death in 1621. These same competences were transmitted to his son Āsaf Khān who, like his father, is praised in contemporary literature for his ability in the fiscal domain; more importantly, he inherited from his father the position of *wakīl*, which he likewise held until his death in 1641. As a matter of fact, statistical studies have shown that the highest offices in Mughal fiscal administration became an Iranian preserve from Jahāngīr's reign on (Ali 1985). Āsaf Khān is also the first member of the family whose commercial activities are known in detail, even though the profile of Khwāja Muhammad Sharīf and his connections with Āqā Muhammad Dawatdār leads one to believe that trade was already part of the portfolio of familial activities back in Iran. Whatever the case may be, the family's involvement in commerce only grew stronger during the second half of the seventeenth century, as shown by Āsaf Khān's and his son Shayista Khān's strong participation in the trade of the Bay of Bengal (Prakash 1985).

Before concluding on this point, it is worth pausing briefly to consider another biography, whose complexity is all the more illuminating. Mīr Jumla Isfahānī hailed from one of the Sayyid clans of Ispahan, whose diversified interests in land property, manufacturing, and commercial activities are otherwise well known. He left Iran at the beginning of the seventeenth century and settled in Golconda where, according to the memoirs of Jahāngīr, he was, for ten years, the factotum of Muhammad Qulī Qutb Shāh (ruled 1580–1612) and the centre of the affairs of the state (Jahāngīr 1999: 258). In 1613, his falling out with the next sultan drove him out of Golconda, and it is only after he had failed to attract the patronage of the neighbouring kingdom of Bijapur that he resolved to go back to Iran. The reasons for this reluctance are made clear by the treatment he received at the court of Shāh 'Abbās. After having tried for a while to exchange a part of the immense wealth he had acquired in India (through his fiscal duties and his likely participation in the lucrative trade of Masulipatnam) for a high position in Safavid administration, Mīr Jumla understood that the Shāh would concede no political participation to him and, in 1618, he therefore decided to leave yet again for the subcontinent

Europe–Mughal India–Muslim Asia

(Bhakkarī 2003: 72). At the Mughal court, the Mīr actually obtained what the Safavid had denied him and henceforth held a series of high positions in the imperial administration until his death in 1637 (Ali 1985: 128, 141). The case of Mīr Jumla Iṣfahānī vividly illustrates how the Iranian merchant-administrators were pushed into the background in Safavid times, driving many of them on to the road to India as a result. Besides, his successful career under Jahāngīr and Shāh Jahān demonstrates the degree to which the Mughals valued the Iranian elites, who combined administrative and commercial expertise. That men such as Mīr Jumla, I'timād-ud-daula, and so many others were also natural vehicles for the diffusion of Shāh 'Abbās' new commercial policy in Mughal territories is beyond doubt. The growing participation of the imperial family and the Mughal elite in maritime trade and the Iranian hegemony in the politico-economic sphere are not, however, the only elements hinting at the Mughals' attraction towards state mercantilism. It is also borne out by some specific directions of Mughal expansion, as well as by the hardening of the dynasty's attitude toward European trade companies.

Contrary to received wisdom, Jahāngīr's reign did not coincide with the complete cessation of the conquest process (re)initiated by Akbar: the new monarch succeeded in subjecting Rājpūt Mewar, kept the Deccani sultanates under continuous pressure, and, more importantly for the present purpose, pursued Mughal expansion into the southern and eastern fringes of Bengal. The main motivation behind this last operation was essentially commercial, the Mughals aiming at seizing Bengal's two principal ports—Hughli to the west and Chittagong to the east—which were then under the control of Portuguese merchants and the Magh dynasty of Arakan, respectively. It is true that nothing came of these expeditions at the time. However, Jahāngīr's efforts were continued by his successors and finally proved successful; Hughli and Chittagong fell to the Mughals in 1632 and 1666 respectively, henceforth providing the dynasty with privileged access to the Bay of Bengal and its lucrative trade.

Jahāngīr not only pursued an aggressive policy on the eastern margins of the empire, he also took a harder line on the European presence on the western coast. The first open conflict broke out in 1613 with the seizure and destruction by the Portuguese of a ship from Surat that was bringing a valuable cargo back from Jeddah, a cargo in which the emperor's mother had an important interest (Flores 2005: 251–261). The scale of Jahāngīr's reaction—all the Europeans living in the empire were put under arrest and had their goods seized—shows that the Mughals were less and less ready to accept European control of sea trade, and indicates, by the same token, their growing interest in this activity. A period of "contained conflict" succeeded the crisis of 1613–1615, which lasted until the end of the reign and saw the Portuguese progressively lose ground against the Mughals' increasing pressure. In this respect, Jahāngīr's 1617–1618 trip to Gujarat appears particularly significant, because of its likely connection with the new commercial policy that was taking shape at the time. During his short stay in Cambay, the monarch actually publicised his willingness to promote traffic between the western coast of the empire and the Red Sea, and to turn Cambay into the most attractive harbour of the whole western Indian Ocean, thanks to the fiscal reforms he intended

142   C. Lefèvre

to introduce there. That he took the opportunity during his stay in Gujarat to assign the government of the province to his son Shāh Jahān is also no coincidence: he thereby made sure that imperial authority would be felt more strongly in the future, especially *vis-à-vis* the Europeans (Jahāngīr 1999: 241, 244).

In this, as in many other cases, Shāh Jahān proved to be an excellent choice. The prince was himself actively involved in Gujarātī trade, and Portuguese archives indicate that he indeed took a harder line against the Estado da Índia (Flores 2005: 262–264). The Portuguese were not, however, the only Westerners to feel the bitter taste of his formidable gift for negotiation, his dealings with the English factors of Surat testifying to his expert use of the carrot and stick method (Faruqui 2002: 187–189). With the support of his father, Shāh Jahān succeeded in establishing, within the context of Gujarat, a steadfast commercial policy whose aim was to develop Mughal interests in international trade, liberate them from Portuguese control and, more generally, to protect them from European appetites. In many respects, the government of the richest province of the empire may thus be said to have been the laboratory where the prince elaborated and put to the test the mercantilist policy he was to develop as king. For, of all Mughal monarchs, Shāh Jahān was certainly the one most deeply involved in maritime trade. Besides, Iranians continued to be massively recruited under his rule and to trust the higher levels of the fiscal apparatus. Last but not least, Mughal mercantilist tendencies grew even stronger at his instigation, as shown, for instance, by the expulsion of the Portuguese from Hughli in 1632, or the attempts to institute royal monopolies on commodities such as indigo, lime, or saltpetre (Chandra 1959: 94–95).

The commercial policy of the dynasty was not, however, the only sphere to bear the imprint of the processes of competition and imitation that informed the relations of Mughal India with the contemporary polities of Muslim Asia throughout the early modern period. Reciprocal influences were also of tremendous importance where state ideology was concerned. As has been argued elsewhere (e.g. Lefèvre 2010; Moin 2010), this holds particularly true for Mughals and Safavids during the seventeenth century, but other examples are not hard to find. To cite but one, Paul Wormser (2009) has recently built on the earlier insight of Denys Lombard to demonstrate how the sultans of Aceh successively turned to Ottoman and Mughal models to legitimise their power and elaborate a sophisticated royal ideology. As far as political ideas and instruments are concerned, there is, then, no denying that the transfers that took place within the Asian-Islamicate ecumene far exceeded the exchanges between Europe and Muslim Asia in early modern times. This is, of course, in sharp contrast with the situation that was to prevail with the advent of European domination in the region from the eighteenth century on.

Bibliography

'Abd-us-Sattār b. Qāsim Lāhaurī. 2006. *Majālis-i Jahāngīrī*, ed. A. Naushahi and M. Nizami. Tehran: Miras-i Maktub.

Abd-us-Sattār b. Qāsim Lāhaurī. *Samarat-ul-falāsifa*. British Library, London, MS. Or. 5893.

Alam, Muzaffar and Sanjay Subrahmanyam. 2009. "Frank disputations: Catholics and Muslims in the court of Jahangir (1608–11)." *Indian Economic and Social History Review* 46/4: 457–511.

Alden, Dauril. 1996. *The Making of an Enterprise. The Society of Jesus in Portugal, its Empire and Beyond, 1540–1750*. Stanford: Stanford University Press.

al-Ḥimyarī. 1938. *Kitāb al-Rawẓ al-miʿṭār fī khabar al-aqṭār*. Partial ed. and tr. E. Lévi-Provençal, *La péninsule ibérique au Moyen Age d'après le Kitāb al-Rawḍ al-Miʿṭār fī ḥabar al-akṭār. Texte arabe des notices relatives à l'Espagne, au Portugal et au Sud-Ouest de la France*. Leiden: E. J. Brill.

Ali, Muhammad Athar. 1985. *The Apparatus of Empire. Awards of Ranks, Offices and Titles to the Mughal Nobility, 1574–1658*. Delhi: Oxford University Press.

Ali, Muhammad Athar. 1992. "Political Structures of the Islamic Orient in the Sixteenth and Seventeenth Centuries." In *Medieval India 1. Researches in the History of India, 1200–1750*, ed. I. Habib. Delhi: Oxford University Press: 129–140.

Bailey, Gauvin A. 1998. *The Jesuits and the Grand Mogul: Renaissance Art at the Imperial Court of India, 1580–1630*. Washington D. C.: Freer Gallery of Art, Arthur M. Sackler Gallery & Smithsonian Institution.

Bailey, Gauvin A. 2000. "The Truth-Showing Mirror: Jesuit Catechism and the Arts in Mughal India." In *The Jesuits. Cultures, Sciences and the Arts*, ed. J. W. O'Malley et al. Toronto-Buffalo-London: University of Toronto Press: 380–401.

Bāqir Khān, Muḥammad (Najm-i Sānī). 1989. *Mauʿiza-i Jahāngīrī*. Ed. and tr. S. S. Alvi, *Advice on the Art of Governance: An Indo-Islamic Mirror for Princes of Muḥammad Bāqir Najm-i Sānī*. Albany: State University of New York Press.

Bhakkarī, Shaikh Farīd. 2003. *Zakhīrat-ul-khawanīn*. Tr. Z. A. Desai, *Nobility under the Great Mughals. Based on the Dhakhīratul Khawanīn of Shaikh Farīd Bhakkari*. Delhi: Sundeep Prakashan.

Calmard, Jean. 1988. "Les marchands iraniens: formation et montée d'un groupe de pression, $16^e–19^e$ siècles." In *Marchands et hommes d'affaires asiatiques dans l'Océan Indien et la Mer de Chine, $13^e–20^e$ siècles*, ed. J. Aubin and D. Lombard. Paris: Éditions de l'EHESS: 91–107.

Camps, Arnulf. 1957. *Jerome Xavier, S.J. and the Muslims of the Mogul Empire: Controversial and missionary activities*. Schöneck-Beckenried: Nouvelle Revue de Science Missionnaire.

Chandra, Satish. 1959. "Commercial Activities of the Mughal Emperors during the 17th century." *Bengal Past and Present* 78/2: 92–97.

Dale, Stephen Frederic. 1998. "The Legacy of the Timurids." *Journal of the Royal Asiatic Society, Series 3* 8/1: 43–58.

Das Gupta, Ashin. 1979. *Indian merchants and the decline of Surat, c. 1700–1750*. Wiesbaden: Steiner.

Digby, Simon. 1999. "Beyond the Ocean: Perceptions of Overseas in Indo-Persian Sources of the Mughal Period." *Studies in History* 14/2: 247–259.

Farooqi, Naimur R. 1989. *Mughal-Ottoman Relations: A Study of Political and Diplomatical Relations between Mughal India and the Ottoman Empire, 1556–1748*. Delhi: Idarah-i Adabiyat-i Delli.

Faruqui, Munis Daniyal. 2002. Princes and Power in the Mughal Empire, 1569–1657. Ph.D.: Duke University.

Flores, Jorge. 2005. "Firingistan" e "Hindustan". O Estado da Índia e os confines meridionais do Imperio Mogol (1572–1636). Ph.D.: Universidade Nova de Lisboa.

Flores, Jorge. 2011. "The Sea and the World of the *Mutasaddi*: A Profile of port officials from Mughal Gujarat (c. 1600–1650)." *Journal of the Royal Asiatic Society, Series 3* 21/1: 55–71.

Habib, Irfan. 1969. "The Family of Nur Jahan during Jahangir's Reign: A Political Study." In *Medieval India. A Miscellany*. Vol. 1. Mumbai: Asia Publishing House: 74–95.

Habib, Irfan. 1980. "Cartography in Mughal India." In *Medieval India. A Miscellany*. Vol. 4. Mumbai: Asia Publishing House: 122–134.

Hasan, Farhat. 1989–1990. "Mughal Officials at Surat and their Relations with the English and Dutch Merchants: Based on a Collection of Persian Documents of the Reigns of Jahangir and Shah Jahan." In *Proceedings of the Indian History Congress, 50th Session*. Delhi: Indian History Congress: 284–293.

Hasan, Farhat. 2004. *State and Locality in Mughal India. Power Relations in Western India, c. 1572–1730*. Cambridge: Cambridge University Press.

Islam, Riazul. 1970. *Indo-Persian Relations: a Study of the Political and Diplomatic Relations between the Mughal Empire and Iran*. Tehran: Iranian Culture Foundation.

Jahāngīr, Nūr-ud-dīn Muhammad. 1999. *Jahāngīr Nāma*. Tr. W. M. Thackston, *Jahāngīr Nāma. Memoirs of Jahāngīr, Emperor of India*. Washington D. C. and New York: Freer Gallery of Art and Arthur M. Sackler Gallery, Smithsonian Institution & Oxford University Press.

Koch, Ebba. 1997. "The Hierarchical Principles of Shah-Jahani Painting." In *King of the World: The Padshahnama: An Imperial Mughal Manuscript from the Royal Library, Windsor Castle*, ed. M. C. Beach, E. Koch and W. M. Thackston. London and Washington D. C.: Azimuth Editions and Sackler Gallery, Smithsonian Institution: 130–143.

Koch, Ebba. 2001. *Mughal Art and Imperial Ideology. Collected Essays*. Delhi: Oxford University Press.

Koch, Ebba. 2009. "Jahangir as Francis Bacon's Ideal of the King as an Observer and Investigator of Nature." *Journal of the Royal Asiatic Society, Series 3* 19/3: 293–338.

Lefèvre, Corinne. 2010. "Jahāngīr et son frère Šāh 'Abbās : compétition et circulation entre deux puissances de l'Asie musulmane de la première modernité." In *Muslim Cultures in the Indo-Iranian World during the Early-Modern and Modern Periods*, ed. D. Hermann and F. Speziale. Berlin and Tehran: Klaus Schwarz and IFRI: 23–56.

Maclagan, Edward Douglas. 1932. *The Jesuits and the Great Mogul*. London: Burn Oates & Washbourne Ltd.

Matthee, Rudolph P. 1999. *The Politics of Trade in Safavid Iran. Silk for Silver, 1600–1730*. Cambridge: Cambridge University Press.

Moin, Ahmed Azfar. 2010. Islam and the Millennium: Sacred Kingship and Popular Imagination in Early Modern India and Iran. Ph.D.: University of Michigan.

Momigliano, Arnaldo. 1982. "The Origins of Universal History." *Annali della Scuola Normale Superiore di Pisa. Classe di lettere e filosofia, 3rd Series* 12/2: 533–560.

Moosvi, Shireen. 1990. "Mughal Shipping at Surat in the First Half of the Seventeenth Century." In *Proceedings of the Indian History Congress, 51st Session*. Delhi: Indian History Congress: 308–320.

Moosvi, Shireen. 2002. "Sharing the "Asiatic Mode"? India and Iran." In *A Shared Heritage. The Growth of Civilization in India and Iran*, ed. I. Habib. Delhi: Tulika Books: 177–188.

Necipoğlu, Gülru. 1993. "Framing the Gaze in Ottoman, Safavid and Mughal Palaces." In *Pre-Modern Islamic Palaces (Ars Orientalis 23)*, ed. G. Necipoğlu. Ann Arbor: University of Oklahoma Press: 303–342.

Paiva, José Pedro. 2006. "Bishops and Politics: The Portuguese Episcopacy During the Dynastic Crisis of 1580." *E-Journal of Portuguese Studies* 4/2: 1–19.

Paulmier-Foucart, Monique (with the collaboration of M.-C. Duchenne). 2004. *Vincent Beauvais et le Grand miroir du monde*. Turnhout: Brepols Publishers NV.

Pearson, Michael N. 1987. *The Portuguese in India (The New Cambridge History of India I/1)*. Cambridge: Cambridge University Press.

Pelsaert, Francisco. 1957. *A Contemporary Dutch Chronicle of Mughal India*, ed. and tr. B. Narain and S. R. Sharma. Kolkata: Susil Gupta (India) Limited.

Picard, Christophe. 2003. "Le passé antique et l'histoire d'al-Andalus chez les auteurs arabes." *Pallas : revue d'études antiques* 63: 97–106.

Prakash, Om. 1985. *The Dutch East India Company and the Economy of Bengal, 1630–1720*. Delhi: Oxford University Press.

Qaisar, Ahsan Jan. 1982. *The Indian Response to European Technology and Culture (A.D. 1498–1707)*. Delhi: Oxford University Press.

Ramaswamy, Sumathi. 2007. "Conceit of the Globe in Mughal Visual Practice." *Comparative Studies in History and Society* 49/4: 751–782.

Sidarus, Adel. 2010. "O Espelho de Príncipes de Jerónimo Xavier SJ dedicado ao Imperador Mogol (1609)." In *Caminhos Cruzados em História e Antropologia. Ensaios de Homenagem a Jill Dias*, ed. P. J. Havik, C. Saraiva and J. A. Tavim. Lisbon: Imprensa de Ciências Sociais: 37–50.

Subrahmanyam, Sanjay. 1992. "Iranians abroad: Intra-Asian Elite Migration and Early Modern State Formation." *Journal of Asian Studies* 51/2: 340–363.

Subrahmanyam, Sanjay. 2005. "Taking Stock of the Franks: South Asian Views of Europeans and Europe, 1500–1800." *Indian Economic and Social History Review* 62/1: 69–100.

Teltscher, Kate. 1995. *India Inscribed. European and British Writing on India (1600–1800)*. Delhi: Oxford University Press.

Terry, Edward. 1777. *A Voyage to East-India* (1st ed., 1655). London: J. Wilkie.

Walker, James Bernard. 1933. *The "Chronicles" of Saint Antoninus*. Washington, D. C.: The Catholic University of America.

Wormser, Paul. 2009. "Un modèle moghol à Aceh au XVIIe siècle?". *Archipel* 77: 69–82.

Xavier, Jerónimo. *Ādāb-us-salṭanat*. School of Oriental and African Studies, London, MS. 7030.

Weighing the Mughal

German Perception of Governmental Structures and the Staging of Power in the Early Modern Indian Mughal Empire

Antje Flüchter

1 Introduction

Twice a year, on his solar and his lunar birthday, the Indian Mughal was weighed before his entire court. For this occasion, many nobles and governors from the provinces came to the place where the Mughal held court. In this solemnity, the Mughal sat, richly clothed and with lots of jewellery, in a huge and sumptuous scale and was weighed several times: against money, against gold and jewels, a third time against precious clothes and spices, and then a last time against cereals, butter, and herbs. Afterwards, the precious items were given to the courtiers, and the money and food to the poor. If the Mughal weighed more than the year before, everybody was happy. Many travellers wrote about this special ritual, travellers who had actually been at the court and could thus observe this ceremony first-hand, such as the French Jean de Thévenot, Jean-Baptiste Tavernier and François Bernier, or Sir Thomas Roe, the first English ambassador at the Mughal court. The ritual was integrated into most of the compilations and in rather general texts about India, such as the ones written by Olfert Dappert (*Asia, Oder: Ausführliche Beschreibung Des Reichs des Grossen Mogols* 1681) or Erasmus Francisci (*Ost- und West-Indischer wie auch Sinesischer Lust- und Statsgarten* 1668), as too into encyclopedias like *Zedlers Universalexicon*. The representation of the Mughal Empire in this single solemnity was also used in a different medium. One of the most famous and precious objects in the *Grüne Gewölbe* (Green Vaults), the treasure chamber in Dresden, is the "Court in Delhi at the Birthday of the Great Mughal Aurangzeb" (*Der Hofstaat zu Delhi am Geburtstag des Großmughals Aurang Zeb*), made by the goldsmith Johann Melchior Dinglinger between 1701 and 1707 on behalf of August the Strong, Elector of Saxony and King of Poland (Warncke 2004; Müller and Springeth 2000). This diorama consists of 165 small golden figures coloured with

---

A. Flüchter (✉)
Karl Jaspers Centre, Voßstr. 2, 69115 Heidelberg, Germany
e-mail: fluechter@asia-europe.uni-heidelberg.de

A. Flüchter and S. Richter (eds.), *Structures on the Move*, 147
Transcultural Research – Heidelberg Studies on Asia and Europe in a Global Context,
DOI 10.1007/978-3-642-19288-3_8, © Springer-Verlag Berlin Heidelberg 2012

enamel and jewel-encrusted, depicting courtiers, servants, ambassadors with presents, exotic animals etc., and, in the centre, the Mughal Aurangzeb (who was still alive when Dinglinger started his work). This piece of art is not a fictional scene; Dinglinger referred in part to several travellers' reports in order to make a true representation of the Mughal's court, and as well he integrated aspects from other Asian courts to produce a representation of the whole of Asia. In the installation today, a huge set of scales is placed, rather forlornly, at the edge of the scene, whereas in the early eighteenth century it was situated near the Mughal and thus indicated the ritual of his weighing (Warncke 1989: 2156). It would seem that if someone wanted to accumulate all the knowledge available about the Mughal Empire and its governance in one scene, this ritual of weighing was the one chosen in the seventeenth and eighteenth centuries. Today, as also in the late eighteenth and throughout the nineteenth century, this gorgeous Indian court life fits the picture of oriental lavishness. The image of India became homogeneous after the second half of the eighteenth century: the Mughal became one amongst the oriental despots, India the country of holy cows and snake charmers. This orientalistic interpretation and construction of the Mughal Empire, its government, as well as of the whole of India was very successful: older pictures and older knowledge were forgotten for a long time. While the impact of the Chinese experience on Europe was never totally forgotten and research on Chinese-European encounters has increased in recent decades (Osterhammel 1998; Appleton 1951; Hobson 2004), the Indian subcontinent stayed as a static world region in the shadow of historical research, at least in Germany.[1]

The present paper tackles two problems. Firstly, Early Modern German knowledge of India must be examined, along with the perception of the Indian Mughal court's governmental structures and technologies of governance. An analysis shall be carried out as regards which political aspects of the Mughal Empire were of interest to a European and most of all German audience, which were well-known and integrated into the discourse on government as knowledge about India. Knowledge is understood as socially constructed (Landwehr 2002; Burke 2002; Berger and Luckmann 1967). Travelogues communicated an individual experience and were read as such. The reception and processing of these texts or particular narratives though the compilation of travelogues and even more by using them for general texts about India can be understood as a process of selection, dividing more reliable elements or those accepted as being true from other parts. The height of generalisation was the integration of information in encyclopaedias, because this genre claimed to present the general knowledge of the time (Schneider 2006; Flüchter 2010). To analyse this transfer or circulation of knowledge through a first case study the narratives of some specimen travelogues are compared with compilation texts from the seventeenth century, most of all those mentioned by Erasmus Francisci and Olfert Dapper, alongside two encyclopaedias of the

---

[1] One exception is the study by Dharampal-Frick (1994); there is also much information, of course, in Lach and Van Kley (1993).

eighteenth and early nineteenth centuries (that is the article "Mogul" in Zedler 1739 and Krünitz 1803). Based on this perception and our assessment, we must, secondly, ask: was Mughal governance credited with a certain superiority which might then have contributed to a willingness to absorb its ideas and technologies of governance? Or did the Mughal Empire oppose European ideals of government? Were elements of later "oriental despotism" already distinguishable at this time? To analyse the German reception of India, two theoretical perspectives are important. First, the recent approaches using transcultural perception and translation have given us new insights into processes of intercultural contact and communication (Budich and Iser 1996; Burghartz 2003; Burke 2007). However, to understand the Early Modern perception of Mughal governance, it is time to integrate as well new cultural approaches to political history. This constructivist perspective understands the political world as socially constructed and as reproduced in every action. Everyone who acts in this sphere must know about this system of symbols. These approaches have led to many new insights into the performative character of the political system of Early Modern Europe (Stollberg-Rilinger 2005, 2009; Landwehr 2003), however, they have been applied, for the most part, solely to intra-European topics. It is time to apply these approaches to Early Modern perceptions of non-European world regions and their technologies of governance. Thus, this paper combines the perspective of this cultural political history with concepts of transcultural perception and ethno-history.[2] Players involved in any intercultural political interaction need political knowledge of the system in which they are participating. In Early Modern times, travellers, diplomats and others brought their European knowledge with them into the transcultural interactions, and then brought their experiences back to Europe, where these influenced new groups of travellers, and were also integrated into theoretical texts about state and state-related topics.

In the seventeenth century, many regions in the Holy Roman Empire were either engaged in fighting the 30 Years' War, or were recovering from its consequences: their political systems had to be completely reorganised; during this crisis the demand for *gute policey*, that is, a policy to establish and maintain a well-ordered community, was high on the agenda. Therefore the process of modern state-building received new impetus and gained an intensification and acceleration. The processes led to a well-ordered state with regard to policy, politics and organisation (Raeff 1975; Härter 2010; Iseli 2009) and involved many actors as recent research concerning state-building from below has analysed and shown (cf. introduction of this volume). The focus of this paper, however, concerns only one group of actors, namely the people who were interested and involved in politics and who were looking for ideas as to how to improve technologies of governance.

---

[2] Important here is Dirks (1987), for his concept of politics, cf. XXIII–XXV. However, while Dirks analysed how the Indian princely states were integrated into the British Empire with the help of a "political economy of honour" and thus preserved in a pre-modern context, the present paper analyses the Indian-European encounter at a time when this symbolic communication was the main mental structure for European culture.

The North Indian Mughal Empire was, in the seventeenth century, one of the richest and most powerful empires in the world. In travelogues and travellers' reports it is mostly considered to be one of the mightiest in the world, or at least in Asia (e.g. Mandelslo 1696: 64; Tavernier 1984: 159; Thévenot 1693: 6), and this assessment was absorbed into many encyclopedias (Zedler 1739: 826; Krünitz 1803: 595).[3] There are only a few works in Europe which analysed the European perception of Indian governmental structures, and the question of whether Europeans learned anything about politics in Asia and then applied this knowledge in the Early Modern state-building process. On the contrary, the modern European state is well understood as a purely European phenomenon, as characteristic of, and unique to, European history (Reinhard 1999: VII–XIV). This paper examines what German-speaking people knew about India in Early Modern times, as a basis for further research on Indian influence in German and European political development. To tackle these questions, certain topics have been chosen to serve as examples. These are, firstly, the central administrative system, customs and the judiciary as instrumental aspects of *policey*, and, secondly, aspects of court life as the main stage for representing power. These topics cover the instrumental and symbolic aspects of early modern rule; both were intertwined and both were important for the functioning of the whole.

2   The Well-Ordered Indian State: The Central Administrative System

Mughal administration was interwoven with military hierarchies, social elites, in the attempts to incorporate very different regional traditions of governance. For this reason it is still an important topic for studies of the history of Mughal India (Richards 1993). The early modern European travellers had difficulty in grasping it in its complexity; nevertheless, governance and administration were topics that were described in many seventeenth century travellers' reports, and that is a proof that this topic was considered important, although the degree of detailed description varied. In his travel report *Orientalische Reise-Beschreibungen*, published in 1669, the German Jürgen Andersen, who travelled to India with the VOC (the Dutch East India Company) gave a detailed description of the main offices of the Mughal's central administration: the "Primo-Visir oder Reichskantzler" (the imperial chancellor) was at the top, followed by the "Wasanbassi oder Schatzmeister" (treasurer), who ruled over 21 "geschworne Schreiber" (scribes who had sworn an official oath) (Andersen and Iversen 1980: 44–45). The terms used in Andersen's text are rather unique among the early modern travel accounts. Maybe his account is not based on

---

[3] This assessment mostly described the power of the Ottoman Empire, Persia and Mughal India, China not being included, as a rule.

Andersen's experience in India at all, but on that of the editor of this text, Adam Olearius. He was not only an erudite man and ducal counsellor, he had also travelled himself with an embassy to Moscow and Persia. As an editor, he is known for his thorough editing and for including information deriving from his own experience or other sources.[4] For this article it is only important to observe what kind of image of Mughal administration was presented in German discourse. Andersen's text communicated a sense of amazement at such a well-organised and very rationally functioning accountancy. The Dutch compiler Olfert Dapper described the administrative system with the same terms Andersen had (Dapper 1681: 149). "Such a shared usage of terminology by these writers underlines the relevance of this as a system of perception for early modern German discourse, whatever its empirical reliability might have been." A similar description of a highly differentiated administrative system, but using somewhat different terms and closer in spirit to modern historiography, can be found in Erasmus Francisci's encyclopedia, where Johannes de Laet's Latin compilation about India and Johann Albrecht von Mandelslo's report on his travels are quoted, the latter author a nobleman from Schleswig-Holstein, whose book was also published by Adam Olearius (Francisci 1668: 1437; De Laet 1928 (reprint New Delhi 1975); Mandelslo 1696). The phrasing of the description in Francisci's text was even more successful than the one by Andersen: Francisci's terminology for the Mughal administration is more or less the same as can be found under the lemma "Mogol" in Zedler's *Universal Lexicon* (Zedler 1739: 828), and also in the entry in Krünitz's *Oeconomische Encyclopädie* (Krünitz 1803: 600). Whilst the Krünitz text used similar terms, it changed the evaluation in essential ways. Whereas the article in the Zedler concluded with the statement that the Mughal could rule his territory using the instrument of a well-ordered administration with absolute power ("unumschränkte Macht"), the author of the same lemma in Krünitz's encyclopedia, written about 70 years later, formulated that the Mughal's governance was despotic, because he ruled absolutely over the life and property of his subjects (Krünitz 1803: 596). Between the appearance of these texts, the shift from admiration to orientalised criticism had taken place.

The administrative system of the Mughal Empire, we may conclude, was considered both interesting for an audience and worthwhile to write about. With this description of the administration, the Mughal Empire is characterised as a systematically organised and well-ordered form of government. There is no explicit comparison with European systems, but the translation into European terminology

---

[4] Adam Olearius' publishing work should be seen in the context of his duke striving to become part of a global trade network. Books on seventeenth century state theory can be understood in a similar context (Hill 2003; Becher 1673; Duchhardt 1986). Because of the thorough rewriting by Olearius of the reports by Andersen and Iversen, Honoré Naber refused to include this work in his series of travelogues (cf. his foreword to Merklein 1930: VIII). In general, and in view of his own travel accounts to Russia and Persia, Olearius is considered to be a very trustworthy author (cf. e.g. Strack 1994).

of, e.g. *Vize-Roy* or *Schatzmeister* is not only a simple translation for the readers, but also means that these offices and their functions can be compared with those of the European system. Although there is no explicit statement that the Indian system was seen as a role model, it was interesting enough that this information was integrated into many compilations. With its inclusion in Zedler's *Universal Lexicon*, it became a socially accepted and highly valued "truth", whereas in the nineteenth century the framing of knowledge had shifted and with it the selection of what could be believed to be "true".

3 The Well-Ordered Indian State: The Customs Administration

As important as the description of the administrative system was, the customs imposed upon everyone entering the Mughal's kingdom was even more significant. Thomas Roe, the first English ambassador at the Mughal's court in the early seventeenth century, complained greatly that the customs officers did not make an exception for him, as the ambassador of the King of England, and his servants (Foster 1967: 42–43). In nearly all travellers' reports the customs practice is described in great detail—it had obviously left a great impression on the authors. Some accounts announced the actual amount of money that had to be paid for customs (Burckhardt 1693: 156; Andersen and Iversen 1980: 22). Jean de Thévenot, a French merchant whose book of travels was translated into many European languages, delivered a very drastic description: the searching was accomplished with much force and very carefully, so that it was impossible to deceive the customs officer. They even had a list with all the merchants' names, so it was obviously very well organised. Thévenot seems undecided as to whether he admires this effective system or is annoyed although he did give vent to his obvious annoyance by writing that he needed all his patience to let the customs officers do their work (Thévenot 1693: 2–4). There were some people who complained about the arbitrariness of the customs practice, about greedy and corrupt officers (Mandelslo 1696: 39–40; Wurffbain 1931: vol. II, 11); however, compared with the description of customs practices in other parts of the world, the perception of a powerful and effective system in the Mughal empire prevailed.[5]

The customs duties were an important source of income for the Mughal and were described as such. However, their detailed description had a wider purpose than just explaining the Mughal's wealth: Mughal rule was based on long experience and seen as powerful and effective by these travellers—not only because of the well-organised examination of goods. The description of the customs practices not only

---

[5] Cf. for example the description of customs practice in Guinea (Hulsius 1606: 60–61). Thévenot, who was rather critical about the customs practice in the Mughal empire, later compared it with that in the kingdom of Golconda, where the officers were even more impertinent and arrogant (Thévenot 1693: 187).

explained how the Mughals increased their wealth, it also illustrated the power relation between the Mughal office-holders and the Europeans. In the travelogues published by Adam Olearius, several occasions were described in which the asymmetries of power relations between European traders and Mughal officers became apparent. In the harbour town of Surat, all European traders had to give up their weapons because of an order which declared that no Christians were allowed to wear weapons in the Mughal's towns (Andersen and Iversen 1980: 22). Moreover, Jürgen Andersen depicted a scene in Ahmedabad where Dutch goods were examined a second time by the Mughal's customs officers. An Indian merchant tried to help the Dutch and calculated the value of their goods as quite low. The customs officers punished him severely, while the Europeans could not help him and had to accept the powerful position of the Mughal's officers (Andersen and Iversen 1980: 27). Thus, the relations of power were clear and the European traders did not dare to challenge this, at least not (or only rarely) in the seventeenth century, when the Mughal supremacy of power was unquestioned. This staging of power asymmetries in the social practice of collecting customs duties may have been a reason why these anecdotes were hardly mentioned in the compilations, and were scarcely of any importance in the *Zedler* and the *Krünitz*. The customs practice was experienced as being impressive and efficient by the travellers, but it did not awaken the interest of authors who processed this information into a learned and rather general discourse. Hence none of these anecdotes were transferred into a compilation or into an encyclopaedia. It was not a particularly Indian technology of governance and it showed the Europeans' weak position in India.

4 The Well-Ordered Indian Police State: The Judiciary

From the modern perspective, the judiciary is considered an important element of government. With the success of Montesquieu's book *L'esprit des lois*, the judiciary or the existence of written laws became an even more important criterion for evaluating forms of governance (Osterhammel 1998: 275–284). Moreover, the practice of administering justice can also be seen as an act of solemnly exercising and thereby presenting one's sovereignty (Neves 1998; Flüchter 2005). Compared with this relevance of the judiciary in modern discourse, judicial practice was only rarely tackled in early travellers' reports. Jürgen Andersen mentioned a building for justice ("Richthaus") in the context of the administrative positions; he also described a "Reichsrichter", whom he compared with a European bishop-judge in criminal affairs (Andersen and Iversen 1980: 45–48; Mandelslo 1696: 63). As explained above, the empirical basis of Andersen's report is sometimes disputable; it is possible that this is some information drawn from other sources by Olearius, or from the latter's own experiences in Persia. This would explain why Andersen did not mention aspects of the Mughal judiciary that were described in many other texts about India.

In the following, three aspects of Mughal judiciary will be analysed: first, the factor of approachability, often described and praised; second, the security in the cities. In a third step, certain critical aspects will be examined. The Mughal administered justice regularly; he thus seemed to be accessible for all his subjects. This aroused the interest of European travellers and many wrote about it. On several occasions Thomas Roe, the English ambassador, wrote in his diary about Jahangir's practice of administering justice personally every day (Foster 1967: 106). The French travellers Jean de Thévenot, as well as Jean-Baptist Tavernier, wrote about the same practice (Tavernier 1984: 62–64; Thévenot 1693: 82–83). This approachability was most tellingly represented in a narrative about golden bells, which everybody who wanted to speak to the Mughal could ring. For the German discourse the report of Johann Albrecht von Mandelslo was most influential in this respect (Mandelslo 1696: 63, footnote (a)). His report was widely read, and the image of the golden bell was very memorable, thereby entering many compilations (Francisci 1668: 1438–1439, 1444; Dapper 1681: 271). This part of his report was also integrated into one of the most important compilations of travel accounts of the eighteenth century (Schwabe 1753: 83). The Mughal's approachability was also stressed in Zedler's lemma for "Mogol" (Zedler 1739), while it was also praised in an important text about state theory by Johann Heinrich Gottlob von Justi. In his *Vergleichung der europäischen mit den asiatischen und andern vermeintlich barbarischen Regierungen* (1762), he compared European and Asian systems of governance. His aim was to reform the territories of the *Alte Reich*, so that they could compete with other, more developed European countries such as France or England. He praised the accessibility of the Indian Mughal, and regarded the practice of regularly and personally administering justice as an advantage of Asian government over European (Justi 1762: 42). In this respect, Justi hoped European rulers would take Asian rule as a role model. The relevance of the Mughal's accessibility, as well as the public practice of administering justice, is apparent if it is compared with the way justice was experienced elsewhere. The antipode of this practice in early modern texts was the Portuguese Inquisition, often criticised because trials did not take place publicly and so nobody knew why a sentence was passed (Tavernier 1984: 100).[6]

If we analyse the perception of this narrative over the course of time, there is an interpretational shift again when we look at the same lemma in Krünitz's encyclopedia, where the daily audience is only understood as an opportunity for the Mughal to carry out some "self-fashioning" and to demonstrate his power (Krünitz 1803: 596).

Justi admired a second particularity of the Mughal's judiciary, as well: the security in the cities. This aspect is mentioned in several travel accounts, mostly French. Jean de Thévenot explained it in the context of his description of Surat. There, the *Coutal*, a kind of police officer, was liable for all criminal offences

---

[6] This comparison between Asian judiciary and Catholic—in this case Portuguese—inquisition was still being made Justi in the eighteenth century (Justi 1762: 252).

committed, which meant that, if he could not find the culprit, he himself had to compensate the victim. However, while Thévenot distinguished here between theory and practice, and thus explained that the *Coutals* were mostly clever enough to avoid this liability (Thévenot 1693: 37), Justi took this practice as an example and a proof of the superiority of Indian government, and complimented the Indian system on its efficiency in general. Also using the example of the port town of Surat, he wrote that there was no violence on the streets, not even arguments, and all because the government was so effective. Similarly to Thévenot, he explained this situation as being due to the government's great effort, and that the system included an efficient driving force to encourage office-holders to care for the security of their subjects. If the *Coutal* could not convict the offender—for example, a thief—he had to compensate the victim for damages suffered. In this case, Justi did not consider the *Coutal*'s liability *per se* as a model for European governance, but he praised the Asian wisdom in considering that public servants needed special motivation, so that public safety did not suffer (Justi 1762: 252–255).

However, there was not only praise for the Mughal Empire's judiciary. Flaws were also mentioned, flaws that can be understood as building blocks for the modern narrative of oriental despotism. Some writers considered the sentences handed down to be rather cruel. This perspective is particularly explicit in the travel accounts published by Adam Olearius. Mandelslo mentioned, for example, that Shah Jahan sometimes passed cruel sentences (Mandelslo 1696: 64), while Andersen wrote that there was no "professional" executioner, but that the judge just called someone out of the crowd to carry out the sentence (Andersen and Iversen 1980: 45).[7] If travelogues include descriptions of punishments in India, they seem rather cruel and drastic. However, this is a rather modern perspective; if we consider early modern criminal law (Dülmen 1988), the early modern traveler might have been less shocked.

In the late eighteenth and nineteenth centuries another aspect of the judiciary in the Mughal Empire, not mentioned so far, became an integral part of the theory of Asian despotism (Richter 1974; Whelan 2001): the lack of written laws. When analyzing the travelers' reports we find, astoundingly, that this lack of written law was especially stressed by English travellers. In 1616, Thomas Roe complained in a letter to Lord Carew: "They haue no written Law. The King by his owne word ruleth, and his Gouernours of Prouinces by that authoritie" (Foster 1967: 110). Jemima Kindersley, one of the few women travellers of the late eighteenth century, characterised the Mughal's way of governing as despotic, because there was nothing like a well-ordered *corpus juris*, only tradition (Kindersley 1777: 158). This lack of a written law is the only one of the many aspects described that Montesquieu integrated as a central argument in his *Esprit des lois*. In chapter 16 of his fifth book the difference between a moderate and a despotic government is given as being that, in the despotism, the ruler's will is the only law (Montesquieu

---

[7] The statement in Andersen's report opposed Thévenot's account, which stressed that nobody could be sentenced to death without the Mughal's permission (Thévenot 1693: 37).

1994: 168). The Mughal's absolute power was also mentioned in many compilations (Francisci 1668: 1442; Dapper 1670: 148); however, it was not always mentioned in a negative manner, and it was also not regarded as the main characterisation of his governmental system.

The shift in approbation can be seen again in Krünitz's lemma, changing the lack of written laws to a lack of laws altogether. Only the Mughal's will was the law, only he could judge, and it was mortally perilous to say anything against his judgement (Krünitz 1803: 596).

The Indian judiciary included some aspects, such as the general approachability of the Mughal and the security in port towns that were appreciated in European texts and, in the case of Justi, even proposed as a role model for European rulers. However, Justi's position seems to be rather isolated. In the eighteenth century, laws and legislation gained more relevance in the perception of India. The lack of written laws was considered an indicator of despotism, and in despotic rule, approachability does not improve the situation. The shift of esteem with regard to the judiciary is even more drastic than that concerning other technologies of governance.

5 Court Life in India

The importance of ceremonial and symbolic practices for European court life is well researched. Between the fifteenth and the seventeenth centuries, there was a shift in Europe from occasionally celebrating great rituals of royalty to permanently and publicly celebrating the daily routine of the court and its hierarchies. In the face-to-face interaction in a European court, ceremonial was used to define the monarch's relationship to his subjects, to the members of court society, and to other monarchs. In Europe, monarchic favours and honours became exactly measurable; everyone who lived at court had to know this elaborate symbolic language, and they constantly had to "read" the ceremonial practice to know the positions of all court members.[8] All these ceremonials, of staging rank, power, and social relations, contrast, in the sense of governance, strongly with the instrumentalised ones analysed in the first part of this article. In pre-modern Europe, symbolic politics were considered as important as instrumental politics. Against this backdrop, it is not surprising that many travelogues included descriptions of Indian court life. In the following, general evaluations of the Mughal court are described first, then two special symbolic practices are analysed (processions and the Mughal's birthday): the French travellers Thévenot and Tavernier both experienced the Mughal's court at first hand and wrote about several *solemnities*. Thévenot wrote only briefly about everyday court life and ceremonies, a fact that he justified with reference to the

---

[8] "Zeremoniell" has become an important analytical instrument for research on Early Modern European or German society; cf. Stollberg-Rilinger (1997); Pecar (2005).

more detailed account by Francois Bernier, who stayed for several years at the Mughal court as one of Aurangzeb's physicians (Bernier 1673). However, Thévenot also wrote about the entrances of several of the Mughal's governors, and about the *solemnities* at the wedding of the Governor of Surat's daughter (Thévenot 1693: 43–45). Tavernier described the audience's reactions (Tavernier 1984: 68). Even so, Adam Olearius complained that, with regard to the importance and wealth of Mughal India, only a few detailed texts about its court life could be found in German or Latin (Mandelslo 1696: 63). This lack of information might be one of the reasons why Olearius fleshed out the corresponding parts of the accounts of India he published. Thus, Andersen and Mandelslo described how huge and gorgeous the court was; Andersen counted 12,000 servants, 1,200 women of the harem, and 600 eunuchs. Mandelslo explained that the Mughal displayed all of his splendour when he gave an audience to foreign ambassadors, or when he went out hunting or to war (Andersen and Iversen 1980: 44; Mandelslo 1696: 66). In later descriptions, the splendour of the Mughal court seems to increase over the course of time. Dapper and Francisci mention a similar number of courtiers to those Andersen gave. Francisci added that the Mughal's court was much more pompous and ceremonious than the court of the Persian king (Francisci 1668, 1436, 1440–1441; Dapper 1670: 142). Concerning the ceremonial, he referred to Thomas Roe, who became an important point of reference regarding knowledge about the Mughal court. In Zedler's article the details mentioned in these reports are repeated, and, as in Francisci's text, the Mughal court was compared with the Persian court (Zedler 1739: 828). In one of the standard works on European ceremonial, the *Theatrum Ceremoniale Historico-Politicum*, the author Lünig explains that he included non-European ceremonials, because the courts in Asia and Africa were very famous in Europe because of their luxuriousness and lavishness (Lünig 1720: 1461). Contrary to criticisms in the later eighteenth century, here lavishness must be understood as praise. Krünitz's general estimation of the Mughal power mirrored that shift; he, too, evaluated it much more negatively than his predecessors in the seventeenth and early eighteenth centuries. He viewed this court life as pure spectacle, without any inner values. One other detail is interesting in his characterisation: he still refers to Thomas Roe, whose experience and information was nearly 200 years old by this time. Krünitz knew that Roe had travelled to India long before his own time, but he justified his reference to Roe by the assumption that oriental societies were more static than European ones. In Krünitz's view, then, Roe's observations could still be applied without any problem to nineteenth century India (Krünitz 1803: 597). Here the image of the static Orient is represented very tellingly by this statement.

Apart from these general observations, some practices were described in more detail. Many authors of travel accounts and compilations wrote about diplomatic ceremonials at the Mughal court. The differences from, as well as the similarities with European diplomacy have still to be analysed more systematically (Subrahmanyam 2005: 152–155). The perception of processions or *adventus* also seemed to be important for the image of the Mughal empire. Andersen depicted one of the Mughal's processions in a way that reminds us of the importance of the

European *adventus* for the performance and understanding of social differentiation.[9] Thus, Andersen wrote about the lavishly decorated elephants, the servants who accompanied the Mughal with a *Kitesol*—a kind of parasol—to offer shade, and a fan made out of peacock feathers to keep him cool.[10] Next came 200 eunuchs, with the Mughal's sons and eight nobles of his court following this group—each of them again with a servant carrying a *Kitesol*—then 600 expensively arrayed riders and huntsmen (Andersen and Iversen 1980: 35–36). Similarly—but not nearly in such detail—Tavernier described the procession with which Aurangzeb went to a mosque, accompanied by his sons, his wives and a large contingent of military personnel (Tavernier 1984: 179). The travellers described these stagings of power and social hierarchies in processions not as a foreign phenomenon, although individual elements were exotic (the parasol, the elephants), but as something which could be read like European court life, and was comparable. Dapper included the description of such a procession in his compilation, and illustrated it impressively (Dapper 1681: 142–144). Zedler also referred to Tavernier's description of the Mughal's procession to the mosque,[11] and regarding this element of Mughal court life even Krünitz's article does not differ in its evaluation.

The last example of Mughal court life and its perception from German texts is the Mughal's birthday. The celebrations of the Mughal's birthday were a very important event for the description of the image of Mughal India as was mentioned at the beginning of this article. Thomas Roe, the first English ambassador, wrote about it, as did French travellers. Thévenot gave his readers many details, as outlined at the beginning of this paper, and the translation of his text was even accompanied by an illustration of this ritual (Tavernier 1984: 175–177, cf. also the description in Thévenot 1693: 93–94; Bernier 1673). Even in some of the reports written by German servants of the Dutch East India Company (VOC) this event is mentioned, such as Burckhardt's, who certainly did not attend this event personally (Burckhardt 1693: 158). Reports like Burckhardt's probably derive from a knowledge of Mughal court life shared by Europeans in India. Thus it seems that this ritual became a topos in describing the Mughal court or even the whole empire; perhaps the weighing of the Mughal was seen as the essence that represented the Mughal Empire as a whole. This hypothesis may be supported by the fact that Lünig included only this one ceremonial in the *Theatrum Ceremoniale*, his standard work about European court ceremonials (Lünig 1720: 1463).

---

[9] Fundamental for the practice of reading a society in the text of a procession is Darnton (1985). Concerning the European relevance of the so-called *adventus*, cf. Schenk (2002).

[10] This fan—and the boy who chased away flies with it—appears to have been an important element in the Indian symbolic household, if somebody wanted to stage his social importance, cf. Thévenot (1693: 206).

[11] Zedler (1739: 832); however, in contrast to Tavernier, Zedler's article distinguishes between a rather secular procession, with many elephants, and the passage to the mosque, when all except the Mughal and his sons went on foot.

Weighing the Mughal 159

This story served several purposes. On the one hand, it showed the opulence of the Mughal court and his expected wealth; the celebration was the opportunity to talk about many aspects of Mughal court life. But on the other hand, there were also criticisms included in these descriptions. Jean de Thévenot questioned the value of the things which were weighed against the Mughal, and he also described the artificial nuts and fruits the Mughal used to throw among his guests as rather worthless (Thévenot 1693: 94). A similar evaluation can be found in the travel report by Christian Burckhardt, mentioned above (Burckhardt 1693: 158). In Francisci's *Statsgarten* the whole ceremonial in its splendour together with the criticism are both described.[12] And it seems significant that Lünig in his *Theatrum Ceremoniale* referred to the less critical Thévenot; in fact, he almost quoted him verbatim (Lünig 1720: 1463). While doubts about the value of some of the gifts was one aspect among others in the travel account analysed, the article in Krünitz's encyclopedia organised the whole description of the weighing around criticism: the Mughal used his birthday to obtain, or even to force, many presents from his guests, and gave them knick-knacks in return. While the seventeenth century travel accounts stressed that most of the things against which the Mughal was weighed were given to the poor, Krünitz put it differently. Mockingly, he wrote that after the ritual came the one good deed ("Wohltat") the Mughal did every year, when he gave away some small pieces of money ("einige kleine Stücke Geld") to the poor, and cheap nuts to his nobles (Krünitz 1803: 600). So the splendour and gorgeousness of the Mughal's court was quite insubstantial, it was showmanship more than substance, altogether something of a sham. The increasing criticism of the way the Mughal celebrated his birthday can be interpreted in the context of the increasing criticism of lavishness at the European courts themselves. The same applies to the description of Indian court life and its splendour in general: the narratives became more critical during the eighteenth and nineteenth centuries, and ceremonial practices were more or less deprived of any instrumental function. But the later image of India is not only a mirror or vehicle for European criticism of Europe. It also marks a shift in the perception of European-Asian power relations—similar to the praise in the preceding period.

The Mughal court was praised and admired for its splendour in the seventeenth century. But was the Mughal court a role model for ceremonial? In some respects, the Mughal court could be understood as the baroque representation of the ideal of the absolute ruler. As such a representation or mirror of the court of August the Strong, Dinglinger had produced his precious *Hofstaat des Großmoguls*, mentioned

---

[12] Francisci was referring to Thomas Roe, Francisci (1668: 1445–1446); interestingly, he quoted the version of Roe's description that Olearius had published as a further remark to accompany Mandelslo's travelogue. Also in Burckhardt, as well as in Francisci, a second critical aspect of this feast can be found: the wastefulness of food and drink—"das Fressen und Sauffen"! Burckhardt (1693: 158–169); Francisci (1668, 1446): "Nach solchem ist die gantze Nacht mit Sauffen zugebracht"—a fact that neither Tavernier nor the more critical Thévenot mentioned (Thévenot 1693: 94).

at the beginning of this article, for the same ruler. In the seventeenth century, the importance of symbolic communication is mirrored in detailed descriptions of ceremonial processions, hunting, and diplomatic encounters at the Mughal court. These appeared as classical, solemn acts to express dominion, power and sovereignty—in Europe as well as in India. Thus, these detailed descriptions prove that the European authors "read" the Indian staging with the same symbolic language they used for European courts; hence, they did not perceive Mughal court life as foreign or strange. However, it should be stressed that handbooks for European ceremonial only rarely included non-European ceremonials. Lünig included the weighing of the Mughal, as he wanted to stress the power of this ruler, but also to point out an exotic ceremonial. It is significant that Lünig did not put the description of this ceremony in the first part of his book, where he collected ceremonies and practices of many European courts (including the Ottoman Empire), but in his 36th chapter where he brought ceremonies from many non-European courts together, that seemed interesting and exotic. In the course of the eighteenth century, the general perception of India changed, but so did the concept of good government in Europe. It is significant that Justi, who wanted to improve European technologies of governance in a modern sense, did not appreciate or use these descriptions and appraisals of Mughal court life in detail, but complained about the pompous extravagance at European courts, and confronted their wastefulness with the economising practice in Asia (Justi 1762: 64–67).

6 Conclusion

The question was whether the Indian experience, or the Mughal Empire in particular, could serve as a type of role model for European development and state building. Governmental structures were part of the Early Modern perception of India; the image of the Mughal Empire encompassed institutions such as customs administration, the administration in general, and the judiciary, as well as the staging and thus performative production of government and power at the Mughal court's ceremonial. All narratives cited that describe the governmental system in the Mughal Empire have elements of admiration and of foreignness or alterity. In seventeenth century travellers' reports, the image and the evaluation of the Mughal Empire are very heterogeneous; the admiration and wonder outweighed the criticism. The English ambassador Roe complained a great deal, yet his view of the Mughal Empire is not that of a barbaric government. The Frenchmen Tavernier and Thévenot described the Mughal system in detail, sometimes mockingly, but most of all as an effectively functioning and well-ordered system.

In the seventeenth century, parts of the German and European audience were interested in Asian and Indian technologies of governance and even more in description of Indian court life. Some texts on India functioned as light reading and entertainment. However, they had more functions than simply entertaining, and were also read and published by people who were interested in governance or state theory. The general, as well as the specific interest in Indian technologies of governance and court life expressed itself in the reception of this information in compilations and encyclopaedias. This has been shown in the examples of the works of Erasmus Francisci, Olfert Dapper, and Zeder's *Universallexicon*. The comparison with Krünitz's encyclopedia shows that the perspective had shifted in the course of the late eighteenth century; this orientalised India could not be a role model of any kind.

In the evaluation and even more so in its change, differences between the topics can be seen. Some aspects of the Indian experience were more important, if Europeans were looking for new ideas of governance, than others. The description of court life aroused the interest of many readers. They were not interested because these ceremonials were so exotic, but because they perceived them as being similar or even better, that is richer, than European practice. A certain amount of learning from Asian court culture might have been possible at the time when court ceremonials in Europe were at their peak. Moreover, if we acknowledge that Early Modern Europeans employed a reservoir of symbols when reading, understanding and structuring their world, we should also acknowledge that they read non-European cultures in the same way. Thus, they could understand the rationality of the Mughal's ceremonial practice, which nineteenth century Europeans could not. As such, some of the texts might have served future travellers or diplomats as a guideline for how to behave abroad,[13] or as a metaphor for court life, as Dinglinger's masterpiece showed, but not as a role model for European courts.

The situation is quite different if we look at the perception and appropriation of the more instrumental aspects of Indian experience, of the description of technologies of governance. Olearius, for example, was, as a ducal counsellor, an important example of this perspective; he was very interested in administrative structures, and it is significant that he as editor fleshed out most of those parts of the travel reports that concerned the Mughal Empire. Also, other actors and brokers in the Indian-European encounter served various German rulers, giving economic advice. Justi, who was looking for ideas for how to reform certain structures in the *Alte Reich*, was more interested in aspects of Indian judiciary than in the customs practice. As far as the technologies of Mughal governance, as they have been analysed in the first part of this paper, were to some extent credited with superiority compared with European governances in several texts, research is still needed to discover whether any of these ideas were transferred into political

---

[13] Christian Wieland in his article in this volume comes to a slightly different conclusion, namely that ambassadors could not really "learn" the customs of foreign courts because they had to represent their own ruler and his culture. However, this has to be argued on different levels: a shared (symbolic) language was necessary so that communication could function at all—and such a common language had been established in European diplomacy since the Middle Ages. Then and only after the establishment of such a shared symbolic language a maintenance of one's own cultural behaviour—as Wieland highlights—had to be stressed.

planning. Justi transferred the information about Indian governments into a theoretical discourse, but his text is an exception.

The perspective at the Mughal court and its technologies of governance changed over the course of time, most of all shifting in the second half of the eighteenth century. Justi's text is an important exception, but an exception nevertheless. With the decline of the Mughal Empire and with the beginning of British territorial rule in India, the Mughal Empire is increasingly described as weak, lavish and despotic, and this perception was projected back to earlier times. Early modern India with its achievements was forgotten.[14]

There are many reasons for this change. The shifting power relations in India are important: the decline of the Mughal empire as well as the rise of British colonialism and in short the process that is summarised under the label *great divergence*.[15] The European interest in technologies of governance changed too. In the eighteenth century, efficiency, for example, became more important than a lavish court-life. This change of interest was connected with an increasing criticism of European court ceremonials and against this background Indian courts were also seen differently.

Moreover, there was not only a change over time, but also selective perception during the transfer from one genre to another should be considered. Compilations and encyclopedias rarely integrated narratives that clearly proved an Indian superiority, and this process began already in the prologues of travelogues. In the European discourse, understood here as texts written in Europe, narratives about India were decreasingly used to express something about India, but to mirror Europe or as an argument in the internal European state discourse. An important example of this process is the oriental despotism as described in Montesquieu's *L'esprit de lois*. Subsequently this image gained a fixed place in state theory. The Mughal court as the baroque representation of the ideal of the absolute ruler—as we may understand Dinglinger's creation of the Mughal court, produced for August the Strong—was not possible any more. India had become the country of lavishly clothed maharajas, snake charmers, and holy cows—other perceptions were forgotten.

---

[14] Already, in Guillaume Raynal's *Histoire des deux Indes* (the German translation was published between 1774–1778), the author praises ancient India as the source of many European achievements, while later times are characterised by decline (Raynal et al. 1988, 48–49, 61, 66). This perspective became even more dominant in Orientalist texts of the nineteenth century, and, for German discourse, Max Müller must be mentioned in this context (Müller 1883).

[15] The literature about the Great Divergence is abundant, cf. the classic studies: Pomeranz (2000); Wong (2000); Vries (2002); and the discussion by Patrick O'Brien: O'Brien (2006).

Bibliography

Andersen, Jürgen and Volquard Iversen. 1980. *Orientalische Reise-Beschreibungen. In der Bearbeitung von Adam Olearius, Schleswig 1669*, ed. Dieter Lohmeier. Tübingen: Niemeyer.

Appleton, W.W. 1951. *A Cycle of Cathay: the Chinese Vogue in England during the 17th and 18th Century*. New York: Columbia University Press.

Becher, Johann Joachim. 1673. *Politischer Discurs von den eigentlichen Ursachen deß Auff- und Abnehmens der Städt, Länder und Republicken. In specie, wie ein Land volckreich und nahrhafft zu machen und in eine rechte societatem civilem zu bringen; auch wird von dem Bauren-, Handwercks- und Kauffmannsstandt derer Handel und Wandel item, von dem Monopolio*. Frankfurt: Zunner.

Berger, Peter L. and Thomas Luckmann. 1967. *The Social Construction of Reality. A Treatise in the Sociology of Knowledge*. New York: Doubleday.

Bernier, François. 1673. *Auffgezeichnete Beobachtungen was sich in dem Reich des Grossen Mogols Begeben und zugetragen hat / In Frantzösischer Sprach beschrieben von Dem Herrn Bernier Auß Derselbigen dem Geschichtliebenden Leser zu Nutzen in die Hochteutsche übersetzet und in offenen Truck befördert Durch Wilhelm Serlin / Buchführer in Franckfurt am Mayn*. Franckfurt am Mayn: Wilhelm Serlin.

Budich, Sanford and Wolfgang Iser. 1996. *The Translatability of Cultures. Figurations of the Space Between*. Stanford: Stanford University Press.

Burckhardt, Christian. 1693. *Ost-Indianische Reise-Beschreibung / Oder Kurtzgefaßter Abriß von Ost-Indien / und dessen angränzenden Provincien, bevorab wo die Holländer ihren Sitz und Trafiquen maintenieren etc.* Halle, Leipzig: Joh. Friedrich Zeitler.

Burghartz, Susanna. 2003. "'Translating seen into Scene?' Wahrnehmung und Repräsentation in der frühen Kolonialgeschichte Europas." In *Berichten – Erzählen – Beherrschen. Wahrnehmen und Repräsentation in der frühen Kolonialgeschichte Europas*, ed. Susanna Burghartz et al., 161–175. Frankfurt am Main: Klostermann.

Burke, Peter. 2002. *A Social History of Knowledge. From Gutenberg to Diderot*. Cambridge: Polity.

Burke, Peter. 2007. *Cultural Translation in Early Modern Europe*. Cambridge: Cambridge University Press.

Dapper, Olfert. 1670. *Umbständliche und Eigentliche Beschreibung von Africa, Und denen darzu gehörigen Königreichen und Landschaften, als Egypten, Barbarien, Libyen, Biledulgerid ... und den Africanischen Insulen*. Amsterdam: Meurs.

Dapper, Olfert. 1681. *Asia, Oder: Ausführliche Beschreibung Des Reichs des Grossen Mogols Und eines grossen Theils Von Indien: In sich haltend die Landschafften Kandahar, Kabul, Multan, Haikan, Bukkar, Send oder Diu, Jesselmeer, Attak, Peniab, Kaximir, Jangapore, Dely, Mando, Malva, Chitor, Utrad, Zuratte oder Kambaye, Chandisch, Narvar, Gwaliar, Indostan, Sanbat, Bakar, Nagrakat, Dekan und Visiapour. Nebenst einer vollkommenen Vorstellung Des Königreichs Persien, Wie auch Georgien, Mengrelien, Cirkassien und anderer benachbarten Länder*. Nürnberg: Hoffmann.

Darnton, Robert. 1985. "A Bourgeois Puts His World in Order. The City as a Text." In *The great Cat Massacre and other Episodes in French Cultural History*, ed. Robert Darnton, 107–144. New York: Vintage Books.

De Laet, Johannes. 1928 (Reprint new Delhi 1975). *The Empire of the Great Mogol. A Translation of De Laet's "Description of India and Fragment of Indian History", translated by John S. Hoyland*. Bombay; Taraporevela.

Dharampal-Frick, Gita. 1994. *Indien im Spiegel deutscher Quellen der frühen Neuzeit (1500–1750): Studien zu einer interkulturellen Konstellation*. Tübingen: Niemeyer.

Dirks, Nicholas D. 1987. *The Hollow Crown. Ethnohistory of an Indian Kingdom*. Cambridge: Cambridge University Press.

Duchhardt, Heinz. 1986. "Afrika und die deutsche Kolonialprojekte der 2. Hälfte des 17. Jahrhunderts." *Archiv für Kulturgeschichte* 68: 119–133.

164   A. Flüchter

Dülmen, Richard van. 1988. *Theater des Schreckens. Gerichtspraxis und Strafrituale in der frühen Neuzeit, 2ⁿᵈ edition*. Munich: Beck.

Flüchter, Antje. 2005. "Konfessionalisierung in kulturalistischer Perspektive? Überlegungen am Beispiel der Herzogtümer Jülich-Berg im 16. Jahrhundert." In *Was heißt Kulturgeschichte des Politischen?*, ed. Barbara Stollberg-Rilinger, 225–252. Berlin: Duncker & Humblot.

Flüchter, Antje. 2010. "'Aus den fürnembsten indianischen Reisebeschreibungen zusammengezogen'. Knowledge about India in Early Modern Germany." *Intersections: The Dutch Trading Companies as Knowledge Networks* 13: 337–360.

Foster, William. 1967. *The Embassy of Sir Thomas Roe to the Court of the Great Mogul 1615–1619 as Narrated in his Journal and Correspondence* (reproduction of the edition 1899: 1899. Nendeln/Liechtenstein: Kraus.

Francisci, Erasmus. 1668. *Ost- und West-Indischer wie auch Sinesischer Lust- und Statsgarten [. . .]; in drey Haupt-Theile unterschieden. Der Erste Theil Begreifft in sich die edelsten Blumen/Kräuter/Bäume/[. . .] in Ost-Indien/Sina/America: Der Ander Theil Das Temperament der Lufft und Landschafften daselbst; [. . .] Der Dritte Theil Das Stats-Wesen/Policey-Ordnungen/Hofstäte/Paläste/[. . .] Aus den fürnembsten/alten und neuen/Indianischen Geschich-Land- und Reisebeschreibungen/mit Fleiß zusammengezogen/und auf annehmliche Unterredungs-Art eingerichtet*. Nürnberg: Endter.

Härter, Karl. 2010. "Security and 'gute Policey' in Early Modern Europe: Concepts, Laws and Instruments." In Karl Härter and Cornel Zwierlein (eg.), *The Production of Human Security in Premodern and Contemporary History*, (Special Issue *Historical Social Research*) 35, 2010/4, 41–65. Cologne: Zentrum für Historische Sozialforschung.

Hill, Thomas. 2003. "Gottorf, Grönland und Guinea. Schleswig-Holstein und die außereuropäische Welt im 17. Jahrhundert." In *Studia Eurasiatica. Kieler Festschrift für Hermann Kulke zum 65. Geburtstag*, Stephan Conermann ed. 65–70. Hamburg: EB Verlag.

Hobson, John M. 2004. *The Eastern Origins of Western Civilisation*. Cambridge: Cambridge University Press.

Hulsius, Levinus. 1606. *Siebte Schiffahrt, das ist: In das Goldreiche Königreich Guineam, in Africa gelegen, so sonsten das Goldgestadt von Mina genannt wirdt, welches von den Portugalesern vngefähr vor 200. Jahren erfunden, von den Holländern jnnerhalb 18. Jahren hero bekannt gemacht*. Franckfurt am Mayn: Hulsius.

Iseli, Andrea. 2009. *Gute Policey. Öffentliche Ordnung in der frühen Neuzeit*. Stuttgart: Ulmer.

Justi, Johann Heinrich Gottlob von. 1762. *Vergleichung der europäischen mit den asiatischen und andern vermeintlich barbarischen Regierungen. In drei Büchern verfaßt*. Berlin, Stettin and Leipzig: Rüdigers.

Kindersley, Jemima. 1777. *Briefe von der Insel Teneriffa, Brasilien, dem Vorgebirge der guten Hoffnung und Ostindien / aus dem Englischen der Mistreß Kindersley*. Leipzig: Weidmann and Reich.

Krünitz, Johann Georg. 1803. "Mogul." In *Ökonomische Encyklopädie oder Allgemeines System der Staats-, Stadt-, Haus- und Landwirtschaft*, Vol. 92, ed. Johann Georg Krünitz, 595–607. Berlin: Pauli.

Lach, Donald F. and Edwin J. VanKley. 1993. *Asia in the Making of Europe. Trade, Missions, Literature*. Chicago: University of Chicago Press.

Landwehr, Achim. 2002. *Geschichte(n) der Wirklichkeit. Beiträge zur Sozial- und Kulturgeschichte des Wissens*. Augsburg: Ed discord.

Landwehr, Achim. 2003. "Diskurs - Macht - Wissen. Perspektiven einer Kulturgeschichte des Politischen." *Archiv für Kulturgeschichte* 85: 71–117.

Lünig, Johann Christian. 1720. *Theatrum Ceremoniale Historico-Politicum, Oder Historisch- und Politischer Schau-Platz Aller Ceremonien, Welche bey Päbst- und Käyser-, auch Königlichen Wahlen und Crönungen [. . .] Ingleichen bey Grosser Herren und dero Gesandten Einholungen [. . .] beobachtet warden, Vol. 2*. Leipzig: Weidmann.

Mandelslo, Johann Albrecht von. 1696. *Des Hoch-Edelgebohrnen Johann Albrechts von Mandelslo Morgenländische Reise-Beschreibung: worinnen zugleich die Gelegenheit und* heutiger Zustandt etlicher fürnehmen indianischen Länder, Provintzien, Städte und Insulen . . . beschrieben werden, herausgegeben durch Adam Olearius. Hamburg: Guth.

Merklein, Johann Jacob. 1930. *Reise nach Java, Vorder- und Hinter-Indien, China und Japan. 1644–1653. Neu hrsg. nach d. zu Nürnberg im Verl. von Endter 1672 gedr. verb. Ausg. des 1663 z. 1. Mal ersch. Textes*. Haag: Nijhoff.

Montesquieu, Charles Louis de. 1994. *Vom Geist der Gesetze*. Stuttgart: Reclam.

Müller, F. Max. 1883. *India, What can it teach us? A Course of Lectures Delivered Before the University of Cambridge*. London: Longmans, Green & Co.

Müller, Ulrich and Margarete Springeth. 2000. "Ein Indien-Reisebericht des Barock aus Gold, Edelsteinen und Perlen: Der Hofstaat zu Delhi am Geburtstag des Großmoguls Aureng-Zeb der Hofjuwelier-Werkstätte von Johann Melchior Dinglinger (Dresden 1701–1707)." In *Beschreibung der Welt: zur Poetik der Reise- und Länderberichte; Vorträge eines interdisziplinären Symposiums vom 8. bis 13. Juni 1998 an der Justus-Liebig-Universität Gießen; Chloe 31*, ed. Xenja von Ertzdorff and Rudolf Schulz, 345–367. Amsterda, Atlanta: Rodopi.

Neves, Marcello. 1998. *Symbolische Konstitutionalisierung*. Berlin: Duncker & Humblot.

O'Brien, Patrick Karl. 2006. "The Divergence Debate. Europe and China 1368–1846." In *Transnationale Geschichte. Themen, Tendenzen und Theorien*, ed. Gunilla Budde et al., 68–82. Göttingen: Vandenhoeck & Ruprecht.

Osterhammel, Jürgen. 1998. *Die Entzauberung Asiens: Europa und die asiatischen Reiche im 18. Jahrhundert*. Munich: Beck.

Pecar, Andreas. 2005. "Das Hofzeremoniell als Herrschaftstechnik? Kritische Einwände und methodische Überlegungen am Beispiel des Kaiserhofes in Wien (1660–1740)." In *Staatsbildung als kultureller Prozess*, ed. Ronald Asch and Dagmar Freist, 381–404. Cologne: Böhlau.

Pomeranz, Kenneth. 2000. *The Great Divergence. China, Europe, and the Making of the Modern World Economy*. Princeton, New York: Princeton University Press.

Raeff, Marc. 1975. "The Well-Ordered Police State and the Development of Modernity in Seventeenth- and Eighteenth-Century Europe. An Attempt at a Comparative Approach." *American Historical Review* 80: 1221–1243.

Raynal, Guillaume et al. 1988. *Die Geschichte beider Indien. Histoire philosophique et politique des établissements et du commerce des Européens dans les deux Indes* . Nördlingen: Greno.

Reinhard, Wolfgang. 1999. "Einführung: Moderne Staatsbildung – eine ansteckende Krankheit." In *Verstaatlichung der Welt? Europäische Staatsmodelle und außereuropäische Machtprozesse*, ed. Wolfgang Reinhard, VII–XIV, München: Oldenbourg.

Richards, John F. 1993. *Power, Administration and Finance in Mughal India*. Aldershot: Variorum.

Richter, Melvin. 1974. "Despotism." In *Dictionary oft the History of Ideas. Studies of Selected Pivotal Ideas*, ed. Philip P. Wiener, 1–18. New York: Charles Scribner's Sons.

Schenk, Gerrit Jasper. 2002. *Zeremoniell und Politik. Herrschereinzüge im spätmittelalterlichen Reich*. Köln: Böhlau.

Schneider, Ulrich Johannes. 2006. *Seine Welt wissen. Enzyklopädien in der frühen Neuzeit*. Darmstadt: WBG.

Schwabe, Johann Joachim. 1753. *Allgemeine Historie der Reisen zu Wasser und Lande oder Sammlung aller Reisebeschreibungen, welche bis itzo in verschiedenen Sprachen von allen Völkern herausgegeben worden/ Vol 11*. Leipzig: Arkstee and Merkus.

Stollberg-Rilinger, Barbara. 1997. "Zeremoniell als politisches Verfahren. Rangordnung und Rangstreit als Strukturmerkmal des frühneuzeitlichen Reichstages." In *Neue Studien zur frühneuzeitlichen Reichsgeschichte*, ed. Johannes Kunisch, 91–132, Berlin: Duncker & Humblot.

Stollberg-Rilinger, Barbara. 2005. *Was heißt Kulturgeschichte des Politischen?* Berlin: Duncker & Humblot.

Stollberg-Rilinger, Barbara. 2009. "The Impact of Communication Theory on the Analysis of the Early Modern Statebuilding Processes." In *Empowering Interactions. Political Culture and the Emergence of the State in Europe, 1300–1900*, ed. Wim Blockmans et al., 313–318. Farnham: Ashgate.

Strack, Thomas. 1994. *Exotische Erfahrung und Intersubjektivität. Reiseberichte im 17. und 18. Jahrhundert. Genregeschichtliche Untersuchung zu Adam Olearius - Hans Egede - Georg Forster.* Paderborn: Igel-Verl.

Subrahmanyam, Sanjay. 2005. *Explorations in Connected History: Mughals and Franks.* New Delhi [u.a.]: Oxford University Press.

Tavernier, Jean-Baptist. 1984. *Reisen zu den Reichtümern Indiens. Abenteuerliche Jahre beim Großmogul, 1641–1667. Edited by Susanne Lausch and Felix Wiesinger.* Darmstadt: Thienemann, Edition Erdmann.

Thévenot, Jean de. 1693. *Deß Herrn Thevenot Reysen in Ost-Indien / in sich haltend Eine genaue Beschreibung des Königreichs Indostan, der neuen Mogols und anderer Völcker und Länder in Ost-Indien; nebenst ihren Sitten, Gesetzen, Religionen, Festen, Tempeln, Pagoden, Kirchhöfen, Commercien, u.a. merckwürdigen Sachen. [. . .].* Franckfurt am Mayn: Fievet.

Vries, Peer. 2002. "Governing Growth: A Comparative Analysis of the Role of the State in the Rise of the West." *Journal of World History* 13: 67–138.

Warncke, Carsten-Peter. 1989. "Der Hofstaat des Großmoguls." *Deutsche Kunst- und Antiquitätenmesse* 59/19: 2152–2157.

Warncke, Carsten-Peter. 2004. "Sehen, Fühlen und Verstehen. Johann Melchior Dinglingers Hofstaat des Großmoguls'." *Dresdener Kunstblätter* 4: 278–281.

Whelan, Frederick G. 2001. "Oriental Despotism: Anquetil-Duperron's Response to Montesquieu." *History of Political Thought* 22: 619–247.

Wong, Roy Bin. 2000. *China transformed. Historical Change and the Limits of European Experience.* Ithaca [u.a.]: Cornell University Press.

Wurffbain, Johann Sigmund. 1931. *Reisen nach den Molukken und Vorder-Indien (1638–1646).* Haag: Nijhoff.

Zedler, Johann Heinrich. 1739. "Mogul." In *Grosses vollständiges Universal-Lexicon aller Wissenschafften und Künste, welche bißhero durch menschlichen Verstand und Witz erfunden und verbesset worden: Darinnen so wohl die Geographisch-Politische Beschreibung des Erd-Kreyses, . . . Wie nicht weniger die völlige Vorstellung aller in den Kirchen-Geschichten berühmten Alt-Väter . . ., Endlich auch ein vollkommener Inbegriff der allergelehrtesten Männer . . . enthalten ist (1731–1754),* vol 21, ed. Johann Heinrich Zedler, 816–826. Halle & Leipzig: Zedler.

Part III
Case Studies: Interaction

Technology, Tactics and Military Transfer in the Nineteenth Century

Qing Armies in Tonkin, 1884–1885

Barend Noordam

In European historiography, there is a school of thought which attributes an important role to the military in the process of state formation[1]. Starting in the early modern period, the introduction of gunpowder weapon technology is thought to have conferred a decisive edge to rulers in Europe, allowing them to consolidate their power against competing aristocratic interests and leading to the centralisation of state power. The military demands of unrelenting warfare in Europe are also supposed to have accelerated this process of state formation, spurred on by a "coercion-extraction cycle", eventually leading to the fiscal military state. This is seen by some scholars as a veritable juggernaut of centralised armed might, which gave European polities a definitive edge over their Asian counterparts from the late eighteenth century onwards (Di Cosmo 2001: 119, 134; Parker 1996; Tilly 1992). For the still-independent Asian polities at this time, European military technology and organisation were their most visible markers of strength, and processes of transfer in the military sector were undertaken to defend against external imperialistic pressures. But, just as important in the context of the historiographical school of thought mentioned above, these processes helped Asian polities in the consolidation of central rule against internal enemies (Horowitz 2005: 458).

This was perhaps nowhere more pronounced than in late Qing China (1644–1911), where many rebellions raged in the mid-nineteenth century. The Chinese had also been faced with the strength of European armies in two Opium Wars (1839–1842 and 1856–1860), and the combination of internal and external threats led a group of reform-minded officials, many of whom had risen to important

---

[1] The present article is based on my MA thesis, which I wrote as part of the history curriculum at Leiden University and which was supervised by Peer H. H. Vries and Petra M. H. Groen. This rewritten and abridged version benefitted greatly from the helpful input of Antje Flüchter.

B. Noordam (✉)
Institute for History, Leiden University, Binnenstadcomplex, Rapenburg 38, 2311 EX Leiden, The Netherlands
e-mail: b.noordam@hum.leidenuniv.nl

A. Flüchter and S. Richter (eds.), *Structures on the Move*,
Transcultural Research – Heidelberg Studies on Asia and Europe in a Global Context,
DOI 10.1007/978-3-642-19288-3_9, © Springer-Verlag Berlin Heidelberg 2012

positions during these upheavals, to initiate the first steps in what would become a process of transfer in the military field between Europe and China (Horowitz 2002: 154–155). This process is interesting to examine in detail, because it allows us to study transfer in the military sector at a time when a clear technological asymmetry existed in favour of Europe, after centuries of a relatively stable military equilibrium. I will argue here that this process constituted not a simple transplantation of European military technology and tactics to a Chinese context, but was mediated by a complex process of ideological negotiation and appropriation, channelled by institutional factors with the occasional aid of European personnel. I understand *transfer* here in the way Matthias Middell has defined it, as "an integration of foreign cultural elements into a culture defined as native" (Middell 2000: 26).[2] Adopting his approach, I opt to focus on the people who were the carriers of transfer processes, the transferred technology, and the Chinese systems of thought legitimising the transfer, as the three main entry points to study this transcultural encounter, which produced hybrid armies incorporating aspects of both European and Chinese military origin. The Sino-French War (1884–1885), the first war China fought with a European power since the start of the transfer process in the 1860's, will be used to illustrate the characteristics of these hybrid armies in action on the battlefields of Tonkin, in the north of present-day Vietnam. This way, the extent and nature of the transfer can be highlighted, relying mainly on accounts by French soldiers and other eye-witnesses, whose familiarity with European techniques of warfare gives us the opportunity to view Chinese armies as seen through contemporary French eyes. However, in order to explicate the transfer process, I deem it necessary first to start with a consideration of the changes which accrued to European warfare, at home and abroad, because of technological developments in the nineteenth century. These changes will have an impact on my analysis of the performance of the Chinese armies during the Sino-French War, further highlighting what the consequences of hybridity were in the context of late nineteenth-century warfare.

1 European Warfare at Home and Abroad: The Consequences of Technological Change

In order to do justice to the complexities of the Chinese response to European warfare in the late nineteenth century, it is first of all necessary to keep in mind that the waging of war was subject to unprecedented technological changes in the era

---

[2] Many scholars still understand transfer to be a process between an active sender and a passive receiver. The latter is assumed to take over the transferred entity without alteration and the receiver's internal dynamics often do not figure at all as a force shaping the transfer process. Similar to Middell's understanding of transfer, there are many other concepts which challenge this model in transcultural and transsocial contexts. Important for this article were current ideas on practices of *appropriation*, Jeremy Black's concept of *tasking*, Stefan Brakensiek and his views on *state-building from below* (in this volume) and Barbara Stollberg-Rilinger's use of *performativity* to elucidate the functioning of social reality (Ashley and Plesch 2002; Black 2004; Stollberg-Rilinger 2009).

after the Napoleonic Wars (1799–1815). Rapidly developing technology changed and improved the fire power, the logistical and infrastructural systems, and the communications of the armies. Furthermore, these developments also had a significant impact upon tactics, and, as the century wore on, different armies tried out different solutions to deal with the challenge that incorporating these new technologies posed. It is therefore problematic to speak of a unitary "European way of war", and this especially holds true for the nineteenth century. European armies were often, sometimes just as much as their non-European equivalents, at a loss as to how best to adapt their military establishment to rapidly changing technological and tactical parameters (Hacker 1977: 50).

The technological advances were most notable in areas of weapon range, accuracy and fire-power. Troops, who at the start of the nineteenth century still mostly fought in dense close-order formations, were more and more forced to disperse on the battlefield, owing to the increased lethality of the weapons used. Smooth-bore muskets, with an effective range of a mere 50 m, gave way to breech-loading rifles accurate up to 550 m, with a higher rate of fire because of improved loading mechanisms. Comparable developments affected the designs of artillery cannons, which could now lob exploding shells over longer distances. The new weapons necessitated training in aimed fire and fire discipline, something which had not been necessary before, since the characteristics of the smooth-bore musket had encouraged tactics maximising the effect of massed salvo fire, offsetting the weapon's inaccuracy. The tactic of dispersing troops also required an increased involvement on the part of the officers and non-commissioned officers (NCOs), who had a more difficult task directing the troops (Presseisen 1965: 69–73; van Creveld 2005: 205–218).

These new demands placed on training, tactics and leadership could be seen during the Franco-Austrian and Franco-Prussian Wars (1859 and 1870–1871, respectively). During the former, the Austrians opted to divide the infantry into smaller close-order formations and position them in such a way as to maximise the number of rifles firing at a given time. The French resorted to the tactics of charging the enemy lines with densely packed columns, which, strangely enough, worked. This was not due to a flaw in the Austrian tactics, but had more to do with their lack of expertise in handling the rifles and utilising their increased accuracy and range. Most of the Austrian soldiers were illiterate peasants from very diverse ethnic backgrounds with correspondingly diverse native tongues. Because of their want of schooling, they were often not able to handle the new tasks that came with the new rifles, such as estimating ranges and adjusting the gun sights accordingly. In addition, the language of command in the Austrian army was German, and the soldiers often did not understand commands given to them on the battlefield, limiting the implementation of the new tactics by officers. The result was that the Austrian units fired blindly and in an uncoordinated fashion and were overrun by French bayonet charges (Deák 1990: 30, 51; Wawro 1995: 408–415). Before the Franco-Prussian War, the French had adopted the Chassepot breech-loading rifle which had twice the effective range of the German rifle (1,200 m vs. 600 m), and also deployed an early version of the machine gun, the *mitrailleuse*. Taking the capabilities of their new weapons into account, the French army, in the Franco-Prussian war, decided to adopt defensive tactics in the field and dig in to defeat the attackers with a combination of machine-gun, rifle, and cannon fire. This seemed like a sound solution, given the greater range of the French Chassepot rifle, and the Prussian army indeed suffered heavy casualties, sometimes even twice the number of French casualties. Nevertheless, the Prussian army prevailed owing to their numerical superiority and better artillery. With more manpower available, the Prussians were able to envelop and attack the French positions on their vulnerable flanks, whilst the French were bombarded by the new breech-loading artillery, which out-ranged the older French muzzle-loading rifled artillery. However, the heavy casualties suffered by the Prussians impressed upon them the need to rely on open dispersed formations. This necessitated an increase in the number of NCOs, and they, together with the ordinary soldiers, had to be trained to function more independently during battle, since officers were no longer able to exercise tight command on the battlefield with the demise of close-order formations. Considerable responsibility devolved on the NCOs, since the coordination of so much dispersed infantry was too demanding for the officers alone. Much attention was also paid to training the soldiers to use their weapons effectively and instilling a kind of fire-discipline, since it was feared that the troops would consume too much ammunition in the excitement generated in the heat of battle (Wawro 2000: 78–94, 100–117). However, many conservative officers resisted these tactical changes and continued to drill their formations in close-order tactics to ensure discipline and control, illustrating the fact that adapting to technological change was a problem not restricted to non-European armies (Jackman 2004). The Franco-Prussian War, as well as the preceding American Civil War (1861–1865), highlighted the increased importance of entrenchments and fortified positions on the battlefield in reaction to the new weaponry.[3] These showed the tendency of weapon developments to work to the advantage of the defence, if the defenders were able to handle their weapons well, and were equipped with adequate artillery which was not out-ranged by enemy batteries. Especially during the American Civil War, there was a marked shift away from offensive bayonet charges to relying on defensive fieldworks supported by artillery (Presseisen 1965: 74–75).

European technology is still quite often seen as the reason for the stunning success of imperialistic ventures in the nineteenth century. Breech-loading rifles, artillery, steam ships, the telegraph and rail-roads caused a technology gap between Europe and the rest of the world, which was hard to bridge. In general, non-European polities tended to offset European superiority in technology by avoiding direct confrontations and waging wars of attrition, employing guerrilla tactics (Headrick 1981; Wesseling 1989: 1–8). European armies adapted to this by dividing their forces into smaller, more mobile units and enlisting indigenous troops,

---

[3] I include the American Civil War here since it mirrors European wars of this period in the weaponry used, and the evolution of tactics employed. Since Native Americans played no notable role in the war, the war resembled a European conflict.

Technology, Tactics and Military Transfer in the Nineteenth Century   173

who were trained and equipped according to European standards. These indigenous troops knew the terrain better, were cheaper, and were more resistant to the climate and diseases (Vandervort 1998: 40–44). These characteristics were all reflected in the functioning of the French colonial armies. Most French overseas ventures were carried out by the French *infanterie de marine* and *artillerie de marine*. These marines conquered Senegal and Cochin-china, the southern part of present-day Vietnam. In Algeria, Senegal and Cochin-china, the French first experimented with training indigenous troops, who would be led by French officers.[4] These forces were known as the *tirailleurs Algériens* (or *turcos*), *tirailleurs Sénégalais* and *tirailleurs Cochinchinois*, and were enlisted on a voluntary basis. Around 1880, 35% of the troops raised under the banner of the French marines consisted of indigenous troops. Besides the French marines and their indigenous levies, the Foreign Legion was the third important unit participating in imperial expansion. This legion consisted mainly of foreign mercenaries, with about a third of the troops having French origins. The troops were commanded by French officers and NCOs of the regular army. The soldiers were expected to be trained enough to adjust the gun sights and to fire at will, with the officers only monitoring the effect of the fire (Anonymous 1885b: 615; Porch 1981: 139–140). Since there was no separate military theory dealing with wars of imperial expansion taught in French military academies, officers were forced to be resourceful and flexible in the field to adapt to local circumstances. These varied enormously, which is not surprising, since the French fought in areas as disparate as Africa and Southeast Asia, and this also explains the lack of a specifically colonial military theory. In general, it could be said that military doctrine, which had arisen as a response to European military problems, often informed the tactics of non-European campaigns. But even here a process of adaptation could be seen, since older tactical solutions, which had lost their value in the context of European warfare, could still be put to good use outside the continent. Close-order infantry charges using the bayonet, for example, were used regularly, and this reflected the less destructive defensive fire that non-European armies could generate (Black 2001: 98–99; Porch 1981: 153–156). Arguably, the conflict which the French army fought in Tonkin more closely resembled a conventional European war, and a contemporary German military observer even thought it worthwhile to study the conflict for its tactical lessons, unlike the French colonial exploits in Madagascar and North Africa (Kunz 1902: III–IV). The Chinese armies facing the French were equipped with modern weapons and received partial training from European instructors, symptomatic of a process of transfer which had, arguably, formed these into hybrid entities prior to the conflict in Tonkin.

---

[4] The French training of Indian sepoys in the eighteenth century constitutes an even earlier example, but there is an institutional discontinuity between the armies of the early modern French East India Company and the nineteenth century French colonial army.

2   Negotiating Transfer in the Military Field: Hybridising Armies in China

China, as well as many other non-European polities, was affected by the accelerating technological change taking place during the nineteenth century. Chinese armies were defeated in the two Opium Wars, and, especially after the second conflict, the growing asymmetry in military capabilities was noted by Manchu and Han Chinese officials alike. That an attempt would be made to transfer the military innovations of Europe to China in order to create parity with Europe was to be expected. China, under the Manchu Qing dynasty, joined the ranks of similarly inclined non-European polities such as Egypt, the Ottoman Empire, and Japan in the nineteenth century to introduce programmes of army modernisation. The case of China, however, demonstrates that such processes of transfer in the military field were never between an active sender and a passive receiving party, which simply incorporated these improvements unchanged in its institutional matrix.[5] Instead, transfer in the military field was as much, perhaps even more, conditioned and channelled by internal variables, as by outside pressure. For the Qing dynasty in the mid-nineteenth century faced an unparalleled series of internal rebellions the size of which simply dwarfed the conflicts with Western powers. These rebellions, in their turn, shaped the institutional context in which transfer from Europe took place (Horowitz 2002: 154–155; Yu 2002: 135).

To deal with the threat of rebellion, new provincial armies arose, since the older armies deployed by the Qing failed in their task of suppression, mainly because of structural problems. They were legacies of the Manchu conquest of China in the seventeenth century, and were characterised by decentralisation and decreasing effectiveness, owing to socioeconomic changes. Decentralisation was deemed important, since the throne feared a concentration of power in the hands of a single official, and a system of checks and balances was maintained to prevent this, but this meant they were unable to effectively deal with, and coordinate a response to the threat posed by large-scale rebellions and invasions of highly mobile European forces in the nineteenth century. Another structural problem was that, because of inflation caused by population growth, the Chinese soldiers' fixed stipends had decreased in value. Out of necessity they had to take jobs to supplement their incomes, and this led to a decrease in fighting value, since less time was spent on training. Technologically, these forces lagged behind the West, using old matchlock muskets, bows and arrows, spears, swords and a variety of cannon dating back

---

[5] Research on military transfer from Europe to the rest of the world in the nineteenth century often assumes the form of a "deficit analysis". As a rule this measures the relative success of the process against the completeness with which the European model was copied, but hardly takes stock of the extent to which internal factors on the part of the receiver shaped and channelled it. Ralston (1991) is an example of this tendency. I will argue below that the Chinese approach to military transfer fitted their political realities and tasking very well and as such did not constitute a "failure".

to the sixteenth and seventeenth centuries (Headrick 1981: 43–50, 90–91; Powell 1955: 3–19; van de Ven 2003: 23–24).

The necessities of war led officials, sent to deal with the rebellions, to organise new forces which dispensed with the disadvantages of the old system. Zeng Guofan (1811–1872), one of these officials, took the lead in this process and created the Hunan Army. It was raised amongst the peasants of Hunan province, and its officers were mainly drawn from amongst the gentry and provincial elites. This gentry consisted mostly of literati who had obtained a degree through the civil services examination, but had not been able to find a place in the bureaucracy. In fact, the majority of degree-holders never became part of the bureaucracy, but their degrees did confer status and authority on them, and they performed a leadership role in local communities. As such they had a stake in defending the established order, represented by the Qing dynasty, against rebellions. The manner of recruitment also assured cohesion within the ranks, since every layer in the hierarchy was responsible for recruiting the layer below. Zeng Guofan chose his own generals, who in turn chose their own subordinates and this process was repeated down to the lowest rank. This was a sharp departure from previous practice, where the Qing had tried to prevent this accumulation of power in the hands of one official, and had also made sure that officers were rotated between units, in order to prevent the creation of personal ties with the men under their command. The troops were thoroughly indoctrinated with Confucianism to ensure discipline and loyalty to the existing order. This was especially important in light of the threat posed by the Taiping (1850–1864), a group of Han Chinese rebels who, based on their interpretation of Christianity, not only wanted to topple the dynasty, but also aimed to overthrow the Confucian social order. The new provincial armies, created on the Hunan Army model and often referred to as *yongying* ("brave battalions"), were primarily funded by a new tax, called the *lijin*, which was imposed on trade commodities (Kuhn 1978: 267–278; Yu 2002, 137, 146–148).

After the conclusion of the Second Opium War, primarily fought to secure the opening of the Chinese market by forcing unequal treaties on the Qing, the European powers were more positively disposed towards China and sought to bolster the dynasty, which guaranteed these desirable treaties, against the internal threat the rebellions posed. This was to be a "push" factor in the dissemination of European techniques and technologies of warfare into China. The "pull" factor was represented by those officials who led provincial armies, and were acquainted with the power of European weapons through personal experience and wanted to use them against internal enemies and external threats. Indeed, a process of ideological negotiation and appropriation was under way to legitimise the use of these European innovations in a Chinese context. Reform-minded officials, amongst whom were a great many leaders of provincial armies who had used European military techniques to suppress the rebellions, coalesced into a group which was collectively called the Self-Strengthening Movement (*Ziqiang Yundong*), or the Foreign Affairs Movement (*Yangwu Yundong*) (Teng and Fairbank 1970: 50–55). They adopted an ideological slogan, "Chinese learning for fundamental principles and Western learning for practical application", as a legitimisation for the appropriation of, amongst other things, weapons technology from Europe (Kwong 1993: 253). *Appropriation* is understood here as the way in which the receiving culture, Confucian China, gained power over Western learning, the Chinese making it their own by giving it a place in the order of things as sanctioned by Chinese thought. This slogan derived its strength from a dualistic concept in Chinese philosophy, namely that between substance and function (*ti* and *yong*). Adapted to a context of cultural transfer, this would come to mean that Chinese cultural values would supply the substance and European technology a function of that substance. It shows that China was not simply a passive receiver of technology transmitted by a "superior culture", but an active agent in the selective process of appropriation. In addition to ti-yong ideology, historical precedent also legitimised technological transfer, since in the seventeenth century the Qing had used Jesuits to cast cannon, draw maps, and impart astronomical knowledge. Ti-yong thinking also had its implications for personnel acquisition. As the nineteenth century progressed, increasing numbers of Chinese were trained as translators, technicians and other specialists needed to transfer European technologies to a Chinese context. There was, however, a perceived danger of cultural erosion involved in this process of transfer, and Chinese educated in European subjects were usually distrusted or looked down upon. Many feared cultural contamination through contact with Europe and its representatives in the Empire. Therefore, personnel trained in European matters were also expected to be thoroughly acquainted with, and educated in, the precepts of Confucian ideology. In such a manner it was believed the perfect hybrid expert would be created, combining the moral fibre of Confucian civilisation with the technical insights derived from Western learning, so as to be able to deal with the problems of the present age (Ashley and Plesch 2002: 2–3; Kwong 1993: 253–268; Waley-Cohen 1993: 1529–1532).[6]

Although ideologically attractive, this programme was hampered by an unwillingness on the part of the Qing court to facilitate further adaptations in the institutional structure. Being an alien dynasty, the Manchu Qing relied on their support for Confucianism for their legitimation and their ideological ties to the majority Han Chinese population of the empire. The emergence of the provincial armies had already greatly increased the power of provincial governors vis-à-vis the throne, since the old system of checks and balances did not apply to these forces, which were now the most significant military units. To prevent further loss of control, the dynasty refused to change the examination system, which tested the candidates' knowledge of Confucian precepts and thus ensured ideological loyalty to the dynasty. In the aftermath of the rebellions, this examination system was reinstated as the principal avenue to a career in the bureaucracy, whilst during the rebellions, upward career mobility had been possible for men who distinguished themselves by

---

[6] The term "hybrid expert" is anachronistic in the context of nineteenth-century China, since the Empire wanted them to be vaccinated against European culture, so that they would not be in danger of cultural contamination. It is only in the present-day understanding of the author that they are considered "hybrid".

practical abilities, without passing the state examinations. These examinations tied the elites of the empire to the throne, and the latter was unwilling to compromise it and create a separate avenue to power for those qualified in Western learning (Horowitz 2002: 161; Smith 1994: 138). The source of the reluctance of the Qing dynasty to change the examinations can be sought in the prime importance of these as a tool for state building. Stefan Brakensiek points out, in his contribution to this volume, that power elites could play an important role in the expansion (and presumably also the maintenance) of state authority in Europe, and this held true of China as well. The state examinations inculcated common values in the servants of the dynasty and provided social mobility. As Brakensiek notes, "increasing the power of their employer would have seemed to be in their [the servants] own best interest" (Brakensiek in this volume, 33), and it is exactly this collusion between the interests of the servants, i.e. the officials, and the powerful binding force of the commonly inculcated Confucian culture which had galvanised the officials into action to defend the existing order against large-scale rebellions (Wright 1957: 79).

Incorporation of Western learning into the curriculum of the state examinations posed, again, the danger of cultural erosion mentioned above. Thus, Foreign Affairs experts were not to be provided with much in the way of incentives to pursue their studies, and it was up to the reform-minded officials themselves to embed them in their own staffs, arsenals and translation bureaus, which were outside the regular bureaucracy (Bays 1970: 335; Elman 2004: 310–312).

Now that we have seen the Chinese system of thought legitimising transfer, I will turn to the carriers of the transfer process, and, in particular, the European military instructors working in conjunction with the yongying armies. Along with weapons technology, Europe was also invited to supply the knowledge of how to use it. In addition to arsenals, established to produce new rifles, artillery and ammunition, training camps were set up to instruct Chinese soldiers in the ways of European warfare. The invitation to Europe was not extended without reservations, and these would only grow stronger as the nineteenth century progressed. During the Taiping Rebellion an army was raised, funded by wealthy Chinese merchants of Shanghai, to protect the city against the approaching rebel forces. This army, known as the Ever-Victorious Army, was trained and led by European and US officers. Chinese officials witnessed this army in action and its effectiveness created an incentive on their part to introduce European weapons and training to the indigenous armies. However, foreign officers directly leading Chinese contingents were regarded as an undesirable infringement upon Chinese sovereignty, and would also make the military establishment vulnerable to outside meddling. As a compromise, training camps were set up under Chinese jurisdiction, in which European instructors would train selected units of the Chinese armies. This system, too, did not last, since Chinese officials grew increasingly belligerent towards the continuing attempts of European powers to intervene in the affairs of these camps. The training camp at Fenghuangshan, for example, fell victim to this when British authorities tried to influence the choice of the British officers employed, and pressed for the increased control of these officers over the internal organisation of the camp. The Chinese, for their part, wanted to retain complete control over the recruitment, organisation and pay of the soldiers, and kept the role of the instructors restricted to just the training of the troops. After the demise of the last training camps in the 1870s, European instructors were only employed on an individual basis in the diverse provincial armies of the Chinese officials themselves (Smith 1976: 217–218; Smith 1994: 120–121, 132–133). Chinese fears of European intervention in military affairs were not ungrounded, and earlier historical examples show that inviting Europe was an extremely perilous courtesy. The Marathas in India had employed European officers in their armies from the late eighteenth century onwards as commanders and instructors, and they wielded considerable authority. In the Second Anglo-Maratha War (1803–1805), the British were able to bribe many of them to desert, greatly decreasing the effectiveness of the Maratha forces. Although it is uncertain whether the Qing dynasty was aware of this particular instance, Asian rulers did have good reason to be cautious about devolving too much power over their military forces to Europeans. This is presumably why drilling and training Chinese forces using commands in foreign languages was seen as a security risk. For this reason, efforts were made to translate these commands into Chinese and to decrease dependence on foreign instruction as soon as possible, although this aim was never achieved (Bidwell 1971: 219–220; Smith 1994: 126–127).

The demise of the training camps meant that there was no central institution through which the acquisition of European military knowledge could be channelled, and thus the process of transfer was entirely confined to the provincial armies themselves. Here, European instructors were employed from various national backgrounds, but mainly British, French, and eventually predominantly German nationals. The latter especially could be seen as participating in a globalised market for German military expertise, as, in the aftermath of the Franco-Prussian War and the concomitant rise of the reputation of the Prussian military model, they found employment in China, Japan, the Ottoman Empire and states in Latin America (Kaske 2002: 15, 21–22). The multinational instructors were the mediators of military transfer, but their reach in China was constrained by many factors.[7] To be sure, recourse to foreign military experts was not perceived as humiliating or as a sign of embarrassing backwardness. Throughout Chinese history, succeeding dynasties had always made use of foreign military personnel, and a body of theories and practices had arisen to deal with the incorporation and use of them. On an ideological level, "barbarians" were expected to show signs of cultural submission to Chinese civilisation, since they were supposed to be drawn to service owing to the moral superiority of the Chinese. These signs of cultural submission would involve what we would call the attributes of acculturation: adopting Chinese language and dress, marrying Chinese women, and (during the Qing dynasty) shaving the forehead (as was expected of all Qing subjects). Next to this, it was recognised that, on a practical level, foreigners came to China for economic gain, and for this category of

---

[7] See Peter Trummer's article in this volume for more on the European instructors in nineteenth-century China.

barbarian it was necessary to ensure that they were bound in a web of personal relations and institutional constraints, combined with economic inducements. In short, they were to have a stake in the existing order. The Europeans in China were problematic, in that they were confident of their own cultural superiority and were also protected by the unequal treaties and the military presence of their own armies. As such, the focus shifted to the practical side of barbarian management, meaning that foreign employees were paid well, kept under close surveillance, and embedded in a web of personal relationships. Various inducements were also offered, and an innovation was made in this respect when the Qing dynasty started issuing European-style medals as a reward for accomplishments (Smith 1975). Using foreign military experts and embedding them in existing institutional structures was not the problem inhibiting transfer; the problem was to be sought more in the institutional make-up of the yongying.

As Elisabeth Kaske concluded in her study of German instructors in China, the extent of transfer in the military field was mostly determined by the attitude of the receiving party, not by the mediators (Kaske 2002: 18). The knowledge they tried to impart to the provincial armies had a hard time becoming accepted. No high premium was placed on knowledge and no institutional requirement needed to obtain it, owing to the absence of military academies. In fact, most officers in the yongying had risen through the ranks during the various rebellions or by other means based on military merit. Chinese military men sent abroad to be trained in European countries, or in the training camps during the rebellions, often did not find acceptance in the units, let alone disseminate their knowledge among the rank and file. Undoubtedly the particular organisational characteristics of the yongying, with every rank selecting the men to serve under them, played a part in inhibiting the transfer of military expertise, since it was hard to integrate outsiders and newcomers into the army structure. Here, the need for internal cohesion served as an obstruction to transfer. This phenomenon equally hindered the foreign instructors; in addition, their status as Europeans who were well paid had a tendency to evoke hostility and resentment. To a certain extent, it was "not done" to excel in European-style military training and drill. Amongst the Chinese officers, there was also a reluctance to engage in European training exercises, since drilling and training together with the rank and file was considered to be below their status (Liu and Smith 1980: 267; Smith 1976: 218; Smith 1978: 23–24). This attitude was exacerbated by the fact that many of these officers were veterans who had fought during the rebellions, and therefore did not automatically see the need to take advice from European instructors who had never seen battle (Kaske 2002: 79–84). In an age when the technological requirements of European warfare tended to increase the necessity of training for officers, this was a serious impediment for reform along European lines. This ensured that, on the battlefield, complex tactics which had evolved in Europe as a response to increasing infantry and artillery fire-power, could not be replicated. It would be naive to see this as Chinese obstinacy in the face of European superiority. Indeed, by this time this superiority was no longer assumed to be so great by many Chinese officers and some even thought the yongying to be superior to Western organisational models, in Chinese perception restoring their superiority vis-à-vis the Europeans. Armed with modern weapons, these armies had suppressed internal rebellions, and they fitted into the Chinese cultural tradition, being inspired by precedents dating back to the sixteenth century (Kaske 2002: 75; Liu 1994: 36; Smith 1978: 19–31). When we consider that social reality is performatively regenerated through acts of communication, it is possible to get a more profound grip on the reasons behind the reluctance of the Chinese military to more fully adopt European drill and tactics, which would seem to the Chinese to be European modes of behaviour (Stollberg-Rilinger 2009: 313). This behaviour can be seen as an act of communication, in which the Chinese soldiers and officers would have to perform as the derided and even hated Europeans. Richard Smith quoted a contemporary observer who noted that Chinese soldiers who excelled in European methods were stigmatised: "To be "smart" [in European drill] was to be "like the hated foreigner and to lose caste"" (Smith 1976: 218). This also affected European instructors when they did not show signs of submission to Chinese culture.

To be sure, more structural problems also plagued the dissemination of European-style training. This was evident in the area of fire discipline training, which was a must for making full use of the benefits of the rifles. Estimating distances and accurately aiming the weapons was neglected, perhaps partly for economic reasons, since practising with live ammunition was an expensive affair. This problem was not merely restricted to non-European polities, since Austria-Hungary also neglected this important area of troop training for similar reasons (Smith 1976: 218; Smith 1978: 28; Wawro 1995: 415–416). Another parallel can perhaps be drawn with respect to the response of conservative Prussian officers to new tactics which called for a greater dispersal of troops on the battlefield. Similarly to their Chinese counterparts, these officers had the final say in the tactics and training employed in their units. Fearing loss of control and desertions during combat, they often opted to use older close-order tactics facilitating cohesion (Jackman 2004: 76, 80–82). It is possible that a similar concern motivated Chinese officers to stick to the tried-and-tested tactics used during the rebellions. We should be cautious about seeing the defects of the yongying armies as a specifically Chinese problem, but rather, this should be placed in the context of a varied and sometimes confused reaction to technological changes by armies across the world.

According to military historian Jeremy Black, investigating failures to make the best possible use of military technology has become an important genre in military literature. He proposes to focus on *tasking*, or the setting of goals, to better understand this phenomenon (Black 2004: 114–115). The yongying arose as a specific response to internal rebellion against the dynasty, representing and upholding traditional Confucian culture. In this they succeeded, and they also thought it to be equivalent to the task of defending this same order against outside aggression. This perception was aided by the fact that since 1860, when actual reform started, there had been no conflict with a European power and the rebellions had been quelled by the hybrid yongying, which mostly coupled European weapons with traditional Chinese tactics and organisation. Steps to increase the effectiveness of these armies along European lines would have required institutional changes, endangering the very order the yongying were meant to defend. Looking at the Chinese nineteenth-century developments this way also gives us an alternative to the war-state building paradigm so well articulated in European historiography. I argue here that tasking, in the context of nineteenth-century China, was determined primarily by political goals, not military. In the words of Black: "in many states, it has been forces other than the regular military that have been primarily responsible for maintaining governmental power" (Black 2004: 137). The Qing dynasty was saved by its loyal Confucian officials and local gentry. They were the source of dynastic power, more so than the armies could ever be, the latter being under much less central supervision than the older armies had been. Instead, these armies and their foreign expertise were to be restricted in their power by diverse policies, since the concentration of too much power in the hands of too few individuals constituted a security risk. Therefore, the provincial armies remained decentralised, with each responsible for their own pay (obtained through the lijin tax), training and equipment, which led to a lack of standardisation in armaments and training. The regional character of the yongying armies worked to the advantage of the throne, conveniently pre-empting the creation of a true state-wide homogeneous army capable of acting in concert to topple the dynasty. Their lack of central institutions, such as military academies, also helped "compartmentalise" Western techniques of warfare within the various armies, preventing the knowledge from spreading. This also had a precedent in the seventeenth century, when measures were taken to limit the circulation of (European) fire-arms, perhaps to prevent them from reaching anti-Qing rebels (Di Cosmo 2001: 134–135).

3   The Limits of Hybridity: Qing Armies in Tonkin 1884–1885

With the nature of the transfer process clarified, it is instructive to see the performance of Chinese armies in action through French eyes. The French fought two provincial armies in Tonkin, those of Yunnan and Guangxi, at first driving the Guangxi back over the Chinese border, before being repulsed, which precipitated a French retreat from Lang Son in the north of Vietnam. This victory did not win the Qing dynasty the war, since French naval activity threatened to stop maritime trade, and any intervention by other powers on behalf of the Qing was not forthcoming. Instead, it was decided to end the costly conflict, which had been embarrassing for both sides, by means of a settlement, with the Chinese relinquishing any claims on Vietnam as a tributary state, but not having to pay a costly indemnity to the French.

Throughout the confrontation in Tonkin, both Chinese forces in general adopted a defensive posture, relying on earthworks and fortresses on top of the many hills in the combat zone. The usual French tactic was to launch an infantry attack on these fortifications, preceded by an artillery bombardment. The bombardment was not sufficient to dislodge the defenders, and the attackers had to resort to bayonet charges and hand-to-hand fighting to secure a Chinese retreat. The Chinese were vulnerable to these tactics for two reasons. One was that on the Chinese side there was usually no artillery present to counter the superior French artillery and help repulse the infantry assaults. The second reason was the defective training of Chinese soldiers when it came to accurately discharging their weapons. During a battle at Bac Le (23 June 1884), Chinese soldiers fired from the comparatively short range of 200 m, whilst their rifles were accurate up to 500 m. Even at these short ranges, Louis Sarrat, a French marine soldier, found that "Leur tir est heureusement fichant et fait peu de mal" (Sarrat 1987: 139). During the French advance to Lang Son, Foreign Legionnaires also witnessed Chinese soldiers tucking their rifle butts in their armpits, instead of firing from the shoulder. They seem to have tried to hit the enemy this way with arcing shots from a long distance, but this technique was also used at short distances of 200 m, which meant the soldiers fired harmlessly into the air instead of taking properly aimed shots at the French (Porch 1991: 208–209, 230). The construction of the Chinese fieldworks also gave evidence of the way they expected to use their fire-power. Whilst generally resistant to French artillery fire, the fieldworks at Hoa Moc were constructed in such a way as to limit the effective range of rifle fire to 100 m. The defenders of the hill fortresses near Lang Son were also only able to fire at French attackers when these were nearly at the top (Grisot and Coulombon 1888: 455; Lecomte 1888: 47–50, 63–67). Apparently not much trust was placed in the long-range precision fire made possible by rifles, or else the defenders were not expected to be proficient enough in the handling of their weapons. This played to the advantage of the attacking French soldiers, who now only had to cross a killing zone of 100 m instead of 500. In a way not dissimilar to what the French experienced during the Franco-Austrian War, a lack of competent long-range gunnery enabled successful frontal assaults. Nevertheless these proved costly enough to lead to a change in tactics. Later in the war, fieldworks were to be attacked from the front and from the flank, threatening to cut off the lines of retreat of the defenders. This caused an early retreat of the Chinese forces, and, thus, fewer casualties on the French side (Porch 1991: 214). This is reminiscent of the tactical solution the Prussians devised against the French fieldworks in the war of 1870–1871, when they encircled the French flanks to dislodge the defenders. As such, the Sino-French War arguably resembled a conventional European war more closely than a war of imperial expansion fought against an elusive enemy who used guerrilla tactics.

The Chinese reliance on the defensive was also not a senseless reaction to the technological developments shaping warfare in the nineteenth century, but it is not known whether this disposition was due to an awareness of these developments. Allen Fung noted that "there was within Chinese military thought a powerful tradition which preferred the defensive to the offensive, unless one enjoys a substantial advantage in manpower over the enemy". He also states that Zeng Guofan believed that defensive tactics would be the key to victory, since bogging down the attacking side would cause them serious logistical problems (Fung 1996: 1019). Causing logistical problems was indeed a tactic employed during the battle at Bac Le, where the Chinese forces made it a point to kill as many coolies, accompanying

Technology, Tactics and Military Transfer in the Nineteenth Century   183

the retreating French, as possible (Sarrat 1987: 140; Thomazi 1934: 196). Furthermore, the two most notable instances of the Chinese going on the offensive occurred when they had a numerical superiority over the enemy. The first took place during the battle at Bac Le, the second just over the Chinese border at Bang Bo near Lang Son (24 March1885). At the former, a French column of 900 men faced 4,000 Chinese regulars, whilst at the latter 1,500 French were nearly overwhelmed by an estimated 25,000–35,000 Guangxi soldiers (Long 1996: 243–245; Elleman 2001: 87; Porch 1991: 232). At Bang Bo the Chinese used a human-wave assault, simultaneously charging at the front and trying to encircle the enemy at the flanks. Hocquard, a French army doctor who spoke to survivors, recorded the following account: "they [the Chinese] advanced in a compact mass and attempted an encircling movement. The one-hundred-and-eleventh saw a human avalanche come towards them" (Hocquard 1999: 467–468). These were comparatively simple and straightforward tactics relying on overwhelming numbers, but yongying also occasionally showed an ability to manoeuvre in a more complex European fashion, recognisable to the French. This happened during the battle at Kep (11 October 1884). The French tried to dislodge troops belonging to the Guangxi army, numbering 3,000 men, with a force of 1,500, supported by artillery. The Chinese were solidly entrenched in two successive lines of fieldworks, but with no artillery support. The fighting here was excessively hard, and the Chinese lines only broke after an artillery bombardment and three infantry charges, culminating in a man-to-man battle. The French also attempted a pincer movement to encircle the defenders, but the Chinese, interestingly, attempted a similar encircling movement of their own, perhaps showing European training. One arm of this movement was met by a French arm of their own pincer movement and was defeated, the other arm almost succeeded in reaching the artillery position of the French, before being driven back by the combined fire-power of rifles and a machine gun (Hocquard 1999: 331–335). Despite this being a French victory, Louis Sarrat was very impressed by the Chinese movements: "Ils (. . .) manoeuvrent à l'européenne" (Sarrat 1987: 166–167). Praise for manoeuvring was also given to the force attacking the French after the Bang Bo defeat. Three columns attacked the French positions on 28 March 1885 and uncharacteristically started discharging their weapons at 1,500 m. The attacks were repelled, but the French general Négrier was wounded and his substitute decided to retreat from Lang Son, fearing the envelopment of his position (Grisot and Coulombon 1888: 466; Thomazi 1934: 256).

I would argue that we see here a hybrid army at work, occasionally trying to replicate Western tactics, but most often relying on the defensive sanctioned by indigenous military thought, and perhaps also by experiences during the many rebellions of the mid-nineteenth century, for many of the commanders involved rose through the ranks during this period. Wang Debang (1837-1893) commanded the troops at Bac Le, and he had served under Zuo Zongtang (1812-1885), an important member of the Self-Strengthening Movement and mastermind behind the suppression of the Panthay Rebellion (1856-1873). Cen Yuying (1829-1889) commanded the Yunnan provincial army at Hoa Moc, and he had climbed through the ranks during the Taiping and Dungan Rebellions (1850-1871 and 1862-1877).

While suppressing the latter, he had used French weapons and advisers to arm and train his troops, and perhaps they also instructed him in the construction of fieldworks, which were used to good effect at the battle of Hoa Moc (2–3 March 1885) (McAleavy 1968: 158; Spector 1964: 307). Ironically, although the appropriation of Western technology had been a relatively successful venture, it was its use that constituted the most glaring weakness of the Chinese armies in Tonkin. Technologically, the Chinese even seem to have enjoyed a certain edge over the French. Many troops were equipped with magazine rifles, which had a higher rate of fire than the French Gras rifles (Sarrat 1987: 138). The French captured impressive stockpiles of weapons from retreating Chinese units on more than one occasion, and their contents led a Dutch military journal to proclaim that no army in the world could be equipped in a more modern fashion, only hot air balloons were lacking. Amongst the loot were machine guns, Gatling guns, magazine rifles, breech-loading rifles, modern Krupp mountain cannon, and huge stockpiles of ammunition (Anonymous 1885a: 1291). Clearly, weaponry and logistics were not the problems undermining the Chinese war effort. The technological gap between China and the West seemed to have been closed, certainly in comparison with 1860, when French and Chinese forces last met on the field of battle (Elman 2004: 316–317). The problem lay in the application of this technology to modern warfare. The lack of accuracy on the part of Chinese soldiers has already been noted and this was one of the most important problems of the war. This shortcoming is also reflected in the number of dead and wounded on both sides after each battle, with the Chinese casualties being invariably much higher, even allowing for French exaggeration. At Kep, for example, the well-entrenched Guangxi army regulars inflicted 93 casualties on the French (32 dead and 61 wounded), but lost 600 men in return (Hocquard 1999: 334–335). This was by no means exceptional, and it showed a lack of training in weapons handling at least as much as deficiencies in tactics, which was actually one of the strengths of the Chinese army at Kep. Any theoretical advantage in fire-power was thus offset by ignorance, and this also played its part with the artillery. Modern artillery was present in the Guangxi army, in the shape of Krupp breech-loading mountain guns, but the only times they show up in French sources is when they are captured as loot after being abandoned by the retreating Chinese (Hocquard 1999: 110). The single time they were mentioned as being effectively used is during the battle of Dong Dang, near Lang Son, on 23 February 1885. The fire of the artillery even forced the French artillery to change position; nonetheless, this appears to have been an exception (Grisot and Coulombon 1888: 460). Liu Yongfu (1837-1917), a Chinese mercenary leader who had fought the French with his irregular Black Flags before the involvement of the Guangxi provincial army, was convinced that the Chinese artillery-men did not know how to use their guns properly, when he observed them at Bac Ninh in March 1884 (McAleavy 1968: 230). Once again, ignorance and the resulting lack of integration of artillery with infantry, one of the strengths of the French, hampered the Chinese war effort.

4 Conclusion

Without personnel properly schooled in the use of Western technology, or at least without proper incentives to learn, the mere presence of modern artillery and rifles did not prevent overall military defeat for the Chinese in the Sino-French War. Transfer in the military field was not just a top-down process between a superior active culture and an inferior passive one, but was shaped by the receiving culture according to its own setting of political goals, or tasking. In addition, technology and institutions were not seen as value-neutral, but had to be appropriated within the receiving cultural context and fitted to the existing structures of power.

Some attributes of European warfare were more difficult to appropriate, given the cultural context of yongying armies, but this was hardly a specifically Chinese problem, as the Austrian and the Prussian armies were also resistant to certain changes. Both European and Chinese experiences during the nineteenth century show that the adoption of modern military technology was not sufficient to win wars if it was not used in conjunction with appropriate tactics and training. This juxtaposition of European and Chinese armies shows that there was no monolithic "European warfare", and suggests a more generalised picture of military forces across the world dealing with comparable (tactical) problems brought about by technological changes.

However, a specifically Chinese problem seems to have been the Qing court's lack of interest in systematically sponsoring European-style reforms in a centralised way, since this might have entailed endangering the system of ideological inculcation which critically bound the throne to elites within the empire. This illustrates that heavier military demands placed on the Qing Empire did not lead to state building along the lines of the "coercion-extraction" model articulated by scholars such as Charles Tilly. Military necessities did not lead to a more interventionist and coercive state increasingly occupied with extracting resources from its population to support growing military efforts. Instead, we see regional power-holders—governors and the local gentry—proactively increasing their military assets and capabilities and applying them in the name of the dynasty. This effort, which in some ways could be regarded as state building from below, could not be fully appropriated by the central court. Instead, the court had to balance the need for increased military capabilities with upholding the institutions which buttressed its ideological legitimisation. This example of transfer in the military field thus shows the multi-faceted nature of state interests and imperatives which came into play, rendering the task of army reform a complex one. The regional power-holders, such as Zeng Guofan, managed to strengthen the state militarily, but their efforts also threatened to weaken the very institutions that state used in order to produce the elites it relied on.

Decentralised transfer on the level of the regional armies also encountered its share of cultural difficulties. In this context, the introduction of drill and tactics, as they had developed in Europe during the nineteenth century, illustrates an important conundrum of transcultural transfer processes: what was the point in defending your culture against Europe if you had to become like the Europeans in order to do so? Other attributes were easier to transfer, especially if they could be sanctioned by historical precedent. The yongying armies were a prime example of a hybridity resulting from the need to offset a power asymmetry whilst also preserving one's own cultural identity. Unfortunately for the Qing, there were limits to this hybridity, and the Sino-French War showed its shortcomings for the first time. Technological change had put a premium on new kinds of training and demanded more of officer and soldier alike. But these demands were hardly recognised in a context where internal conditions of the Qing Empire were responsible for the creation of a demand for Western military expertise, and these shaped the process of transfer decisively.

Bibliography

Anonymous I. 1885. "De Fransche oorlogvoering in Tonkin." *Indisch Militair Tijdschrift* 16/7-12: 1290–1291.
Anonymous II. 1885. "De vechtwijze der Franschen in Tonkin." *Indisch Militair Tijdschrift* 16/1-6: 611–619.
Ashley, Kathleen and Véronique Plesch. 2002. "The Cultural Processes of "Appropriation"". *Journal of Medieval and Early Modern Studies* 32/1: 1–15.
Bays, Daniel H. 1970. "The Nature of Provincial Political Authority in Late Ch'ing Times: Chang Chih-tung in Canton, 1884–1889." *Modern Asian Studies* 4/4: 325–347.
Bidwell, Shelford. 1971. *Swords for Hire. European Mercenaries in Eighteenth-Century India.* London: John Murray.
Black, Jeremy. 2001. *Western Warfare, 1775–1882.* Bloomington: Indiana University Press.
Black, Jeremy. 2004. *Rethinking Military History.* London: Routledge.
Long Zhang 龍章 (1996) Yuenan yu Zhong Fa Zhanzheng 越南於中法战争. Taibei: Taiwan shangwu yinshu guan 台北: 台湾商务印書館
Deák, István. 1990. *Beyond Nationalism. A Social and Political History of the Habsburg Officer Corps, 1848–1918.* New York: Oxford University Press.
Di Cosmo, Nicola. 2001. "European Technology and Manchu Power: Reflections on the "Military Revolution" in Seventeenth-Century China." In *Making Sense of Global History*, ed. Sølvi Sogner, 119–39. Oslo: Universitetsforlaget.
Elleman, Bruce A. 2001. *Modern Chinese Warfare, 1795–1989.* London: Routledge.
Elman, Benjamin A. 2004. "Naval Warfare and the Refraction of China's Self-Strengthening Reforms into Scientific and Technological Failure, 1865–1895." *Modern Asian Studies* 38/2: 283–326.
Fung, Allen. 1996. "Testing the Self-Strengthening: The Chinese Army in the Sino-Japanese War of 1894–1895." *Modern Asian Studies* 30/4: 1007–1031.
Grisot, Paul-Adolphe and Ernest-Auguste-Ferdinand Coulombon. 1888. *La légion étrangère de 1831 à 1887.* Paris: Berger-Levrault.
Hacker, Barton C. 1977. "The Weapons of the West. Military Technology and Modernization in 19th-Century China and Japan." *Technology and Culture* 18/1: 43–55.
Headrick, Daniel R. 1981. *The Tools of Empire. Technology and European Imperialism in the Nineteenth Century.* New York: Oxford University Press.
Hocquard, É. 1999. *War and Peace in Hanoi and Tonkin. A Field Report of the Franco-Chinese War and on Customs and Beliefs of the Vietnamese (1884–1885).* Bangkok: White Lotus Press.

Horowitz, Richard S. 2002. "Beyond the Marble Boat: The Transformation of the Chinese Military, 1850–1911." In *A Military History of China*, ed. David A. Graff and Robin Higham, 153–174. Boulder: Westview Press.

Horowitz, Richard S. 2005. "International Law and State Transformation in China, Siam, and the Ottoman Empire during the Nineteenth Century." *Journal of World History* 15/4: 445–486.

Jackman, Steven D. 2004. "Shoulder to Shoulder: Close Control and "Old Prussian Drill" in German Offensive Infantry Tactics, 1871–1914." *The Journal of Military History* 68/1: 73–104.

Kaske, Elisabeth. 2002. *Bismarcks Missionäre. Deutsche Militärinstrukteure in China 1884–1890*. Wiesbaden: Harrassowitz.

Kuhn, Philip A. 1978. "The Taiping Rebellion." *The Cambridge History of China. Volume 10. Late Ch'ing, 1800–1911, Part 1*, 264–317. Cambridge: Cambridge University Press.

Kunz, Hermann. 1902. *Taktische Beispiele aus den Kriegen der neuesten Zeit. 1880–1900. Drittes Heft: Die Feldzüge der Franzosen in Tonkin. 1883 bis 1885*. Berlin: Mittler.

Kwong, Luke S.K. 1993. "The T'i-Yung Dichotomy and the Search for Talent in Late-Ch'ing China". *Modern Asian Studies* 27/2: 253–279.

Lecomte, Jean François Alphonse. 1888. *Marche de Lang-Son à Tuyen-Quan. Combat de Hoa-Moc; Déblocus de Tuyen-Quan (13 février - 3 mars 1885)*. Paris: Berger-Levrault.

Liu, Kwang-ching. 1994. "The Confucian as Patriot and Pragmatist: Li Hung-chang's Formative Years, 1823–1866." In *Li Hung-chang and China's Early Modernization*, ed. Samuel C. Chu and Kwang-ching Liu, 17–47. New York: M.E. Sharpe.

Liu, Kwang-ching and Richard J. Smith. 1980. "The Military Challenge: The North-West and the Coast." In: *The Cambridge History of China. Volume 11. Late Ch'ing, 1800–1911, Part 2*, ed. Denis Twitchett and John K. Fairbank, 202–273. Cambridge: Cambridge University Press.

McAleavy, Henry. 1968. *Black Flags in Vietnam. The Story of a Chinese Intervention*. London: George Allen and Unwin.

Middell, Matthias. 2000. "European History and Cultural Transfer." *Diogenes* 48/1: 23–30.

Parker, Geoffrey. 1996. *The Military Revolution. Military Innovation and the Rise of the West, 1500–1800*. Cambridge: Cambridge University Press.

Porch, Douglas. 1981. *The March to the Marne. The French Army, 1871–1914*. Cambridge: Cambridge University Press.

Porch, Douglas. 1991. *The French Foreign Legion: A Complete History*. LondOn: MacMillan.

Powell, Ralph L. 1955. *The Rise of Chinese Military Power 1895–1912*. Princeton, New Jersey: Princeton University Press.

Presseisen, Ernst L. 1965. *Before Aggression. Europeans Prepare the Japanese Army*. Tucson: University of Arizona Press.

Ralston, David B. 1991. *Importing the European Army. The Introduction of European Military Techniques and Institutions into the Extra-European World, 1600–1914*. Chicago: University of Chicago Press.

Sarrat, Louis. 1987. *Journal d'un Marsouin au Tonkin, 1883–1886*. Paris: Éditions France-Empire.

Smith, Richard J. 1975. "The Employment of Foreign Military Talent: Chinese Tradition and Late Ch'ing Practice." *Journal of the Hong Kong Branch of the Royal Asiatic Society* 15: 113–138.

Smith, Richard J. 1976. "Foreign-Training and China's Self-Strengthening: The Case of Feng-huang-shan, 1864–1873." *Modern Asian Studies* 10/2: 195–223.

Smith, Richard J. 1978. "The Reform of Military Education in Late Ch'ing China, 1842–1895." *Journal of the Hong Kong Branch of the Royal Asiatic Society* 18: 15–40.

Smith, Richard J. 1994. "Li Hung-chang's Use of Foreign Military Talent: The Formative Period, 1862–1874." In *Li Hung-chang and China's Early Modernization*, ed. Samuel C. Chu and Kwang-ching Liu, 119–142. New York: M.E. Sharpe.

Spector, Stanley. 1964. *Li Hung-chang and the Huai Army. A Study in Nineteenth-Century Chinese Regionalism*. Seattle: University of Washington Press.

Stollberg-Rilinger, Barbara. 2009. "The Impact of Communication Theory on the Analysis of the Early Modern Statebuilding Processes." In *Empowering Interactions. Political Cultures and the Emergence of the State in Europe 1300–1900*, ed. Wim Blockmans, André Holenstein and Jon Mathieu, 313–318. Farnham: Ashgate.

Teng, Ssu-Yu and John K. Fairbank. 1970. *China's Response to the West. A Documentary Survey 1839–1923*. New York: Atheneum.

Thomazi, A. 1934. *La Conquête de l'Indochine*. Paris: Payot.

Tilly, Charles. 1992. *Coercion, Capital and European States, AD 990–1992*. Cambridge, Massachusetts: Blackwell.

Van Creveld, Martin. 2005. "Technology and War I: To 1945." In *The Oxford History of Modern War*, ed. Charles Townshend, 201–223. Oxford: Oxford University Press.

Vandervort, Bruce. 1998. *Wars of Imperial Conquest in Africa, 1830–1914*. London: UCL Press.

Van de Ven, Hans. 2003. "Military Mobilization in China, 1840–1949." In *War in the Modern World since 1815*, ed. Jeremy Black, 20–40. London: Routledge.

Waley-Cohen, Joanna. 1993. "China and Western Technology in the Late Eighteenth Century." *American Historical Review* 98/5: 1525–1544.

Wawro, Geoffrey. 1995. "An "Army of Pigs": The Technical, Social, and Political Bases of Austrian Shock Tactics, 1859–1866." *The Journal of Military History* 59/3: 407–433.

Wawro, Geoffrey. 2000. *Warfare and Society in Europe, 1792–1914*. London: Routledge.

Wesseling, H.L. 1989. "Colonial Wars: An Introduction". In *Imperialism and War: Essays on Colonial Wars in Asia and Africa*, ed. J.A. de Moor and H.L. Wesseling, 1–11. Leiden: E.J. Brill.

Wright, Mary Clabaugh. 1957. *The Last Stand of Chinese Conservatism. The T'ung-Chih restoration, 1862–1874*. Stanford, California: Stanford University Press.

Yu, Maochun. 2002. "The Taiping Rebellion: A Military Assessment of Revolution and Counter-revolution". In *A Military History of China*, ed. David A. Graff and Robin Higham, 135–151. Boulder: Westview Press.

Exporting Military Revolutions and the Changing Clausewitzian Triad between People, Armed Forces and Ruler at the Turn of the Nineteenth Century

Peter I. Trummer

Using the Turks as an example and as a way of indirectly criticising France, one of the most successful French generals of the eighteenth century, the Maréchal de Saxe (1696–1750), in his *Mes Rêveries* pondered on the difficulties of nations to learn (written 1732, published posthumously in 1757) (Parker 1991: 174). "It is hard for one nation to learn from another, either from pride, idleness or stupidity. Inventions take a long time to be accepted (and sometimes, even though everyone accepts their usefulness, in spite of everything they are abandoned in favour of tradition and routine)."

Military organisations have experienced throughout history that they have to learn lessons and that the swift as well as successful adaptation and incorporation of military lessons prove to be decisive for the survival not only of the military but for the entity the military was supposed to protect: the ruling dynasty, the empire or the state and its respective political order and society.

This essay will try to develop some questions for further research on the general topic of the transfer of military culture, meaning the import and export of military techniques and institutions. It will also try to demonstrate that the transfer of military cultures and military revolutions is based on and shaped by the transfer of structures and technologies of analysis. "Military structures on the move" did not only consist of new military technologies and techniques but essential parts of the flow were tools and technologies for the analysis of the existing military culture in the exporting and the importing countries. The starting point is a look at Prussian-German military missions to China during the last 20 years of the nineteenth century. This stands as a case study for the frictions involved in the transfer of military culture and military revolution(s). The debate on "military revolution (s)"—initiated in the 1950s—will then extend the historical dimension to European experiences of military revolutions with a focus on the eighteenth century to the

---

P.I. Trummer (✉)
Karl Jaspers Centre, University of Heidelberg, Voßstr. 2, 69115 Heidelberg, Germany
e-mail: trummer@asia-europe.uni-heidelberg.de

A. Flüchter and S. Richter (eds.), *Structures on the Move*,
Transcultural Research – Heidelberg Studies on Asia and Europe in a Global Context,
DOI 10.1007/978-3-642-19288-3_10, © Springer-Verlag Berlin Heidelberg 2012

early nineteenth century. To get an understanding of the truly revolutionary dimension of the importing of European military techniques and military culture, the Clausewitzian triad of relations between the ruler, the people and the armed forces will be introduced. Attempts at copying and introducing Central European military culture meant for China as well importing a rather different Clausewitzian triad. Modernising the military was coupled with changing the power relations within the Clausewitzian triad in a revolutionary way. This triad is based on the theory of Carl von Clausewitz (1780–1831) who devoted his life to the analysis of war in a time of revolutionary change.

Key for the understanding of the export of "military revolutions" and the transfer of military culture is to get a better understanding of the character of the military culture and civil-military relations in the exporting country, in our case Prussia. Suitable examples for this will therefore be presented in more detail. The main focus will be on the effects of military revolution(s) around the turn of the nineteenth century and for civil-military relations within the framework of the state during the nineteenth century.

The triad opens up the possibility to discuss the complexity of the changing character of war and thereby the changing character of civil-military relations within and for the state. Three aspects within the Clausewitzian triad will be described in more detail:

(a) The changing image of the individual soldier and of the military in society
(b) The citizen as soldier and the concept of general conscription
(c) Patriotic professionalism and the diminishing influence of class and money

These three aspects have been selected because they are important connections within the framework of the Clausewitzian triad especially between the spheres of the people and the armed forces in the context of the state. They have also been chosen because they may demonstrate the hidden and truly revolutionary dimension of the importing of European military techniques, institutions and culture. This is especially of importance for the transfer of European military culture after the French Revolution and the Napoleonic wars. In several cases the ruler who initiated the introduction of European military techniques underestimated the "hidden political cost" that resulted. The introduction of new techniques included in most cases more than merely introducing new weapons or technology while retaining the traditional military culture. As a conclusion a pattern of military learning is presented which also constitutes a bridge between the approaches to war, military revolutions and military culture from Early Modern times, through the nineteenth century, up to the early twentieth century.

1 The Case of Prussia

In several ways Prussia was a very special case even in the league of its European rivals. Until the late nineteenth century Prussia only had military experience on battlefields in Central Europe but not on the periphery of Europe or in far-away colonies as had the British, the French, the Russians or the Austrian-Hungarians with their military border with the Ottoman Empire. Even so the global "Prussian military model" of the nineteenth century already had its predecessor in the inner-European "Prussian military model" of the eighteenth century. It was from the 1860s onwards that the Prussian armed forces became a model not only for military reforms in European countries and territories but also outside of Europe.

What were the reasons for the attractiveness of learning from the Prussian military model for extra-European rulers? Was it only the fascination of military efficiency or also the rather conservative character of the existing reality of the Clausewitzian triad in Prussia and after 1871 in the German Empire with the strong position of the ruler as supreme military commander? Whatever the motivations of looking into the reform of one's armed forces were, for extra-European rulers the Prussian model seemed to be strengthening the position and control of the ruler over the armed forces. The Prusso-German experiences during the nineteenth century also stressed an interpretation of the armed forces as the centre-piece for the building of a strong and unified German Empire.

From the 1860s on, the Prusso-German military model was copied globally and after the creation of the German Empire actively exported to non-European countries, namely the Ottoman Empire (already since the 1830s), as well as to countries in South America and Asia, including Japan and China. In his path-breaking book from 1990, *Importing the European Army*, David B. Ralston stated in his conclusion that the import of European-style military techniques and institutions into Russia, the Ottoman Empire, Egypt, China and Japan—mainly during the nineteenth century—was "a significant first step, probably an irreversible one, in the modernization of these countries" (Ralston 1990: 173). Ralston also stated that all of the five cases he studied had developed a "noteworthy level of civilization. None was a primitive or tribal society (. . .)." His central thesis was that voluntary military reforms started by "the indigenous ruling elite" did lead to "the Europeanization of armed forces" in the respective countries (Ralston 1990: 173).

One parallel of circumstances in the countries initiating reform in the case of Prussia, Europe and outside of Europe is striking: they all were confronted with major military defeats—in the case of China even a series of military defeats during the late nineteenth century—that were considered to be humiliating and which led to strong reform movements. Another parallel is that also in the extra-European cases—especially again China—military reforms had to come in waves over an extended time period to show lasting effect. The circumstances for creating reform pressure may be manifold but national humiliation by military defeat may have been considerably increased by propaganda of superiority before and during an armed conflict. For the Chinese this was the case in a number of internal uprisings and military defeats against external opponents, especially during the late nineteenth century in the French-Chinese war (1884–1885) and the defeat by the Japanese in the Japanese-Chinese war (1894–1895). The latter was an especially humiliating defeat as the victorious Japanese army had been trained by Prussian-German military missions. The Chinese case gives a good example of the multiple motives and initiatives for reform. Even before those two defeats there were agents of military reform in China who studied successful European models of armies. Prussia, and after 1871 the German Empire, were considered to be just such a successful model of military modernisation. "Successful" in military categories is often interpreted as meaning victorious in battles and wars, with its victories in the Wars of German Unification (1864 against Denmark and 1866 against Austria and a coalition of Southern German territories) and by its success against France in 1870–1871—against a French army that was at the time considered to be one of the most modern land armies in the world—Prussia had acquired the aura of a phoenix that had risen out of the ashes of defeat in 1806 and had become a rising star in Europe (Eberstein 2007: 127–157). Since the 1860s a self-strengthening movement had begun to become of importance in China (Ralston 1990: 107–141; Jing 2002). The first group of German military instructors was hired by the Chinese representative of the Embassy in Berlin, Li Fengbao, while the French-Chinese war was going on (1884–1885) (Kaske 2002). This body of 30 military instructors was still a group of (all Prussian) officers and non-commissioned officers (NCOs) who left the Prussian army and were directly contracted into Chinese service. This happened against the intentions of the German foreign office which had anticipated the negative French responses (Kaske 2002: 37–39). Later military missions became official military missions of the German Empire which shows the shifting and growing official interest in such quasi "military ambassadors" of the German Reich. These early military instructors were mainly hired to teach special military (technical) skills to selected members of again selected elements of regional military formations. Together with "contract-instructors" of other nationalities—mainly French, British and US-American—they should thus not be seen as the introduction of an external military reform process. They are much more elements of an early wave of an internal Chinese struggle for military reforms. In the Chinese military organisation with its strong regional elements these reform impulses also became entangled in political power struggles. Importing Western weapons technology seems to have been much easier and much less confrontational for internal power relations than inviting external military expertise for the employment of these new weapons. Seen over a longer period of time the founding of the military school at Tianjin in 1885 may have been one of the most important initiatives for the transformation of Chinese military culture until the beginning of the twentieth century (Kaske 2002: 117–132). In the end it took several waves of military modernisations for China to really achieve a military revolution in the first decade of the twentieth century (Dreyer 1995: 9–39). Here all the components for a true revolution in military affairs—as will be described in the following example of Prussia—also came together in China.

2 On Military Revolutions: The Debate

One of the most interesting and influential discussions initiated by Early Modern historians was the Military Revolution debate. Its roots can be traced to the 1950s and Michael Roberts' thoughts on *The Military Revolution, 1560–1660 in Central*

Europe.[1] Various aspects of military revolution(s) have been discussed and expanded since then (Roberts 1956). The debate will not be rehearsed in full here, but in summary, the debate has focused on military technological as well as tactical innovations and their close connections with changes in political and societal structures. An important second wave of debate was initiated in the 1980s by Geoffrey Parker and William H. McNeill. One of the most important aspects of this renewal of the debate during the 1980s was the theme of the revolution in the Western way of war in the context of Western global expansion.

As already mentioned, the term *military revolution* may be misleading as it suggests swift, revolutionary changes. More often military revolutions are actually military evolutions over a longer period of time. From looking at case studies, the author's impression of military revolutions, transformations, or reforms is that one of their main characteristics is that they are never swift and they tend to come in "revolutionising waves".[2] For our case it is therefore necessary to go further back than just the eighteenth century to understand lines of development in military revolutions in Europe for the eighteenth century. On many occasions it is a specific combination of several technological revolutions over time which leads to a "revolutionary quantum leap" such as the one after 1789. In this paper such a fundamental change brought about by a combination of revolutionary factors will be called a change in the character of war and military affairs. The term "military affairs" underlines that not only war and military culture, but the Clausewitzian triad and civil-military relations per se underwent fundamental changes in Central Europe at the turn of the nineteenth century. Those changes were not only technological revolutions, but a combination of changes in several fields with an emphasis on doctrinal changes and fundamental changes in civil-military relations. The latter are the core changes, the ones that are really revolutionary in the sense of the word. While military technological revolutions are numerous, such changes in the political character of warfare are rare. They are culmination points in long-lasting processes of change with numerous setbacks for the "revolutionary forces" and the agents of reform. Often they end as incomplete reform processes, watered down considerably from their initially revolutionary thoughts and beginnings. Without having the space to elaborate here on this topic, the Prussian army reforms of the early nineteenth century may be considered as one of those incomplete reform processes (Walter 2003). The terminology of military "reform", "reorganisation", "transformation", and "modernisation" itself was constantly undergoing reform, adaptation and reinterpretation in different historical and political contexts (Rink and von Salisch 2010: 1–25). The naming of the commission may serve as one example. It was decreed in 1807 by the Prussian King Friedrich Wilhelm III (1770–1840) to address the conclusions for the military organisation drawn from the Prussian defeat by Napoleon in 1806: it was named *Reorganisationskommission*

---

[1] The lecture was held in 1955 at Queen's University, Belfast. It was first printed in Belfast 1956.

[2] The image of "revolutionary waves" is inspired by Samuel Huntington's "waves of democratization" (Huntington 1991).

(reorganisation commission) and not "reform commission". The term *Preussische Refom(en)* is a historiographic term which was coined by the interest of German liberal historians in those reforms during the middle of the nineteenth century. Its first lexicographical reference is only from 1863, by Rotteck and Welcker (Koselleck 1984). In extra-European countries importing European military culture and techniques was also often not labelled as "reform" but came in linguistic disguise as, for example, "self-strengthening" in China during the nineteenth century.

Importing a military revolution therefore is more than simply importing military technology or arms. To stress this distinction John A. Lynn's concept of military culture may be introduced here. He stresses "... the essential value of using a cultural approach in military history is precisely in distinguishing the mental from the material." (Lynn 2008, xix) He distinguishes between three cultural realms: societal, military and strategic: "Many aspects of societal culture impact upon the military, matters such as religion and masculinity, for example. Armed forces also create their own cultures, influenced by, but distinct from, those of society. [...] Both societal and military cultures combine in strategic culture, a useful category comprising the way a state's political and military institutions conceive of and deal with armed conflict. Strategic culture derives from civil values and practices as well as from military conceptions and capabilities." (Lynn 2008, xx) Aspects of these three cultural realms shall be described for the military revolutions in Europe.

3 Revolutionary Military Changes in Europe During the Eighteenth Century

The revolutionary changes of the eighteenth and early nineteenth century did not appear out of the blue; they had their foundation in military reforms and a series of tactical and technological revolutions starting as early as the sixteenth century (Rogers 1995: 37–54). The major impact of these military revolutions had been the creation of standing armies of unprecedented size in Central Europe. Revolutionary new ways of financing armed forces were a central factor as the majority of these standing armies were comprised of a considerable number of non-nationals. During times of heightened tension they had to be considerably augmented by mercenary forces to become ready for a military campaign. New weapons, new ways of organisation and administration in the military sphere, new uniforms and higher numbers of forces had to rest on a sound financial basis—or on loans and debts.

To give some impression of the augmentation of force numbers for the eighteenth century, here are some figures for Prussia: in 1700 there were around 80,000 soldiers including about 34% foreigners; in 1740 there were still around 80,000 soldiers (with a population of 2.2 million the ratio was 1:27) but including about 66% foreigners; in 1763 166,000 soldiers (with a population of 4.5 million, ratio 1:28) including about 56% foreigners; in 1786 194,000 soldiers (with a population of 5.7 million, ratio 1:29) including about 50% foreigners; and in 1794, at the beginning of the war with France, around 200,000 soldiers.[3] The fact that while total numbers of forces are growing, the ratio to the even-faster-growing population increases only slightly, hints at the potential for immense force mobilisations based on a *levée en masse* also in Prussia. This will be addressed later.

In the seventeenth century it was the Dutch who first not only introduced the well-known Oranean Army reform (1690s) but also optimised techniques of financing war. This was based on the growing Dutch trade and the European commercial and financial centre, Amsterdam. In combination with the prompt payment of interest and repayment of loans, it became a model for modern state and military financing. After about 1660 population and wealth had been steadily growing and thereby increased the basis for governmental income through taxation in Central Europe (Rogers 1995: 46). In 1689 the so-called "Dutch finance" was adopted in England. Geoffrey Parker states: "The foundation of the bank of England, Parliament's guarantee of all government loans, and the organization of a sophisticated money market in London made it possible for a British army of unprecedented size—90,000 men—to fight overseas for years; while in France the credit network of Samuel Bernard and other Swiss bankers financed Louis XIV's later wars" (Parker 1995: 48, also Parker 1974). It was mainly English money that financed the military enterprises on the European mainland and outside of Europe during the eighteenth century and especially funded the struggle against France until 1815. Larger standing armies had also led to the introduction of administrative and organisational structures, which in addition to central taxes strengthened central governments and administrations. Without going into details, Parker states "It is interesting to note that major waves of administrative reform in Western Europe in the 1530s and 1580s and at the end of the seventeenth century coincided with major phases of increase in army size" (Parker 1995: 45). At the end of the seventeenth century the size of armed forces had reached its "natural limit"—for the time and the existing conditions. The primary reasons were the financial limitations especially for financing mercenary forces, the population base upon which the formations, especially the infantry, had to rely,[4] and the techniques and technology of command and control, as well as logistics, which could not manage ever larger armies in the field. The maximum force limit for the management of operations of an army was discussed in the contemporary literature of the eighteenth century and in modern research literature as being roughly 50–60,000 soldiers (McNeill 1982: 144–184). To avoid any misunderstandings: 50,000 thus constitutes not the total number of armed forces of a country since it may have had

---

[3] Data compiled from: Thomson (1994, 29) and for numbers with ratios: Kroener (2008a: 222).

[4] Eastern European countries, especially Russia with large un-free peasant populations, constituted the exceptions to the rule and raised the topic of differences between the centre and the periphery for Europe.

more than one army in several theatres of operation at the same time, but means the manageable size in battle.

The well-established military power of France was severely bruised by defeats during the mid-eighteenth century in Europe but also in North America and India. The rising star around the mid-eighteenth century was Prussia. By this time as well the public response to such defeats as the one France suffered at Minden was undergoing considerable changes. The ideas of the Enlightenment strengthened the notion of the citizen and saw the sovereign and his state administration as responsible for such a series of defeats. Reforms were proposed and not only discussed by military experts but also by a broadening intellectual elite and circles considering themselves to be part of such an enlightened elite culture. At the centre of the critique in mid-eighteenth century France was the image of the officer and his lack of professionalisation. Above all the sale of officer patents and offices was considered at the base of "unprofessional performance" on the battlefield. Almost all the critics agreed that at the centre of reform had to be the French officer (Bien 1979: 70f.). Consequently this reform debate was also indirectly a highly political debate not only about the military but the abilities of the nobility as "natural born leaders" on and off the battlefield. Moreover learning from the enemy, which meant after the military successes of Frederick the Great especially learning from Prussia, became an important topic.[5] The quest for military reforms in France mainly focused on new military technology, especially reforms of the artillery, as well as on new tactical formations, which were intensely discussed in the "line versus divisional column" debate. However, military learning and professionalisation of training also became important issues. New military schools like the *École Militaire* were established in 1751, and from 1776 onwards military schools in the provinces were available to noblemen who could afford to attend them (Bien 1979: 71). The elimination of the purchase of office proved to be much more difficult and, first projected for the 1760s, endured well into the 1780s. Summarising the French experience before 1789 it can be stated that the ideas of the preceding decades, the conduct of battle, training for it, and theories for analysing military affairs, had all been undergoing evolutionary changes. True revolutionary changes are rare and are never constituted just by tactical or techno-logical innovations. Looking at the evolution of army style in the Western world between 800 and 2000, John A. Lynn stated: ". . . neither technology nor the course of major wars nor the careers of great commanders dictate the character and chronology of the stages set out there" (Lynn 1996: 507). The exogenous shock of military defeat can be identified as one factor for initiating military reforms. At the same time the French example demonstrates that the process took almost 30 years and was far from being comprehensive. Only the political revolution in 1789 brought a properly fundamental new organisation of the French armed forces,

---

[5] Our colleague at the Historical Institute of the University of Heidelberg, Dr. Isabelle Deflers, is currently working on an extensive study on Flows of ideas about Prussia in France between 1763 and 1806.

doubtless based on former reforms and the ideas of earlier reformers, but mainly by putting the whole military organisation into a new, revolutionary political context. Carl von Clausewitz spent all his adult life analysing war and its relationship to the state. Based on his theory[6] the following attempt will be made to create a framework for the analysis of the relations between the people, the armed forces and the ruler.

4 The "Clausewitzian Turn": The Revolution in the Analysis of War at the Turn of the Nineteenth Century

Revolutionary France challenged the European monarchies after 1789 militarily but especially in ideological terms. Describing this new character of French revolutionary warfare Clausewitz gets to the heart of it in *On War*: "... in 1793 a force appeared that beggared all imagination. Suddenly war again became the business of the people—a people of 30 millions, all of whom considered themselves to be citizens. We need not study in detail the circumstances that accompanied this tremendous development; we need only note the effects [...].The people became a participant in war; instead of governments and armies as heretofore, the full weight of the nation was thrown into the balance. The resources and efforts now available for use surpassed all conventional limits; nothing now impeded the vigor with which war could be waged, and consequently the opponents of France faced the utmost peril" (Clausewitz 1976: 591–592). Clausewitz was trying to bring order not only into the chaos of battle, but also into the chaos of warfare. Yet he chose an approach quite different from the many military analysts in the eighteenth century. The study of war and its changing characters included for Clausewitz a strong historical element.[7] He was as much a child of the early and mid-eighteenth century as a scholar and a contemporary of the outgoing eighteenth century and beginning of the nineteenth century.

Clausewitz engaged in extensive studies of military campaigns and also in reading and excerpting writings of military theoretical works of the eighteenth century.[8] In particular the campaigns of Frederick II were a central part of his empirical basis for

---

[6] Clausewitz himself (modestly) would not have defined his writings as a theory of war but only as "preliminary notes for a possible theory of war". For English introductions to the person and his theories see Paret (1985) and Strachan (2008). See also the introductory essay Bernard Brodie in Clausewitz (1976). All quotes from *On War* in this essay are taken from this edition and quoted as: Clausewitz. *On War*.

[7] On Clausewitz and history see especially Paret (1985: 78–89, 327–355). Also Paret (1992: 130–142). For selected historical and political writings by Clausewitz in English see Clausewitz (1992).

[8] In a footnote Hans Rothfels named some of the authors on whom Clausewitz wrote excerpts, among them Montecuccoli, Folard, Maurice de Saxe, Turpin, Guibert, Lloyd, Tempelhoff, Mauvillon, Venturini, Turenne, Herzog von Braunschweig. (Rothfels 1920: 29–30, note 5)

the analysis of the changing character of war. Thus Clausewitz is standing on the shoulders of the military analysts—whether civilian or military—of the eighteenth century and their discussions about the art and science of war (Gat 2001: 13–137). However, in a very special way he is also more than simply a link between the thinking on war of the eighteenth century and the nineteenth century, because he added a new dimension of analysis to the "traditional" approaches of the eighteenth century. Azar Gat sees Clausewitz as part of "the reaction against Enlightenment" (Gat 2001: 142).[9] One of the main antagonists to Clausewitz' analysis of war came in the person of Antoine Henri Jomini (1779–1869) who set about "synthesizing the legacy of the Enlightenment with Napoleonic warfare" (Gat 2001: 108). For Clausewitz the discussion about whether it is better for analysing the manifestations and new dimensions of the French revolutionary war to speak of the "art of war" or "science of war" in the end is not really fruitful. In *On War* he weighs up the arguments in a special chapter. He puts forward arguments for both points of view but comes to a different conclusion which leads beyond the argumentation of the eighteenth century. One central point of his revolution of the theory of war may be found in his following statement: "War is an act of human intercourse. We therefore conclude that war does not belong in the realm of arts and sciences; rather it is part of man's social existence (*Gebiet des gesellschaftlichen Lebens*). War is a clash between major interests, which is resolved by bloodshed—that is the only way in which it differs from other conflicts. [...] Politics, moreover, is the womb in which war develops—where its outlines already exist in their hidden rudimentary form, like the characteristics of living creatures in their embryos" (Clausewitz 1976: 149). This challenged the opponents of Napoleonic France to the extreme as it brought up the question of whether the military challenge could be met without revolutionising—and eventually even toppling—the existing monarchical systems themselves. During the ensuing years this topic caused the major friction and problems amongst the Prussian reformers, the king and conservative elites. The basis for the revolutionary change of the character of war in France after 1789 is therefore not to be found in new tactical or military technological innovations, even if they might have been enforcing factors. Instead it lies in the fundamental reversal of the political order and the power triangle between "people"—"armed forces" and—"ruler".

5 The Clausewitzian Triad and the Clausewitzian Trinity as Frameworks of Analysis

The real revolutionary response to the French challenge was in the analysis of war: the revolutionary new theory for analysing the changing character of war and the dynamic relationship of civil-military-relations[10] by Carl von Clausewitz. The

---

[9] Gat argues that the ways in which Clausewitz was subsequently received actually contributed to a rapidly decreasing interest in the out-dated theories of war of the "military enlightenment".

[10] The term *civil-military relations* is not from Clausewitz or his time, but it is taken from the mid-twentieth century to give my points more clarity. A discussion of the translation and interpretation

following focus will concentrate on the "Clausewitzian triad", which is to be distinguished—even though they are closely linked—from the "Clausewitzian trinity of war".[11] The "triad" focuses on war and the military instrument in the context of society, state policy and politics, and is much more "practice-oriented" than the "trinity". The relations between the three spheres of the triad are highly dynamic, with action and counteraction continuously at work (Herberg-Rothe 2007: 104–117). In this respect the following statement by Clausewitz on the dynamics of war can be transferred to the concept of the Clausewitzian triad: "The essential difference is that war is not an exercise of the will directed at inanimate matter, as is the case with the mechanical arts, or a matter which is animate but passive and yielding, as is the case with the human mind and emotions in the fine arts. In war, the will is directed at an animate object that reacts" (Clausewitz 1976: 149). Within the framework of state and society, the three spheres of "ruler" (King of Prussia), "the people or citizens", and the "armed forces" comprised of all ranks, together form the triad. Establishing a parliament as a representation of the will of the people and as an organ of control over the military was a point of controversy arising from the early discussions on the responses to the French revolutionary and then Napoleonic challenge. For this reason it is in italics in the diagram below. The triad exists in times both of peace and war.

WITHIN THE BORDERS OF THE STATE THREE "SPHERES" FORM THE TRIAD

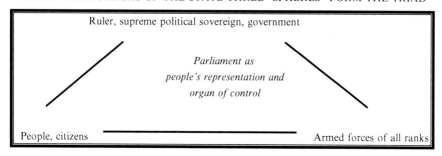

The Clausewitzian trinity focuses on the character of war within the larger context of society, policy and politics. It deals with the "chameleon war", or to put it differently: the "trinity" deals with the (philosophical) framework for the "triad" in times of war. It is much more concerned with the *Wesen des Krieges* (character of war) than with its *Erscheinungen* (manifestations of war) which makes it much more theory-oriented than the triad. The most important link

---

of terms central to Clausewitz has been on-going at least since the publication of the English edition and translation of *On War* by Michael Howard and Peter Paret in 1976.
[11] The Trinity cannot be discussed here. A superb discussion of "Clausewitz's Legacy: The Trinity" may be found in Herberg-Rothe (2007).

between the trinity and the triad and also within themselves is Clausewitz's famous dictum "... that war is not merely an act of policy, but a true political instrument, a continuation of political intercourse, carried on with other means" (Clausewitz 1976: 87).

The trinity is composed of three tendencies which are variable in their relationship to one another:

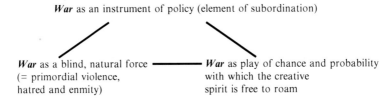

Using the triad and the trinity it is possible to analyse and characterise the new quality of the changes in military theory, military strategy, doctrine and civil-military relations during the (long) nineteenth century. They may well address different levels of analysis and different topics, but the author considers them to be always related. The thesis is that there is no change in the character of war without a fundamental change in civil-military relations or more complex, a considerable change in the relations in the Clausewitzian triad.

The types of manifestation (*Erscheinungsformen*) in both the triad and the trinity underwent fundamental changes during the late eighteenth and nineteenth century (revolutionary and evolutionary, technological and theoretical). An interesting question for the global analysis of war and society as well as for the changing dynamics of civil-military relations is to what degree and when different manifestations or the sum of them come to represent as well a point of culmination (*Umschlagpunkt*) of the character of war and/or the character of civil military relations.

From the complex relations and entanglements of the spheres of the Clausewitzian triad two areas of change will be looked at more closely. Firstly the focus will be on the military in society and especially on the evolution of the soldier from "social outcast" to "citizen in uniform". The citizen in uniform is also a concept which links the people to the state, at least the male part which was considered "worthy of military service" ("*wehrwürdig*") in the Prussian armed forces. Secondly, the citizen soldier and the concept of general conscription will be described. As a third aspect the evolution of a "patriotic professionalism" and the diminishing influence of class and money will be addressed. The primary goal is to give an impression of the new quality of linkage between the multiple identities of the individual as citizen as well as political and military subject which emerged from the confrontation with the French Revolution and French military expansionism under Napoleon Bonaparte.

6 Reshaping the Image and Role of the Soldier and the Military in Society

Even today the image of the common soldier of the eighteenth century evokes a number of pejorative associations. In the German language *der gemeine Soldat* has in the course of time even come to carry a double meaning as "the common soldier" but also the "mean soldier". Countless portrayals—especially by military and political leaders—shaped the image of soulless low-lives of society who had to be shaped by brute force into machine-like military organisms.

Recent research has moderated that impression of the individual soldiers forming the bulk of the infantry (Kroener 2000; Kroener 2008a, b, c). It seems that the soldiers were much more a part of society, especially in garrison-cities and towns, than isolated outcasts. Bernhard Kroener has since the late 1970s given an excellent overview of this development in a new German military history of Early Modern times. One important emphasis is to move towards research on the military *in* society and not only on the military *and* society. The focus has shifted from the military as organisation to the individual soldier in his multiple social contexts. Kroener makes an excellent point when he states that our image of military life in Early Modern society and the relationship between military and society has to be "... liberated from the burden of misinterpretation originating from the nineteenth century..." ("... *(ist) vom interpretatorischen Ballast des 19. Jahrhunderts zu befreien* ...") (Kroener 2000: 288). This seems true as well for the iconographic impressions of the eighteenth and early nineteenth century which in Germany are often still based on images by famous patriotic artists of historical and military topics like Adolf Menzel and Richard Knötel[12] from the mid to late nineteenth century.

Actually the soldiers of the eighteenth century lived mostly not in military barracks but literally in the middle of the city population, in the houses of citizens in which the soldiers were quartered. This definitely was not an isolated position in everyday life and even made common soldiers part of the (political) communication within the city population (Pröve 1995; Kroll 1997). Once the image of the soldier is moderated from being an isolated outsider several interesting questions are raised. One is whether and how living in the midst of civil society influenced the political awareness of common soldiers or even "revolutionised" their thinking. Another is how the rather high percentage of soldiers from foreign countries has to be looked at in this context. A third topic is the question of gender relations between the soldiers living in the midst of city society, not least questions about the

---

[12] Adolf Menzel (born in Breslau 1815, died in Berlin 1905) became famous for his images of "Friedrich dem Großen und seiner Taten" ("Frederick the Great and his achievements"). For a contextualisation of Menzel in "Art as History and History as Politics" see Paret (1990/1988). Richard Knötel (1857–1914) is also well known among experts for his illustrated work *Uniformkunde* in 18 volumes.

economic situation of (formal or informal) soldier families during times of war and the loss of the male *pater familias*.

Within the military organisation the human and emotional components such as compassion for one's fellow soldier, one's comrade, in a unit will certainly have played a much larger role than evoked by the mechanical image of the soldier. The small human unit of 6–8 men per tent—the *Zeltgemeinschaft* (tent-community)—may have played a considerable role in cohesion during battle (Epkenhans et al. 2006). Reducing cohesion and performance during combat for these soldiers to only being the result of drill and pressure actually reduces in a way the individuals to their pejorative stereotype as marionettes or cogs and bolts. Already in contemporary literature and theatre plays in the eighteenth and early nineteenth century the soldier and the military system were portrayed in a more nuanced way and even constituted a specific genre, the *Soldatenstück* (soldier play).

These considerations may suffice here to make the point that the common soldier of pre-revolutionary times was much less an "outcast military automaton" than already a member of civil society. The evolution of mass armies of citizen soldiers during and after the French (and American) Revolution may therefore have had a more solid base in society, civilian and military culture than commonly thought.

The main link between the infantry of the line of the eighteenth century and the new model of the revolutionary citizen soldier has to be sought in the formations and tactics of light infantry. This linkage is not only one in military terms, but also carried a political aspect in itself. The revolutionary political importance of the individual had in military culture already emerged out of military (tactical) necessity for the individual light infantry soldier.[13] He was not led in closely supervised formations but was used as a skirmisher in front and on the flanks of the line infantry to screen the latter and to harass the enemy. Reliance on individual skills, autonomous target selection and fire, intelligent use of the terrain and most often acting independently within the larger order of battle, the light soldier personified the absolute opposite of the image of the spiritless, machine-like soldier of the line infantry. The evolution of the famous German *Auftragstaktik* (mission command), giving the subordinate military leader and soldier large freedom of decision, is closely linked to this tactical development (Oetting 1993: 11–77). This was also a kind of military organisation with which the citizen could identify more easily. While light infantry formations were considered to be elite formations, the question was how large these new formations of generally much less skilled and trained citizen soldiers could become, but still be efficient in combat and such that a commander would not loose overall command and control in battle. One of the new characteristics of the wars of the French Republic and the Napoleonic wars was a further increase in size of the armies deployed. They now jumped to one million

---

[13] My focus here is on the infantry soldiers as they were much more numerous than the light cavalry and therefore played a more important role in the evolution of these units into units of citizen soldiers and in forming the nucleus for citizen armies. For an overview of the development of the light units and small war in Prussia see Rink (1999).

men raised by the *levée en masse* in Revolutionary France. This phenomenon of mobilising the hitherto untapped parts of the population base was founded on the introduction of general conscription and thereby created the new citizen soldier. Not to be underestimated is the decoupling of the common soldier from society which came with the ideal of the unmarried male conscript. In combination with the stationing of the conscript armies in newly built military barracks—mainly on the outskirts of cities and towns—the conscript citizen soldier was actually moving away from the centre of city life. These measures were also meant to tighten the control of the ruler—standing for the state—over the citizen soldier.

7 The Citizen as Soldier and the Concept of *General Conscription*

The dimension of "people/citizen" and its relation to the ruler and the state is one of the elements within the triad, which changed so fundamentally between the 1790s and 1815 that one may speak of a new quality in the power relations among the three dimensions of the triad.

The initiating event was the declaration of general conscription in the famous decree of the revolutionary French Republic regarding the *levée en masse* of August 23, 1793.[14] Already in December of 1789 the member of the French national assembly, Dubois de Crancé, had demanded "Tout citoyen doit être soldat, et tout soldat citoyen."[15] The surprising military victories of the ill-trained and ill-organised revolutionary French troops against a coalition of European monarchies between 1792 and 1797 had introduced the principle of general conscription into war (Cohen 1985). One of the most obvious results of the French general conscription had been that large armies were created for the Republic, which could almost always lead to far superior numbers on the battle-field. These numbers in combination with revolutionary élan resulted in a number of stunning victories for the revolutionary troops over the anti-French coalition even before the supreme command of Napoleon Bonaparte and his "military genius".

For Prussia, real study of the new and by then further developed French system came with the crushing Prussian defeats at Jena and Auerstädt in 1806 (Aaslestad and Hagemann 2006: Hahn 2008; Paret 2009; Schnitter 1994). Between 1807 and 1815 several reforms were initiated in Prussia, and that concerning the armed forces was developed and led by the military reform commission. Clausewitz himself was

---

[14] Initiated by Lazare Carnot—later often called "the organiser of victory"- in the wars of the coalition. For a critical approach to the historical appraisal of the levée en masse see Cohen, especially chapter 2: 42–59.

[15] *Archives Parlementaires de 1787 à 1860*, vol. IX, 1877: 520–521. Quoted after Michael Sikora in Baumgart et al. (2008: 135). Details about the French conscription and its problems are described in Woloch (1986). Also in Moran and Waldron (2003: 1–7).

a member of this commission and a close confidant of the head of the commission, Gerhard von Scharnhorst. The reforms were oriented on the French model and by studying them one may come to the conclusion that the Prussian army reform was actually more directed to the original, French revolutionary model than to the already watered-down Napoleonic practice. Additional inspiration came from practices in Prussia and other German territories during the eighteenth century, for example the *Defensionspflicht* as a forerunner of general conscription.[16] A discussion of proposals raged between 1809 and 1813 (Friedeburg 2005: 881–916); the plans of the commission were deemed to be so "revolutionary" that they were blocked by anti-reform circles and could not be introduced until the outbreak of the Prussian war of liberation in spring of 1813 (Stübig 1994; Neugebauer 2008).

The main points of the new general conscription were:

- All male Prussian subjects, without exception, could now be recruited. Before, the inhabitants of several cities (including the capital Berlin), certain professions, the clergy, the nobility and most parts of the emerging "middle class" were exempted from being called up or even "pressed" into the army.
- Abolition of the institution of *Stellvertretung*, a replacement for someone called up for military service paid by a person wealthy enough to do so.
  This practice had developed into a (legal) business, even with some forms of "insurance agencies" of which one could become a paying member to be insured in the event of being picked for military service.
- The end of recruitment of non-Prussian citizens (which earlier had accounted for up to 66% of the forces).
- The abolition of the brutal system of capital punishment and the moderation of the (in-) famous "Prussian drill"—the latter being closely linked to the introduction and enlargement of new formations and units as for example the *Jäger*.

In practice this meant the rise of the "bourgeois element" in the armed forces as well as more recruits who came from the cities. A number of innovations were introduced, many based on already existing examples. Thus formations and systems were especially "tailored" to the middle-class/bourgeoisie such as the *Jäger*, the creation of new army formations in addition to the main body of the army ("troops of the line") like the *Landwehr* and *Landsturm*, the *Krümper* system (short service times distributed over the calendar year, also intended to train more soldiers by still adhering to the troop limit set by the French for the Prussian army), the concept of the "1-year volunteer" for the middle-class and students who in this way could more quickly obtain officers' positions in the *Landwehr* and *Landsturm*.

These examples should suffice to show the broad range of military innovations. Some of the reforms were revoked after the victory over Bonaparte, but by the time of the large Prussian army reform of the 1860s, most of the principles had become

---

[16] Schnitter (1994). For the ideas of major reformers concerning general conscription see Kessel (1987).

Exporting Military Revolutions and the Changing Clausewitzian Triad   205

established. Successfully waging war in central Europe was not possible any more without the mobilisation of large, well-trained and well-motivated armies. The concepts of universal conscription and total war mobilisation also created new linkages between citizenship rights and military duty for the young male citizen. The introduction of the reforms meant not only the shifting of power in the triad with an increasing relevance of all citizens as "man-power basis", but by introducing reserve structures like the *Landwehr* and the *Landsturm* with their posts of part-time citizen officers pressure was also increased on the future political representation of the "people element", especially the middle-class within the state. Access to military service as a duty and a right had opened the door to a struggle for more universal, political participation rights. It cannot be discussed here, but it should not be overlooked that the new Prussian citizenship concepts not only created new inclusions but also new boundaries of exclusion, notably in the categories of gender and religion (Lohmann and Mayer 2007: 7–27). The strengthening of parliaments as political bodies demanding participation in decisions, and of control like the "power of the purse"—not least in military questions—became a field for political power struggle in Prussia and the German Reich for the rest of the nineteenth century (Walter 2003). The examples of "peoples in arms" driving war to its extreme of "absolute war", such as the anti-Napoleonic guerrilla war, as per note in Spain, the Tyrol, and in Russia had also demonstrated that such an armed population constituted a possible threat which should not be underestimated in the event of internal revolt against the existing monarchies.[17] As the character of war itself had changed—as Clausewitz had observed and stated during the reform process for example in several *Denkschriften*—the military reforms posed formidable challenges for the Prussian monarchy. A central dilemma for traditional elites was that attempting to beat Napoleon with his own techniques would itself lead to a revolutionary power shift in the triad, a shift which once conceded could not easily be reversed. The frustration of the slow reforms and political opposition from conservative circles actually led Clausewitz to resign from Prussian service in 1812 and made him join the Russian Czarist army in the anti-Napoleonic fight until 1814. This personal struggle between loyalty to the Prussian king as supreme commander and his patriotic sentiments to do the best for the Prussian fatherland is exemplary for the changing interpretation of loyalties and patriotism during those times.[18] For Clausewitz this decision seems to have especially been linked to the opposition by reform sceptics of the concept of citizen soldiers in its absolute form: the concept of people's war (*Volkskriegskonzept*). With the revolutionary change in the triad new concepts of military professionalism developed as well.

---

[17] It is not possible to address the concepts of "absolute war", "total war" and their relation to "guerrilla war" or "people"s war" in this context.

[18] For Clausewitz and his struggle see "*The Logic of Patriotism*" in Paret (1985: 209–221).

8 "Patriotic Professionalism" and the Diminishing Influence of Class and Money[19]

Military professionalism definitely existed before the French Revolution, Napoleon and the Prussian military reforms of 1807–1815 (Cohen 1985). In fact the Prussian king and his generals had trusted in the glorious tradition of military professionalism in the Prussian army before the humiliating defeats of 1806. Those defeats clearly demonstrated the need for fundamental reform (Paret 2009: Koselleck 1967).

Samuel Huntington measured the "development of professional expertise, responsibility, and corporateness ... in terms of the evolution of five key institutions of the military vocation: (1) the requirements for entry into the officer corps; (2) the means of advancement within the officer corps; (3) the character of the military educational system; (4) the nature of the military staff system; and (5) the general *esprit* and competence of the officer corps."[20] Without having the space to discuss the definition, I would at least add (6) the nature and organisation of the military administration.

The new quality of Prussian professionalism—a quasi-post-Frederick-the-Great professionalism—may especially be seen in the combination of large numbers of conscripts with their high motivation to risk their lives for "king and country". Its roots are much older and are easily traced for Prussia to the eighteenth century and the times of Frederick II and the Seven Years War (Hagemann 2002: 45–71). One exceptional example pleading that patriotism is not only possible in a republic but also in a monarchy is Thomas Abbt's *Vom Tode für das Vaterland* from 1761 (Abbt 1996: 589–650; Commentary: 971–1008). If the monarch is also a just *Landesvater* and fully engaged in the interest of the fatherland then patriotism is also possible in a monarchy (Munch 1982). For the time between 1765 and 1767 Nicholas Vazsonyi spoke of a "National Spirit Debate" in Germany.[21] Inspired by Montesquieu and made popular in Germany also through the Swiss Johann Georg Zimmermann's *Von dem Nationalstolze* (1758) a number of German thinkers, including Friedrich Carl von Moser and Johann von Justi, had developed their own ideas and engaged in a debate which may be called the *Nationalgeistdebatte* (national spirit debate) (Vazsonyi 1999; 227). The new concept of a citizen-in-arms and the new military

---

[19] My gratitude for comments and inspirations on this part goes especially to the scholars present at the workshop *Being an Official: The Sale of Public Offices and its Effects in Comparative Perspective* held at the Fairbanks Centre for Chinese Studies, Harvard University, April 25, 2009, organised by Dr. Elisabeth Kaske.

[20] Huntington (1957, 20), Abrahamson (1972). For a brief summary of the overwhelming literature on the main theories concerning civil-military relations see Schiff (1995).

[21] Vazsonyi (1999). One of the editors of this volume, Dr. Susan Richter, is an expert on these German thinkers of the eighteenth century, notably Justi and Moser. For more see her contribution in this volume and a number of forthcoming articles.

Exporting Military Revolutions and the Changing Clausewitzian Triad 207

professionalism built on such concepts, but also created a new quantity and quality of these ideas.

As such the new quality of professionalism around the turn of the nineteenth century will here be called "patriotic professionalism" that is paying allegiance to a *patria*, a fatherland, and a sovereign. The later form of patriotism, which puts the nation first, could be called "national patriotism", and ergo its respective professionalism would be "national professionalism".[22]

With the increasing importance and size of technical troops new technical skills and knowledge became a necessity for the professional officer, "outranking" by far nobility, a long line of military ancestors, political connections or the money to buy an officer's patent. Artillery especially became the branch for advancement of officers without a noble background. The increasing number of armed forces, as mentioned, along with the casualties resulting from long periods of war certainly outgrew the "human resources" of the limited number of noble families. Not only did the ranks have to be increased by general conscription but also the respective number of officers had to be provided for by opening officer positions up to non-noble citizens. This was also a result of the patriotic move of reducing or even banning the (general) service of non-nationals in officer positions in the new national armies (Thomson 1994). The other aspect of this concept of "nationalising the military profession" was over time the banning of citizens from military service in foreign military contingents. This concept of "nationalising" the military profession took some time but became the dominant approach in the nineteenth century. It was coupled to the general prohibition of the service of national citizens in foreign armed forces, although military instructors of training missions fell into a special category.

Furthermore the management of larger, more complex bodies of troops, the increased demands of training, operations, logistics etc. created the necessity for a new generation of well-educated and trained officers as well as a professionalised military organisation. Later to become one of the most admired Prussian military institutions, the rise of the Prussian general staff was one of the outcomes of these new demands and reorganisations (Thomson 1994).

After crowning himself French emperor, Napoleon had in many respects restored elements of the old, pre-revolutionary military system. Because of the long duration of wars and with mounting French casualties more and more non-French troop contingents from conquered territories were fighting on the French side. As a high-water mark we may consider the Russian campaign and the *Grande Armée*, which consisted to a large degree of non-French elements.

---

[22] Clausewitz is one of the examples of a Prussian patriot and professional since he went into Russian service when Prussia was obliged to become an ally of the French. At Tauroggen, 1812, he participated as a Russian staff officer in convincing the Prussian general Ludwig von Yorck to "neutralise" his troops and not to support the French contingent any more. This actually meant valuing Prussia higher than the King of Prussia, an act that later was regarded as treason. For the historical context (in English) see Paret (1966).

The Prussian reforms were in many respects closer to the revolutionary French model of the 1790s than the later Napoleonic practice. The patriotic element, combined with anti-French propaganda, was a driving force for the broad mobilisation of forces and public support in Prussia during the War of Liberation (*Befreiungskrieg*, 1813–1814) from French rule (Görlitz 1967). This important role of linking the citizen (the people), the armed forces and the ruler fell to patriotic propaganda, which in the Prussian example during the anti-Napoleonic struggle also included the striving for a united German nation (Hagemann 2002).

The foundation for the patriotic professionalisation of the Prussian army had been laid between 1806 and 1809 with the forced retirement of 86 and the expulsion of 17 Prussian generals out of a total of 142 (Clark 2008: 380). In 1808 the privilege whereby only the nobility could become officers was ended (Baumgart et al. 2008: 72–95). The basis for becoming an officer was now founded on acquiring knowledge at the three newly established war schools and passing an exam of an also newly created central examination board. The curricula of the war schools contained mainly topics taken from the educational ideals of the emerging middle-class together with the sciences (Hagemann 2002). The solid resistance of the nobility against losing its officer privilege was a continuous struggle for decades and is mirrored in the discussion concerning the curricula and the constant restructuring of the war schools. There were also requirements, often unofficial, stemming from the nobility concerning how one might become an officer in a number of "traditional units"—such as guard units of the cavalry—and some of these remained influential until the First World War.

The most thoroughly and most quickly reformed branches were the technical ones like the artillery, the engineers and the increasingly numerous units of the light elite infantry (such as the *Jäger*). The highest training institution for officers became the war academy (*Allgemeine Kriegsschule*) in Berlin. For 3 years officers were trained to be receptive to progressive ideas in the field of military science and the art of war, an ideal again heavily contested over the years. This educational approach was combined with the introduction of more realistic training for the soldiers in preparation for battle (for example combat training and reducing formation drill, shooting at targets and training the individual soldier in marksmanship). These innovations led to the dissolution of close (infantry) formations. The new, looser formations were harder to command and control, and as a result the soldier could not essentially be forced to fight, but intrinsic motivation and initiative became increasingly important. Rapidly, a new type of soldier was required and was developing.

Of central importance for the question of purchase of office were the reorganisations of the military organisation, especially the logistical system and the abolition of the so-called *Kompaniewirtschaft* (company economy) in 1808. This was considered to have been one of the sources of defeat, as the economic gain for the military commander during times of peace often seems to have been of more importance than training the unit for future combat. The *Kompaniewirtschaft* had given the head of larger military formations, from the *Kompanie* (company, around 120–150 infantry soldiers) upwards, the opportunity to make a lucrative income.

Officers had personally used and abused money allocated to them for the payment and supply of their soldiers. Therefore it had also been lucrative for the nobility to purchase an officer's patent and to become the head of a military unit. The abolition of the company economy also abruptly ended the opportunity to turn a military command into a lucrative business. Certainly, abuses and fraud were still possible after the reform, but to a much smaller degree than before and were now strictly punished. In addition high-ranking career officers were now rotated between units—normally also geographically—when promoted. This also prevented them from becoming "entangled" (too deeply) in a specific regional network or to establish dependencies over a longer period of time. Very telling for the new understanding of a military unit now being part of the "national capital" and not an officer's private capital was the termination of naming units after their commander. This had been a tradition in Prussia until the military reforms. To establish and control this system a new branch of military administration was introduced, the *Intendantur* (loosely translated as the accounting and auditing administration). It was responsible for organising the logistics of the movement of larger goods for the units (mostly on the regimental level) as well as the money transfer to the individual soldier so fraud could be diminished. The military administrators were not part of the disciplinary chain of command of the unit they were attached to, but were directly responsible to the military economy department of the "war ministry" (*Kriegsministerium* or *Kriegsdepartment*), which started its work in March of 1809.

The importance of money and class had thus begun to change significantly towards patriotism and professionalism as driving factors for military careers. The linkage between the multiple identities of the individual as citizen as well as political and military subject had undergone a revolutionary change and a new quality of civil-military relations was established. The struggle over the implementation of these qualitative changes in the form of adaptations or the revolutionising of political structures of the state continued in Prussia and Germany for over a century. This is a reminder of the dynamic character of the Clausewitzian triad based on action and counter-action. For a long time "the new" and "the old" existed beside each other. Reforms came in waves, sometimes being broken against cliffs of stiff resistance and at other times petering out. Indeed, over a period of around 50 years their cumulative effects changed the organisation and structure of the Prussian armed forces fundamentally. For the observer the Prussian military victories in the wars of 1864 against Denmark, 1866 against Austria and 1871 against one of the leading military powers, France, seemed to prove that a successful Prussian military example had been created. Prussia developed into a model for military reorganisation and "patriotic professionalisation". Before the "global export" of the Prussian military model began it was first copied and exported to the armed forces of other German territories (von Salisch 2010: 89–106), incorporated into the German *Bundesarmee*, but kept their distinctive military culture, for example, uniforms and separate military training institutions, until the end of the First World War. Over a long period of time the model of the Prussian export of military organisation remained a "horizontal" export instead of a top-down "vertical". This may have been one of the sources of its success as a model.

At the same time, looking at the fundamental changes in so many aspects of military culture during the reform process gives an impression of how fundamental and highly political the reform process was for the extra-European military organisations engaging in it, in the course of attempting to import the Prussian military model.

9 The Revolution in Military Learning and the Migration of Military Thought and Technology

The main conclusions from the processes in Prussia described are:

- Preceding and accompanying the Prussian military reforms there was above all a true revolution in military learning and education.
- The military reforms combined material and non-material aspects.
- The military reforms initiated a fundamental power struggle within the existing Clausewitzian triad in Prussia.

The example of Prussia demonstrates that military learning, adopting lessons and initiating fundamental change is much more likely in times after a decisive defeat than when functioning as a model of success, exactly as the Prussian army perceived itself and was perceived by all major European militaries until its defeat in 1806. Tactical and technological innovations, especially among the technical troops like the artillery, had already been introduced into the Prussian as well as into the French army during the eighteenth century. However, the principles and thereby the power constellations within the Clausewitzian triad did not alter fundamentally in France until the French Revolution in 1789 and for Prussia not until the defeat at Jena and Auerstädt in 1806. This shows that military revolutions in technology or tactics may occur without leading to a revolution in the character of military affairs and military culture. All too often the not so obvious developments in military culture, for example institutional developments and reforms, are more important than obvious and easily visible changes such as in tactical formations. Importing military revolutions was a difficult and complex undertaking especially when rather different military cultures of the "exporting" and the "importing" militaries were involved. Jeremy Black makes the point when he writes: "... there was a major difference between technology which was relatively easy to acquire though less so to copy proficiently, and technique, which was culturally based and therefore very difficult to adopt. This was particularly so in the case of tactical developments" (Black 1995: 105).

Systematic learning from others, even enemies, and the increased communication between various Western European military communities had only started in the sixteenth century. In his *The Art of War in the XVIth Century* Sir Charles Oman stated that the European wars of the fifteenth century could "be described, not inaccurately, as being shut up in many water-tight compartments" (Oman 1937: 3).

With the election of Charles I of Spain as Holy Roman Emperor Charles V in 1519 "Spain" and "Austria" were united in the same empire "causing European-wide exchanges of personnel and cross-fertilization of ideas" (Rogers 1995: 302). Charles VIII's invasion of Italy and the Spanish response to it in the sixteenth century "... immediately and irrevocably ruptured the boundaries between three of these compartments and compromised the rest. The immediate result [...] was that the premier military establishments of Western Europe learned an extraordinary amount from one another in a very short time" (Rogers 1995: 303). In the eighteenth century the debate on learning lessons took place in the context of the Enlightenmen (Hohrath 2000; Stübig 2010). Specifically Military Enlightenment challenged through several military revolutions and through general debate the pillars of the art of war and the organisation of armed forces. From the middle of the eighteenth century onwards the volume of literature published on military affairs increased significantly. Azar Gat states: "The middle of the eighteenth century, therefore, marked a revolutionary growth in military publications" (Gat 2001: 27).[23] This literature was read in the trans-national context of an emerging new military professionalism. The Military Enlightenment began in France but became even stronger in Prussia when it began there in earnest about a generation later, around 1770 (Gat 2001: 27–54 and 56–68).

Remembering the remarks of the Maréchal de Saxe concerning the difficulty of nations to learn lessons, this is remarkable and demonstrates that the learning process and first reforms of the Prussian military system had already started before the *annus horribilis* for Prussia of 1806. For the deeper reforms threatening the existing power relations of the Clausewitzian triad the shock of total defeat in 1806 was essential. It was followed by another wave of rapid learning.

10   Conclusion: Ways of Military Learning and Transfer of Military Culture

Trans-cultural military learning between a European nation like Prussia and an Asian empire like China was even more challenging. As a conclusion an attempt shall be made to extract the major ways of learning between European military organisations which may also be used for an analysis of extra-European learning. They are presented here in the form of a preliminary list and must be studied in more detail and depth.[24]

---

[23] He bases his verdict on J. Pöhler's *Bibliotheca historic-militaris*. Leipzig, 1887–1897.

[24] My gratitude for encouraging further work in this direction goes to the organisers and participants of the workshop "The Early Modern Ottoman Empire as Contact Zone" (June 10 and 11, 2010) at the Institute for Advanced Study, Princeton University, and to Peter Paret for the time he took to discuss aspects of my work.

- Attending traditional military educational institutions and the successors of the princely education or noble *Ritterakademien*. These had a rather limited curriculum and were open almost exclusively to high nobility.
- Military "training on the job". "Apprenticeships" with regiments for future officers who could start as "cadets" at a rather young age.
- Military manoeuvres as practical exercises. Troop reviews following detailed scripts were increasingly transformed into realistic tactical exercises in Prussia after 1806.
- War experience. The character of experience from war engagements was rather different in Prussia from that of neighbouring global, colonial powers like France or Austria with its military border with the Ottoman Empire.
- Garrison duty with time for self-study of military literature. Here the evolution of regimental and public libraries played an important role. Into the nineteenth century military literature was chiefly published in French and was linguistically quite accessible to interested and educated scholars.
- Attending courses at higher military educational institutions. Even before Prussia's defeat the reformed War Academy (*Kriegsschule*) in Berlin introduced the first 3-year course in 1801. The later famous reformer Scharnhorst initiated a reform of the academy as its director.
- Becoming a member of military societies as circles of enlightened discussion of military affairs. Military societies were also an excellent place for professional and societal networking.
- Staff duty as military adjutant with a high-ranking (commanding) officer or even at the court.
- More war experience in a higher position, often also in a different theatre of war.
- Experience of foreign or enemy countries either as part of occupation forces, as prisoner of war or attending courses at foreign military schools and institutions.
- Active participation in reforms. For example, Carl von Clausewitz became part of the circle of reformers and in different positions was involved in the process between 1808 and 1812. This included intense discussions of proposals for reform and possible lessons to be learned from other countries.
- Service in foreign armed forces and personal experience in foreign military service. For a long time, serving in the military contingents of other rulers was perceived as a legitimate form of seeking advancement and complementing one's experience especially among European nobility. Another form of experience in foreign military service would be participating in foreign military training missions, which became increasingly important from the 1770s.
- Experience in combined campaigns with allied forces was very common in the European wars during the eighteenth and early nineteenth century.
- Experience in diplomatic service or as a war observer in foreign countries. In the early nineteenth century the position of military attaché became established among European powers.
- Information provided by spies.

Comparing these elements of military learning in Europe between the outgoing eighteenth century and the 1830s with corresponding elements in China shows one considerable difference: the high degree of external military experience of European officers and the rather easy accessibility of military literature by its publication in French. A key question remains: what role for the importing of European military culture was played by Chinese officers training and learning outside of China? Military learning for leading Prussian officers involved in military reforms seemed to be inseparably linked to experiences, including personal service, beyond one's national border. This component seems to have been much less the case for China during the late eighteenth to mid nineteenth century.

The revolution in military learning based on the Military Enlightenment begun during the eighteenth century and made trans-national military learning much easier for a Prussian officer. The language barrier seems to have been one of the fundamental hindrances for a faster importation of European military culture in China. "Second-hand learning", for example, through importing Japanese translations and adaptations of Prusso-German military literature, was an important factor for the wave of military revolution in China beginning after 1895. The hiring of Prussian military instructors for training Chinese troops in 1884/1885 by Li Fengbao seems to have initiated an attempt at a coordinated process of military learning from Europe for China by using external instructors beyond immediate training for battle, and especially by setting up new military academies after Western models, namely the military school at Tianjin in 1885 (Kaske 2002: 117–132). Before then an import of modern, European military culture was mainly limited to importing modern arms technology and technical military training for their use and to contracting—mostly high-ranking—Western mercenaries to lead Chinese troops into battle, as during the crushing of the Taiping rebellion (Ralston 1990: 107–141). Around the turn of the twentieth century the next important wave of importing a military revolution to China took place. By then military learning from foreigners was turning into a Chinese revolution in military learning and became to large degree learning from the master-pupil of the Prussians in Asia, the Japanese. This also included sending Chinese junior and senior officers to military schools and training in Japan.

It may not come as a surprise that the wave of another generation of German military instructors came to China after the First World War. They brought with them their new and more radical interpretations of "lessons" from the war and of military theory, including the Clausewitzian triad. This created another wave of military transformation in China which cannot be further elaborated in this article.

Bibliography

Aaslestad, Katherine and Karen Hagemann 2006. "Collaboration, Resistance, and Reform: Experiences and Historiographies of the Napoleonic Wars in Central Europe." *Central European History* 39: 547–579.

Abbt, Thomas. 1996. "Vom Tode für das Vaterland (1761)" in *Aufklärung und Kriegserfahrung. Klassische Zeitzeugen zum Siebenjährigen Krieg*, ed. Johannes Kunisch, 589–650.

214 P.I. Trummer

Commentary: 971–1008 (= Bibliothek der Geschichte und Politik, ed. Reinhart Koselleck, vol. 9). Frankfurt/Main: Deutscher Klassiker-Verlag.

Abrahamson, Bengt. 1972. *Military Professionalization and Political Power*. Beverly Hills et al.: Sage Publications.

Baumgart, Peter, Bernhard R. Kroener and Heinz Stübig (eds.) 2008. *Die preussische Armee zwischen Ancien Régime und Reichsgründung*. Paderborn: Schöningh.

Bien, David D. 1979 "The Army in the French Enlightenment: Reform, Reaction and Revolution." *Past & Present* No. 85: 68–98.

Black, Jeremy. 1995: "A Military Revolution? A 1660–1792 Perspective." In *The Military Revolution Debate*, ed. Clifford J. Rogers, 95–114. Boulder (CO): Westview Press.

Clark, Christopher. 2008. *Preußen. Aufstieg und Niedergang 1600–1947*. (Translated from the 1st edition in English: *Iron Kingdom. The Rise and Fall of Prussia, 1600–1947*. London 2006), Munic: Pantheon.

Cohen, Eliot A. 1985: *Citizens and Soldiers. The Dilemmas of Military Service*. Ithaca et al.: Cornell University Press.

Cole, Howard. 1972. *Minden*. London: C. Knight.

Clausewitz, Carl von. 1976. *On War*. Edited and translated by Michael Howard and Peter Paret with an introductory essay by Bernard Brodie. Princeton (NJ): Princeton University Press.

Clausewitz, Carl von. 1992. *Historical and Political Writings*. Edited and translated by Peter Paret and Daniel Moran. Princeton (NJ): Princeton University Press.

Dietze, Anita and Walter (eds.). 1989. *Ewiger Friede. Dokumente einer deutschen Diskussion um 1800*. Leipzig and Weimar: Kiepenheuer.

Dreyer, Edward L. 1995. *China at War, 1901–1949*. London et al.: Longman.

Eberstein, Bernd. 2007. *Preußen und China*. Berlin: Duncker & Humblot.

Epkenhans, Michael, Stig Förster and Karen Hagemann (eds.). 2006. *Militärische Erinnerungskultur. Soldaten im Spiegel von Biographien, Memoiren und Selbstzeugnissen*. (*Krieg in der Geschichte* vol. 29). Paderborn et al.: Schöningh.

Friedeburg, Robert von. 2005. "The Making of Patriots: Love of Fatherland and Negotiating Monarchy in Seventeenth-Century Germany." *Journal of Modern History* 77: 881–916.

Gat, Azar. 2001. *A History of Military Thought. From Enlightenment to the Cold War*. Oxford et al.: Oxford University Press.

Görlitz, Walter. 1967. *Kleine Geschichte des deutschen Generalstabs*. (1st ed. Frankfurt 1950), Berlin: Haude&Spenersche Verlagsbuchhandlung.

Guilmartin Jr., John F. 1995. "The Military Revolution: Origins and First Tests Abroad." In: *The Military Revolution Debate*, ed. Clifford J. Rogers, 299–333. Boulder (CO): Westview Press.

Hagemann, Karen. 2002. *"Mannlicher Muth und Teutsche Ehre". Nation, Militär und Geschlecht zur Zeit der Antinapoleonischen Kriege Preußens*. (*Krieg in der Geschichte*, vol. 8, ed. Stig Förster, Bernhard R. Kroener, Bernd Wegner) Paderborn et al.: Schöningh.

Hahn, Hans-Werner. 2008. "Machtpolitischer Umbruch und innenpolitischer Aufbruch. Jena 1806 und die Folgen." In *Das Jahr 1806 im europäischen Kontext. Balance, Hegemonie und politische Kulturen*, ed. Andreas Klinger, Hans-Werner Hahn and Georg Schmidt, 1–19. Cologne: Böhlau.

Herberg-Rothe, Andreas. 2007. *Clausewitz's Puzzle. The Political Theory of War*. Oxford: Oxford University Press. (First published in German in 2001)

Hochedlinger, Michael. 1990. *Johannes Nikolaus Graf Luckner (1722–1794). Söldnertum zwischen Ancien Régime und Revolution*. (Militärgeschichtliches Beiheft zur Europäischen Wehrkunde/Wehrwissenschaftlichen Rundschau. Vol. 6 (December) 1990).

Hohrath, Daniel. 2000. "Spätbarocke Kriegspraxis und aufgeklärte Kriegswissenschaften. Neue Forschungen und Perspektiven zu Krieg und Militär im ‚Zeitalter der Aufklärung.'" In: *Die Kriegskunst im Lichte der Vernunft. Militär und Aufklärung im 18. Jahrhundert*. Part 2, ed. Daniel Hohrath and Klaus Gerteis, 5–47. Hamburg: Meiner.

Huntington, Samuel P. 1957. *The Soldier and the State. The Theory and Practice of Civil-Military Relations*. Cambridge, MA: Belknap Press.

Huntington, Samuel P. 1991. *The Third Wave of Democratization*. Norman: University of Oklahoma Press.

Jing, Chunxiao. 2002. *Mit Barbaren gegen Barbaren. Die chinesische Selbststärkungsbewegung und das deutsche Rüstungsgeschäft im späten 19. Jahrhundert*. (Europa-Übersee. Historische Studien. Vol. 13 ed. Horst Gründer) Münster et al.: Lit-Verlag. (Dissertation at the University of Münster)

Kaske, Elisabeth. 2002. *Bismarcks Missionäre. Deutsche Militärinstrukteure in China 1884–1890*. (Asien- und Afrikastudien der Humboldt-Universität zu Berlin. Vol. 11) Wiesbaden: Harrassowitz.

Kessel, Eberhard. 1987. "Die allgemeine Wehrpflicht in der Gedankenwelt Scharnhorsts, Gneisenaus und Boyens." In *Militärgeschichte und Kriegstheorie in neuerer Zeit. Ausgewählte Aufsätze*, ed. and introduced by Johannes Kunisch, 175–188. Berlin: Duncker and Humblot.

Koselleck, Reinhart. 1967. *Preußen zwischen Reform und Revolution. Allgemeines Landrecht, Verwaltung und soziale Bewegung von 1791 bis 1848*. Stuttgart: Klett.

Koselleck, Reinhart. 1984. "Revolution, Rebellion, Aufruhr, Bürgerkrieg" in *Geschichtliche Grundbegriffe. Historisches Lexikon zur politisch-sozialen Sprache in Deutschland*, ed. Otto Brunner, Werner Conze and Reinhart Koselleck, 653–788, vol. 5, Stuttgart: Klett.

Kroener, Bernhard R. 2000. "Militär in der Gesellschaft. Aspekte einer neuen Militärgeschichte der Frühen Neuzeit." In *Was ist Militärgeschichte*, ed. Thomas Kühne and Benjamin Ziemann, 283–299. Paderborn et al.: Schöningh.

Kroener, Berhard R. 2008a. *Kriegerische Gewalt und militärische Präsenz in der Neuzeit*. Paderborn: Schöningh.

Kroener, Bernhard R. 2008b. ",Des Königs Rock'. Das Offizierskorps in Frankreich, Österreich und Preußen im 18. Jahrhundert – Werkzeug sozialer Militarisierung oder Symbol gesellschaftlicher Integration?" In *Die preussische Armee zwischen Ancien Régime und Reichsgründung*, ed. Peter Baumgart, Bernhard R. Kroener and Heinz Stübig, 72–95. Paderborn: Schöningh.

Kroener, Bernhard R. 2008c. "Vom "extraordinari Kriegsvolck" zum "miles perpetuus". Zur Rolle der bewaffneten Macht in der europäischen Gesellschaft der Frühen Neuzeit. Ein Forschungs- und Literaturbericht." In *Kriegerische Gewalt und militärische Präsenz in der Neuzeit. Ausgewählte Schriften*. ed. Ralf Pröve and Bruno Thoß for the Militärgeschichtliche Forschungsamt, 3–63. Paderborn et al.: Schöningh.

Kroll, Stefan. 1997. *Stadtgesellschaft und Krieg. Sozialstruktur, Bevölkerung und Wirtschaft in Stralsund und Stade 1700 bis 1715*. Göttingen: Schwartz.

Lohmann, Ingrid and Christine Mayer. 2007. "Educating the Citizen: Two Case Studies on Inclusion and Exclusion in Prussia in the Early Nineteenth Century." *Paedagogical Historica*, vol. 43, No. 1 (February): 7–27.

Lynn, John A. 1996 "Army Style in the Modern West, 800-2000". *The International Historical Review* 18, 3–4: 505–535.

Lynn, John A. 2008. *Battle. A History of Combat and Culture*. 2nd, updated edition with a new epilogue, New York: Westview Press.

McNeill, William. 1982. *The Pursuit of Power*. Chicago: Chicago University Press.

Moran, Daniel and Arthur Waldron (eds.). 2003. *The People in Arms. Military and National Mobilization since the French Revolution*. Cambridge: Cambridge University Press.

Münch, Paul. 1982. "Die "Obrigkeit im Vaterstand" – zu Definitionen und Kritik des "Landesvaters" während der Frühen Neuzeit", *Daphne's 11*: 15–40.

Neugebauer, Wolfgang. 2008. "Staatsverfassung und Heeresverfassung in Preußen während des 18. Jahrhunderts." In *Die Preussische Armee zwischen Ancien Régime und Reichsgründung*, ed. Peter Baumgart, Bernhard R. Kroener and Heinz Stübig, 27–44. Paderborn: Schöningh.

Oetting, Dirk W. 1993. *Auftragstaktik. Geschichte und Gegenwart einer Führungskonzeption*. Bonn: Report Verlag.

Oman, Charles W.C. 1937. *The Art of War in the XVIth Century*. London: Methuen.

216   P.I. Trummer

The Oxford Companion to Military History. Edited by Richard Holmes 2001. Oxford: Oxford
   University Press.
Paret, Peter. 1966. *Yorck and the Era of Prussian Reform.* Princeton: Princeton University Press.
Paret, Peter. 1985. *Clausewitz and the State. The man, his theories, and his times.* 2nd, revised
   edition, Princeton (NJ): Princeton University Press.
Paret, Peter. 1990. *Kunst als Geschichte. Kultur und Politik von Menzel bis Fontane.* Munich:
   Beck. (English edition 1988 under the title: *Art as History: Episodes in the Culture and Politics
   of Nineteenth-Century Germany.* Princeton (NJ): Princeton University Press)
Paret, Peter. 1992. "Clausewitz as Historian". In *Understanding War. Essays on Clausewitz and
   the History of Military Power*, ed. Peter Paret, 130–142. Princeton (NJ): Princeton University
   Press.
Paret, Peter. 2009. *The Cognitive Challenge of War: Prussia 1806.* Princeton (NJ): Princeton
   University Press.
Parker, Geoffrey. 1974. "The emergence of modern finance in Europe." In *The Fontana Economic
   History of Europe*, vol. II, ed. C.M. Cipolla, 560–582. London: Collins/Fontana.
Parker, Geoffrey. 1991. "Europe in the wider world, 1500–1750: the military balance."
   In *Politicial Economy of Merchant Empires. State Power and World Trade 1350–1750*, ed.
   James D. Tracy, 161–195. Cambridge: Cambridge University Press.
Parker, Geoffrey. 1995. "The "Military Revolution'1560-1660" – A Myth?" In *The Military
   Revolution Debate*, ed. Clifford J. Rogers, 37–54. Boulder (CO): Westview Press.
Pröve, Ralf. 1995. *Stehendes Heer und städtische Gesellschaft im 18. Jahrhundert. Göttingen und
   seine Militärbevölkerung 1713–1756.* München: Oldenbourg.
Ralston, David B. 1990. *Importing the European Army. The Introduction of European Military
   Techniques and Institutions into the Extra-European World, 1600–1914.*Chicago: University
   of Chicago Press.
Rink, Martin. 1999. *Vom "Parteygänger" zum Partisan. Die Konzeption des kleinen Krieges in
   Preußen 1740–1813.* (Europäische Hochschulschriften 851) Frankfurt a.M. et al.: Lang.
Rink, Martin and Marcus von Salisch. 2010. "Zum Wandel in deutschen Streitkräften von
   den preußischen Heeresreformen bis zur Transformation der Bundeswehr." In *Reform,
   Reorganisation, Transformation. Zum Wandel in deutschen Streitkräften von den preußischen
   Heeresreformen bis zur Transformation der Bundeswehr.* Edited for the Militärgeschichtliche
   Forschungsamt by Karl-Heinz Lutz, Martin Rink and Marcus von Salisch, 1–25, München:
   Oldenbourg.
Roberts, Michael. 1956. *The Military Revolution, 1560–1660.* Belfast: Boyd. Extended version
   reprinted in Clifford J. Rogers (ed.) *The Military Revolution Debate. Readings on the Military
   Transformation of Early Modern Europe.* 13–35, Boulder (CO): Westview Press.
Rogers, Clifford J. (ed.). 1995. *The Military Revolution Debate. Readings on the Military
   Transformation of Early Modern Europe.* Boulder (CO): Westview Press.
Rothfels, Hans. 1920. *Carl von Clausewitz. Politik und Krieg. Eine ideengeschichtliche Studie.*
   Berlin: Duemmler.
Salisch, Marcus von. 2010. "Das Beispiel Sachsen: Militärreformen in deutschen Mittelstaaten. "
   In *Reform, Reorganisation, Transformation. Zum Wandel in deutschen Streitkräften von den
   preußischen Heeresreformen bis zur Transformation der Bundeswehr.* Edited for the
   Militärgeschichtliche Forschungsamt by Karl-Heinz Lutz, Martin Rink and Marcus von
   Salisch, 89–106, München: Oldenbourg.
Saxe, Maurice Comte de. 1757. *Mes Rêveries. Ouvrage posthume de Maurice Comte de Saxe.
   Augmenté d'une histoire abrégée de sa vie, et de différentes pièces qui y ont rapport par
   Monsieur l'Abbé Pérau.* 2 vols., Amsterdam and Leipzig.
Schiff, Rebecca L. 1995. "Civil-Military Relations Reconsidered: A Theory of Concordance."
   Armed Forces & Society vol. 22, no. 1 (Fall): 7–24.
Schnitter, Helmut. 1994. "Die überlieferte Defensionspflicht. Vorformen der allgemeinen
   Wehrpflicht in Deutschland." In *Die Wehrpflicht. Entstehung, Erscheinungsformen und*

politisch-militärische Wirkung, ed. Roland G. Foerster for the Militärgeschichtliche Forschungsamt. 29–37, Munich: Oldenbourg.

Strachan, Hew. 2008. *Carl von Clausewitz's* On War. *A Biography.* London, Atlantic.

Stübig, Heinz. 1994. "Die Wehrverfassung Preußens in der Reformzeit. Wehrpflicht im Spannungsfeld von Restauration und Revolution 1815–1860. " In *Die Wehrpflicht. Entstehung, Erscheinungsformen und politisch-militärische Wirkung,* ed. Roland G. Foerster for the Militärgeschichtliche Forschungsamt. 39–53, Munich: Oldenbourg.

Stübig, Heinz. 2010. "Das höhere militärische Bildungswesen im Zeichen der Aufklärung." In *Reform, Reorganisation, Transformation. Zum Wandel in deutschen Streitkräften von den preußischen Heeresreformen bis zur Transformation der Bundeswehr,* edited for the Militärgeschichtliche Forschungsamt by Karl-Heinz Lutz, Martin Rink and Marcus von Salisch, 29–42, München: Oldenbourg.

Thomson, Janice E. 1994. *Mercenaries, Pirates, and Sovereigns. State-building and Extraterritorial Violence in Early Modern Europe.* Princeton, (NJ): Princeton University Press.

Vazsonyi, Nicholas. 1999. "Montesquieu, Friedrich Carl von Moser, and the "National Spirit Debate" in Germany, 1765–1767." *German Studies Review* vol. 22, no. 2 (May): 225–246.

Walter, Dierk. 2003. *Preußische Heeresreformen 1807–1870. Militärische Innovation und der Mythos der ‚Roonschen Reform'.* (Krieg in der Geschichte vol. 16) Paderborn et al.: Schöningh.

Woloch, Isser. 1986. "Napoleonic Conscription: State Power and Civil Society." *Past & Present* 111: 101–129.

Approaches to State-Building in Eighteenth Century British Bengal

Sebastian Meurer

1 Suddenly Sovereign?

Since the early seventeenth century, English, and later British trade to South and South-East Asia was conducted by the English East India Company, a privately owned joint-stock trading corporation endowed with a royal charter. In the eighteenth century, the Company increasingly acted as a political and military player in India, which was characterised by power struggles within the framework of the Mughal Empire, following the gradual decline of the Emperor's central authority. The beginning of British colonial rule in India is usually marked by the battle of Plassey in 1757, when the East India Company used the dynamics of an internal struggle to become the power behind the throne of the Nawab ("provincial governor"), the ruler of Bengal in the northeast of India. The Company defended its position as the dominant power in Bengal in the Battle of Buxar in 1764, beating the combined forces of the Nawab and the Mughal Emperor. This Emperor, Shah Alam II (1728–1806), who afterwards was in dire need of allies, acknowledged the Company's position with the grant of the Diwani, the privilege entailing the collection of land-taxes and the civil jurisdiction over Bengal. The leading officers of the Company in Bengal, located at Fort William, the Company's headquarters in Calcutta, tried to fulfil their new role by constructing a system of government, placed as they were between the directives of the Company's Court of directors—and increasingly the British ministry in London—and the necessities faced on the spot (Marshall 1987a: 70–136, id. 2006: 487–507; Mann 2000: 33–93; Chaudhury 2000; Bowen 2006).

The grant of the Diwani started a dynamic that no one involved could fully apprehend. The development of colonial governance over the next decades

---

S. Meurer (✉)
Karl Jaspers Centre, University of Heidelberg, Voßstr. 2, 69115 Heidelberg, Germany
e-mail: meurer@asia-europe.uni-heidelberg.de

A. Flüchter and S. Richter (eds.), *Structures on the Move*,
Transcultural Research – Heidelberg Studies on Asia and Europe in a Global Context,
DOI 10.1007/978-3-642-19288-3_11, © Springer-Verlag Berlin Heidelberg 2012

constitutes a particularly dense period of institutional change, taking place in an encounter between European and South Asian notions of government. It therefore seems to be an outstanding example for transcultural "state-building" on the brink of modernity. In the following, I aim to delineate this historical case, then to use it as an example for the heuristic utility and limitations of the term "state-building" for historical analysis, especially in consideration of the widened historiographical focus of world history. The article is therefore divided into two parts.

First, I would like to delineate the specific forms and radical change of colonial governmentality—the discourses and practices of colonial rule—in Bengal during the transition between the "first" and the "second British Empire", focusing on the tenures of Warren Hastings (1772/73–1785) and Charles Cornwallis (1786–1793) as governors-general of India. The outline is thus restricted to the British agents' perspectives, with the focus on the change in the central assumptions and ideas underlying their respective approaches to state-building. These conceptualisations of "British Bengal" must be understood in the context of the evolving British imperial framework and the state-building processes in Britain itself. I will therefore also try to relate them to the beginning of the far-reaching reform processes beginning in the late eighteenth century, which ultimately led to the bureaucratised state of Victorian Britain.

The second part of this article deals with the more general conceptual problems inherent in the current scholarly usage of the terms "state-building" and "state-formation". Two excellent studies have recently reshaped the state of research on the discourse on government in Bengal, which I will examine with regard to these terms as a starting point for my further analysis: Robert Travers" *Ideology and Empire* focuses on Warren Hastings" attempt to tackle the problems at hand by adapting the logic of the "Ancient Constitution" from the English constitutional discourse to a fabricated image of the Bengal political tradition (Travers 2007), while Jon Wilson's *The Domination of Strangers* argues that, from the perception of governmental crisis underlying the reforms of Charles Cornwallis, the first distinctly modern state of the British Empire developed in Bengal (Wilson 2008). Both Travers and Wilson use the terms "state-building" and "state-formation" in a rather clear-cut, yet not expressly defined way, which partly shapes their perspectives on their topics. These findings in mind, I will then widen the focus by trying to indicate more generally the usage of the terms in recent historiography, which is much less congruent and well-grounded than one might suspect. There is, in particular, no established distinction between the two terms. By contrast, such a differentiation has recently emerged in political science, though not out of epistemological reflection, but rather from the differentiation of current fields of research, which I will demonstrate in another short sketch. On the basis of this twofold overview of the state of research, I will, in conclusion, suggest a differentiated application of these concepts, the epistemological consequences of which I will again try to demonstrate through the Bengal case study.

Approaches to State-Building in Eighteenth Century British Bengal   221

2   A Company State in Bengal?

The decision to participate in the coup d'état in 1757 and the subsequent unsystematic takeover in Bengal had been decided by the Calcutta Council alone. Looking to England, it can be said that during the first years after the Company had come to power in Bengal there was hardly a concept for colonial rule, let alone a colonial state. The sudden volatility of the company stock courses made the East India Company's central administration fall prey to the short-term interests of investors, leading to frequent changes in the directorate of the Company (Bowen 2006: 53–68). For the British government, on the other hand, what was dubbed the Indian Question played an increasing role in British politics, but it was mainly seen as a domestic and fiscal problem caused by the East India Company, while the developments in India mainly figured as the private business of the Company. Besides, intervention in the chartered rights of the Company was a controversial issue. And, while the British ministry started to intervene in Company affairs, it was always in reaction to problems that mounted towards a crisis of the Company that could not be ignored. Thus, the most notable intervention of the 1770s, the Regulating Act of 1773,[1] that strongly intervened in both the domestic structures of the Company and the government in Bengal, only occurred when it was more than obvious that the Company was unable to handle its own crisis. Not only had there been many accounts of rampant corruption in India after the great Bengal famine, which resulted in the loss of life of up to a third of Bengal's population, but, more significantly, the Company could only be saved from financial collapse by massive public loans. The Regulating Act marked a momentous intervention in the Company's affairs in India—for example, the governor of Bengal now became a crown-appointed governor-general—but it did not include an assertive concept for the form of government that was to be established in Bengal (Bowen 2002; Mann 2000: 166–77).

2.1   The Question of Sovereignty

In Bengal, however, the management at Fort William quite decidedly saw their work in the establishment of a fully fledged power state. Even before he became the first governor-general of India, Warren Hastings described his work as "the dominion of an extensive kingdom, the collection of a vast revenue, the command of armies, and the direction of a great political system"[2] (Gleig 1841: 290). This very

---

[1] Officially "An Act for Establishing certain Regulations for the better Management of Affairs of the East India Company, as well in India as in Europe" (13 Geo. III, cap. 63).

[2] Warren Hastings to George Colebrooke, Chairman of the East India Company's Board of Directors, 3 March 1773.

much sums up the domain of a sovereign state in the contemporary European sense—the problem being that Hastings did not represent a power that could claim formal sovereignty over Bengal. On the contrary, it was a hallmark of the legitimisation of the Company rule that it was only acting in the name of the Mughal Emperor, who had granted the Diwani, thereby fitting into the structure of the late Mughal Empire: the company even paid a considerable yearly tribute to the Emperor, which the Nawabs of Bengal had long ceased to do.[3] And the initial system of revenue collection had indeed been set up along these lines, Company personnel had only been introduced into the highest layers of the Nawab's administration (Khan 1969: 101). On the other hand, the Company had established and maintained military supremacy and quickly reduced the Nawab to a decidedly subordinate position (Mann 2000: 87–93). For Warren Hastings, it was the lack of formal sovereignty and the constraints of his own authority by the India Council, as well as the lack of clearly defined hierarchies, that obstructed his government (Sen 1997: 61): "The want of clear and distinct lines to mark the different parts of which the Government of Bengal is composed is the greatest of the many defects which clog this establishment." Without a clearly defined constitution, including a strong central authority (his own), he repeatedly voiced his fear that "the government, for want of a power to preside and rule it, must fall into anarchy"[4] (Gleig 1841: 289f.). When he set about moulding his vision of the Company state, he very much had to do so on the basis of a factual sovereignty, the frame of the government being backed up by military force that ensured that the rule was rarely challenged openly from within. While formal British sovereignty would only be claimed in 1813, this factual sovereignty, together with the claim of undisputed government for the Company, was very distinct from the early 1770s (Dodwell 1929; Bayly 1996; Sen 1997: 59–81). There is not much room for doubt in Hastings' formulation of this subject: "Every intermediate power is removed, and the sovereignty of this country wholly and absolutely vested in the Company" (Gleig 1841: 293).

Warren Hastings is usually characterised as a man of action who based his decisions on his profound experience of the Indian situation, not as a political thinker whose actions were based on theoretical abstractions. Part of his unease with the set-up of the British government certainly stemmed from the restraints caused by the necessity of a constant struggle with his internal opponents in council. Nevertheless, it can be clearly seen that, in the conceptualisation of his constraints,

---

[3] For the East India Company the question was essential for the defence of its property rights. According to a legal opinion (the "Pratt-Yorke Opinion" of 1757), conquered territory would fall under British sovereignty as property of the Crown, while any acquisitions made by treaty or through grant from an Indian ruler would belong to the Company. For the domestic concerns this was also the question of international politics; not only might European rivals be aggravated, but the Indian dominions would be drawn into any European conflict as well. In the end, Parliament also shied away from the responsibility and potential ramifications of officially taking over, preferring regular payments and the Company as an intermediary (Travers 2007: 43–49; Bowen 2002: 53–55; Dodwell 1929: 589–608).

[4] Warren Hastings to George Colebrooke, 7 March 1773.

Approaches to State-Building in Eighteenth Century British Bengal 223

but also of his positive goals, he had to draw on the contemporary European language of politics. And as his ideas centred on Bengal, he envisioned the erection of a state, based on a supposedly revitalised Constitution for Bengal (Sen 1997: 66).

2.2 Perfecting the Ancient Constitution

While the official version of the Company only executing a privilege inside the Mughal system can be characterised as a legal fiction, this does not mean that the envisioned Company state would try to impose a thoroughly new system of government. Hastings had lived in India for more than 20 years and mastered several South Asian languages. He admired Indian culture and engaged in the patronage of Indian art (Lawson 1993: 114; Marshall 1973). In short, he did not doubt his profound intimacy with Indian culture and political notions. Moreover, before the struggles in Bengal that had allowed the British take-over in the first place, he and some of the older Company officers had got to know a relatively well-functioning Nawabi administration under the Nawab Alivardi Khan (1740–1756) (Travers 2007: 106). He therefore proposed to base the Company state on what he perceived to be the "first principles' of Mughal rule, perfecting it in the process. "The remedy which I would recommend to these distractions is obvious and simple. It is not to introduce fresh innovations but to restore the government to its first principles. [...] Many correspondent Regulations will be necessary, but not one perhaps which the original constitution of the Mogul Government hath not before established or adopted, & thereby rendered familiar to the People"[5] (Monckton-Jones 1918: 150f.).

This original or "Ancient Constitution" was a concept that had figured very prominently in the English constitutional discourse since the early seventeenth century. It was based on the assumption that the English constitution had at one point been set up in perfect form in the distant past—for example, by the Saxons— and that constitutional problems of the present could be explained as aberrations from its original principles. Thus, a static (but vague) ideal model was constructed by means of history as a frame for arguments aiming at the present political situation (Pocock 1957; Burgess 1992; Kidd 1999). The adaptation of this concept to the Indian situation helped to reconcile British notions of governance with the practice encountered, while at the same time legitimising changes to the Bengal elites, as well as to the British (Cohn 1996: 27, 60–2; Travers 2007: 137f.).

This approach can be clearly seen in the reform attempts of the Bengal legal system. Consciously overstepping the boundaries of the Diwani, central courts for civil and criminal justice were established at Calcutta. For the code of law, Muslim as well as "Hindu" legal documents were translated and systematised according to

---

[5] Warren Hastings to George Colebrooke, 26 March 1772.

the presumptions of English legal thought (Travers 2007: 115–32, 181–206). In England, the common law was still often held to be one of the pillars of continuity, not only for the English constitution, but for ethnic identity as a whole (Pocock 1957: 229–51; Kidd 1999: 83–98). Analogously, the approach in enquiring into Hindu and Muslim legal tradition focused not so much on the codification of positive law, but aimed at "the essence" of the Mughal (or even Indian) constitution in a rather broad sense. This is the beginning of the early British Orientalism, with its tendency to enshrine sometimes ancient legal texts, constructing a basically static picture not only of Indian law and religion, but also of its society and culture (Rocher 1993: 215–244). There is another important element to this paradigm of the "ancient Mughal constitution. While Hastings respected the Mughal state as a working administration, he understood it in terms of "Asiatic Despotism", a widespread but ambiguous concept of contemporary political theory.[6] While the laws were supposedly established along the lines of customary practice, the boundaries were set by reference to (European) natural law, interfering to correct supposedly inhumane legal practices stemming from that despotic tradition (Travers 2007: 104–107, 115–126; Monckton-Jones 1918: 157f.). In this view, arguments based on the despotic character of the Mughal constitution served both as a motivation, or often a pretext, and as the constitutional basis for interventions, because the Company was held to have inherited a form of absolute ("despotic") sovereign authority from the Mughal Emperor.

This Janus-faced argumentation also pervades the field of governance that was by far the most prominent for the agents involved: revenue collection. In order to maximise the gains from revenue, Hastings enforced a system whereby the taxation right for any given district was auctioned off for a period of 5 years, with the intention of establishing a market that would yield a realistic estimate of a district's economic capabilities. Yet the right to taxation was, in most cases, part of the hereditary privileges of Zamindars ("land-holders"), local elites, whose exact status and function in the "Mughal constitution" eluded systematistion. Comparing the Mughal constitution to a form of European medieval feudalism, Hastings asserted that there was no understanding of (freehold) property in India, all the land ultimately belonging to the Mughal Emperor. By succession, it was therefore principally the right of the Company to reallocate the right of taxation if the

---

[6] The concept of (Asiatic/Oriental) despotism had been very prevalent in eighteenth-century European political discourse and theory ever since it had been popularised by Montesquieu. The concept had two semantic levels, one descriptive and one pejorative, of which the emphasis differed. On the one hand, it was used initially to neutrally denote a system of government in which absolute sovereignty was concentrated in the ruler and in which no private property right existed. On the other, this form of government, which is often associated with Turkey, but also with East and South Asia, often served as a negative counter-model in discussions about European states. As such, it was associated with slavery and rule by fear, and rejected by the majority of authors (Richter 1973; Curtis 2009: 72–102). When applying the concept to Mughal India, the arbitrary character of rule was stressed, property, as well as offices or honours, being solely dependent on the will of the Mughal Emperor (Cohn 1996: 62–65).

previous Zamindar did not manage to win the auction. At the same time, Hastings substantiated the necessity of the reorganisation with the despotic nature of the Nawabi system, in which the Zamindars had allegedly been "left at liberty to plunder all below them"[7] (Prasad 1960: 420). The revenue reform thus constituted was a constant bone of contention, especially in the ruling council itself. But even Hastings" antagonist Philip Francis largely shared the basic assumptions just sketched. He criticised Hastings on the basis of a different reading of the "ancient Mughal constitution", citing precedents from Indian history, building his arguments by the logic of the common law[8] (Mann 2000: 182–196; Travers 2007: 112–132, 171).

2.3   An "Imperial Revolution in Government?"[9]

Outlined above is the perspective or approach to state-building of Warren Hastings, the first governor-general of India, which he tried to enforce during this 13 years in this office. This is not the place to go into the details of the actual process, in which many of the foundations for British rule were laid. The assessment of his rule is still a much disputed matter (Travers 2007: 100). In the short term, the establishment of a stable state system can be seen as having, in all likelihood, failed. The revenue system still did not yield enough to satisfy the demands of the Company, nor had Hastings succeeded in establishing a legal system in working order when he left for London. Moreover, there was a sense of crisis, as the British had been hard pressed by Tipu Sultan in the second Anglo-Mysore war, and were, as a consequence, again struggling with debt (Marshall 2005: 366–70; Wilson 2008: 47–9).

It is certain that, at the end of his tenure, Hastings' reputation in England was not at its best. In the 1780s, the Indian issue was again very present in British politics. Already, in 1783, the Select Committee of the House of Commons, which was charged with the investigation, came to a very severe judgement, put into words by Edmund Burke, who would later elaborate it during the impeachment trial of Warren Hastings[10]: "This System of Government appears to Your Committee to be at least as much disordered, and as much perverted from every good Purpose, for which lawful Rule is established, as the trading System has been from every just

---

[7] Public letter from Warren Hastings and Council to the Court of Directors, 3 Nov. 1772.

[8] Francis compared the Zamindars to the English landed gentry, thereby interpreting them as the very backbone of the Mughal constitution. He also acted as the defender of their ancient, pre-Mughal rights against Hastings' executive tyranny. He strongly insisted that Mughal despotic rule and property rights went hand in hand. Therefore he proposed a system by which the revenue would be permanently set at a moderate level, allowing (following physiocratic reasoning) for the improvement of the economical situation (Travers 2007: 163–180; Weitzmann 1929).

[9] Heading taken from Bayly (1989: 116).

[10] The Hastings Trial from 1788 to 1795, although it plays a prominent role in the English discussion of the question of Indian government, cannot be discussed here. See Dirks (2006: 87–132); Pavarala (2004: 291–336).

Principle of Commerce." (Burke 1981: 306) In particular, the charges of widespread corruption in India were very audibly voiced in the reports, and in parliament debates, but also in public.

But then, not only the Company was reproached for being corrupt. In fact, in light of the gigantic national debt, the whole British political elite was accused of abusing the state apparatus, primarily to strengthen their personal patronage networks. Moreover, the British central administration was depicted as inefficient, outdated and corrupt. And this pressure was no longer applied by an insignificant group of radicals, but by a broad alliance, including parts of the Anglican Church traditionally loyal to the ministries. Scandalous news from India as well as the perception of returned Company men who had made their fortune in India—so called "nabobs"—as pretentious *nouveaux riches* often served as outstanding examples of the perceived corruption of the elites and the decrepit condition of the state system (Harling 1996: 31–42; Edwardes 1991).

One of the results of this reform moment was the constitution of the "Commissioners for Examining the Public Accounts". From 1780 to 1787 they conducted a detailed survey of the central administration, not only checking the accounts, but also comparing the practices in the different state agencies, and developing concrete proposals for reform, reporting to Parliament. Although many of the deficiencies of public administration had been voiced much earlier, they were, for the first time, formulated in a set of abstract principles. In a nutshell, these already anticipated the reforms that would lead to the modern, Victorian bureaucracy by the middle of the nineteenth century (Torrance 1978; Breihan 1977: 48–58). The widespread reform sentiment also played a significant role in the fall of the Fox-North Ministry over the Indian issues in 1783, and the subsequent ascent of William Pitt the Younger, who had the reputation of being disinterested and reform-oriented.[11]

Certainly the 1784 India Act of the Pitt Ministry marked a profound restructuring of the East India Company and its regime in Bengal. The shareholders were almost completely disempowered. In their place, a Board of Control was established, closely controlled by the ministry. While it was kept on a short leash from London, the office of the governor-general of India was vested with considerably enhanced executive powers (Mann 2000: 281–321; Lawson 1993: 123f.).

The Pitt Ministry, with Henry Dundas as its Indian expert, also began to develop a more distinct imperial policy. The 13 North American colonies had been finally lost in the peace of Paris of 1783, and India played a steadily increasing role in the geopolitical concerns of Great Britain. Especially after the French Revolution, India was to serve as a counterweight to France, to interrupt the French trade, but most of all, it was to become quiet and predictable, providing a steady income. It was hoped that the Company would once again concentrate on its trading activities. Especially

---

[11] After a first phase of reforms, Pitt's reforming fervour much declined. Apart from the wars, this can be ascribed to his determination not to yield competences of the executive to Parliament (Breihan 1984).

against the backdrop of the French Revolution and the coming of the Wars of the Coalitions, there was a growing patriotic zeal, supporting the ministry and even favouring a new and more authoritarian approach to government (Bayly 1989: 109–121; Lawson 1993: 124–128; Marshall 1987b: 115–120).

2.4 Government Without a History

The man who was chosen as the ministry's arm in India was Charles Cornwallis, who had been a somewhat unlucky general in the American War of Independence, but enjoyed the reputation of being a reliable and decisive administrator. While Hastings had learned his trade in direct contact and communication with Indian officials and was an admirer of Indian culture, Cornwallis neither had a comparable background, nor was he overly interested in India. Where Hastings and Francis had made constant use of Indian informants, Cornwallis based his judgment solely on the advice of experts from within the Company. He certainly did not lack confidence as an experienced administrator, and saw himself as a man appointed to fulfil the task of establishing order in the Bengal government and finances (Travers 2007: 212f., 232). First and foremost, he presented himself as "a rigid, but I flatter myself not an unpopular economist"[12] (Ross 1859: 276). As he perceived it, the situation he came upon when he superseded the interim governor-general John Macpherson left much to be desired: "the late Government had no authority, and the grossest frauds were daily committed before their faces; their whole conduct, and all their pretensions to economy [...] was a scene of delusion"[13] (Ross 1859: 238). His disdain also included the East India Company's Court of Directors in London: "If the essence of the spirit of economy of the whole Court of Directors could be collected, I am sure it would fall very short of my earnest anxiety on that subject"[14] (Ross 1859: 290). His own undivided loyalties lay with the British government, reporting to Henry Dundas and William Pitt, even to the point of consciously passing over the official channels of communication (the Secret Committee),[15] discussing important matters only in explicitly private correspondence: "I have purposely [...] given you opinions that you will perceive are [...] intended to be perfectly confidential between us; I mean always including Mr. Pitt"[16] (Ross 1859: II, 172).

---

[12] Cornwallis to the Duke of York, 20 July 1787.

[13] Cornwallis to Henry Dundas, 15 Nov. 1786.

[14] Cornwallis to Henry Dundas, 26 Aug. 1787.

[15] For theory and practice of the collaboration of the involved institutions—Governor General, Secret Committee of the Board of Directors, and the government Board of Control, in which Dundas was the central figure—cf. Bowen (2006: 73–83).

[16] Cornwallis to Henry Dundas, 18 June 1792. Dundas had given clear instructions on exactly this procedure years before, in a letter marked "private and confidential": "We never before had a

228   S. Meurer

While Cornwallis could not quite avoid waging war, he focused on the reform of the government, i.e. the administrative and fiscal system, in order to deliver the tranquil and reliable Indian colony Dundas and Pitt desired (Lawson 1993: 129). Still, the new approach to state-building developed in Bengal and not in England, as Jon Wilson forcefully argues (Wilson 2008: 62f.). One of the hallmarks of Cornwallis" reforms is the "Permanent Settlement" of 1793, which settled the amount of the land-tax at a permanent, unchangeably fixed amount. The idea had already been voiced by Warren Hastings" great rival Philip Francis, but it had been based on an utterly different rationale. While Francis had aimed at a re-establishment of a presumed older Mughal constitution and argued with constitutional rights of the Zamindars, for Cornwallis it was a clean break with all Mughal precedent, for the first time introducing some sort of reliable property rights. Its aim was to introduce a systematic and institutionalised fiscal system that was to provide a reliable income, while leaving the dealings with the actual peasants to local, landed elites. At the same time, it was to demonstrate the long-term commitment to economic development on the basis of landed property.[17]

The decision to break with the Mughal constitution approach did not originate in England. Francis' version of Zamindar property rights grounded in the Mughal constitution was very present in Fox's India bill, and had also been included in Pitt's India legislation (Wilson 2008: 54–58). However, in the eyes of Cornwallis, the attempts to base the tax assessment on experience and research in the Mughal constitution had not yielded conclusive results, but left "the revenue affairs of this country in the singular state of confusion"[18] (Firminger 1969: 486).

This break and the idea of setting up an entirely new order were explained by reference to a much changed concept of "Asiatic Despotism". In Hastings' version, the Mughal despotism had been a system with some faults that occasionally required correction. Cornwallis and his fellow administrators by contrast used the concept to discredit not only all Mughal precedent, but to devalorise the very character of the Indians, attributing something close to a racial trait to them, which supposedly explained the failure of former attempts to introduce a stable polity based on reliable knowledge. In the words of Cornwallis' close advisor and successor John Shore: "property in the soil, must not be understood to convey the same rights in India, as in Britain; the difference is as great as between a free constitution and arbitrary power. Nor are we to expect under a despotic government fixed principles, or clear definitions of the rights of the subject; but the general practice of such a government, when in favour of its subjects, should be admitted as

---

Government in India, both at home and abroad, acting in perfect unison together; upon principles of perfect purity and integrity; [...] You may depend upon my giving the most exact attention to every suggestion you communicate to me, not only in your publick despatches, but in your private letters; and indeed there are many things which you cannot with propriety communicate to me otherwise." Henry Dundas to Cornwallis, India Board 21 March 1787, received 26 Aug. 1787 (Ross 1859: 292f.). Cf. Mann 2000: 337–339.

[17] The standard account of Cornwallis' revenue reforms is Guha (1982); also see Islam (1979).

[18] Minutes of the governor-general (Cornwallis), 3 Feb. 1790.

an acknowledgement of their rights"[19] (Firminger 1969: 205). There was to be a clear break, no more association with such an intrinsically corrupt constitution. Ironically, while faulting Hastings with an "Asiatic despotic" government, what the Cornwallis cadre set up in a long series of reforms in the early 1790s can be aptly characterised as a form of European "enlightened despotism". Where Hastings had decided to selectively overstep the boundaries of the "Mughal inheritance", Cornwallis tried to establish a distinctly new constitution for Bengal. Often discussed in patronising terms like "benevolent" or "improving government" this authoritarian approach pervades the comprehensive regulations of 1793, known as the "Cornwallis Code", most of which would stay in force throughout the nineteenth century (Lawson 1993: 129; Clarke 1854: 1–248).

2.5 The Government of Strangers

Even so, the exercise of absolute sovereignty could be legitimised (now only to a British public!) with the Hindus' supposed "national character", bred through despotic rule: "their manners partake of the nature of the Government under which they have lived. As this has been arbitrary or despotic, the natives are timid and servile [...], have little sense of Honour" and "are wholly devoid of public virtue." To introduce a system in which, for example, revenue collection and the judiciary lie in the same hands, might be "repulsive" to Englishmen, but "[p]eople long accustomed to a despotic authority should only look to one master."[20]

This new government was to be carried out by a thoroughly reformed administrative apparatus. These reforms very much followed along the principles developed by the "Commissioners for Examining the Public Accounts", mentioned above. Thus, the scope of duties of the various offices was clearly defined, relatively high salaries and pensions were introduced, recruitment and promotion were based on qualification, and the training was intensified. Abstract rules and regulations were introduced as a key to the new system (Lawson 1993: 129f.; Aspinall 1931: 1–40). Jon Wilson suggests that an important factor for the shift of paradigm under Cornwallis was the increasing estrangement of the Company officers from those governed, accompanied by the anxiety and frustration in a situation experienced as a crisis. One of the measures taken was the exclusion of Indians from higher offices. The long-term consequence of the reforms that is often stressed most is the introduction of an *esprit de corps* and a moral code among the administrators, based on "pride and incorruptibility". This may be an overly sympathetic view of an utterly changed cadre of administrative office-holders, who became increasingly professional, but also secluded and disdainful to the Bengalis (Wilson 2008: 66–74). Under Cornwallis and his successors, this change of governmentality

---

[19] Minutes of John Shore, 14 June 1789.

[20] John Shore, remarks on the Mode of Administering Justice to the Natives of Bengal, 18 May 1785, IOR P/50/58, 382, 387ff., cited in Wilson (2008: 64f.).

continued, the regime growing ever more authoritarian, especially with the extensive wars of conquest following the tenure of Robert Wellesley (1797–1805), openly represented in the quasi-royal splendour flaunted by the governors-general (Bayly 1989: 100).

The impulse for institutional reform continued, while in England, partly because of the wars of the coalition, partly for political reasons, reform efforts did not come up to the expectations raised during the reform discourse of the 1780s. Major administrative reforms were only again tackled after 1815, whereas the East India Company even introduced an institutionalised education system for their servants with the founding of Fort William College in 1800, and Haileybury College in England in 1806. Eventually, the Company administration would develop into the Indian Civil Service, the first fully-fledged modern Civil Service in the English-speaking world (Bayly 2004: 256; Ghosal 1944).

3 "State-Building" and "State-Formation" as Research Terms

On the basis of the case study just delineated, I will now discuss the advantages and problems in the use of the terms "state-building" and, closely related, "state-formation". Is the change of governmentality in eighteenth-century British Bengal to be understood as "state-building", and if so, what consequences does this lead to? The terms are regularly used in the research literature on this topic, recently, for instance, in the works of Robert Travers and Jon Wilson mentioned above. Neither author defines "state-building" or "state-formation". Yet for both, they serve as helpful tools to classify their subjects and to integrate them into the larger context. In the following, I will identify the authors' usage of the terms in order to show the consequences of the perspectives they generate, before broadening the perspective to the more general use of the terms in historiography.

Robert Travers denotes British Bengal conventionally as a "colonial state", with the word "state" remaining a rather undefined term used to describe different sorts of polities, notably "the post-Mughal regional states", which, as he asserts, "revealed evidence of rapid commercialization [...] and the growth of centralizing "military-fiscal" regimes tapping into new forms of wealth to pay for growing armies" (Travers 2007: 11). Here, Travers highlights similarities between Indian polities and European states, but the signifying term for this is "military-fiscal regime", not "state". The "colonial state" can, in Travers' usage, appear as an agent, when he holds, for instance, that "indigenous categories [...] were put to new uses by the colonial state" (Travers 2007: 14). He justifies his work, insisting that "the historicist and constitutionalist aspects of early colonial thought deserve careful study as a critical aspect of colonial state-building" (Travers 2007: 17). Indeed, he specifies the subject of the book—the approaches to colonial governance he has described—as "a distinctive style of colonial state-building that has tended to be buried under later notions of the British civilizing mission" (Travers 2007: 6). Thus what he describes by "colonial state-building" is the aggregate of the discourse and practice of government by colonial officials, who were actively trying to shape the polity. He argues "that British imperial ideology was formed at the intersection of exported European concepts and appropriated indigenous categories that were put to new uses by the colonial state" (Travers 2007: 14).

He points out that most academic approaches either "emphasize the capacity of empire to build alliances with colonized elites based on shared [sic!] in unequal benefits" or "emphasize more the violent subordination of Indians and their interests in a colonial regime of conquest", while he sees his own approach as one which "fruitfully" combines "the paradigms of "negotiated empire" and the Imperial rule of force," which he sees as "inseparable dimensions of colonial state-formation" (Travers 2007: 14). To rephrase, "state-formation", as the actual institutional change, was driven by the interplay of coercion and negotiation, and this means by an encounter with indigenous forms of political thought and governmental practice. "State-building" appears to be a set of purposeful actions in the course of this encounter, while "state-formation" relates to the actual process taking place, constantly shaping the context in which "state-building" is attempted: "Colonial state-building, as a top-down process of demand and extraction, was also entangled with longer histories of state-formation, a more dispersed process in which local interests tried to appropriate the authority of the central state for local purposes" (Travers 2007: 90).

Initially, Jon Wilson likewise uses "colonial state" in a broad sense to designate the polity in Bengal since the grant of the Diwani.[21] Yet his central argument deals with the emergence of the much more closely defined "modern state": "Britain's first modern state emerged in Bengal" (Wilson 2008: ix). He highlights the similarities of eighteenth-century Britain and Bengal, both of which he characterises as based on networks of personal ties or personal rule. Therefore, he challenges the notion that the "modern state"—not really in existence in England—can be assumed to have been exported from there to Bengal (Wilson 2008: 19–44). On the contrary, he argues that, in the mood of crisis and estrangement after the failure of early attempts at governance, "colonial thought came to be dominated by an obsession with the search for general, abstract rules, which could be applied mechanistically by an authoritarian state" (Wilson 2008: 3). In his interpretation, this "modern state" is characterised, on the one hand, by mechanistically treating its subjects as strangers, and, on the other hand, by a future-oriented relation to time; it is constantly trying to reform by reference to a rationalistically constructed ideal model located in the future, which the state aspires to turn itself into (Wilson 2008: 15f., 73f.).

"In other words, the project of colonial state-formation was structured by prior British perceptions of the failure of government in India. [...] This book suggests the modern colonial state was not something that was merely described or "represented" in a static fashion by contemporaries. When it was written about, it

---

[21] E.g. "Throughout the period examined in this book, the colonial state remained an unstable, restless entity, never quite certain what it was doing, how it should act or whom it was acting for." (Wilson 2008: 8).

was situated in a story about a future-oriented project of state-formation, in which human action relied on a complicated sense of the relationship between past, present and future" (Wilson 2008: 15).

To Wilson, it is the wrong approach to start with a general definition of "the state" that is then applied to the actual facts. Rather, he is interested in "the genealogy of an idea of the state as an entity with the capacity to cause transformative effects" (Wilson 2008: 14). "State-formation", as Wilson uses it, is the coming into existence of a polity to which the idea of the modern state is central. "Not experiencing either revolution or invasion, Britain did not undergo quite the same dramatically self-conscious process of state-formation" (Wilson 2008: 187). Thus, it is a structural process of change of discourse and change of practice. Wilson also distinguishes this terminologically from the agent-driven attempts of institutional build-up: "Efforts of active state-building were only partially successful of course; failure was always a component of the attempt to produce a social world governable in rational rules to some degree" (Wilson 2008: 186).

While there are important differences between Travers' and Wilson's perspectives on the state and on events in eighteenth-century Bengal, their usage of "state-building" and "state-formation" seems to be based on shared assumptions about the general differentiation between the terms. "State-building" refers to conscious efforts of officials aiming at the implementation of institutional change, while "state-formation" points towards the more general process of the emergence of the (modern) state. This conformity, however, does not mirror a general consensus in the wider field of historical research—on the contrary, both terms often seem to be used indeterminately, both in relation to each other and to the underlying comprehension of "the state". As there has not been much explicit discussion of the terms, I will, in the following, highlight some aspects and problems of their usage in historiography, and, as a heuristic contrast, sketch the differentiation between them as it has recently emerged in political science.

3.1 The Concepts of "State-Building" and "State-Formation" in Historiography

Though the perspectives on it have been changing, the "state" has continued to serve as an important focal point for continental and especially German historical research since the nineteenth century.[22] And, since the 1960s, this has also been true of the historiography of the English-speaking world (Bayly 2004: 249–252; Brewer 1989: xiii–xxii; Brewer 1996). Much attention has been paid to the process by which the modern state emerged—a process that began in late medieval times, but is widely seen as one of the key signatures of the early modern period in Europe and

---

[22] The centrality of the state in German historical research can ultimately be dated back to German idealism and its influence on the foundations of historism in the nineteenth century. See Ameriks and Stolzenberg (2004); Iggers (1968). An in-depth analysis of the term "state" itself is beyond the scope of this article.

arguably its main legacy to the modern world. Building on the work of historical sociologists such as Charles Tilly or Michael Mann, the historical understanding of this complex process has been much deepened by historical research during the last three decades, particularly by the work of Wolfgang Reinhard (Tilly 1975; id. 1990; Mann 1986; Blockmans and Genet 1995–2000; Reinhard 2000). From this perspective, the state is a very specific political formation that was "invented" in Europe in the course of a unique historical process and then "exported" to the rest of the world[23] (Reinhard 2000: 15–20). It is to this multi-faceted process and the corresponding scholarly discussion that the terms "state-building" and "state-formation" (among others) usually refer. While the historical process has thus seen much clarification in terms of content, little has been done to determine and differentiate the use of the signifying terms. Reinhard himself prefers to speak of the "growth of state power", yet one of the decisive miscellanies he has edited is called "Power Elites and State Building", without any discussion of that term.[24]

Matters are complicated by translation for instance between Anglophone and German languages and also research traditions. The German "Staat" is much more closely connected to the concept of the modern power state than the English "state". Nevertheless "state-building" and "state-formation" are usually translated into German indiscriminately as "Staatsbildung", which does not help terminological clarity.[25] It is also because of the more open character of the English term "state" that "state-building" is frequently used to specify the increase of density or institutionalisation in any sort of political entity. For example, Bernard Bachrach labelled a collected volume of his papers centring on the tenth century *State-building in medieval France*, noting in the introduction: "The twelve articles reprinted here represent key studies in the process by which the stirpes Tortulfi created a great dynasty and built a successful state in Francia Occidentalis." (Bachrach 1995: ix) This raises the question whether the term can be meaningfully used only if there is an explicit historical connection to

---

[23] "Export" of the state does not mean unproblematic or unchanged adoption. Indeed, the spreading of the state is seen as a topic that has to be approached in a highly differentiated way; it does mean, however, that "state and state-power are so conclusively of European origin that even that designation of origin appears to be dispensable." ("Staat und Staatsgewalt sind so eindeutig Europäischen Ursprungs, daß sogar diese Herkunftsbezeichnung entbehrlich erscheint"), Reinhard (2000: 15); for Reinhard's analysis of the "export", ibid.: 480–536.

[24] In the introduction, labeled "Power Elites, State Servants, Ruling Classes, and the Growth of State Power", Reinhard occasionally uses both "(process of) state building" and "state formation", besides the omnipresent "growth of state power", indiscriminately (Reinhard 1996b: 2, 4, 17 (state building); 4, 6 (state formation)).

[25] A recent and, because it is a German-English Miscellany, especially vivid example of this is "Hexenprozess und Staatsbildung—Witch-Trials and State-Building", where the terms "State-Building", "State-Formation", "Staatsbildung", and "entstehende Staatlichkeit" are used side by side. Johannes Dillinger's introduction, which is presented both in German and in English, translates both state-formation and state-building as "Staatsbildung" (pp. 12, 22), while in the title of the introduction "entstehende Staatlichkeit" is rendered as "State-Building". Last, but not least, the editors offer the term "Verdichtung von Staatlichkeit" in the preface (Dillinger et al. 2008).

the modern power state. While there is certainly no consensus in historical research as to when exactly a "fully-fledged" state can be seen to exist, the phenomenon is usually dated to the period between the sixteenth and eighteenth centuries, at the latest in the aftermath of the French Revolution. The emergence of the specific Modern European State is sometimes even dated later, with the industrialisation surge of 1850–1870.[26]

A similar question to this historical or chronological demarcation of the term "state-building" is that of its cultural or geographical applicability. Does "state" refer to a specific form of political organisation, namely the European power state, and can it be used for pre-colonial polities? (Bayly 1998; Doornbos and Kaviraj 1997). If so, the terms "state-building" or "state-formation", if applied to the pre- and extra-colonial world, are at risk of presupposing a likeness of the processes of European and Asian state-formation, thereby arguing in a potentially very teleological way.[27] The explanation of the more or less unchanged diffusion of the European state by way of the colonial state does not carry much conviction. Instead, in the recent syntheses on world history a relative predominance of the modern nation state is only dated to the second third of the twentieth century, while, for the nineteenth century, the diversity of forms of political organisation is emphasised. This diversity is characterised through a tentative typology of either different models of states, or different polities beside the state[28] (Bayly 2004: 254–261; Osterhammel 2009: 822–826).

There have also been attempts to formulate a specifically South Asian concept of state-formation. Frank Perlin, for instance, describes a process in which the colonial period is no longer seen as the interruption of a much longer continuity, but only one episode in a long and intrinsically interconnected history (Perlin 1981: 275–302; id. 1985: 415–480).

---

[26] The problematisation of "the state" as a unique political configuration in the second half of the twentieth century also led to the emphasis of the processual character of the state. Cf. Reinhard (1998: 1–9). For a reserved assessment of the assertiveness of the modern state before the twentieth century, see Bayly (2004: 249).

[27] This is a matter much disputed in post-colonial research. In the critical approach of the Subaltern Studies group, for instance, a term like "pre-colonial" is seen to be problematical as such, because it is based on Western conceptions of "progress" and "modernity". For Dipesh Chakrabarty, for example, the state is a problematical concept, in so far as it is part of "political modernity", whereby the categorisation as "state" can become part of a normative chronology that tends to exclude certain phenomena as "pre-political". Cf. Chakrabarty (2000: 3–16); Iggers and Wang (2008: 284–290).

[28] Both Bayly and Osterhammel stress the necessity of dynamic models. Osterhammel explicitly questions the validity of a state-based typology of forms of government and the fixed correlation of state and territory (Osterhammel 2009: 825f.). Similarly, Bayly stresses the co-existence of different forms of "statishness", a neologism that, like the German "Staatlichkeit", can be used to signify aspects of governmentality, without presupposing a centralised state: ""statishness" could take a variety of forms in the nineteenth century-world." (Bayly 2004: 253).

3.2 The Differentiation Between "State-Building" and "State-Formation" in Political Science

"State-building" and "state-formation" have also been prominent terms in the social sciences. As a heuristic contrast I will therefore examine whether the usage of the terms in political science can help to advance clarity. In political science, "state-" as well as "nation-building" has initially been closely connected with modernisation theory of the 1950s and 1960s (e. g. Deutsch 1953; Lerner 1958; cf. Smith 1986: 231–235). It was assumed that the post-colonial states would undergo a similar, but accelerated process to that which led to the modern nation-state in Europe. The terms could therefore relate both to the historical process of European state-formation—a term that was used as well—as to ongoing processes of emerging states assumed to be equivalent. With the failure of these expectations and the corresponding stigmatisation of modernisation theory as essentially teleological, "state-building" was largely discarded. This was also partly because the state itself went out of fashion. The dominant behavioural and systems analysis approaches had little use for "state" as an analytical concept or point of reference up to the 1970s, preferring "political system" (Shepsle 1995: 276–282; Farr 1995: 206–215; Evans et al. 1985: 4–7; Pereira 2005).

This began to change by the mid-1980s, when institutions came back into focus, and with them, the demand to "bring the state back in" (Evans et al. 1985; Hall 1986). Gradually, usage of the terms "state-formation" and "state-building" diverged. "State-formation", on the one hand, was, and is still, used to refer to the *longue-durée* process—often seen as an informative prelude to the present subject of political science. In addition to that, the term marks a growing field of research concerned with the study of state-formation from a comparative perspective, contrasting very loosely defined "states", often across huge temporal and geographical distances, in order to enhance the understanding of "the state" (Vu 2010).

"State-building", on the other hand, has very much come back into focus in the field of development policy, where it stands for a new paradigm, replacing the "good governance" approach. As "failed" or "fragile" states are increasingly seen as a risk for international security (especially since the 9/11 terrorist attacks), the question arises of how external agents can actively advance stable state structures. Different approaches to this question can be categorised either as "state-building" (in a narrower sense) or "nation-building", depending on the scope of intervention deemed possible (Debiel and Lambach 2007: 89–92).[29] Exponents of state-building in this narrower sense aim at "a shortcut to the Weberian state" (Ottaway 2002: 1004), bypassing the long historical process through the intentional construction of the institutional apparatus of government (e.g. Fukuyama 2004a).[30] "Nation-building"

---

[29] Many thanks to Daniel Lambach for useful hints and an enlightening discussion on this subject.

[30] It is rather revealing that this book's title ("State-building") has been (correctly) translated into German as "Staaten bauen" and not "Staatsbildung" (Fukuyama 2004b).

is an even wider and more optimistic approach, envisioning the construction of a well-ordered nation-state based on an integrated society (Debiel and Lambach 2007: 90–92).[31] To sum up, "state-formation" points to *longue-durée* processes by which states come into existence, especially the process of European state-formation, while "state-building", as it is used in current political science, focuses on the intentional construction of a certain set of institutions, (hopefully) leading to a stable state.

4 Conclusion

The distinction between "state-formation" and "state-building" that has emerged in political science follows from issues that are not directly applicable to historical research. However, the comparison markedly reveals the ambiguity of the historiographical usage. By and large, the terms "state-building" and "state-formation" are used synonymously in historiography to signify the *longue-durée* process of the development of the modern state, while the former especially can additionally be used to signify individual instances of institutional change, often, but not always, associated with the long-term process.

What I suggest is the consistent distinction of these aspects on a terminological level. In analogy to political science, "state-formation" should be exclusively used to signify a *longue-durée* process through which a state has emerged—whether this means the narrative of European state-formation, a specific Asian state-formation, or even a hypothetical transcultural synthesis of processes leading to a globally shared political modernity.

"State-building", on the other hand, should be used for distinct short- or medium-term processes of institutional densification. The term is maybe most fitting for periods in which historical agents have tried (successfully or not) to construct institutions related (by direct reference or by ex-post classification) to the state.[32] A methodologically sound assessment of "success" or "failure" of such measures only becomes possible, indeed, by the initial separation from state-formation—without this separation, the very classification as "state-building" *a priori* suggests the teleological integration in a state-formation narrative. The distinction also holds true without the focus on intentional actions, e.g. in approaches stressing "state-building from below".[33] In both perspectives, the

---

[31] In practice, the terms are often used interchangeably, and approaches can overlap. Also, there is a call for the "embedded state-building" approach, which focuses on the institutions, but pays close attention to the institutions' connectedness to a given society and cultural context.

[32] This relation is, of course, very dependent on the applied definition of the state. The basic terminological distinction suggested here should, however, be largely independent of the individual concretisation of "the state".

[33] Cf. the article by Stefan Brakensiek in this volume.

conscious integration of cases in the *longue-durée* account of state-formation will, of course, be an informative second step.

I will try to exemplify these thoughts by means of the transition in eighteenth-century Bengal. The British governance in early colonial Bengal can be described simply as a series of reactions to rapidly evolving problems at hand. This is certainly true for the involved parties in London. It is, in many respects, also true for those responsible at Fort William in Calcutta—assuredly they were not in control of the processes of transition of the government. Nevertheless they developed—maybe needed to develop—a concept of the political system they were trying to erect. It is therefore easy to categorise the British colonial efforts as "state-building". The governor-general certainly aimed at the build-up of stable institutions, and their approaches developed in reference both to the European state-discourse and the situation at hand. For Robert Travers, "colonial state-building" thus helps to summarise governmental decisions and identify a "style of colonial state-building", the discursive and ideological presumptions of these decisions. Warren Hastings and other "old hands" of the East India Company had experienced the Mughal Empire from the perspective of British enclaves in the imperial structure. Therefore, they envisioned a state based on the logic of the Mughal Empire as they understood it. They applied the traditional concept of the "Ancient Constitution" from the English Constitutional Discourse to translate their experiences and perceptions to their own notions of government. At the same time, Hastings did not hesitate to interfere with the perceived constitution, justifying this, on the one hand, with necessity or *raison d'état*, but also with the "Asiatic Despotic" character of the Mughal Constitution the Company had inherited.

The state-building approach heralded by Cornwallis and Dundas, on the other hand, proceeded from the geopolitical logic of the second British Empire, even though its conclusive form developed in Bengal. In the increasingly asymmetrical narrative underlying British governmentality, European notions of government were seen as plainly superior, and their implementation not least legitimised by the supposedly beneficial influence this rule would have on the subjects. Moreover, the Bengali elites were no longer seen as partners (albeit inferior ones), but increasingly forced into the position of mere subjects and strangers, who were to be coercively assigned the role they had to play in the new system. This was presented as a distinct break with the despotic Mughal past. Nevertheless, the legal fiction of Mughal sovereignty was kept up—maybe it was only now really becoming a fiction.

By specifying the actions and perceptions as "state-building", it is initially unnecessary to decide whether a "state" stood at the end of the process and whether the Mughal Empire or Bengal ruled by the Nawabs can be called a "state"—Bengali institutions, agents and political thought played an important role in the process anyhow. It certainly does not mean that their actions were the all-deciding factor for the actual outcome of the transition. While this state-building process was initiated by the British seizure of territorial dominion in Bengal, its outcome was the result of a multi-faceted transcultural process. Without pushing the analogy of early modern state-building and the prospects of present-day development policy too far, they have in common that they were, and are, complex and often entangled processes, with a huge gap between intentional approaches and the actual outcome that was, and is, hard to predict.

With the categorisation as "state-building", nothing is yet said about the placement of these events within the narratives of "state-formation". Conversely, such a placement is—as a conscious interpretation—assuredly possible and can be meaningful. The events outlined, for instance, not only figure as antecedents for the modern Indian state or, as Frank Perlin suggests, as one of many episodes of the specific South Asian state-formation. They certainly also have their place in the very British or European state-formation, especially considering the prototypical significance of the Indian Civil Service in the history of public administration. And if you follow Jon Wilson's argument, they constitute the very moment of birth of a distinctly modern, "future-oriented project of state-formation" (Wilson 2008: 15).

Bibliography

Ameriks, Karl and Jürgen Stolzenberg. 2004. *Der Begriff des Staates = The Concept of the State* (= International Yearbook of German Idealism, vol. 2). Berlin: de Gruyter.

Aspinall, A. 1931. *Cornwallis in Bengal: The Administrative and Judicial Reforms of Lord Cornwallis in Bengal, together with Accounts of the Commercial Expansion of the East India Company, 1786–1793, and of the Foundation of Penang, 1786–1793* (= Publications of the University of Manchester, vol. 216). Manchester: Manchester University Press.

Bachrach, Bernard S. 1995. *State-building in Medieval France: Studies in Early Angevin History* (= Collected studies series, vol. 486). Aldershot: Variorum.

Bayly, Christopher Alan. 1989. *Imperial Meridian: The British Empire and the World, 1780–1830. Studies in Modern History.* London: Longman.

Bayly, Christopher Alan. 1996. "The British Military-Fiscal State and Indigenous Resistance: India 1750-1820". In *An Imperial State at War. Britain from 1689 to 1815*, ed. L. Stone, 322–354. London, New York: Routledge.

Bayly, Christopher Alan. 1998. *Origins of Nationality in South Asia. Patriotism and ethical government in the making of modern India.* Delhi et al.: Oxford University Press.

Bayly, Christopher Alan. 2004. *The Birth of the Modern world 1780–1914: Global Connections and Comparisons* (The Blackwell history of the world). Malden, Mass.: Blackwell.

Blockmans, Wim and Jean-Philippe Genet (eds.) 1995–2000. *The origins of the modern state in Europe, 13th to 18th Centuries.* 7 vols. Oxford et al.: Clarendon Press.

Bowen, Huw V. 2002. *Revenue and Reform: The Indian Problem in British Politics 1757–1773* (2nd ed.). Cambridge et al.: Cambridge University Press.

Bowen, Huw V. 2006. *The Business of Empire: The East India Company and Imperial Britain.* Cambridge et al.: Cambridge University Press.

Breihan, John Robert 1977. *Economical Reform, 1785–1810.* Unpublished DPhil Dissertation. Cambridge.

Breihan, John Robert. 1984. "William Pitt and the Commission on Fees, 1785-1801". *Historical Journal*, 27 (1), 59–81.

Brewer, John. 1989. *The Sinews of Power: War, Money and the English State, 1688–1783.* London et al.: Unwin Hyman.

Brewer, John. 1996. "The Eighteenth-Century British State: Contexts and issues". In *An Imperial State at War. Britain from 1689 to 1815*, ed. Lawrence Stone, 52–71. London, New York: Routledge.

Burgess, Glenn. 1992. *The Politics of the Ancient Constitution. An Introduction to English Political Thought, 1600–42*, Basingstoke, London: Macmillan.

Burke, Edmund. 1981. "Ninth Report of Select Committee, 25 June 1783". In *The writings and speeches of Edmund Burke. Vol. V: India: Madras and Bengal, 1774–1785*, ed. Peter James Marshall, 194–333. Oxford: Clarendon Press.

Cohn, Bernard S. 1996. *Colonialism and its forms of knowledge: The British in India*. (= Princeton studies in culture/power/history). Princeton, NJ: Princeton University Press.

Chakrabarty, Dipesh. 2000. *Provincializing Europe: Postcolonial thought and historical difference* (= Princeton studies in culture/power/history). Princeton, NJ: Princeton University Press.

Chaudhury, Sushil. 2000. *The prelude to empire: Plassey revolution of 1757*. New Delhi: Manohar Publishers & Distributors.

Clarke, Richard (ed.). 1854. *The Regulations of the Government of Fort William in Force at the End of 1853...*, vol. 1: *Regulations from 1793 to 1805*. London: Cox.

Curtis, Michael. 2009. *Orientalism and Islam. European Thinkers on Oriental Despotism in the Middle East and India*. Cambridge et al.: Cambridge University Press.

Debiel, Tobias and Daniel Lambach. 2007. "From "Aid Conditionality" to "Engaging Differently": How Development Policy Tries to Cope with Fragile States". *Journal für Entwicklungspolitik*, 23 (4), 80–99.

Deutsch, Karl W. 1953. *Nationalism and Social Communication: An Inquiry into the Foundations of Nationality*. New York, London: Technology Press of the Massachusetts Institute of Technology.

Dillinger, Johannes, Jürgen Michael Schmidt, and Dieter R. Bauer. 2008. *Hexenprozess und Staatsbildung = Witch-trials and state-building* (= Hexenforschung Vol. 12). Gütersloh: Verlag für Regionalgeschichte.

Dirks, Nicholas B. 2006. *The scandal of empire: India and the Creation of Imperial Britain*. Cambridge, Mass.: Belknap Press of Harvard University Press.

Dodwell, Henry Herbert. 1929. "The Development of Sovereignty in British India". In *Cambridge History of India, vol. 5: British India 1497–1858*, ed. Henry Herbert Dodwell, 589–608. Cambridge: Cambridge University Press.

Doornbos, Martin and Sudipta Kaviraj(ed.). 1997. *Dynamics of State Formation. India and Europe Compared*. (Indo-Dutch studies on development alternatives, vol. 19). New Delhi; Thousand Oaks.

Edwardes, Michael. 1991. *The Nabobs at Home*. London: Constable.

Evans, Peter B., Dietrich Rueschemeyer and Theda Skocpol (eds.). 1985. *Bringing the state back in*. Cambridge: Cambridge University Press.

Farr, James. 1995. "Remembering the Revolution: Behavorialism in American Political Science". In *Political science in history. Research programs and political traditions*, ed. J. Farr, J.S. Dryzek, S.T. Leonard, 198–224. Cambridge: Cambridge University Press.

Firminger, Walter Kelly (ed.). 1969. *The Fifth Report on East India Company Affairs – 1812, Vol. 2: Introduction and Bengal Appendices*. Reprint. New York: Cambray.

Fukuyama, Francis. 2004a. *State-building: Governance and world order in the 21st century*. Ithaca, NY: Cornell University Press.

Fukuyama, Francis. 2004b. *Staaten bauen: Die neue Herausforderung internationaler Politik*. Berlin: Propyläen.

Ghosal, Akshoy Kumar. 1944. *Civil Service in India under the East India Company: A Study in Administrative Development*. Calcutta: Calcutta University Press.

Gleig, G.R. (ed.). 1841. *The Memoirs of the Life of the Honourable Warren Hastings, First Governor General of India: Compiled from Original Papers*. London: Richard Bentley.

Guha, Ranajit. 1982. *A Rule of Property for Bengal: An Essay on the Idea of Permanent Settlement* (2nd ed.). New Delhi et al.: Orient Longman.

240 S. Meurer

Hall, John Anthony. (ed.) 1986. *States in History*. Oxford: Basil Blackwell.

Harling, Philip. 1996. *The waning of "Old corruption": The Politics of Economical Reform in Britain, 1779–1846*. Oxford: Clarendon Press.

Iggers, Georg G. 1968. *The German conception of history: The National Tradition of Historical Thought from Herder to the Present*. Middletown: Wesleyan University Press.

Iggers, Georg G. and Q. Edward Wang. 2008. *A Global History of Modern Historiography*. Harlow: Pearson/Longman.

Islam, Sirajul. 1979. *The Permanent Settlement in Bengal: A Study of its Operation 1790–1819*. Dacca: Bangla Academy.

Khan, Majed Abdul. 1969. *The Transition in Bengal 1756–1775. A Study of Saiyid Muhammad Reza Khan*. Cambridge: Cambridge University Press.

Kidd, Colin. 1999. *British identities before nationalism: Ethnicity and nationhood in the Atlantic World, 1600–1800*. Cambridge: Cambridge University Press.

Lawson, Philip. 1993. *The East India Company: A History* (= Studies in Modern History). Harlow: Longman.

Lerner, Daniel. 1958. *The Passing of Traditional Society: Modernizing the Middle East*. Glencoe, Ill.: The Free Press.

Mann, Michael. 1986. *The Sources of Social Power: A History of Power from the Beginning to A.D. 1760*. Cambridge: Cambridge University Press.

Mann, Michael. 2000. *Bengalen im Umbruch: Die Herausbildung des britischen Kolonialstaates 1754–1793*. Stuttgart: Steiner.

Marshall, Peter James. 1973. "Warren Hastings as Scholar and Patron". In *Statesmen, Scholars and Merchants*, ed. A. Whiteman, 242–262. Oxford: Clarendon Press.

Marshall, Peter James. 1987a. *Bengal: the British Bridgehead: Eastern India, 1740–1828* (= The New Cambridge History of India. Indian states and the transition to colonialism 2). Cambridge: Cambridge University Press.

Marshall, Peter James. 1987b. "Empire and Authority in the later Eighteenth Century". *Journal of Imperial and Commonwealth History* 15: 105–122.

Marshall, Peter James. 2005. *The Making and Unmaking of Empires: Britain, India, and America c.1750-1783*. Oxford: Oxford University Press.

Marshall, Peter James. 2006. "The British in Asia: Trade to Dominion", 1700–1765. In *The Oxford History of the British Empire: Vol. 2. The Eighteenth Century*, ed. Peter James Marshall, 487–507. Oxford: Oxford University Press.

Monckton-Jones, M.E. 1918. *Warren Hastings in Bengal*. Oxford: Clarendon Press.

Osterhammel, Jürgen. 2009. *Die Verwandlung der Welt: Eine Geschichte des 19. Jahrhunderts*. Munich: Beck.

Ottaway, Marina. 2002. "Rebuilding State Institutions in Collapsed States". *Development and Change* 35 (5): 1001–1023.

Pavarala, Vinod. 2004. "Cultures of Corruption and the Corruption of Culture: The East India Company and the Hastings Impeachment". In *Corrupt Histories. Studies in comparative history*, ed. E. Kreike and W.C. Jordan, 291–336. Rochester, NY et al.: University of Rochester Press.

Pereira, Charmaine. 2005. Article "State, the". In *New Dictionary of the History of Ideas*, ed. M. Cline Horowitz, 2250–2257. Detroit et al.: Gale.

Perlin, Frank. 1981. "The Precolonial Indian State in History and Epistemology: A Reconstruction of Societal Formation in the Western Deccan from the Fifteenth to the Early Nineteenth Century". In *The Study of the State* (= New Babylon. Studies in the Social Sciences, vol. 35), ed. H.J.M. Claessen and P. Skalník, 275–302. The Hague et al.: Mouton.

Perlin, Frank. 1985. "State Formation Reconsidered: Part Two". *Modern Asian Studies,* 19: 415–480.

Pocock, John Greville Agard. 1957. *The Ancient Constitution and the Feudal Law: A Study of English Historical Thought in the 17th Century*. Cambridge et al.: Cambridge University Press.

Prasad, Bisheshwar (dd.). 1960. *Fort William - India House Correspondence: And other Contemporary Papers Relating Thereto, 1770–1772* (= Indian Records Series, vol. 6). Delhi.

Reinhard, Wolfgang (ed.) 1996a. *Power Elites and State Building* (The origins of the modern state in Europe, 13th to 18th Centuries). Oxford et al.

Reinhard, Wolfgang. 1996b. "Introduction: Power Elites, State Servants, Ruling Classes, and the Growth of State Power". In *Power Elites and State Building*, ed. Wolfgang Reinhard, 1–18. Oxford et al.: Clarendon Press.

Reinhard, Wolfgang. 1998. "Frühmoderner Staat – moderner Staat". In *Die Entstehung des modernen Europa. 1600–1900* (Wirtschafts- und sozialhistorische Studien Vol. 7), ed. Olaf Mörke and Michael North, 1–9. Cologne: Böhlau.

Reinhard, Wolfgang. 2000. *Geschichte der Staatsgewalt: Eine vergleichende Verfassungsgeschichte Europas von den Anfängen bis zur Gegenwart* (2nd ed.). Munich: Beck.

Richter, Melvin. 1973. Article "Despotism". In *Dictionary of the History of Ideas. Studies of Selected Pivotal Ideas*, ed. Philip P. Wiener, vol. 2, 1–18. New York: Scribner.

Rocher, Rosane. 1993. "British Orientalism in the Eighteenth Century: The Dialectics of Knowledge and Government". In *Orientalism and the postcolonial predicament. Perspectives on South Asia* (= South Asia seminar series), ed. C.A. Breckenridge, 215–244. Philadelphia: University of Pennsylvania Press.

Ross, Charles (ed.). 1859. *Correspondence of Charles, First Marquis Cornwallis*, 2 vols. (2nd ed.) London: Murray.

Sen, Neil. 1997. "Warren Hastings and British Sovereign Authority in Bengal, 1774-80". *Journal of Imperial and Commonwealth History*, 25 (1): 59–81.

Shepsle, Kenneth A. 1995. "Studying Institutions: Some Lessons from the Rational Choice Approach". In *Political science in history. Research programs and political traditions*, ed. J. Farr, J.S. Dryzek and S.T. Leonard, 276–295. Cambridge: Cambridge University Press.

Smith, Anthony D. 1986. "State-Making and Nation-Building". In *States in History*, ed. J.A. Hall, 228–263. Oxford: Basil Blackwell.

Tilly, Charles. (ed.) 1975. *The Formation of National States in Western Europe*. Princeton, London: Princeton University Press.

Tilly, Charles. 1990. *Coercion, capital, and European states: AD 990–1990. Studies in social discontinuity*. Cambridge, Mass.: Blackwell.

Torrance, John. 1978. "Social Class and Bureaucratic Innovation: The Commissioners for Examining the Public Accounts 1780-1787". *Past and Present*, 78, 56–81.

Travers, Robert. 2007. *Ideology and Empire in Eighteenth-Century India: The British in Bengal* (= Cambridge Studies in Indian History and Society, vol. 14). Cambridge: Cambridge University Press.

Vu, Tuong. 2010. "Studying the State through State Formation". *World Polities*, 62 (1): 148–175.

Weitzmann, Sophia. 1929. *Warren Hastings and Philip Francis*. Manchester: Manchester University Press.

Wilson, Jon E. 2008. *The domination of strangers: Modern governance in Eastern India, 1780–1835* (Cambridge imperial and post-colonial studies series). Basingstoke: Palgrave Macmillan.

State-Building in a Transcultural Context: The Case of the French in India during the Early Eighteenth Century[1]

Gauri Parasher

My ongoing research, of which this paper is a provisional and brief exposition, examines the history of the French in India, particularly in Pondicherry, during the early decades of the eighteenth century. It analyses the administration that developed in Pondicherry during this period, often referred to as a precursor to the colonial state. I will argue that this administration was in fact transcultural and presents an instance of state-building in a transcultural context. In this two-part paper, the first part presents the theoretical framework and the second part presents the scope of the empirical research where the main research questions are raised.

Before proceeding, I would like to delineate the main conceptual underpinnings of this paper: the state, transculturality and state-building from below. The concept of "state" is mostly identified with the concept of the modern European national state i.e. "a territorially bound, highest power organization of a nation." Various forms of state "embrace a fixed territorial space with marked boundaries, and have government and laws, and instruments to execute those laws and protect the members of the nation" (Doornbos and Kaviraj 1997: 56–57). For a long time now, it has been the ideal of the well-ordered, western, modern political community and considered to be the model which any political community that strove towards modernity was expected to embrace (Axtmann 2004: 259). However, as the focus of this research is India, a geographical region beyond Europe and the pre-national epoch, this paper considers the concept of state in a broader sense – namely, a space of interaction, a network of institutions and agents. To analyse state-building in an early-modern and a transcultural context, it is first necessary to step outside the pale

---

[1] This paper is part of an ongoing doctoral thesis and should not, on any account, be regarded as finished. It delineates, necessarily in a limited manner, the main hypothesis, the central arguments and the conceptual framework of the ongoing research. Criticism, suggestions and remarks are most welcome and should be sent to parasher@asia-europe.uni-heidelberg.de.

G. Parasher (✉)
Karl Jaspers Centre, University of Heidelberg, Voßstr. 2, 69115 Heidelberg, Germany
e-mail: parasher@asia-europe.uni-heidelberg.de

A. Flüchter and S. Richter (eds.), *Structures on the Move*,
Transcultural Research – Heidelberg Studies on Asia and Europe in a Global Context,
DOI 10.1007/978-3-642-19288-3_12, © Springer-Verlag Berlin Heidelberg 2012

of these aspects limited reference to Europe, modernity and national state. The term "state" is not to be understood as a socio-scientific model, but as a result of communication and interaction.

The idea of "state" as a result of interaction has been recently brought to the forefront in the recent theory of state-building from below. Speaking of European state-building, André Holenstein postulates that the articulation of interests, moral concepts and need by communities, corporate entities, interest groups and subjects from local society play a determining role in the processes of state-building. "From this perspective, state-building [...] seems to be the unintended outcome of interactive processes, which brought about and fostered the emergence of a state" (Blockmans, Holenstein and Mathieu 2009: 4–5). Now, when applied to Pondicherry in the early modern period, these interactive processes are not within one but between two different cultures. Hence, the idea of state-building in a transcultural context.

The term transcultural refers to a cross-cultural phenomenon that results from an interaction between two or more cultures. To study its practical bearing on state-building processes, the notion of hybridity is employed. Hybridity commonly refers to "the creation of new transcultural forms within the contact zone produced by colonisation" (Ashcroft et al. 2003: 118). In this case-study, these "new transcultural forms" are necessarily those produced in the field of governance and administration. Thus, the transcultural nature of state-building in Pondicherry will be determined through the analysis of these hybrid institutions of administration that resulted from the interaction between the French and the Indians. The aim of this study of the early administration in Pondicherry is not to test a preset model of development of state or colonial state but rather to enquire into the form of governance that grew as a result of transcultural interaction and that was determined as much from below as from above.

In 1674, with the permission of Sher Khan Lody, governor of the Carnatic under the Bijapur Sultanate, François Martin set up a trading post in Pondicherry. As its first governor, he is credited with having consolidated French trade and administration there. By the beginning of the eighteenth century, the town had superseded Surat as the trade capital of the French East India Company's commercial network in India and had become the seat of French affairs in India. Apart from the 6-year occupation by the Dutch from 1693 to 1699, Pondicherry remained under uninterrupted French control for almost a hundred years before being overrun by another European power, the English, in 1761.[2]

When the French, under François Martin, took repossession of Pondicherry in 1699, their first concern was to raise fortifications in order to have a well-protected territory relatively free from external dangers and which was imperative for conducting smooth commercial operations. By 1702, fortifications had been built

---

[2] For general history of the French in India: G.B. Malleson in *Histoire des français dans l'Inde: depuis la fondation de Pondichéry jusqu' à la prise de cette ville (1674–1761)*, S.P. Sen in *The French in India: First Establishment and Struggle.*, Aniruddha Ray in *The Merchant and the State: the French in India, 1666–1739.*

and the town was able to offer a degree of security in order to attract merchants and weavers to settle there. By 1706, the population had reached nearly 60,000 and went on to reach 100,000 in the coming years. The town had developed an administrative infrastructure headed by the *Conseil Supérieur de Pondichéry*. Created in 1701 by an edict of Louis XIV, its primary function was to impart justice in civil and criminal matters to his subjects living in Pondicherry. In time, its functions included administration and commerce and became an organ of administration. Within the next decade Pondicherry had started minting its own coins and had acquired the right to collect revenue. It had developed into a self-sustaining commercial town.[3]

As such, Pondicherry, in the early eighteenth century, was much more than a French trading-post. It was a French colony, i.e. "a type of socio-political organisation" governed by the French. However, it is important to keep in mind that during this period the French territories in India were free of imperialism as a system of domination, economic or political. In his discussion on the relation between colonialism and imperialism, from an economic point of view, Jürgen Osterhammel warns against the dangers of associating this term to early modern colonial empires as they were in a position to achieve "a capitalist penetration of large economic areas." According to him "colonial empires without imperialism were the rule during the early modern period" (Osterhammel 1997: 21–22). In the case of Pondicherry during the early eighteenth century this idea is further supported by Sudipta Das who, equating all forms of imperialism with domination, refutes the common belief that French imperialism existed in India during the early eighteenth century. She sets out to dispel one of the most prevalent and persistent assumptions concerning the French venture in India, i.e. that they aspired to build a colonial empire in this part of the Eastern world. Historically, France did not have any ambition for an empire in India, especially after 1763. In fact, the origins of the idea of French imperialism may be traced back to Joseph François Dupleix, Governor of Pondicherry from1742 to1754 (Das 1992). However, in relation to the period immediately preceding Dupleix, i.e. when the French settlements were under the governorship of Pierre Christoph Lenoir (1726–1735) and Pierre Benoit Dumas (1735–1741), and before them Guillaume André d'Hébert and François Martin, "there was nothing in the conduct of Lenoir or Dumas that allows us to credit the Company with political views and still less ideas of conquest; its factories were more or less fortified but for the motives of simple security against the Dutch or the English; and although it enlisted troops it used them only for the purposes of defence. But after 1742, political motives clearly overshadow the desire for commercial gain . . ." (Das 1992: 4–7). Clearly then, the pursuit of profitable commerce rather than colonial domination was central to the system of governance that developed in Pondicherry during this time.

---

[3] In fact, as a Jesuit priest observed, it "had become a French town with regular administrative infrastructure and headquarters of all commercial posts of the French established in the Indies." Letter by Father P. Bolu from Pondicherry, 1. October, 1704 in BN, f 56. As quoted in Sen, *The Merchant and the State: the French in India, 1666–1739*: 401.

This idea is also reflected in the statutes and rules governing the French East India Company. The Company's primary objective in India was trade and its policy was against the employment of resources for anything but commerce. An abstract from the statutes and rules of the Company in India states: "The Company is first and foremost an institution of commerce. France in forming a "Compagnie des Indes" believes in the obligation to bequeath to it substantial privileges and a certain degree of power ... as a point of support of commerce, very important and to be exercised at all times, the Company so privileged, must never lose from view that the means thus granted to it have been solely for the purpose of commerce, and it can never employ them for purposes of aggrandizement or of conquest to the detriment of its real spirit of commerce."[4]

Thus, the Company was foremost an organ of commerce.[5] This status of the Company was also reflected in the ground realities in Pondicherry: the French were not in a powerful position to dominate. They were heavily dependent on the merchants and inhabitants of the town for their commerce. This commercial dependence clearly reveals itself in the early legislation formulated by the *Conseil Supérieur*. For example, in 1702, François Martin, under pressure from the pressure of the Jesuits, passed a law that prohibited the Hindus, the majority of the population, from taking part in processions and celebrating their festivals. The entire Hindu population, including merchants, masons and weavers, decided to quit Pondicherry, leaving behind their shops and houses, rather than accept the dictates of the French. Consequently, François Martin was obliged to revoke the law for the very survival of the French East India Company's commercial enterprise (Ray 2004; Malleson 1874). Thus, at this time when commercial priorities were foremost in the mind of the French administration, it is too early to speak of colonialism as a "system of domination" in the context of Pondicherry.

It is with this background in mind, when the power asymmetries between the French and the Indians were still not as clearly defined as in the later colonial period, that my research analyses the early eighteenth century administration in Pondicherry. While there is no dearth of material on the history of the French in India or on the activities of the French East India Company,[6] or on the lives of governors,[7] the transcultural aspect of the administration seen in conjunction with the concepts of hybridity and state-building from below, still remains to be analysed. Of the transcultural elements in the interaction and in the networks of

---

[4] *Prospectus des Statuts et Règlements concernant la Compagnie des Indes de France* (1767), Archives Nationales, Paris, Colonies, Vol. 51, Compagnie des Indes: 62. These statutes were established during the inception of the Company and again republished in 1767.

[5] For works on the French East India Company see Indrani Ray in *French East India Company and the Trade of the Indian Ocean*, Paul Kaeppelin in *La Compagnie des Indes Orientales et Francois Martin*, Phillipe Haudrere in *La Compagnie Francaise des Indes au XVIIIe siecle*,

[6] Ibid.

[7] Cf. Philippe Haudrere on François Martin, Alfred Martineau on the life of Dupleix in *Dupleix. Sa vie et son oeuvre.* and *Dernieres Annees de Dupleix.*

agents that comprise the governance of Pondicherry during this particular time, this study first focuses on the judicial framework of the colony.

The significance of records of courts and tribunals lies in that "they document how past peoples thought they should be and how they were, their ideals and their realities, theories and practices, rules and expectations" (Dobson and Ziemann 2009). They hold great potential as sources for the lives of people from all strata of society and clues to their common problems. Furthermore, in the context of state-building, archival records from courts provide clues to the policy-making that went on at the time. As mentioned earlier, by his edict dated 1701, Louis XIV had established the *Conseil Supérieur* to provide justice, both civil and criminal, for the French subjects living in Pondicherry. At the same time, the Indian inhabitants attended the *Tribunal de la Chaudrie* (Chaultry) for disputes among themselves. However, the cultural orientation of the function of both these judicial institutions was not quite as distinct. Records of the deliberations held at the *Conseil Supérieur* are replete with examples of trials concerning Indian parties. Together, these two institutions formed the judicial framework of the Pondicherry administration which catered to French and Indians alike. While most historians mention this fact, their functioning as an administrative institution in the light of the transcultural social make-up of the territory remains to be examined in more detail. What was the need to go to court? What were the underlying principles and policies that governed these two institutions? Where was the entanglement to be found – at the level of policy or practice or both? In a recent two-volume com0pilation of the judgements delivered by the *Tribunal de la Chaudrie*, Claude Bonnan states that the setting-up of this tribunal in the society of the day and its role in constituting a Franco-Indian law still remains to be investigated. Answers to these questions are perhaps crucial to understanding the entanglement and appropriation as constituents of the early judicial set-up in Pondicherry. The co-dependence between the jurisprudence of these two organisms determines how they reflect the multicultural nature of state and society in which they functioned (Bonnan 1999).

The next part of the study focuses on the role and contribution of the intermediary agents in regard to the functioning of the early administration. Like all other European powers present in India, with interests in commerce, the French were heavily dependent on the Indians, from the regional governors to local merchants. While research on the English in India has produced several studies on the roles of these intermediaries,[8] the French situation, particularly pertaining to this period, is not extensive. Moreover, in the study of transcultural state-building, the study of intermediaries in the French context provides us with a case different from that of the British model and thus highlights different aspects of transculturality in formations of governance. Therefore, in order to study in depth the role of the

---

[8] Cf. Susan Neild Basu in *The Dubashes of Madras* (Journal Article), Farhat Hasan, *Indigenous Cooperation and the Birth of a Colonial City: Calcutta, c. 1698–1750* (Journal article) Kanakalatha Mukund in *The View From Below: Indigenous Society, Temples and the Early Colonial State in Tamilnadu; 1700–1835.*

intermediaries it is necessary to bring together scattered studies relating to them in French research.[9] The French often had to employ the *dubashes*, the local societies of merchants, the left- and right-hand caste-leaders and the agents in negotiations with various regional political powers. In order to fully understand these intermediaries' involvement and contribution in administrative practices it is here argued that it is necessary to make a joint study of the role played by the intermediaries in order to establish the extent of their involvement as well as their contribution in the consolidation of the administration.

Of these intermediaries, the term *dubash* is of common usage. The word *dubash* or rather *dubashi* literally means a man of two languages or interpreter and connotes the role of a go-between or broker. His linguistic skills, as interpreter and translator, were essential to his role but the usefulness of the *dubash* extended far beyond his knowledge of languages. The range of *dubashi* functions varied from being a kind of advisor, a guide, a broker to, inevitably, a money-lender for the new arrivals in town. Thus, as the port town developed, the institution of *dubash* rose to prominence and emerged as a necessary commercial, cultural and administrative interface between the local population and the Europeans.

In consequence, through the study of these aspects of the early French administration in Pondicherry in the early eighteenth century, I hope to highlight the transcultural elements of this state-building that resulted from appropriation and interaction between different societies. The French did not bring the "colonial state" with them nor can the state that developed during this time be called colonial. The administration that emerged was an example of a type of state-building in a transcultural context and gives us clues to the nature of early modern pluralism in societies and states.

Bibliography

Ashcroft, Bill, Gareth A Griffiths and Helen Tiffin. 2003. *Post-Colonial Studies: The Key Concepts.* London: Routledge.

Axtmann, Roland. 2004. "The State of the State: The Model of the Modern State and Its Contemporary Transformation." *International Political Science Review* 25: 259–279.

Blockmans, Wim and Andre Holenstein. 2009. Empowering Interactions: Political Cultures and the Emergence of the State in Europe 1300-1900. Farnham/Burlington: Ashgate.

Bonnan, Jean-Claude. 1999. *Jugements du tribunal de la Chaudrie de Pondichéry: 1766–1817.* Pondicherry: Institut français de Pondichéry.

Das, Sudipta. 1992. *Myths and Realities of French Imperialism in India: 1763–1783.* New York: Lang.

---

[9] Even though in her book, *The View from Below: Indigenous Society, Temples and the Early Colonial State in Tamilnadu 1700–1835,* Kanakalatha Mukund focuses mainly on the early colonial state in Madras, it does discuss partially the *dubashes* under the French during the late eighteenth century.

State-Building in a Transcultural Context 249

Doornbos, Martin R. and Sudipta Kaviraj. 1997. Dynamics of State Formation: India and Europe Compared. Sage Publications.

Doornbos, Martin. 1997. *Dynamics of State Formation: India and Europe Compared*. New Delhi: Sage.

Holenstein, André. 2009. "Introduction." In *Empowering Interactions: Political Cultures and the Emergence of the State in Europe, 1300–1900*, ed. Wim Blockmans, 1–31. Farnham: Ashgate.

Malleson, George B. 1874. *Histoire des français dans l'Inde: depuis la fondation de Pondichéry jusqu' à la prise de cette ville (1674–1761)*. Paris: Librairie de la Société Bibliographique.

Mukund, Kanakalatha. 2006. *The View From Below: Indigenous Society, Temples and the Early Colonial State in Tamilnadu; 1700–1835*. Hyderabad: Orient Longman.

Osterhammel, Jürgen. 1997. *Colonialism: A Theoretical Overview*. Princeton: Markus Wiener Publishers.

Ray, Aniruddha. 2004. *The Merchant and the State: The French in India, 16661739*. New Delhi: Munshiram Manoharlal Publications.

Sen, S.P. 1947. *The French in India: First Establishment and Struggle*. Calcutta: University of Calcutta.

Verhoeven, Claudia. 2009. "Court Files." In *Reading Primary Sources: The Interpretation of Texts from Nineteenth- and Twentieth-Century History*, ed. Miriam Dobson, 90–105. London: Routledge.

Ziemann, Miriam and Benjamin Dobson. 2009. Reading Primary Sources - The Interpretation of Texts from Nineteenth and Twentieth Century History. London. New York: Routledge.

Visualising "State-Building" in European-Ottoman Diplomatic Relations

Visual Ceremonial Descriptions and Conflicting Concepts of Early Modern Governance in the Late Seventeenth and Early Eighteenth Centuries

Dorothee Linnemann

1 Introduction

When the French ambassador travelled to Constantinople in 1724, he was instructed by Louis XV to ensure that "the power of the Turks always remains an object of fear to the House of Austria" (Mansel 2002: 45). This strategic thought indicates, on the one hand, a highly affiliated process of clear division of inner-European political entities, and, on the other hand, a more or less defined border between a European alliance and the Ottoman Empire in the first half of the eighteenth century. That implies the interests of different European courts in political relations to the Ottoman Empire being strongly related to intense competition and differentiation of European governments, and the diplomatic European-Ottoman court relations taking part in this process. This article concentrates on the political and diplomatic contacts between the European courts and the Ottoman Empire, and their visual representation in European media in the late seventeenth and early eighteenth centuries because "the Ottoman Empire was not only a military power [...] it also ruled an area of immense economic and religious significance to Christian powers. Constantinople became one of the diplomatic capitals of Europe." (Mansel 1996: 44) Several studies have already recapitulated, in general, these close political, especially diplomatic relations between the Ottoman Empire and Europe (Coles 1968; Mansel 1996; Goffman 2002; Faroqhi 1999: esp. Chap. 7). The Ottoman Court at Constantinople was one important and central place of communications in the political process described by scholars as early modern European "state-building". Hence, in the following I will describe this process as a communicational one, strongly related to diplomatic practice and media coverage. The article will outline possibilities and practices of certain types of image production in early

---

D. Linnemann (✉)
Westfälische Wilhelms-Universität Münster, Domplatz 20-22, 48143 Münster, Germany
e-mail: dorothee.linnemann@uni-muenster.de

A. Flüchter and S. Richter (eds.), *Structures on the Move*,
Transcultural Research – Heidelberg Studies on Asia and Europe in a Global Context,
DOI 10.1007/978-3-642-19288-3_13, © Springer-Verlag Berlin Heidelberg 2012

modern European-Ottoman contacts, and most importantly, their functioning and efficacy in European court politics.

This close relation between politics and media, particularly visual media, in processes of construction of socio-political reality, of authorisation and legitimising power—especially with regard to the Ottoman-European diplomatic contacts in early modern history—has hitherto hardly been described by general European historical and art historical research. In fact, several studies of art history point out a strong connection between arts and the European "discovery" of the world, which touches as well upon the long-established relations to the Ottoman Empire (Boppe 1911; Cirakman 2001; Mansel 2002; Renda 2005; Nefedova 2009). Research in historical science during the last decade, in particular, as well as exemplary international exhibitions since the 1980s—which have been affected by ideas of the "cultural turn" and have tended to deal with certain topics of communication, the discourse on "identity", "alterity", and "hybridity", of geographical, ethnological, political etc. knowledge about the Ottoman Empire in Europe and vice versa— have underscored the current need for interdisciplinary studies (i.e. Sievernich and Budde 1989; Theunissen 1990; Saule 1999; Yapp 1992; Kafadar 1996: 614–625). But even now, historical research and art history research on Ottoman-European contacts in early modern times tend mostly to be divided into traditional historical fields of research, here politics as the central and most important component of society (i.e. state structures, administration, war, diplomacy, etc.), and there the arts (i.e. performative events like theatre or ceremonies, paintings and book-illustrations etc.) as decoration, potentially as instruments of politics, too (i.e. Coles 1968; Goffman 1990). Often these studies point out that the Ottoman Empire had an important impact on European politics, particularly after 1648, mainly because of its military power, its administrative progressiveness, and its economic power and trade monopoly. Arts and other media, if mentioned at all, are cited as secondary instruments, which informed a wide contemporary public about political "facts".[1] Rarely, however, does the question arise of how the media constructed and implemented images of "otherness" in "European society" (Windler 1997; Höfert 2003; Bisaha 2004).

The present article refers at this point to a general thesis: early modern European state-building is no predetermined reality between the classical dates 1648 and 1806. On the contrary, early modern European state-building is a communicational process in which the borders of a conglomerate of governments were negotiated and defined. And this negotiating was not an isolated process between the governments

---

[1] Notably, some German and Austrian historical research, until the end of the twentieth century, was affected by previous nationalist directions in the research of the early and mid-twentieth century, which led to a concentration on the history of the military and war between the Holy Roman Empire and the Ottoman Empire. This often implies a preconception of the image of the "Turks" as a non-Christian and martial antithesis, a preconception which influences the analysis of sources, even in art history, i.e. Bernhart (1915), Historisches Museum der Stadt Wien (1983); critical and progressive: Kurz (2005). For a survey of the literature see Gräf (2005).

inside the developing borders; rather it was a dynamic process of including and excluding of participants. The building of Europe as a state formation depends in this meaning on describing included as "equal" and excluded as "others". The Ottoman Empire was in this respect geographically and politically a perfect stage, and we have to consider the special impact of the media, especially "images", by way of this communicational process. Because European diplomacy played a decisive role in this process of early modern European "state-building", as I will point out in the first part of this article, I will concentrate on images of European-Ottoman diplomatic relations.

This will be discussed in two ways. First, owing to the lack of systematic studies on this subject, I will summarise small sections of current European research on visual media in the history of diplomacy and "state-building". Following this, I will use a communication methodology, the theory of the symbolic communication of cultural history, in particular, to examine the results in connection with the process of early modern European "state-building", analysing more concrete processes in relation to the historical actors responsible. Secondly, I will apply these methodological conclusions to examples of visual representation of European-Ottoman diplomacy, as one important field of image-production, approximately between the second half of the seventeenth century and the first half of the eighteenth century in relation to iconographical traditions and contemporary new artistic developments.

2 "State-Building" as a Communicational Process and its Relation to Early Modern European Art

In his contribution to the discussion of German historical research on early modern European "state-building", the historian Wolfgang Reinhard argues: "By definition, state-building is a top-down process, because it originates from, and is based upon, the interests of the people in the centre" (Reinhard 2009: 18). Research on early modern European "state-building" surely has to broaden its approach, away from concentrating on the ruler's acts, for example, to emphasising the adoption of mechanisms of dominance on the part of subjects.[2] Nevertheless, I agree with Reinhard that we still have to concentrate our research on the top-down process, and within this on the process of elite pooling in particular, because both have an outstanding impact and are, in a way, essential elements in European "state-building" in the seventeenth and eighteenth centuries (Black 1990; Reinhard 1999).

From this perspective, I will analyse early modern European "state-building", concentrating on the process of elite pooling, and especially on the formation of a

---

[2] For current research discussions on these different perspectives, see Antje Flüchter's introduction and Barbara Stollberg-Rilinger's article in this volume.

diplomatic elite, but from a viewpoint in which communicational theory takes centre stage. This theory essentially questions and deconstructs abstract, structural processes such as "state-building", and within this, in turn, institutions such as "diplomacy"—which seem to be unchangeable, naturalised, or stable developments cited as "facts". The view of the actors and their acts, which create and shape meaning, importance, authority and legitimisation, and as a result of this, world views and abstract structures, is placed at the centre (Stollberg-Rilinger 2009b). Diplomacy in this view, like other classical fields of historical research (warfare, peace treaties etc.), has to be understood as a socio-political institution which is communicationally created by the people, the media, and the public involved, through their acts, which, at the same time, give it its meaning. As Pierre Bourdieu has pointed out in his studies on rituals, symbolisation, and behaviour, this social practice of the construction and reception of socio-political hierarchies, status and institutions by means of symbolic acts is a performative strategy (Bourdieu 1982: Chap. 2). This perspective takes into account that the trigger for conflicts surrounding power and authority is to be found in people's actions, and, in early modern society, ceremonial, or, in a wider sense, symbolic acts. At European courts, ceremonial was used to construct, to demonstrate and to define the relationship of the ruler(s) to his/their subjects, to the members of court society, or to other rulers (Muir 2005; Stollberg-Rilinger 2000).

In the seventeenth century we find two important changes in ceremonial which refer especially to the process of early modern European "state-building" and the role of diplomacy within this process. First, in Europe, more and more actors were competing for authority. Within the framework of this change, favour and honour had to become more and more exactly measurable in terms of symbolic acts, and everybody who lived at a European court had to know this elaborated symbolic language (Roosen 1980; Bély 1993). As a result, the ancient European system of court relations, arranged as mostly isolated relationships between several courts, changed to a highly affiliated system of political participants, with a strong division between "sovereigns" and "non-sovereigns". And this "sovereignty" was contemporarily not a question of "states", but still an attribute of an individual person. Like former legitimisations of power—for example divine grace—"sovereignty", too, was strongly associated with the personal appearance of the ruler. This was constructed and demonstrated in the ceremonial. Thus, at the peace congress of Westphalia, for example, the diplomats had to claim and demonstrate the "sovereignty" of their rulers in the ceremonial, mostly by their official arrivals being accompanied by all other representatives of "sovereign" rulers. Within this ceremonial, the persons involved accepted each other as "sovereigns" and demonstrated their exclusiveness against other, excluded pretenders, who became, from that time on, "non-sovereign" (Bély 2000; Stollberg-Rilinger 2009a).

This leads to the second important change of ceremonial. Because of the fact that, from the end of the sixteenth century onward, diplomats increasingly took on the central function of representing the ruler (as a natural result of the rise of court administration from the end of the sixteenth century), to constitute, embody and heighten the ruler's rank in public, the focus of representation changed from an "authentic" face-to-face communication between rulers to indirect communications of representatives among each other, such as those mentioned in the example of the arrivals at the Westphalia Peace Congress. This initiated the formation of a European diplomatic elite from the end of the sixteenth century on.

Because of this political and administrative process, it is not surprising that since the end of the sixteenth century in Europe images of diplomatic acts were created systematically in large numbers, by the use of visual mimetic concepts that were mostly composed in a manner close to historical paintings, and, as formerly, the rulers' ceremonial was commemorated.[3] On this account, the relation of arts and politics in the development of the early modern European political constitution of "state-building" has become the subject of several current studies in the history of politics. They concentrate on an intra-European context, in which "state-building" has become visualised by media. These studies suggest that, from the Westphalia Peace Congress in 1648 on, the emerging European "state system" was directly visualised and represented in public, particularly by visual media presenting the European peace treaties, such as the famous painting of Gerard Ter Borch of the Spanish-Netherlands' Peace Treaty (Burkhardt 1998; Kaulbach 1997; Kettering 1998; Bussmann and Schilling 1998). These studies assert that such visual media are a representation of this new political constitution because of their "mimetic" and, through this, "authentic" character. These paintings and prints are all composed with close similarity to historical paintings, which means that interiors and actors, here the diplomats themselves, who are swearing the peace, are presented in a highly realistic manner. But these depictions of political institutional processes, in their media representations, as "truthful" historical sources of the political events as "facts" lead here to a self-referential system in such studies, and this is to be criticised.

Basically, we must describe such paintings in their (art) historical contexts. With this in mind, and in view of my topic of diplomacy in visual media, one should remember that, through their composition, all these visual media conceive these personal symbolic practices among political actors. They show the contemporary diplomatic ceremonials and their historical subjects. Therefore they must be analysed as visual ceremonial descriptions in relation to, and in the tradition of, contemporary ceremonial theory, practice and description with regard to diplomatic missions (Linnemann 2009). That offers wider possibilities of analysing media in early modern socio-political contexts, and we are able to take the visual media into account when analysing early modern European "state-building".

---

[3] Of course, visual media had already been used earlier, and commonly, to represent ceremonial acts in the form of historical paintings. Clearly, there is a strong connection between art and ceremonial, because of the contemporary belief in both kinds of communication basing their significance on aesthetic expression, and within this, their affect on the recipient. With the arrangement of space, decoration and time, the entire event was marked for contemporaries as a so-called "solemn" event, which means it was an extraordinary, juridically binding political act for all participants, and through the media this was represented to another public. For further reading, see Turner (1977), Rahn (2006).

We can discern a new quality of authorisation in politics and a change in the perception of political constitution and its legitimisation in the visualisations mentioned of peace treaties in late seventeenth—and eighteenth century Europe.[4] There is a noticeable increase in visual media containing mimetic composition schemes in the seventeenth century in political practice. That means that the events and actors, mostly the diplomats, are "entering on to the stage". The visual media suggest established political "facts", authorised by the evidence of eye-witnesses, in the compositions. A wider public than just those attending could participate in and anticipate the occasions, but was always confronted with a version coloured by intent, however realistically it manifested itself in the medium. The diplomats present themselves as the leading protagonists in the making of politics, which led consequently to the (self-)image of an exclusive diplomatic elite.

3 Diplomatic Publicity: Ottoman-European Political Relations in Paintings and Prints

On this account, it is clear that most of the visual media concerning diplomatic acts at the Ottoman Court were commissioned by the diplomatic elite themselves. But the reception of diplomatic Ottoman court ceremonial in the case of European diplomats in relation to their commemoration has rarely been analysed. Especially the art relations between Venice and the Ottoman Empire, shown through the paintings of Gentile Bellini or other Italian artists in the Renaissance, are central topics in various studies focusing on artistic developments, their stylistic characterisation, or their importance as objects of cultural transfer (Kangal 2000; Carboni 2007). Other artistic relations in the seventeenth century are only seldom mentioned, but there are various studies concerning particular cases of diplomats and their commissions of paintings and prints at Istanbul, or on their journey to the Ottoman Empire in the seventeenth century, a few cases of which are presented in the following. In contrast, the period which is important for the questions posed in this paper is strongly connected with one French artist, Jean-Baptiste Vanmour,

---

[4] We can also ascertain a change in the presentation of diplomatic practice at the peace treaties: not the oath—as yet a central ritual of peace-making—but the ratification of the treaties is shown more and more from 1700. The production and perception of this new representation concentrates increasingly on a more functionalised view of political acts, by focusing on political documents as the legitimisation of political systems, by reducing the diplomatic elite from their anciently representative aura to simple juridical functions, cf. Kaulbach (1997), Linnemann (2009). This last development is primarily an outcome of European visualisations of peace treaties, and is, for the most part, irrelevant for the discourse on European-Ottoman political contacts, because generally the court missions—also between European courts—were still referring to an anciently representative aura. Consequently, I would argue that European audiences and images of diplomacy were naturally varied, too, and adapted to different political contexts, e.g. the court public, diplomatic groups, or theoreticians of state; see Rahn (2006), Linnemann (2009).

who has been dealt with in various studies, who was the archetype for later artists such as Francesco Guardi or Antoine Watteau, and who contributed to the creation of an artistically homogeneous image of the "orient" (Bettagno 2002; Gopin 2002). Besides, printed copies after Vanmour's paintings—promptly incorporated in travelogues and costume books commissioned by diplomats for a European public—animated these painters to create an image without any self-awareness of the "orient" or the "Ottoman Empire" (Mansel 1996: 48; Renda 2005: 290; Boppe 1911: 188–277).

I shall now briefly present several of Vanmour's paintings and relate them, summarising current research, to their iconographical traditions. Was his artistic manner indeed so pioneering, or was it contemporary and typical style to imagine the Ottoman Court in the particular way Vanmour did? In 1699, the 28-year-old Flemish painter Vanmour arrived in Istanbul with a French delegation headed by the ambassador the Marquis de Ferriol. When this embassy left Istanbul, Vanmour stayed on and lived there for about 20 years. He built up his own workshop, and there he painted on behalf of different European embassies (Boppe 1911; Broos 1992; Gopin 1994). Today, we find in his œuvre these ceremonial paintings showing audiences, meals and a few of the ambassadors' arrivals. In these ceremonial paintings, apart from the landscapes or costumed figures, the main visual theme for every commission by a diplomat was the audience with the Sultan, as the painter's remaining œuvre, especially in the Rijksmuseum Amsterdam, illustrates (Luttervelt 1958: 5–18; Broos 1992). Count d'Andrezel, the permanent French ambassador in Istanbul who was appointed in 1724, for example, commissioned Vanmour to paint a picture of his official audience with the Sultan in that very year (Fig. 1). Besides the audience, Vanmour painted another typical ceremonial station

Fig. 1 Jean-Baptiste Vanmour. 1724. *The Sultan giving an audience to the French ambassador Count d'Andrezel in 1724*. 90 × 121 cm, oil on canvas. Musée des Beaux-Arts, Bordeaux/© bpk – Bildagentur für Kunst, Kultur und Geschichte

Fig. 2 Jean-Baptiste Vanmour. c. 1730. *The Sultan giving an audience to a diplomat.* 88 × 121 cm, oil on canvas. Rijksmuseum, Amsterdam

in the ritual of reception on behalf of d'Andrezel, the meal with the Grand Vizier before the audience with the Sultan.[5] The painting showing the audience is highly decorated, with distinctly composed interiors. The extraordinary main subject of the image, the Sultan in the left background, is enthroned on a raised platform beneath a canopy. Next to the Sultan, his children are standing to the left of him, and the grand vizier to the right. The latter is looking directly at the ambassador, who is standing on the right side of the painting, surrounded by court officials. The scene actually shows the moment at which the embassy has reached the Sultan's apartment. The persons are painted in a detailed manner; every member of the embassy can be identified from other portraits. Also, the costumes are painted very delicately and exactly. Count d'Andrezel wears a precious caftan, which was compulsory dress for every diplomatic audience with the Sultan. Diplomats like d'Andrezel often commissioned several scenes of the whole ceremony, but never forgot to have the audience appear as the highlight, for example, as did Cornelis Calkoen (Abelmann 1990) or the Venetian ambassador Francesco Gitti—who commissioned Vanmour to paint the largest series, most likely in 1725 (Nefedova 2009: 129, 137, ill. 133). Vanmour arranged all his ceremonial paintings with audiences, arrivals, or meals in the same manner, as paintings show that were commissioned by the Marquis de Bonnac, the predecessor of Count d'Andrezel in 1724 (Boppe 1911: 24–34, ill. 294), and by the Dutch ambassador Cornelis Calkoen in 1727 (Fig. 2).[6]

---

[5] Auguste Boppe first identified Vanmour as the painter of this series, cf. Boppe (1902). D'Andrezel passed the paintings on to his children who, impoverished, sold the art collection of their father to the Royal Collection. In 1803, the paintings were brought to Bordeaux, cf. Museum für Kunsthandwerk (1985: 192, No. I/4), Archives de la ville Marseille (1982: 198f).

[6] The second illustration presents, in typical style, Sultan Ahmed III giving an audience to an unknown ambassador. The painting was brought to the Netherlands as part of the collection of the

As the ceremonies proceeded according to a strict ritual, it is not surprising that the resulting paintings are largely formulaic. In this regard, Marianne Broos sums up: "The procedure of the receptions was arranged by a very strict and traditional protocol which had not changed for centuries. [...] The importance of the reception paintings by Vanmour lies in the fact that he formalised the genre. [...] The compositions are put together in the same way, only with different ambassadors and numbers of delegates. Some authors see this as a proof of Vanmour's lack of talent and technique. I would argue that this is a sign for the immutability of the Ottoman ceremony and of the taste of his customers" (Broos 2002: 180).

I would argue, in addition to this, and with reference to the perspective of symbolic communication, that the paintings themselves standardised the ceremonial for the recipients, constituting a kind of scale of socio-political relation by their very realism, especially by their perspective of the "eye-witness" (Burke 2001). Most remarkable, however, is the fact that none of the images shows an ambassador demonstrating respect for the Sultan, for example, when a prostration or a bow was necessary, or the ambassador had to kiss the Sultan's vestments. Every ambassador is depicted standing to the right of the Sultan, either before or after demonstrating his respect for the monarch. Of course, the highlight of every diplomatic mission to the Ottoman Court was the audience in the Topkapi Serayi in Istanbul, where the total success of the mission was at stake (Burschel 2007; Selveni 2005).

In a way, the large number of paintings from 1700 until the end of the eighteenth century shows the political rivalry between the diplomats as the commissioners of these paintings. It was a necessary consequence of the European rivalry, and—almost—of the very calm atmosphere in European-Ottoman relations after 1683, when the Ottoman armies besieging Vienna were defeated. "Ambassadors now obtained rights which were inacceptable for the Ottoman Empire before: Especially they gained a victory concerning their audiences in the Sultan's throne room: most ambassadors henceforth stood firm when their escorts tried to make them prostrate themselves before the Sultan, 'and keep themselves upright with all their strength'" (Mansel 1996: 107). It is thus not surprising that most of the images show this scene, but without any conflict and with little connotation of the exotic.

There was no interest in focusing on cultural or political misunderstandings, conflicts or frontiers in this type of representation. Consequently, the ambassadors could present themselves in an important symbolic act demonstrating superiority, and create a successful image and self-description, besides the more detailed textual descriptions. The outcome of this is that, apart from Vanmour, other contemporary painters from the 1750s on continually painted and etched the same ceremonial topics, although in varying compositions. While Venetian embassies commissioned paintings in the compositional tradition of Vanmour, French embassies commissioned painters such as Antoine de Favray, who created "close-ups" of Vanmour's

---

Dutch ambassador Cornelis Calkoen. His nephew Nicolaas bequeathed the painting in 1817 to the directorate of the Levant Trade Company in Amsterdam; cf. Gopin (1994).

Fig. 3 Robert Pranker after Francis Smith. c. 1764. *The Sultan giving an audience to a British ambassador*. 39.2 × 48 cm, engraving. National Portrait Gallery, London

compositions (Broos 2002: 182 ff.). For example, the French diplomat de Vergennes commissioned de Favray to do two paintings and gouaches (Sotheby's 1996). British embassies referred to earlier iconographical traditions, above all watercolour paintings and etchings of the late seventeenth century. This is shown by Francis Smith's watercolour paintings of diplomatic audiences at the Ottoman Court around 1750, which were promptly copied by the engraver Robert Pranker in London (Fig. 3) (Nefedova 2009: 162, ill. 157 and 158).

The iconographical tradition of this varied composition lies in the image production from the middle of the seventeenth century onward, which was mostly commissioned by Imperial diplomats. Of course, these diplomatic missions attracted attention in illustrated travelogues from the middle of the sixteenth century, and were also depicted in paintings from the middle of the seventeenth century—as a portrait of the Count of Schwarzenhorn shows (Fig. 4). In the background of the painting, we see on the right the depiction of Schwarzenhorn's audience with the Ottoman Sultan in 1651; this is an early prototype of Vanmour's later paintings. Early archetypes for the watercolour series of the mid-eighteenth century are, for example, the largest series of ceremonial paintings in the seventeenth century, which were commissioned by the Imperial diplomat Hans von Kuefstein in 1628, and which were also painted as preparatory gouache studies (Fig. 5) (Teply 1976: 58–109, ill. 112–135), or the pen drawings of Zacharias Wehme, commissioned by the Saxonian court at the end of the sixteenth century (Schnitzer 1995).

Visualising "State-Building" in European-Ottoman Diplomatic Relations

Fig. 4 Hieronimus Joachims. 1651. *Johann Rudolf Schmid Freiherr von Schwarzenhorn and his visit to the Sultan in 1651*. 67.7 × 83 cm, oil on copperplate. Sammlungen des Fürsten von und zu Liechtenstein, Vaduz – Wien

Fig. 5 Franz Hörmann, Hans Gemminger, Valentin Müller (attr.), *The Sultan receives the Imperial ambassador Hans von Kuefstein in 1628*. 26.4 × 39.3 cm, gouache on parchment. Osmanenmuseum Perchtoldsdorf

The increasing translation of this cultural contact into etchings and paintings by artists and printmakers created these new modes of expression, but they never had such a systematic impact as did later, comparable paintings in the period around 1700–1750. Paintings at this time were more systematically used for forming a distinct diplomatic identity to distinguish the diplomatic elite from other nobles at court and the court administration. In the course of this process, European competition for "sovereignty" was increased and exacerbated, so that everybody wanting to take part in this game had to have himself represented by European court media as in good standing with the superior Ottoman Empire, a situation constituted due to ceremonial.

This self-image of the diplomatic elite is a trans-European one, and is focused on the same social and political opportunities of its members (court dynasties, social and material success, ennoblement etc.). And it agrees with the self-image of their rulers to present themselves as "sovereign", the head of a socio-politically and territorially closed governmental sphere. The visual representations were carefully chosen to reach different kinds of public. Most of the paintings were presented in the courtly or ambassadorial art collections, while some paintings were systematically copied for the print market. That forced the division between an informational sphere of the diplomatic elite and that of other types of informed public (cf. Watanabe-O'Kelly 1995; Kaenel and Reichardt 2007; Schlögl 2008: esp. 614). The art collection of Cornelis Calkoen, Liechtenstein's art collection, or the one belonging to Ludwig von Kuefstein are famous examples of such a well-directed use (Broos 2002; Baumstark et al. 1990; Teply 1976).

The rivalry between the European rulers was also created and expressed by diplomatic ceremonial and its pictorial representation, when Ottoman embassies, which appeared rather rarely throughout the seventeenth and up to the middle of the eighteenth centuries, arrived at European courts. The self-proclaimed status of the French king as the most powerful of the "sovereigns" was thus demonstrated through court paintings, both in the reign of Louis XIV and that of Louis XV (Saule 1999; Hochedlinger 1994). Both commissioned various paintings with compositions in a historical, realistic style, which represented the glorious ceremonies of European and non-European diplomatic missions (Saule 1999; Hochedlinger 1994). Louis XV, in particular, commissioned paintings with regard to the Ottoman diplomatic missions at his court. In 1720, the court painter Charles Parrocel painted two pictures in panel format showing the Ottoman embassy arriving in the Tuileries in front of the Louvre, of which one was presented at the Parisian Salon in the late 1720s as a symbol of the king's glory (Fig. 6) (Nefedova 2009: 40; Clements 1996). For the same diplomatic occasion, Pierre Denis Martin, also a French court-painter, was commissioned to paint the departure of the embassy after the audience (Saule 1999: 256, ill. ibid.). There is no hint that a painting of the audience scene itself was commissioned in this year or after—while in 1742, when the next glorious Ottoman embassy arrived, such an audience scene was commissioned, although it was not finished as a painting, but as a pen drawing by Charles-Nicolas Cochin the Younger (Foster 2001: esp. 263, ill. 3). In the paintings of the meeting in 1720 we cannot find any demonstration of symbolic acts between the two sides—maybe Louis XV tried to prevent a comparison with his first meeting with an Ottoman embassy following the death of his predecessor. Nevertheless, the paintings show the architectural centre of the king's power, the Louvre—even without any of the personal contact. And, as in the paintings of the European-Ottoman audiences in Istanbul, the less negatively connoted "exotic

Fig. 6 Charles Parrocel. Second quarter of the eighteenth century. *The arrival of the Ottoman ambassador at the Tuileries in Paris 1721*. 228 × 329 cm, oil on canvas. Musée national du Château de Versailles et de Trianon, Versailles/© bpk – Bildagentur für Kunst, Kultur und Geschichte

strangeness" of the Ottomans, evoked mainly through the vestments, the horses' trappings, and the interiors, is part of a strategy to display this event as extraordinary and unrivalled.

However, this visual strategy can easily be compared, as a shared visual concept, with other visual compositions of the presentation of diplomatic credentials or arrivals at European Courts, for example, that of the Polish ambassador Jerzy Ossolinsky in Rome in 1633, sketched by the Italian artist Stefano della Bella 1633, which was, a century later, painted by Bernardo Belotto for the Polish king (Ilg 2003; Łukaszewicz 2006: 146). Like the visual ceremonial description of European-Ottoman diplomatic contacts, Polish or Russian embassies were also connected with exotic "strangeness", mostly to underline their role as relative outsiders in the European court system.[7] I would agree with Helge Vogel: "What was additionally symbolic and emblematic was used to indicate specific, individual characteristics of the subject and place them in an appropriate historical context or local expressions of style. However, the exotic, oriental elements of depictions amounted to nothing more than an ethnographic interest for picturesque display of Turkish court dress with its conspicuous turbans, decorative feather trimmings, pearls, and other garments with its required accessories and accoutrements such as: sabres, various foreign weapons indicating their social rank that were very comparable to representations in the West" (Vogel 2007: 157).

---

[7] These cases show the need for research which analyses the differentiated strategic system of creating "identities" and "alterities" among the Courts in Europe, particularly by means of media, cf. Kugler et al. (2006).

Fig. 7 Johann David Schleuen. 1763. *The arrival of the Ottoman ambassador in Berlin in 1763.* 14.24 × 38.08 cm, engraving. Staatsbibliothek zu Berlin – Preußischer Kulturbesitz, Handschriftenabteilung, Berlin

Such a visual strategy was used very systematically and became more and more standardised. This can be shown with one last example, the Prussian princely dynasty. They tried to legitimise and demonstrate their kingship, and primarily their "sovereignty", of course, by using visual media, too (Fig. 7). For instance, Frederick I of Prussia had to struggle hard to be granted the same ceremonial order as other European kings, at least in their eyes. For this reason he demonstrated his claimed status at his coronation in 1701 in an exaggerated fashion, as well as by diplomatic missions to other courts, and not least also by the use of media (Stollberg-Rilinger 2002). These attempts to raise his own rank, and that of the dynasty, and be "sovereign" were also strongly connected to the reception of Ottoman embassies. Consequently, in 1763 Frederick II received the first Ottoman embassy in Prussia (Theilig 2008). Diplomatic relations had already existed for some decades, but in 1763, after the peace of Hubertusburg, the confirmation of Prussia's territorial borders and its acceptance as a sovereign power in Europe, the public representation of diplomatic relations with the Ottoman Empire marked one of the highlights in this process. In this situation, the ceremonial was of the greatest importance, as Frederick II wrote to his minister Finckenstein. They thus informed themselves by examining all ceremonial protocols about Ottoman missions to European courts which the Prussian administration could obtain (Volz 1907: 11). Correspondingly, visual and textual media were used to demonstrate this particular claim, expressed in the ceremonial (Theilig 2008: 147–157): the solemn arrival of the Ottoman ambassador in November 1763 was reported in printed broadsheets, accompanied by textual explanations for a wider public.

4 Summary: Early Modern European "State-Building" from the Perspective of Diplomatic Ceremonial and its Visualisations

How can the classically described period of early modern European "state-building" between the second half of the seventeenth century and the first half of the eighteenth century be perceptively rotated in relation to the European-Ottoman contacts and their media transformation? Within this period we can assume that an increasing and excessive use of visual media was established to legitimise and interpret the relations between the European powers as a "conglomerate of states", especially by way of their relations to the more foreign countries, e.g. the Ottoman Empire. On this abstract process of "state-building" by elite coercion and closure of political frontiers a naturalised character was bestowed by visual media, owing to their credible strategy of depicting ancient diplomatic ceremonial from the viewpoint of an eye-witness. From a theoretical perspective, this also means that "state-building" consists, above all, of communicative acts of an emerging political elite, particularly the diplomatic elite.

So which special part was enacted by the government of the Ottoman Empire in this process? In the images of political-diplomatic ceremonial acts, particularly arrivals and audiences of the European Diplomats at the Ottoman Court, the Ottoman political system was used as a mirror. It was a very important and increasingly standardised foil for the European diplomatic struggle over "sovereignty", because of its known "otherness". The visualisations of Ottoman embassies in Europe offered a chance, within this European competition, to claim and demonstrate one's own rank and status, as shown by the example of Louis XV of France or Frederick II of Prussia. But it was mainly the diplomats themselves who presented continuously their glorious mission at home to advance their own careers, and those of their family members, at court (Hobhous 1988: esp. 11).

In these instrumentalisations of visual media and their circulation, the separation of political elites, in particular the separation of a diplomatic elite and its self-image as participant in a "state corps", was constructed and made visible. In so doing, this production of images was part of the formation of the diplomatic elite which produced increasingly standardised images of European diplomacy and political representation. This was the main reason for the large number of such paintings, and I conclude, in agreement with Philip Mansel, that "the power of the Ottoman Sultan, the allure of his capital and ambassadors' desire for commemoration, were not only reasons why so many ambassadors commissioned pictures. Other capitals such as Madrid, Vienna and Rome were exotic and imposing between 1703 and 1741—at the same time as Vanmour was working in Constantinople—Carlevarijs, Joli, Richter and Canaletto painted spectacular ceremonial pictures of ambassadors arriving by gilded barge at the Doge's Palace in Venice" (Mansel 1996: 49).

In all this, the Ottoman Empire's "otherness" was seldom mentioned and obviously used primarily to show the glory and exclusivity of the European diplomat's own mission, which was a non-recurring attribute of these paintings, as opposed to others showing the diplomatic ceremonial between European courts. It must be said that diplomatic relations with a country like the Ottoman Empire, which was characterised by the image of a more or less common "otherness" in Europe, thus stressed the image of nearness to European conventions. However, the analysis of these diplomatic ceremonial paintings does not lead to the conclusion that a better and more positive view of the Ottoman Empire was to be found in diplomatic circles than in the European general public, a view which was, for example, expressed in paintings and prints; in the seventeenth century, these presented images of military confrontations with the "unholy Ottomans", from the beginning of the eighteenth, with the lassitude of odalisques or eye-catching spectacles in travelogues or prints. Within the different contemporary European perspectives on Ottoman government, the diplomatic one was not the more serious, but an outstanding, deliberated political strategy in the process of early modern European "state-building".

Bibliography

Abelmann, Annelies. 1990. "Cornelis Calkoen op audiëntie bij sultan Ahmed III." In *Topkapi & Turkomanie. Turks-Nederlandse ontmoetingen sinds 1600.* ed. Hans Theunissen, 26–36. Amsterdam: De Bataafsche Leeuw.

Archives de la ville Marseille. 1982. *L'Orient des Provençaux dans l'histoire. Marseilles:* Imprimerie Municipale.

Baumstark, Reinhold et al. (eds.). 1990. *Joseph Wenzel von Liechtenstein. Fürst und Diplomat im Europa des 18. Jahrhunderts.* Einsiedeln: Eidolon.

Bély, Lucien. 1993. "Souveraineté et souverain. La question du cérémonial dans les relations internationales à l'époque modern." *Annuaire-Bulletin de la Société de l'Histoire de France:* 27–43.

Bély, Lucien (ed.). 2000. *L'Europe des traités de Westphalie. Esprit de la diplomatie et diplomatie de l'esprit.* Paris: Presses Universitaires de France, vol. 106.

Bernhart, Max. 1915. "Die Türken im Wandel des historischen Urteils." *Monatshefte für Kunstwissenschaft* 8: 69–80.

Bettagno, Alessandro (ed.). 2002. *I Guardi. Vedute, capricci, feste, disegni e "quadric turcheschi".* Venice: Fondazione Giorgio Cini.

Bisaha, Nancy. 2004. *Creating East and West. Renaissance Humanists and the Ottoman Turks.* Philadelphia: University of Pennsylvania Press.

Black, Jeremy. 1990. "Essay and Reflections: On the "Old System" and the "Diplomatic Revolution" of the Eighteenth Century." *The International History Review* 12: 301–323.

Boppe, Auguste. 1902. "Les deux Tableaux "Turcs" du Musée de Bordeaux." *Revue Philomathique de Bordeaux et du Sud-Ouest* 5: 3–11.

Boppe, Auguste. 1911. *Les peintres du Bosphore au XVIIIᵉ siècle.* Paris: Hachette.

Bourdieu, Pierre. 1982. *Ce que parler veut dire. L'économie des échanges linguistiques.* Paris: Librairie Arthème Fayard.

Broos, Marianne. 1992. *De audiëntietaferelen van Jean-Baptiste Vanmour (1671–1737) in Constantinopel.* Rosendal/State University of Leiden (unpublished).

Broos, Marianne. 2002. "Paintings of Receptions of the Ambassadors at the Sublime Porte by Jean-Baptiste Vanmour (1671–1737) and their Influence in Constantinople and Venice." In: *I Guardi. Vedute, capricci, feste, disegni e "quadric turcheschi"*, ed. A. Bettagno, 179–185. Venice: Fondazione Giorgio Cini.

Burke, Peter. 2001. *Eyewitnessing: The Uses of Images as Historical Evidence*. Ithaca: Cornell University Press.

Burkhardt, Johannes. 1998. "Auf dem Weg zu einer Bildkultur des Staatensystems. Der Westfälische Frieden und die Druckmedien." In: *Der Westfälische Friede. Diplomatie – politische Zäsur – kulturelles Umfeld – Rezeptionsgeschichte*, ed. Heinz Duchhardt, 81–114. Vienna, Munich: R. Oldenbourg Verlag.

Burschel, Peter. 2007. "Der Sultan und das Hündchen. Zur politischen Ökonomie des Schenkens in interkultureller Perspektive." *Historische Anthropologie* 15: 408–421.

Bussmann, Klaus and Heinz Schilling (eds.). 1998. *1648 – Krieg und Frieden in Europa*. Münster: Veranstaltungsgesellschaft 350Jahre Westfälischer Friede, vol. 3.

Carboni, Stefano (ed.). 2007. *Venezia e l'Islam 828–1797*. Venice: Marsilio.

Cirakman, Asli. 2001. "From Tyranny to Despotism: The Enlightenment's Unenlighted Image of the Turks." *International Journal of Middle East Studies* 33: 49–68.

Clements, Candace. 1996. "The Duc d'Antin, the Royal Administration of Pictures, and the Painting Competitions of 1727." *The Art Bulletin* 78: 647–662.

Coles, Paul. 1968. *The Ottoman Impact on Europe*. London: Harcourt, Brace & World, Inc.

Faroqhi, Suraiya. 1999. *Approaching Ottoman history. An introduction to the sources*. Cambridge: Cambridge University Press.

Foster, Carter E. 2001. "Charles-Nicolas Cochin and Festival Design for the Menus-Plaisirs." *Master Drawings* 39: 260–278.

Goffman, Daniel. 1990. *Izmir and the Levantine World, 1550–1650*. Seattle: University of Washington Press.

Goffman, Daniel. 2002. *The Ottoman Empire and Early Modern Europe*. Cambridge: Cambridge University Press.

Gopin, Seth. 1994. *Jean-Baptiste Vanmour. Painter of Turqueries*. Rutgers/State University of New Jersey (unpublished).

Gopin, Seth. 2002. "The Influence of Jean-Baptiste Vanmour." In *I Guardi. Vedute, capricci, feste, disegni e "quadric turcheschi"*, ed. A. Bettagno, 153–163. Venice: Fondazione Giorgio Cini.

Gräf, Holger Th. 2005. "„Erbfeind der Christenheit" oder potentieller Bündnispartner? Das Osmanenreich im europäischen Mächtesystem des 16. und 17. Jahrhunderts – gegenwartspolitisch betrachtet." In *Das Osmanische Reich und die Habsburgermonarchie*, ed. Marlene Kurz et al., 37–51. Wien, München: R. Oldenbourg Verlag.

Historisches Museum der Stadt Wien. 1983. *Die Türken vor Wien. Europa und die Entscheidung an der Donau 1683*. Wien: Österreichischer Bundesverlag.

Hobhous, Neil (ed.). 1988. *At the Sublime Porte. Ambassadors to the Ottoman Empire (1550–1800)*. London: Hazlitt, Gooden & Fox.

Hochedlinger, Michael. 1994. "Die französisch-osmanische "Freundschaft" 1525–1792. Element antihabsburgischer Politik, Gleichgewichtsinstrument, Prestigeunternehmung – Aufriß eines Problems." *Mitteilungen des Instituts für Österreichische Geschichte* 102: 108–164.

Höfert, Almut. 2003. *Den Feind beschreiben. "Türkengefahr" und europäisches Wissen über das Osmanische Reich 1450–1600*. Frankfurt (Main): Campus Verlag.

Ilg, Ulrike. 2003. "Stefano della Bella and Melchior Lorck: The Practical Use of an Artists' Model Book." *Master Drawings* 41: 30–43.

Kaenel, Philippe and Rolf Reichardt (eds.). 2007. *Interkulturelle Kommunikation in der europäischen Druckgraphik im 18. und 19. Jahrhundert*. Hildesheim: Olms.

Kafadar, Cemal. 1996. "The Ottomans and Europe." In *Handbook of European history, 1400–1600. Late Middle Ages, Renaissance, and Reformation*, ed. Thomas A. Brady et al., vol. 2, 589–636. Leiden: Brill.

Kangal, Selmin (ed.). 2000. *The Sultan's Portrait: Picturing the House of Osman*. Istanbul: Türkiye İş Bankası Kültür Yayınları.

Kaulbach, Hans-Martin. 1997. "Zur Ikonographie von Friedenskonzepten vor und nach 1648." *De zeventiende eeuw*: 323–334.

Kettering, Alison M. 1998. *Gerard Ter Borch and the Treaty of Münster*. Zwolle: Waanders Publishers.

Kugler, Heidrun et al. 2006. "Einführung." In *Internationale Beziehungen in der Frühen Neuzeit*, ed. Heidrun Kugler et al,, 21–33. Hamburg: LIT Verlag.

Kurz, Marlene et al. (eds.). 2005. *Das Osmanische Reich und die Habsburgermonarchie*. Wien, München: R. Oldenbourg Verlag.

Linnemann, Dorothee. 2009. "Die Bildlichkeit von Friedenskongressen des 17. und frühen 18. Jahrhunderts im Kontext zeitgenössischer Zeremonialdarstellungen und diplomatischer Praxis." In *Diplomatisches Zeremoniell in Europa und im Mittleren Osten in der frühen Neuzeit*, ed. Ralph Kauz et al., 155–186. Wien: Verlag der Österreichischen Akademie der Wissenschaften.

Van Luttervelt, Remmet. 1958. *De "Turkse" schilderijen van J.-B. Vanmour en zijn school. De verzameling van Cornelis Calkoen, ambassadeur bij de Hoge Porte, 1725–1743*. Istanbul: Nederlands Historisch-Archaeologisch Institut.

Łukaszewicz, Piotr (ed.). 2006. *Die Blume Europas. Meisterwerke aus dem Nationalmuseum Breslau (Wrocław)*. Wolfratshausen: Minerva.

Mansel, Philip. 1996. *Constantinople. City of the World's Desire 1453–1924*. New York: John Murray General Publishing Division.

Mansel, Philip. 2002. "Art and Diplomacy in Ottoman Constantinople." *History Today* 46: 43–49.

Muir, Edward. 2005 (2nd edition). *Ritual in Early Modern Europe*. Cambridge: Cambridge University Press.

Museum für Kunsthandwerk. 1985. *Türkische Kunst und Kultur aus osmanischer Zeit*. Recklinghausen: Bongers, vol. 1.

Nefedova, Olga. 2009. *A journey into the world of the Ottomans. The art of Jean-Baptiste Vanmour (1671–1737)*. Milan: Skira Editore.

Rahn, Thomas. 2006. "Sinnbild und Sinnlichkeit. Probleme der zeremoniellen Zeichenstrategie und ihre Bewältigung in der Festpublizistik." In *Zeichen und Raum*, ed. Peter-Michael Hahn and Ulrich Schütte, 39–48, München: Deutscher Kunstverlag.

Reinhard, Wolfgang. 1999. *Verstaatlichung der Welt? Europäische Staatsmodelle und außereuropäische Machtprozesse*. Wien, München: R. Oldenbourg Verlag.

Reinhard, Wolfgang. 2009. "No Statebuilding from Below! A Critical Commentary." In *Empowering interactions. Political cultures and the emergence of the state in Europe, 1300–1900*, ed. Pieter W. Blockmans et al., 299–312. Farnham [u.a]: Ashate.

Renda, Günsel. 2005. "The Ottoman Empire and Europe. Cultural Encounters." In *Cultural Contacts in Building a Universal Civilisation*, ed. Ekmeleddin İhsanoğlu, 277–303. Istanbul: Research Centre for Islamic History, Art and Culture.

Roosen, William.1980. "Early Modern Diplomatic Ceremonial: A System Approach." *Journal of Modern History* 52: 452–476.

Saule, Béatrix (ed.). 1999. *Topkapi à Versailles. Trésors de la cour ottomane*. Paris: Réunion des Musées Nationaux.

Schlögl, Rudolf. 2008. "Politik beobachten. Öffentlichkeit und Medien in der Frühen Neuzeit." *Zeitschrift für historische Forschung* 35: 581–616.

Schnitzer, Claudia. 1995. "Ein "Spionagebericht in Bildern" aus Istanbul. Das Ungnadsche Türkenbuch und seine Kopie von Zacharias Wehme." *Dresdner Kunstblätter* 39: 98–105.

Selveni, Bart. 2005. "Representation and Self-Consciousness in 16th century Habsburg Diplomacy in the Ottoman Empire." In *Das Osmanische Reich und die Habsburgermonarchie*, ed. M. Kurz et al., 281–294. Wien, München: R. Oldenbourg Verlag.

Sievernich, Gereon and Hendrik Budde (eds.). 1989. *Europa und der Orient 800–1900*. Berlin: Bertelsmann Lexikon Verlag.

Sotheby's. 1996. *The Turkish Sale. Auction: Friday, 11 October, 1996*. London, Lot 232.

Stollberg-Rilinger, Barbara. 2000. "Zeremoniell, Ritual, Symbol. Neue Forschungen zur symbolischen Kommunikation in Spätmittelalter und Früher Neuzeit." *Zeitschrift für Historische Forschungen* 27: 389–403.

Stollberg-Rilinger, Barbara. 2002. "Honores regii. Die Königswürde im zeremoniellen Zeichensystem der Frühen Neuzeit." In *Dreihundert Jahre Preußische Königskrönung*, ed. Johannes Kunisch, 1–26. Berlin: Duncker & Humblot.

Stollberg-Rilinger, Barbara. 2009. "The Impact of Communication Theory on the Analysis of the Early Modern State-Building Processes." In *Empowering interactions. Political cultures and the emergence of the state in Europe, 1300–1900*, ed. P.W. Blockmans et al., 313–326. Farnham: Ashgate.

Stollberg-Rilinger, Barbara 2009[a]. "Völkerrechtlicher Status und zeremonielle Praxis auf dem westfälischen Friedenskongress." In *Rechtsformen internationaler Politik. Theorie, Norm und Praxis vom 12. bis zum 18. Jahrhundert*, ed. Martin Kintzinger and Michael Jucker, 20 pages. (in press). Berlin: Duncker & Humblot.

Teply, Karl. 1976. *Die kaiserliche Großbotschaft an Sultan Murad IV. 1628. Des Freiherrn Hans Ludwig von Kuefsteins Fahrt zur Hohen Pforte*. Wien: Schendl.

Theilig, Stephan. 2008. "Die erste osmanische Gesandtschaft in Berlin 1763/64: Interkulturalität und Medienereignis." In *Europäische Wahrnehmungen 1650–1850. Interkulturelle Kommunikation und Medienereignisse*, ed. Joachim Eibach and Horst Carl, 131–160. Hannover: Wehrhahn.

Theunissen, Hans (ed.). 1990. *Topkapi & Turkomanie. Turks-Nederlandse ontmoetingen sinds 1600*. Amsterdam: De Bataafsche Leeuw.

Turner, Victor W. 1977. "Variations on a Theme of Liminality." In *Secular Ritual*, ed. Sally Falk Moore and Barbara G. Myerhoff, 36–52. Assen: Van Gorcum.

Vogel, Gerd Helge. 2007. "In the Splendour of the Half-moon: Turqueries in European Art During the Enlightenment. A Significant Example of Dialogues Between Cultures." *International Yearbook of Aesthetics* 11: 154–193.

Volz, Gustav Berthold. 1907. "Eine türkische Gesandtschaft am Hofe Friedrichs des Großen im Winter 1763/64." *Hohenzollern-Jahrbuch* 11: 17–54.

Watanabe-O'Kelly, Helen 1995. "Firework Plays, Firework Dramas and Illuminations – Precursors of Cinema?" *German Life and Letters* 48: 338–352.

Windler, Christian. 1997. "Normen aushandeln. Die französische Diplomatie und der muslimische „Andere" (1700–1840). "*Ius Commune* 14: 171–210.

Yapp, Malcolm E. 1992. "Europe in the Turkish Mirror." *Past & Present* 137: 134–155.

The Consequences of Early Modern Diplomacy: Entanglement, Discrimination, Mutual Ignorance—and State Building

Christian Wieland

1 The Development of an Ambassadorial System in Early Modern Europe

From the Renaissance onwards, in the south of Europe "states"—if the entities under consideration merit this somewhat anachronistic label—began to exchange mutual and stable embassies with each other; it was one of the defining and genuinely "modern" features of the late fifteenth and early sixteenth centuries, if we are to believe Jacob Burckhardt, Garret Mattingly, and Donald Queller, each in his way a doyen of Renaissance history whose judgements have proved to be very influential and persistent up to the present day (Watkins 2008: 2). The tradition of *ad-hoc* legations, on the other hand, was by no means an invention of the city-states of Renaissance Italy; this diplomatic practice had its roots in the culture of antiquity, and it was continued throughout the whole of the medieval period, in order to exchange congratulatory messages, to sign peace treaties, to arrange dynastic marriages etc. But the development of a true diplomatic "system" was definitely something new, not only in that embassies changed from short-term events to permanent institutions (Frigo 2008: 15), but also inasmuch as the group of entities which participated in this very specific sort of indirect communication—those who were allowed to express themselves in a diplomatic way and who were addressed diplomatically by others—was increasingly restricted to the sovereigns of the European power system (Roosen 1980: 458–461; Frigo 2008: 15, 26–27; Krischer 2007: 3–10). As far as the beginning of the Early Modern age is concerned, it is not easy to distinguish between the person—normally the monarch—and his territory—the state (Roosen 1980: 455, 462); both could be considered "sovereigns" (Roosen 1980: 459). But whether a concrete human being or an

---

C. Wieland (✉)
Institut für Geschichte, Neuere und Neueste Geschichte, Technische Universität Darmstadt,
Residenzschloß, 64283 Darmstadt, Germany
e-mail: wieland@pg.tu-darmstadt.de

A. Flüchter and S. Richter (eds.), *Structures on the Move*, 271
Transcultural Research – Heidelberg Studies on Asia and Europe in a Global Context,
DOI 10.1007/978-3-642-19288-3_14, © Springer-Verlag Berlin Heidelberg 2012

abstract entity—only sovereigns were allowed to send and to receive permanent diplomats; only those who participated in the ambassadorial system were considered sovereigns by others. The claim to the right of calling one's representatives "ambassadors" was not only a matter of ceremony; it was also, indeed mainly, a vital question of political and legal status.[1]

While diplomacy became an important and increasingly institutionalised factor of statehood, the practice of "doing diplomacy" underwent a process of professionalisation (De Franceschi 2008: 196). Instead of being a momentary interruption of one's ordinary task as a courtier or a magistrate—however glamorous and honourable the membership in such a legation might have been—it became a long-term occupation, although, at least during the fifteenth-seventeenth centuries, the office of ambassador relatively often served as an interlude between several administrative and courtly career steps.[2]

What was to become the diplomacy of Early Modern Europe did not originate only in Italy; and even within the Italian peninsula, it was not just the city republics which were the forerunners of modernity. More often than not, it was not the republics as such that sent and received diplomatic envoys, but their leading families (notably the Medici of fifteenth-century Florence), thereby consciously transcending the boundaries between the public and the private.[3] Ancient and more recent principalities, established and modern dynasties,[4] Venice (Watkins 2008: 3) and, most remarkably, the popes, they all contributed to shaping a network of professional diplomats throughout the whole of Europe. The curia's nuncios, who represented the interests of the pope, the papal state, and the Catholic Church in Italy and at the most important courts of Catholic Europe, could be considered the avant-garde of modern diplomacy. In the course of the sixteenth and seventeenth centuries, the diplomatic network covered most of southern, western and even northern Europe; this network was, at least in part, characterised by confessional patterns, though it was by no means determined by religion. The fact that states did not share the same interpretation of the Christian faith might have complicated diplomatic practice, but it did not preclude diplomatic relations. In this respect, the curia—although the nunciaturae were much more formalised and professionalised than most embassies of the secular monarchies—must be considered an exception,

---

[1] Krischer 2007: 8. In the Early Modern period, the question of sovereignty was always highly controversial and the respective degrees of sovereignty accorded to the actors of the international game varied to a great measure; the free imperial cities of the Holy Roman Empire managed to participate in the Empire's ambassadorial system without ever really achieving the same extent of liberty, nobility and sovereignty as other estates of the Empire. Cf. Krischer (2007: passim.)

[2] For the Early Modern differentiation between the offices of diplomat and courtier, cf. Powell (2005: 416); Watkins (2008: 9).

[3] In so far as participation in the diplomatic game was most important for the strengthening of the prince's (or would-be prince's) acceptance in his own country; by gaining acceptance by other sovereigns, he ensured his supremacy at home. Cf. Roosen (1980: 473–474).

[4] For the weight given to diplomatic ceremonial by the house of Savoy, cf. Roosen (1980: 463–464).

The Consequences of Early Modern Diplomacy 273

rather than a rule, in view of the fact that the popes' diplomatic contacts were strictly limited to Catholic countries.

Eastern Europe, on the other hand, and non-European countries never really became part of this closely woven diplomatic network; there existed diplomatic contacts between European monarchs and some African countries, the Tsar (Jansson 2005: 350), China, and India, but these relations were never transformed from *ad-hoc* legations into permanent institutions; one might argue that diplomacy between Europe and the rest of the world remained medieval in form for the whole of the Early Modern period.

From the fifteenth century onwards, diplomacy in the strict sense of the word became an integral part of a foreign policy which was characterised by a growing entanglement between "states"; still, there were and there continued to be many other actors of external communication: artists and scholars, soldiers, merchants, clergymen, and clients abroad, who—in many ways—made points of contact between states and whose relative importance sometimes superseded that of the official representatives (Frigo 2008: 20; Wieland 2002, passim). Nevertheless, in the course of the sixteenth century, the figure of ambassador became the undoubted key element of interstate affairs; the other persons' activities continued to play an important role in the making of the relationships between one monarch (or republic) and another, but their doings were coordinated by the ambassador, who acted as a sort of "manager" of his country's friends abroad; he transformed them into a defined and homogeneous group, and his expertise, his knowledge, and, most of all, his authority by far superseded that of the other protagonists of the "international" game.[5]

Besides this task of coordinating, supervising and controlling this network of his country's clients (and, of course, of writing home about their doings), the ambassador had to fulfil a variety of functions, which it is by no means easy to describe concisely. The fact that he was the official representative of his monarch (or country) implied a set of duties such as negotiations, a sort of inter-princely brokerage, information about any- and everything.[6] As opposed to the embassy's secretary, who, as a trained lawyer, more often than not had to deal with legal affairs in the stricter sense, and who was supposed to embody rather freely his monarch's sympathies and antipathies towards specific governments and personal networks—who, in short, was a specialist– the ambassador was meant to be a generalist on the international stage (Frigo 2008: 24; Wieland 2004a: 373). He was responsible for everything, and most of all for the display of aristocratic impartiality.

---

[5] Wieland 2004b: 403–406. For the professionalisation of the role of ambassador, cf. Carrió-Invernizzi (2008: 886).

[6] For a contemporary definition of "negotiation"/"*négotiation*", see Avvertimenti, et Instruttione, "DHI, Minucciana, MS. 41" f. 30; cf. De Franceschi (2008: 200); Watkins (2008: 8); Frigo (2008: 17).

274   C. Wieland

2   The Figure of Ambassador as an Object of Sixteenth- and Seventeenth-Century Tract Literature

Political theory at the beginning of the modern age manifested itself in a growing Mirror of Princes literature. One could consider the numerous tracts about the princes' servants—notably secretaries and the like—a sort of derivation of this genre; and the various books which were written about the figure and the duties of the ambassador—one of the most popular examples was Juan Antonio de Very y Figueroa's *El embaxador*, first printed in 1620—were, for their part, nothing but a concretisation of the reflections on how the ideal office-holder and representative of a prince should behave.[7] In many respects, most of these tracts were variations on Machiavelli's *The Prince* (Russell 2005)—mostly in that Machiavelli served as a negative counterpart, from which the writer's own maxims differed substantially. Still, the virtue of *prudenza* (prudence) served as a key element in all studies on ambassadorial behaviour (Frigo 2008: 25). Very often, the offhand refusal of Machiavelli's maxims went hand in hand with a more than tacit acceptance of his guiding principles (De Franceschi 2008: 193–194, 203).

Consequently the ambassador should, firstly, be interpreted as being nothing but one ordinary "politician" among others, such as councillors or secretaries of state, one who was subject to the same rules and to whom the same codes of conduct applied (Idea 1654: 9). Secondly, however, the role an ambassador had to play was very specific: as opposed to his colleagues at court, he did not serve "at home", at the government's very centre, but abroad; his being far away from his prince, from the central bureaucracy, and from court life, was the very essence of his professional existence, his *raison d'être*. This meant that he could not be controlled by his prince or his fellow office-holders—at least not directly and continuously—and that it was impossible for him to receive direct and immediate orders at all times and for all sorts of occasions. Of course, the process of bureaucratisation intensified enormously during the Early Modern period, which meant that the principle of orality was more and more replaced by scripturality; nevertheless, sixteenth- and seventeenth-century court culture was still marked by a very high degree of immediate oral communication, and the ambassador—although considering himself a sort of courtier (Frigo 2008: 24)—represented a marked exception within this communication network.[8] Communication between a prince and his ambassador was characterised by the "gap principle" (as I would like to put it): there was an endemic tension between the prince's instruction and its interpretation by the ambassador (Frigo 2008: 20–21; Larminie 2006: 1318–1319); the geographical distance between the prince and his servant implied that the princely order and

---

[7] De Franceschi 2008: 195; for the vast tract literature on the office of ambassador, cf. Frigo (2008: 16).

[8] Watkins (2008: 9–10) argues that because of the bureaucratisation of diplomacy, ambassadors were fundamentally different beings from "mere" courtiers.

The Consequences of Early Modern Diplomacy

the diplomat's concrete political action were necessarily separated by a specific amount of time (Powell 2005: 425). It will be argued that because of these presuppositions, the requirements for loyalty were much higher for a diplomat than for any other office-holder in the service of the prince (Thiessen 2004: 49; Frigo 2008: 21–22); and that, as a consequence of these demands, the ambassador came to embody the epitome of the devoted civil servant, loyal to his "king and country".

To a much higher degree than other courtiers, the ambassador had to react to unforeseen circumstances. Whereas in many instructions he was told to speak to his "host monarch" or his principal ministers as if the words which his "native monarch" had ordered him to convey were his own (he was commanded to transform the persona he represented into the person he was, to blur the boundaries between role and self), this only applied to situations which could be planned down to the last detail. When this was not the case (and, as the course of a conversation could hardly ever be predicted precisely, this was usually not the case), the ambassador had to pronounce his own thoughts, reflections and arguments as if they were those of his lord and master (Powell 2005: 426); he had to transform the person he was into the person he represented.[9] In order to be able to do this—in order to convincingly play these multiple roles and not to have to retract later what he had said before after having received renewed instructions from his own country—in order to be able to speak and to react correctly in any given situation without damaging his monarch's interests, or his own standing and career opportunities in his prince's service, the ambassador had to be able to anticipate what was expected of him (Idea 1654: 195–202, 282–285). He had to acquire an *a priori* knowledge of his lord's wishes, he had to internalise the structures and guidelines of his own government's policy—in many respects, he had to embody, he had to *be* these maxims. Again, it was necessary that the difference between his person and his role as his monarch's mouthpiece was no longer distinguishable for those with whom he dealt in his diplomatic practice. The complicated interplay between "representing" on the one hand and "being" on the other, as far as the ambassador's professional standing was concerned, was in great part due to the fact that the Early Modern concept of "representation" was, in many respects, decidedly corporeal (Rade 1680: 3): the monarch was considered the embodiment of his country, he therefore was his country (Powell 2005: 425), and the ambassador, as his monarch's representative, embodied and at the same time was his sovereign's persona (Roosen 1980: 455–456, 462). His representing the prince meant that he was supposed to really play the role of his "prince *per procuram*", imitating even his gestures and mimicking his voice (Rade 1680: 3); and in order to be a good representative of his monarch, the ambassador had to be of aristocratic descent

---

[9] Cf. Powell 2005: 417–423; Watkins 2008: 9: "[. . .] the ambassador must submerge his identity as fully as possible in the image of the prince that he represents."

himself, he had to be noble, rich and beautiful—not to the same degree as the prince he represented (Idea 1654: 220–221), but his personal condition ought not to be too far removed from that of his lord and master. As opposed to an actor, who could represent virtually anyone, but only for a limited period of time, the ambassador, who was not allowed to leave his role as long as he acted, had to display a certain natural closeness to the demands of his role. It was essential that he shared the same sense of honour with his monarch, in order to be able to perceive every assault on his own person as an attack on his monarch's sovereignty (Idea 1654: 320–321) (Frigo 2008: 17; Larminie 2006: 1324–1325). This should not be understood too technically. Even in modern times, injuries to the immunity of diplomats are considered assaults on their states' sovereignty, but in the Early Modern period, the ambassador's very person was much more closely connected with his office.

Still, the ambassador had to be aware that, while his display of princely splendour before the auditorium of an alien court had to be as unambiguous as humanly possible, he was not his monarch. He was just his image and shadow, his "*imago et umbra*" (Rade 1680: 3; Wieland 2004b: 511), and he had to be careful to avoid the impression that he was no longer able to distinguish between his role and his person, especially in the dealings with his own government and his monarch himself. In other words, the delicate balance between the representing and the being forced him to continuously change roles, according to the different arenas in which he had to perform (Idea 1654: 203–204). He had to be able to cope with the tension between a quasi-sovereign position abroad, and the position of a loyal subject at home (Powell 2005: 428).

Ideally, the objectives of the diplomatic practice were the monarch's honour and interests (Idea 1654: 247–251) (Rade 1680: 6; Roosen 1980: 457), whereas the diplomat's honour and interests were to be taken into consideration only as far as they affected those of the monarch. In other words, the ambassador had to become highly proficient at abstaining from his own self. The ideas about how an ambassador could best achieve the goal of promoting his monarch's interests differed in the course of the Early Modern period, and according to "national" political cultures. It was by no means clear whether dissimulation ("*dissimulatio*") was an accepted means of policy-making (DHI, Minucciana, MS. 41: 33), or whether transparency and frankness were not more suitable instruments to represent the prince's majesty (Idea 1654: 145–149) (De Franceschi 2008: 201–205). Was it advisable to subordinate everything—including sincerity and a keen sense of honour—to the virtue of prudence ("*prudenza*")? And should a diplomat completely control his passions? (Idea 1654: 12) Or was it not more suitable that he should not do so when his prince's honour was in danger? (De Franceschi 2008: 208)

These differences in opinion about ideal ambassadorial behaviour, however, cannot conceal that, in the tract literature on diplomacy, the ambassador tended to become the epitome of a professional person who completely abstained from his own self in order to serve a higher, impersonal goal.

3 The Ambassador Between Professional Role and Interested Individual

As was common with most "professions" in pre-modern Europe, there existed nothing like a standardised schooling for future diplomats, no specific professional formation, except that most ambassadors and their secretaries were university-trained lawyers, but then they shared this sort of higher education with all the other members of the political and administrative élites of their times, from bishops to councillors and secretaries of state. If they didn't read manuals of the Figueroa-kind, they acquired the necessary professional skills mostly "by doing" the diplomatic practice, by participating in diplomatic missions, and by imitating their superiors and predecessors.[10] From the second half of the sixteenth century onwards, the pope's diplomats, the nuncios, were all high-ranking clerics (at least bishops, mostly archbishops[11]) from the urban patriciates in the northern half of the Italian peninsula, and the ambassadors of secular princes came from the upper ranks of their monarchs' territories; both factors were considered indispensable: the shared territorial identity of the monarch who sent his servant abroad and the diplomat who was sent seemed to ensure the latter's loyalty (Idea 1654: 234); and his high social standing was judged important, not only because his breeding made him a more fitting image of his prince, but also because in matters of precedence—which were all-important in the society of princes, not merely ephemeral aspects which did not really affect the substance—the rank of the represented (the monarch who had sent his diplomat) and the rank of the representative (the diplomat himself) were not necessarily neatly distinguished (Roosen 1980: 455–456). Consequently, the envoy's social role could become a decisive factor for his professional role, and, at the same time, for his monarch's standing within the system of the Early Modern states (Roosen 1980: 458–460, 464–465). Again, the diplomats of the sixteenth to eighteenth centuries had to maintain a delicate balance between their different, and often competing roles, their two "persons".

This is also true for their interests in the stricter sense of the word; of course, in theory an ambassador had to look first to his sovereign's honour, then to his prince's interests, and then to those of his country—and to nothing else (Roosen 1980: 457). In theory, the ambassador simply had no personal interests; on the other hand, since he was elected to his post because he was the aristocratic person he was, because of his family background and his social standing within his country's élite, it was—more or less officially—acknowledged that he not only had personal interests, but that he even had the right to pursue them—within strictly confined boundaries

---

[10] [Idea 1654, 267–280]. For the formation of an ambassadorial role through the imitation of models, cf. Powell (2005: 431).

[11] Cardinals acted as papal diplomats, but never as nuncios: if a cardinal was sent to perform a temporary diplomatic mission on behalf of the Pope, he bore the title of papal legate. For the diplomacy of the popes, cf. Graham (1967).

(Metzler 2004: 209). Those personal interests, though, were to be subordinated to the professional ones, not only as a matter of fact, but also symbolically. This complicated interplay of denial and acknowledgement as far as the existence and legitimacy of the ambassador's personal interests are concerned, as well as their symbolic subordination to those of "king and country", are reflected in the instructions for the Spanish ambassadors at the papal court. The king's wishes were to be expressed by the ambassador himself; those of the subjects of the Spanish monarchy— "*particulares*", as they were called—by the embassy's agent; and those of the ambassador by a third person not officially connected with the diplomatic apparatus. The fact that, in practice, the ambassadors of the Catholic kings articulated all matters of patronage themselves, and especially those concerning themselves and their own friends, clients and relatives, should not be interpreted as a proof for the total ineffectiveness of bureaucratic norms in the Early Modern period, but rather as an indicator of the more or less harmonious coexistence of two differing patterns of behaviour—one referring to the abstract good of the monarchy, the other to the concrete well-being of the family (Thiessen 2004: 53–56). Still, the ideal that ambassadors had to distinguish between their office and their person was acknowledged by all contemporaries. When a diplomat openly put his own and his clients' interests before those of his sovereign and his dynasty, this almost certainly meant that his career was at an end. Nuncio Caetani, extraordinary envoy of Pope Paul V at the court of Madrid, for example, managed to have Philip III bestow the dignity of grandee of Spain on his own nephew, when he was supposed to induce the Catholic king to make the pope's nephew, Marcantonio Borghese, a grandee (Thiessen 2004: 50). This total lack of concealment of his family preferences cost the prelate the Pope's good-will, but then, maybe, after having achieved his goal, the representative of an established Roman baronial family could bear this cost with relative equanimity.

In general, though, those personal interests of a diplomat which were acceptable were to have nothing whatsoever to do with his field of action abroad, but rather with his own *patria*. He was supposed to increase his prestige through his irreproachable professional behaviour, and, in due course, promote his career at home (Roosen 1980: 475). This was best achieved by a nearly complete dissolution of his private personality (Watkins 2008: 10).

4   Ambassadors and the Experience of Otherness

Since foreign countries were the "natural" field of action for ambassadors, the latter were exposed to the continuous experience of otherness (Burschel 1998: 264); they were not simply visitors who came and left again after a short while, but they had to endure their environment's strangeness for a considerable period of time, and, simultaneously, to act as translators or interpreters of one political system to another (Windler 2006: 5). Certainly, the degree of strangeness experienced by ambassadors varied considerably: the internal Italian diplomatic system, for example, offered comparatively few experiences of complete strangeness or a total lack of understanding for its protagonists, as compared to diplomatic relations between, for example, the Curia and the kingdom of Poland; it made a significant difference whether a diplomat moved within an identical religious context or whether he had to cross confessional boundaries in the performance of his professional duties, and it was of vital importance whether the diplomatic communication took place between monarchies or between a monarchy and a republic. Furthermore, although most European states confined their regular and stable diplomatic relations to Europe (even Russia did not form part of the established European diplomatic system for most of the Early Modern period), to Christendom, as it was conceived by the majority of Early Modern contemporaries, legations between European and non-European, even non-Christian states in Africa and Asia, were exchanged, though these were considered remarkable, strange and highly exceptional occurrences.

For an ambassador it was of vital importance to acquire some sort of intimate knowledge about the political system whose guest he was; it was an essential prerequisite for the successful performance of his services, a "conditcio sine qua non", his professional *raison d'être* (Windler 2006: passim). As a stranger who had to interact with strangers, and who had to continually send reports about his interactions to his home country, the ambassador might be considered the prototype of the anthropologist (*avant la lettre*): a professional of otherness, of participatory observation.

A closer look at diplomatic correspondence, however, reveals that this was precisely not the case; on the contrary, reports of Early Modern ambassadors can be characterised as mere reproductions of otherness once experienced (or, better, once constructed) by distant authorities and never substantially altered. They were repetitions of stereotypes which were not based on genuine experiences or even the foreign countries' self-representations, but on preconceived notions which had their origins in the diplomats' own home countries. Images, perceptions and prejudices about the "other", where the future ambassador was supposed to spend a considerable period of time, found their way into the instructions which were given at the beginning of each diplomatic mission. These instructions, characteristic documents for pontifical diplomacy in particular, but also for most other monarchies of the Early Modern period (Reinhard 1998: 217), certainly had some basis in previous diplomatic experience; but they were written with the specific experiences of the indigenous bureaucratic and political elites at home in mind, and they were not meant to alter their respective preconceptions, but instead to confirm them by providing some sort of apparent empiricism (Reinhardt 1998: 287). Thus, the instructions which shaped the ways in which ambassadors perceived their new sphere of action and, even more importantly, showed them the way in which their superiors wanted it to be perceived, hardly left room for new perceptions, modifications and changes; instead, they provoked the constant repetition of the patterns which lay at the bottom of these texts and which remained remarkably stable throughout the whole of the Early Modern period (Burschel 1998: 270).

The reports of the papal nuncios in Switzerland provide a colourful example of the tenacity of patterns of perception, irrespective of all "real" experience.[12] Switzerland, as it was characterised—once and for all—by the Italian humanists, was the exotic counter-world to civilised Italy[13]; in these mountainous regions somewhere between Germany, France and Italy, it seemed that the widely accepted rules of Europe, i.e. European rationality, did not apply (Windler 2006: 30–31). As the Germanic tribes of antiquity had resisted Roman civilisation, nowadays the Swiss seemed completely immune to the blessings of Italian Renaissance and Baroque culture (Reinhardt 1998: 295). True, even the Curia's elite had some knowledge of irrational beings, notably the lower orders, but the existence of this class of people in familiar Italy was mollified by the existence of a sufficient number of social equals. In Switzerland, however, there did not seem to be any equals for the papal diplomats; its society seemed to consist entirely of proletarians, and therefore Switzerland became the epitome of the "other" within Europe, both in cultural and social terms. In the nuncios' perception of the country's social and political structure, instability was the only predictable structure of a society which, as a whole, was characterised by confusion and chaos (Windler 2006: 27). Solely the proverbial avarice of the Swiss (Windler 2006: 30)—itself a mark of their moral and intellectual depravity—was considered a constant feature marking the solitary stable guideline for the nuncios' behaviour towards their hosts (Reinhardt 1998: 296–297). In the instructions to their envoys in Lucerne, the popes and their secretaries of state did not fail to encourage the papal diplomats to feign acceptance of Switzerland's political system (Reinhardt 1998: 291); one might assume that a necessary prerequisite for hypocrisy is real understanding, but in this case the request to practise hypocrisy conveyed the conviction that there was in reality nothing worth comprehending in Switzerland.

Even the encounter with alien cultures whose representatives frequented the capitals of the European monarchies did not contribute much to any deepened knowledge or any sort of mutual understanding.[14] When embassies, for instance, from Christian kingdoms in Africa visited the royal court in Lisbon or the Holy See in Rome in the sixteenth and seventeenth centuries, the African diplomats were forced to dress and behave in as "European" a manner as possible; they were despoiled of all outer signs of otherness, de-Africanised, as it were. At the same time, they served to project an image of biblical and classical Africa, instead of a real and authentic contemporary one; after diplomatic meetings of this sort, the image of Africa did not undergo any differentiation, but, instead, myths and learned preconceptions of the Dark Continent continued to be spread and believed. Antique

---

[12] For the following, cf. Reinhardt (1998). See also Windler (2006: 31).

[13] Spanish and French diplomats, too, considered the political functioning of the Swiss Confederation the one great exception in Europe; cf. Windler (2006: 28–29).

[14] For the following, cf. Lowe (2007).

The Consequences of Early Modern Diplomacy

and humanistic judgements obviously prevailed over experience, or, to be more precise, these intellectual preconceptions shaped all experience beforehand.[15]

Furthermore, there were other barriers to the ambassadors becoming truly and intimately acquainted with their host countries, apart from their (and their superiors') intellectual biases. They were not allowed to know their counterparts too intimately, to interpret their political system too analytically, let alone to fraternise with the foreign elites, since this entailed the danger of the ambassadors losing the aloof dignity which was an essential prerequisite for the representation of their monarch's dignity.[16] They were not only pardoned, if they did not acquire the language of their host country, they were even explicitly told to use their mother tongues during audiences and make use of a good interpreter, so as not to degrade themselves (and their sovereign). If ambassadors became too closely connected with one set among the courtly factions, they ran the risk of alienating other influential groups and, hence, losing them as potential allies. The most important obstacle to their becoming genuine experts of the "other", though, was that this would have caused them to be suspected of being disloyal to their home country and of putting their own, private interests before those of their monarchs.[17]

In this respect, the Roman pontiffs were particularly careful; it seems, for example, that Pope Paul V's nuncios in Tuscany, Antonio Grimani and Pietro Valier, were at least as much defined by their Venetian origin as by their Florentine field of action, in order to exclude too close a proximity between the papal diplomats and the grand ducal government (Wieland 2004b: 189). On the other hand, it seems that the popes had more reason than other monarchs to be suspicious of their diplomats' loyalty. When, in 1613, Grand Duke Cosimo II of Tuscany sent auxiliary troops to the Duke of Mantua, and Tuscan soldiers crossed the territory of the state of the Church, this was contrary to the Pope's explicit wishes, for he feared that this might damage his image as *"padre comune"* of all Christian princes, and be interpreted as an act of partiality towards the Medici and the Gonzaga dynasties, and, consequently, as an act of hostility towards the house of Savoy (Wieland 2004a: 360–361). The nuncio in Florence was suspected by the Pope and his nephew, Cardinal Borghese, of having deliberately omitted to mention his previous knowledge of the grand ducal plans because of his allegiance to the noble house of Medici, whose resources could appear more promising to an ambitious Venetian patrician than those of the *nouveaux-riches* Borghese (Wieland 2004a: 366–367). The nuncio's reply to these reproaches (and they were severe reproaches, indeed!) is a beautiful illustration of how little weight an Early Modern diplomat's host

---

[15] Lowe 2007 115, 118–119, 122. Similarly, the Polish legations to Islamic courts seem to have served to strengthen established sentiments of European superiority over eastern barbarism, not to the development of any sort of differentiated observation; cf. Kołodziejczyk (2003: 253–254).

[16] [Idea 1654, 174–176]. Furthermore, ambassadors were supposed to keep their own governments' secrets and not to convey them to their hosts; cf. Hanotin (2008: 300).

[17] The Milanese envoy to Switzerland, Marso, was suspected of heresy and called home because of his obviously too close relations with the canton of Zurich; cf. Windler (2006: 37).

country had in his self-definition as his prince's faithful servant. He depicted his acceptance of the nunciatura in Florence as an act of faithfulness towards the new Pope; even Florence was, for him, a sort of exile either from his native *patria*, Venice, or from his adopted *patria*, Rome, and his acting as nuncio had proved by no means financially rewarding, in so far as he had spent the entire income of his diocese on the nunciatura's heavy expenses; furthermore, he had lost his privileged position within Venice's communication network by his removal to Florence, and his efforts to obtain the Grand Duke's good graces had only served to improve his ability to convey information to Rome. He concluded: "Here [in Florence], I cannot have the smallest interest, and all my fortune depends upon His Holiness and your most illustrious lordship ..." (Wieland 2004b: 235–236).

Seen within this context, it becomes quite clear why ambassadors were not allowed to accept gifts during their periods of service (whereas it was quite common for them to receive generous gifts from their host monarchs at the time of their leaving their post). This rule not only served to minimise the danger of bribery, but also to make sure that they remained strangers while abroad.[18] When, for example, Sir Thomas Wyatt, Henry VIII's ambassador in Spain, openly declared himself a Protestant by distributing theological pamphlets in the streets of Madrid and, for this reason, was observed by the Spanish Inquisition, this definitely did not serve to ingratiate him with Charles V and the Spanish court society, but it was a means of proving his unquestionable loyalty to his own prince and country (Powell 2005: 415). Similarly, Sir Isaac Wake, who served as James I's diplomatic representative in Turin, Venice and Paris, did everything in his power to support the Protestant cause, which gained him more recognition in England than in Italy or France (Larminie 2006: 1302, 1311, 1321, 1326).

Diplomatic correspondence is full of requests to be allowed to return home, of complaints about the hardships of living abroad, and of the longing to be transferred to another post in close proximity to the prince himself (Larminie 2006: 1325; Reinhardt 1998: 299). The "homecoming wish" was a topos which constituted an integral part of a diplomat's self-fashioning, since it served to underline his absolute loyalty. This does not necessarily mean that the ambassadors' frequently expressed dislike towards their host countries was not genuine and real; next to the financial risks which formed a constant threat to the notoriously underpaid diplomats, they obviously perceived their station abroad as an "exile" (Larminie 2006: 1302; Powell 2005: 424), never as home. And the carefully maintained "otherness" had additional advantages: it served as a most welcome excuse for the occasional lack of success in diplomatic dealings (Windler 2006: 43).

---

[18] [Idea 1654, 226–232]. For the practice of gift-giving in Early Modern diplomacy, cf. Carrió-Invernizzi (2008: passim); Jansson (2005: 364–368).

The Consequences of Early Modern Diplomacy 283

5 Early Modern Ambassadors as Prototypes of Modern Bureaucrats?

The good thing about state servants was (and is) that they are ideal scapegoats for the political failings of their superiors; this is particularly true of such officials not serving at the centre, but on the periphery (e.g. as provincial governors), or—even better—abroad. In this, diplomats fulfil a vital function for the stability of the political system as a whole (Larminie 2006: 1301).

Diplomacy, more than other state functions, is based on scripturality; to quite some extent, the development of an ambassadorial system contributed to the process of bureaucratisation of power, to the rationalisation and formalisation of the bureaucratic apparatus, and to the gradual supplanting of personal interaction by formal organisation. As has been shown, ambassadors personified everything a prince's servant (or a state servant) should be. They were perfect projections of all ideals of service—of loyalty and trustworthiness (not so much of professional expertise)—brought to a peak (Idea 1654: 13) (Frigo 2008: 21–22). And diplomats shaped the political culture of their countries to a high degree: when they returned to their monarchs' courts and central administrations, they re-imported the internalised obedience they had had to practise—and embody—abroad.

The ambassadors' relationship to their fields of action was marked by a pronounced distance, by a demonstrative fear of being absorbed by the foreign political and social system and their respective networks.[19] "Going native" was not an option for diplomats, if they wanted to further their careers at home. The worry, though, of being suspected of too high a degree of closeness to another court did not concern countries and monarchies which were indeed far away from the diplomats' *patriae*—in terms of geography, culture and religion. The Polish envoys to Istanbul, for example, expressed an unwillingness to participate in the Sultan's court ceremonial, since they felt that this involved practices which were degrading to their country's honour and their own, and they described their hosts as uncivilised and barbarous. These strategies of producing and reproducing established images of otherness seem to imply that a preformed exoticism could serve as a commodious barrier for the suspicion of self-interest (Kołodziejczyk 2003: 251, 253–254).

In summary, it seems that diplomacy in the Early Modern period was not concerned with the *other*, but rather with the self. It did not really contribute to a deepened knowledge of foreign state structures, but it contributed to the process of state-building precisely because of the endemic lack of knowledge which was demanded by its protagonists, and which they did not hesitate to reproduce for the sake of their own careers. Foreign countries helped to shape states, since

---

[19] Diplomats were supposed to show a pronounced distrust towards presents offered them by influential persons from their host countries, and, more often than not, to refuse them; cf. Carrió-Invernizzi (2008: 893–895).

284   C. Wieland

they served as laboratories for the production of their most important material: servants who were able to convincingly feign complete ignorance and absolute loyalty.[20]

Bibliography

Burschel, Peter. 1998. "Das Eigene und das Fremde. Zur anthropologischen Entzifferung diplomatischer Texte." In *Kurie und Politik. Stand und Perspektiven der Nuntiaturberichtsforschung* (Bibliothek des Deutschen Historischen Instituts in Rom, 87), ed. Alexander Koller, 260–271, Tübingen: Max Niemeyer Verlag.

Carrió-Invernizzi, Diana. 2008. "Gift and Diplomacy in Seventeenth-Century Spanish Italy." *The Historical Journal* 51: 881–899.

De Franceschi, Sylvio Hermann. 2008. "Les valeurs de l'honnête négociation. Prudence et imprudence diplomatique au temps de l'interdit vénitien (1606–1607)." *Revue d'histoire diplomatique* 122: 193–221.

Deutsches Historisches Institut in Rom, Minucciana, MS. 41, Avvertimenti, Discorsi et Instruttioni, "Avvertimenti, et Instruttione data da un Ambasciatore Catt.co in Roma al suo Successore". [DHI, Minucciana, MS. 41]

Frigo, Daniela. 2008. "Prudence and Experience: Ambassadors and Political Culture in Early Modern Italy." *Journal of Medieval and Early Modern Studies* 38: 15–34.

Graham, Robert A. ι7. *Vatican Diplomacy. A Study of Church and State on the International Plan.* Princeton: Princeton University Press.

Hanotin, Guillaume. 2008. "L'ambassadeur et la pièce de monnaie: représenter le souverain et dissimuler ses intérêts." *Revue d'histoire diplomatique* 122: 291–303.

Idea del perfetto Ambasciadore. Dialoghi Historici, e Politici, portati nuovamente dall'Idioma Francese nell'Italiano, Venedig 1654. [Idea 1654]

Jansson, Maija. 2005. "Measured Reciprocity: English Ambassadorial Gift Exchange in the 17th and 18th centuries." *Journal of Early Modern History* 9: 348–370.

Kołodziejczyk, Dariusz. 2003. Semiotics of Behavior in Early Modern Diplomacy: Polish Embassies in Istanbul and Bahçesaray. *Journal of Early Modern History* 7: 245–256.

Krischer, André. 2007. "Das diplomatische Zeremoniell der Reichsstädte, oder: Was heißt Stadtfreiheit in der Fürstengesellschaft?" *Historische Zeitschrift* 284: 1–30.

Larminie, Vivienne. 2006. "The Jacobean Diplomatic Fraternity and the Protestant Cause: Sir Isaac Wake and the View from Savoy."*English Historical Review* 121: 1300–1326.

Lowe, Kate. 2007. ""Representing" Africa: Ambassadors and Princes from Christian Africa to Renaissance Italy and Portugal, 1402–1608." *Transactions of the Royal Historical Society* 17: 101–128.

Metzler, Guido. 2004. "Die doppelte Peripherie. Neapel als römische Kolonie und als spanische Provinz." In *Römische Mikropolitik unter Paul V. Borghese (1605–1621) zwischen Spanien, Neapel, Mailand und Genua* (Bibliothek des Deutschen Historischen Instituts in Rom, 107), ed. Wolfgang Reinhard, 179–334, Tübingen: Max Niemeyer Verlag.

Powell, Jason. 2005. ""For Caesar's I am": Henrician Diplomacy and Representations of King and Country in Thomas Wyatt's Poetry." *The Sixteenth Century Journal* 36: 415–431.

---

[20] Wieland 2004a: 378. It is by no means clear whether professional expertise or personal loyalty were more important for the successful fulfilment of the state servant's (and, consequently, the ambassador's) role; within the context of the Curia, personal loyalty seems to have been by far the more secure way to success; cf. Metzler (2004: 203).

Rade, Johannes Josua 1680. *De Repraesentativa Legatorum Qualitate*, Heidelberg: Samuel Anemon.

Reinhard, Wolfgang. 1998. "Nuntiaturberichte für die deutsche Geschichtswissenschaft? Wert und Verwertung eines Editionsunternehmens." In *Kurie und Politik. Stand und Perspektiven der Nuntiaturberichtsforschung* (Bibliothek des Deutschen Historischen Instituts in Rom, 87), ed. Alexander Koller, 208–225, Tübingen: Max Niemeyer Verlag.

Reinhardt, Volker. 1998. "Nuntien und Nationalcharakter. Prolegommena zu einer Geschichte nationaler Wahrnehmungsstereotypen am Beispiel der Schweiz." In *Kurie und Politik. Stand und Perspektiven der Nuntiaturberichtsforschung* (Bibliothek des Deutschen Historischen Instituts in Rom, 87), ed. Alexander Koller, 285–300, Tübingen: Max Niemeyer Verlag.

Roosen, William. 1980. "Early Modern Diplomatic Ceremonial: A Systems Approach." *Journal of Modern History* 52: 452–476.

Russell, Greg. 2005. "Machiavelli's Science of Statecraft: The Diplomacy and Politics of Disorder."*Diplomacy and Statecraft* 16: 227–250.

Thiessen, Hillard von. 2004. "Außenpolitik im Zeichen personaler Herrschaft. Die römisch-spanischen Beziehungen in mikropolitischer Perspektive." In *Römische Mikropolitik unter Paul V. Borghese (1605–1621) zwischen Spanien, Neapel, Mailand und Genua* (Bibliothek des Deutschen Historischen Instituts in Rom, 107), ed. Wolfgang Reinhard, 21–177, Tübingen: Max Niemeyer Verlag.

Watkins, John. 2008. "Toward a New Diplomatic History of Medieval and Early Modern Europe." *Journal of Medieval and Early Modern Studies* 38:1–14.

Wieland, Christian. 2002. "Parteien in Rom, von Florenz aus gesehen. Eine römische Gruppe im diplomatischen Dienst der Medici während des Pontifikats Pauls V. (1605–1621)." *Quellen und Forschungen aus italienischen Archiven und Bibliotheken* 82: 490–528.

Wieland, Christian. 2004a. "Diplomaten als Spiegel ihrer Herren? Römische und florentinische Diplomatie zu Beginn des 17. Jahrhunderts." *Zeitschrift für Historische Forschung* 31: 359–379.

Wieland, Christian. 2004b. *Fürsten, Freunde, Diplomaten. Die römisch-florentinischen Beziehungen unter Paul V. (1605–1621)* (Norm und Struktur, 20). Cologne, Weimar, Vienna: Böhlau Verlag.

Windler, Christian. 2006. "Diplomatie als Erfahrung fremder politischer Kulturen. Gesandte von Monarchen in den eidgenössischen Orten (16. und 17. Jahrhundert)." *Geschichte und Gesellschaft* 32: 5–44.